Prentice Hall

AMERICA

HISTORY OF OUR NATION

Interactive Reading and Notetaking Study Guide

ADAPTED VERSION

Cover image: iStockphoto.com

ISBN 0-13-129869-0
5 6 7 8 9 10 09 08

Upper Saddle River, New Jersey
Boston, Massachusetts

Contents

How to Use This Book

The *Interactive Reading and Notetaking Study Guide* was designed to help you understand the content in your *America: History of Our Nation* textbook. It will also help you build your notetaking and historical-thinking skills. Please take the time to look at the next few pages to see how it works.

The unit opener page prepares you to read and think about the chapters in each unit. Section Summary pages provide an easy-to-read summary of each section.

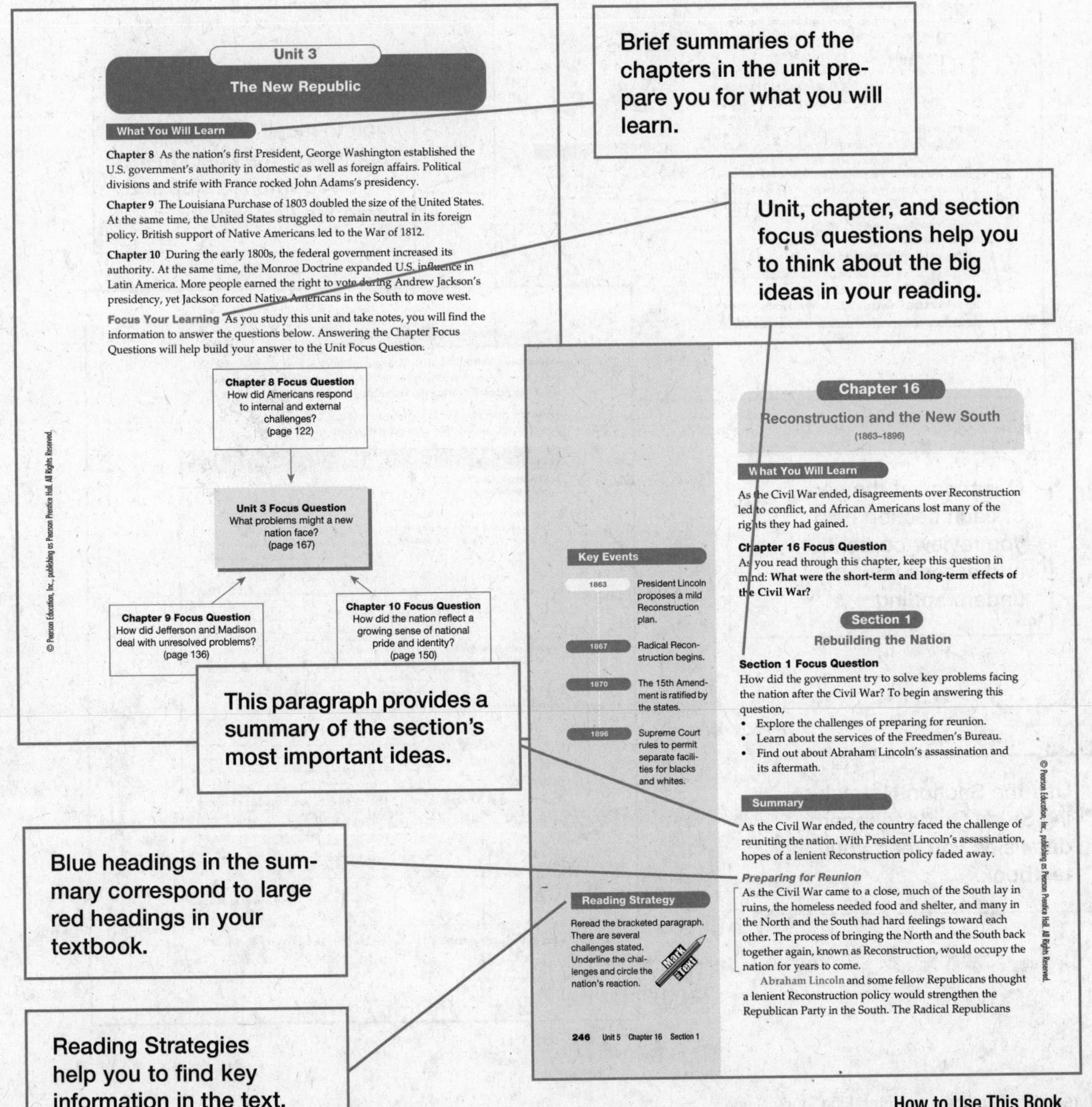

Unit 3
The New Republic
What You Will Learn
Chapter 8 As the nation's first President, George Washington established the U.S. government's authority in domestic as well as foreign affairs. Political divisions and strife with France rocked John Adams's presidency.
Chapter 9 The Louisiana Purchase of 1803 doubled the size of the United States. At the same time, the United States struggled to remain neutral in its foreign policy. British support of Native Americans led to the War of 1812.
Chapter 10 During the early 1800s, the federal government increased its authority. At the same time, the Monroe Doctrine expanded U.S. influence in Latin America. More people earned the right to vote during Andrew Jackson's presidency, yet Jackson forced Native Americans in the South to move west.
Focus Your Learning As you study this unit and take notes, you will find the information to answer the questions below. Answering the Chapter Focus Questions will help build your answer to the Unit Focus Question.
Chapter 8 Focus Question How did Americans respond to internal and external challenges? (page 122)
Unit 3 Focus Question What problems might a new nation face? (page 167)
Chapter 9 Focus Question How did Jefferson and Madison deal with unresolved problems? (page 136)
Chapter 10 Focus Question How did the nation reflect a growing sense of national pride and identity? (page 150)
Brief summaries of the chapters in the unit prepare you for what you will learn.
Unit, chapter, and section focus questions help you to think about the big ideas in your reading.
This paragraph provides a summary of the section's most important ideas.
Blue headings in the summary correspond to large red headings in your textbook.
Reading Strategies help you to find key information in the text.
Chapter 16
Reconstruction and the New South
(1863–1896)
What You Will Learn
As the Civil War ended, disagreements over Reconstruction led to conflict, and African Americans lost many of the rights they had gained.
Chapter 16 Focus Question
As you read through this chapter, keep this question in mind: What were the short-term and long-term effects of the Civil War?
Key Events
1863 President Lincoln proposes a mild Reconstruction plan.
1867 Radical Reconstruction begins.
1870 The 15th Amendment is ratified by the states.
1896 Supreme Court rules to permit separate facilities for blacks and whites.
Section 1
Rebuilding the Nation
Section 1 Focus Question
How did the government try to solve key problems facing the nation after the Civil War? To begin answering this question,
• Explore the challenges of preparing for reunion.
• Learn about the services of the Freedmen's Bureau.
• Find out about Abraham Lincoln's assassination and its aftermath.
Summary
As the Civil War ended, the country faced the challenge of reuniting the nation. With President Lincoln's assassination, hopes of a lenient Reconstruction policy faded away.
Preparing for Reunion
As the Civil War came to a close, much of the South lay in ruins, the homeless needed food and shelter, and many in the North and the South had hard feelings toward each other. The process of bringing the North and the South back together again, known as Reconstruction, would occupy the nation for years to come.
Abraham Lincoln and some fellow Republicans thought a lenient Reconstruction policy would strengthen the Republican Party in the South. The Radical Republicans
Reading Strategy
Reread the bracketed paragraph. There are several challenges stated. Underline the challenges and circle the nation's reaction.
Mark the Text
246 Unit 5 Chapter 16 Section 1

Questions and activities in the margin help you recall information from the summary. Section Notetaking Study Guides help you take notes as your read your textbook.

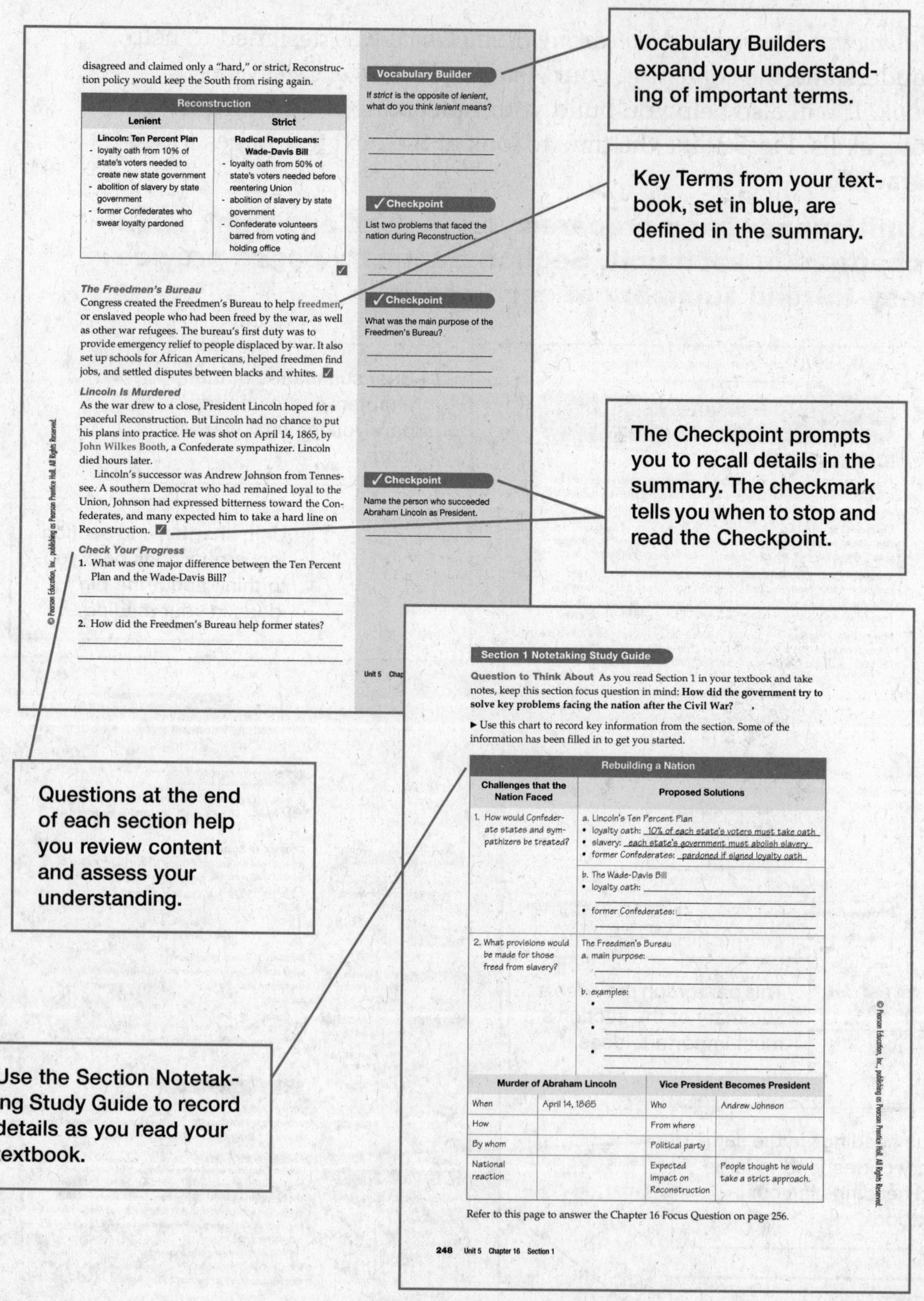

disagreed and claimed only a "hard," or strict, Reconstruction policy would keep the South from rising again.
Reconstruction
Lenient
Strict
Lincoln: Ten Percent Plan
- loyalty oath from 10% of state's voters needed to create new state government
- abolition of slavery by state government
- former Confederates who swear loyalty pardoned
Radical Republicans: Wade-Davis Bill
- loyalty oath from 50% of state's voters needed before reentering Union
- abolition of slavery by state government
- Confederate volunteers barred from voting and holding office
The Freedmen's Bureau
Congress created the Freedmen's Bureau to help freedmen, or enslaved people who had been freed by the war, as well as other war refugees. The bureau's first duty was to provide emergency relief to people displaced by war. It also set up schools for African Americans, helped freedmen find jobs, and settled disputes between blacks and whites.
Lincoln Is Murdered
As the war drew to a close, President Lincoln hoped for a peaceful Reconstruction. But Lincoln had no chance to put his plans into practice. He was shot on April 14, 1865, by John Wilkes Booth, a Confederate sympathizer. Lincoln died hours later.
Lincoln's successor was Andrew Johnson from Tennessee. A southern Democrat who had remained loyal to the Union, Johnson had expressed bitterness toward the Confederates, and many expected him to take a hard line on Reconstruction.
Check Your Progress
1. What was one major difference between the Ten Percent Plan and the Wade-Davis Bill?
2. How did the Freedmen's Bureau help former states?
Vocabulary Builder
If strict is the opposite of lenient, what do you think lenient means?
✓ Checkpoint
List two problems that faced the nation during Reconstruction.
✓ Checkpoint
What was the main purpose of the Freedmen's Bureau?
✓ Checkpoint
Name the person who succeeded Abraham Lincoln as President.
Vocabulary Builders expand your understanding of important terms.
Key Terms from your textbook, set in blue, are defined in the summary.
The Checkpoint prompts you to recall details in the summary. The checkmark tells you when to stop and read the Checkpoint.
Questions at the end of each section help you review content and assess your understanding.
Use the Section Notetaking Study Guide to record details as you read your textbook.
Section 1 Notetaking Study Guide
Question to Think About As you read Section 1 in your textbook and take notes, keep this section focus question in mind: How did the government try to solve key problems facing the nation after the Civil War?
► Use this chart to record key information from the section. Some of the information has been filled in to get you started.
Rebuilding a Nation
Challenges that the Nation Faced
Proposed Solutions
1. How would Confederate states and sympathizers be treated?
a. Lincoln's Ten Percent Plan
• loyalty oath: 10% of each state's voters must take oath
• slavery: each state's government must abolish slavery
• former Confederates: pardoned if signed loyalty oath
b. The Wade-Davis Bill
• loyalty oath:
• former Confederates:
2. What provisions would be made for those freed from slavery?
The Freedmen's Bureau
a. main purpose:
b. examples:
Murder of Abraham Lincoln
When
April 14, 1865
How
By whom
National reaction
Vice President Becomes President
Who
Andrew Johnson
From where
Political party
Expected impact on Reconstruction
People thought he would take a strict approach.
Refer to this page to answer the Chapter 16 Focus Question on page 256.
248 Unit 5 Chapter 16 Section 1

Questions help you to assess your progress. Chapter Notetaking Study Guides help you to pull together the notes you took for each section and focus on important ideas.

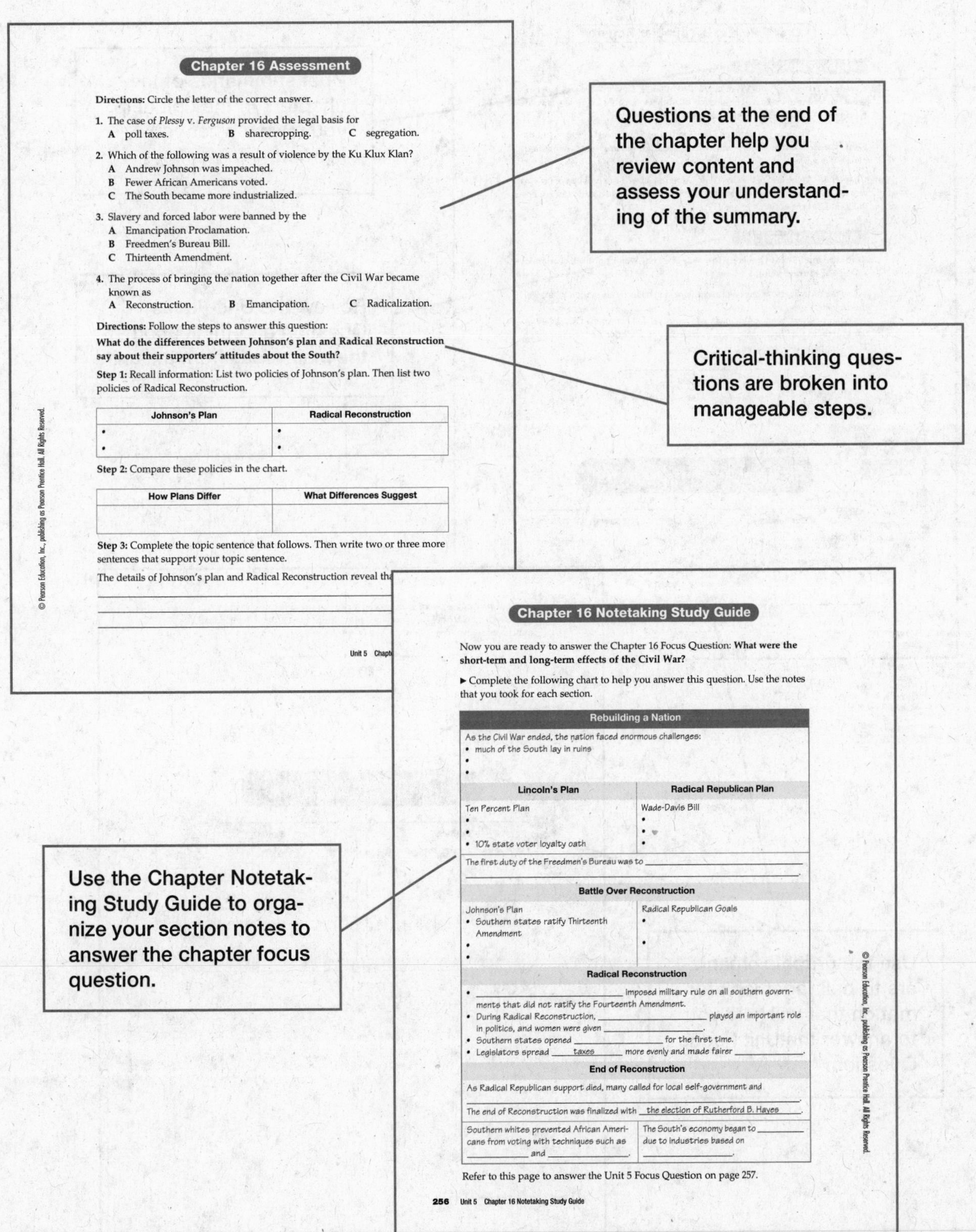

Chapter 16 Assessment

Directions: Circle the letter of the correct answer.

1. The case of *Plessy* v. *Ferguson* provided the legal basis for
   A poll taxes. B sharecropping. C segregation.
2. Which of the following was a result of violence by the Ku Klux Klan?
   A Andrew Johnson was impeached.
   B Fewer African Americans voted.
   C The South became more industrialized.
3. Slavery and forced labor were banned by the
   A Emancipation Proclamation.
   B Freedmen's Bureau Bill.
   C Thirteenth Amendment.
4. The process of bringing the nation together after the Civil War became known as
   A Reconstruction. B Emancipation. C Radicalization.

Directions: Follow the steps to answer this question:

What do the differences between Johnson's plan and Radical Reconstruction say about their supporters' attitudes about the South?

Step 1: Recall information: List two policies of Johnson's plan. Then list two policies of Radical Reconstruction.

Johnson's Plan	Radical Reconstruction
•	•
•	•

Step 2: Compare these policies in the chart.

How Plans Differ	What Differences Suggest

Step 3: Complete the topic sentence that follows. Then write two or three more sentences that support your topic sentence.

The details of Johnson's plan and Radical Reconstruction reveal tha

Unit 5 Chapt

Chapter 16 Notetaking Study Guide

Now you are ready to answer the Chapter 16 Focus Question: **What were the short-term and long-term effects of the Civil War?**

▸ Complete the following chart to help you answer this question. Use the notes that you took for each section.

Rebuilding a Nation

As the Civil War ended, the nation faced enormous challenges:
- much of the South lay in ruins
-
-

Lincoln's Plan	Radical Republican Plan
Ten Percent Plan • • • 10% state voter loyalty oath	Wade-Davis Bill • • •

The first duty of the Freedmen's Bureau was to ______

Battle Over Reconstruction

Johnson's Plan	Radical Republican Goals
• Southern states ratify Thirteenth Amendment • •	• •

Radical Reconstruction

- ______ imposed military rule on all southern governments that did not ratify the Fourteenth Amendment.
- During Radical Reconstruction, ______ played an important role in politics, and women were given ______.
- Southern states opened ______ for the first time.
- Legislators spread ___taxes___ more evenly and made fairer ______.

End of Reconstruction

As Radical Republican support died, many called for local self-government and ______

The end of Reconstruction was finalized with ___the election of Rutherford B. Hayes___.

Southern whites prevented African Americans from voting with techniques such as ______ and ______.	The South's economy began to ______ due to industries based on ______.

Refer to this page to answer the Unit 5 Focus Question on page 257.

256 Unit 5 Chapter 16 Notetaking Study Guide

Questions at the end of the chapter help you review content and assess your understanding of the summary.

Critical-thinking questions are broken into manageable steps.

Use the Chapter Notetaking Study Guide to organize your section notes to answer the chapter focus question.

The Pulling It Together Activity helps you to look back on your reading and focus on the unit's big ideas.

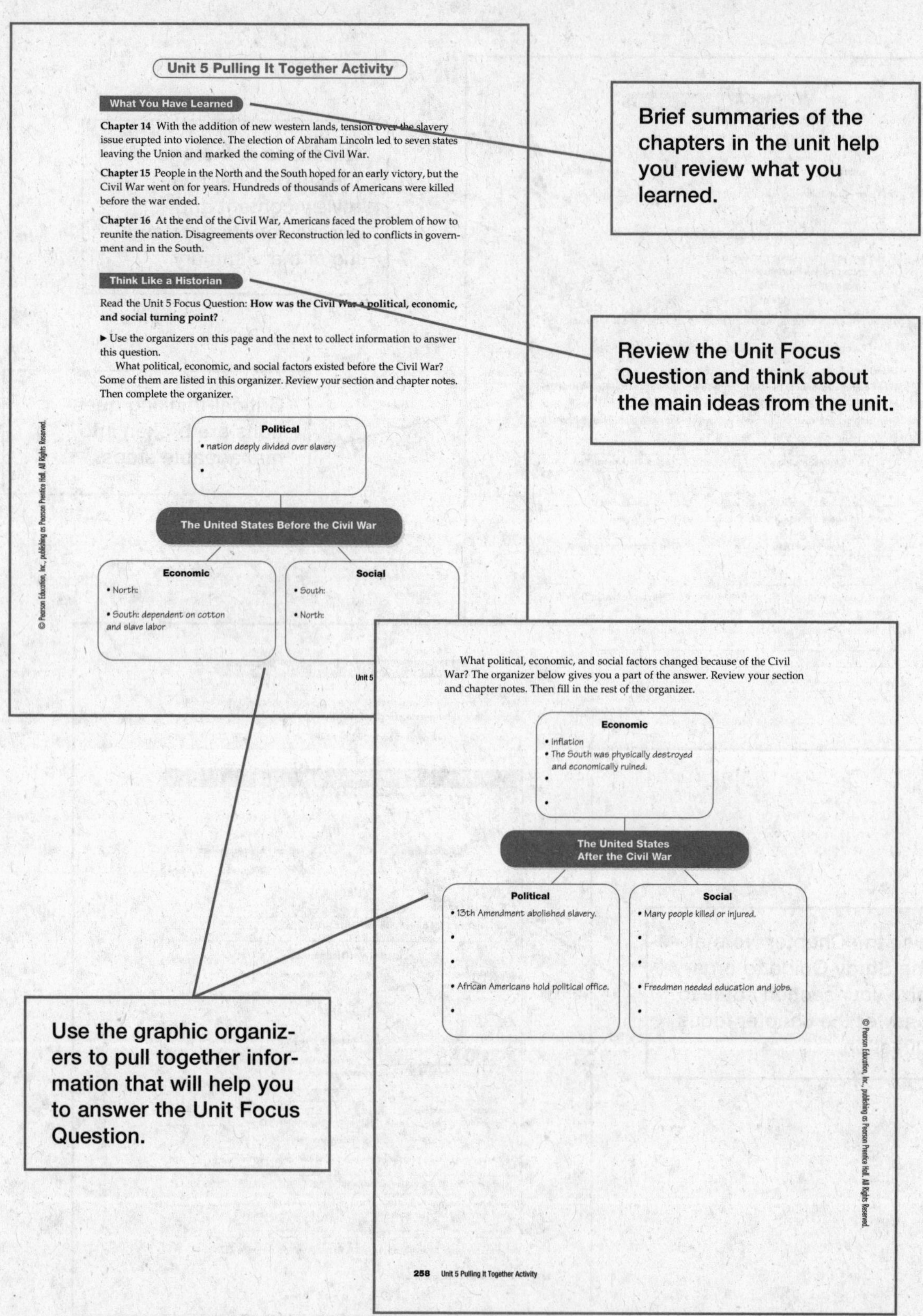
Unit 5 Pulling It Together Activity
What You Have Learned
Chapter 14 With the addition of new western lands, tension over the slavery issue erupted into violence. The election of Abraham Lincoln led to seven states leaving the Union and marked the coming of the Civil War.
Chapter 15 People in the North and the South hoped for an early victory, but the Civil War went on for years. Hundreds of thousands of Americans were killed before the war ended.
Chapter 16 At the end of the Civil War, Americans faced the problem of how to reunite the nation. Disagreements over Reconstruction led to conflicts in government and in the South.
Think Like a Historian
Read the Unit 5 Focus Question: How was the Civil War a political, economic, and social turning point?
▶ Use the organizers on this page and the next to collect information to answer this question.
What political, economic, and social factors existed before the Civil War? Some of them are listed in this organizer. Review your section and chapter notes. Then complete the organizer.
Political
• nation deeply divided over slavery
The United States Before the Civil War
Economic
• North:
• South: dependent on cotton and slave labor
Social
• South:
• North:
What political, economic, and social factors changed because of the Civil War? The organizer below gives you a part of the answer. Review your section and chapter notes. Then fill in the rest of the organizer.
Economic
• inflation
• The South was physically destroyed and economically ruined.
The United States After the Civil War
Political
• 13th Amendment abolished slavery.
• African Americans hold political office.
Social
• Many people killed or injured.
• Freedmen needed education and jobs.
258 Unit 5 Pulling It Together Activity
Brief summaries of the chapters in the unit help you review what you learned.
Review the Unit Focus Question and think about the main ideas from the unit.
Use the graphic organizers to pull together information that will help you to answer the Unit Focus Question.

Unit 1

Beginnings of American History

What You Will Learn

Chapter 1 Early people spread across the Americas and built civilizations. As cultures grew in North America, trade linked Africa, Asia, and Europe.

Chapter 2 In the 1400s, European explorers first met Native Americans. For the next three centuries, European explorers and settlers expanded their influence across North and South America.

Chapter 3 In the 1600s, colonies were settled in North America. They included the New England Colonies of the Puritans, the Middle Colonies known for religious tolerance, and the Southern Colonies, which had slavery.

Chapter 4 European traditions shaped England's 13 North American colonies, but colonists had their own ideas as well. By the 1700s, slavery was a part of American life. Religion and the European Enlightenment spread new ideas.

Focus Your Learning As you study this unit and take notes, you will find the information to answer the questions below. Answering the Chapter Focus Questions will help build your answer to the Unit Focus Question.

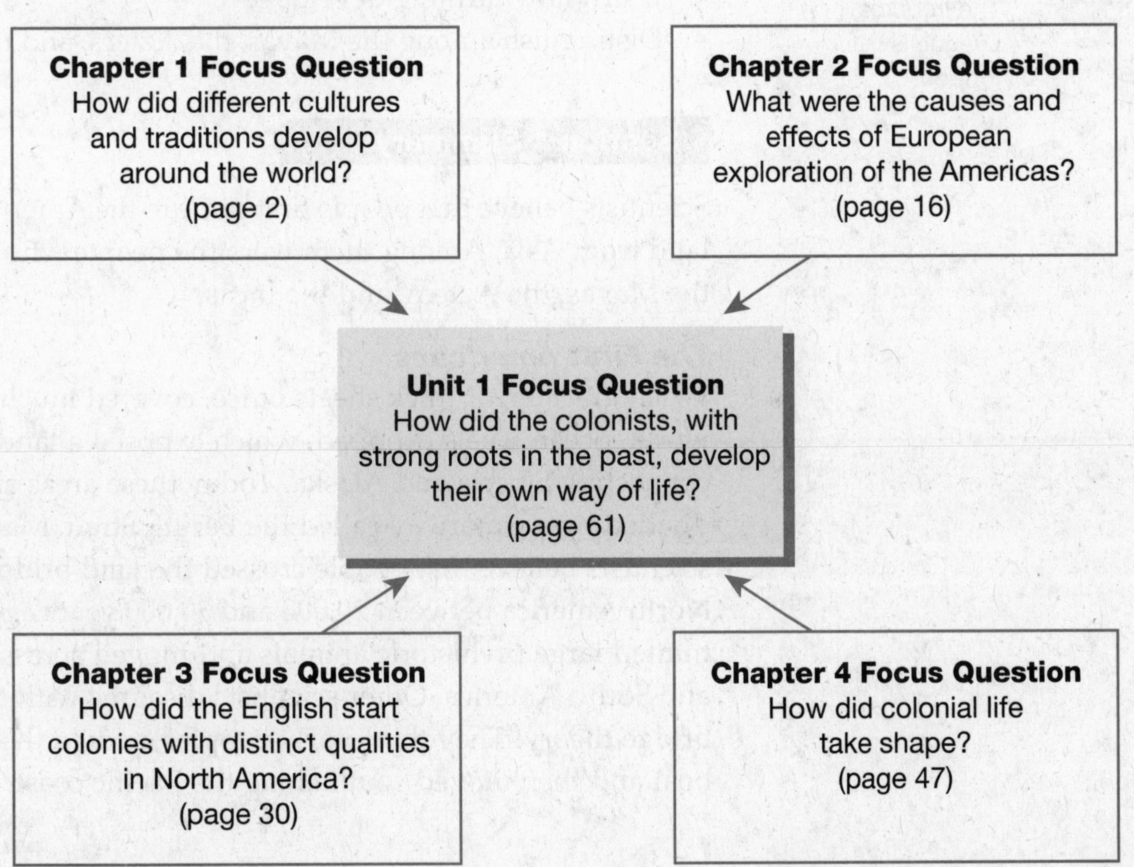

Chapter 1 Focus Question
How did different cultures and traditions develop around the world?
(page 2)
Chapter 2 Focus Question
What were the causes and effects of European exploration of the Americas?
(page 16)
Unit 1 Focus Question
How did the colonists, with strong roots in the past, develop their own way of life?
(page 61)
Chapter 3 Focus Question
How did the English start colonies with distinct qualities in North America?
(page 30)
Chapter 4 Focus Question
How did colonial life take shape?
(page 47)

Chapter 1

Roots of the American People

(Prehistory–1500)

What You Will Learn

Early people spread across the Americas and built three great civilizations. As the Maya, Aztec, and Inca developed in North America, trade linked Africa, Asia, and Europe.

Chapter 1 Focus Question

As you read this chapter, keep this question in mind: **How did different cultures and traditions develop around the world?**

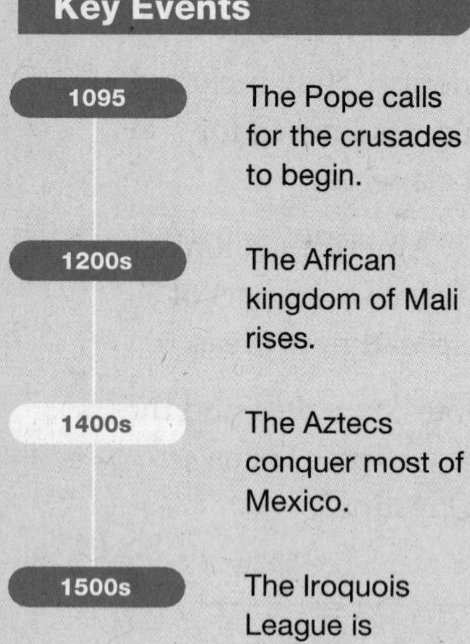

Key Events
1095
The Pope calls for the crusades to begin.
1200s
The African kingdom of Mali rises.
1400s
The Aztecs conquer most of Mexico.
1500s
The Iroquois League is formed.

Section 1
The Earliest Americans

Section 1 Focus Question

How did early civilizations develop in the Americas? To begin answering this question,

- Find out how people first came to the Americas.
- Learn how farming developed.
- Distinguish among the Mayas, the Aztecs, and the Incas.

Section 1 Summary

Scientists believe that people first came to the Americas over land from Asia. Among them were the people who became the Mayas, the Aztecs, and the Incas.

The First Americans

When **glaciers,** or thick sheets of ice, covered much of the world, ocean levels dropped, which exposed a land bridge connecting Siberia and Alaska. Today these areas are divided by a waterway called the Bering Strait. Many scientists believe that people crossed the land bridge into North America between 20,000 and 30,000 years ago. They hunted large prehistoric animals and moved across North and South America. Other scientists disagree with the land-bridge theory. They think early peoples crossed the seas by boat and then moved south along the Pacific coast.

As larger animals disappeared, people changed from hunting to gathering food. About 8,000 years ago, gatherers in Mexico grew squash, lima beans, and many other plants. The discovery of farming completely changed life. Families could now settle in one place instead of constantly moving in search of food. Farmers in dry areas developed **irrigation,** a method to water crops by channeling water from rivers or streams. They also raised livestock and traded their **surplus,** or extra, food with others. With a steady food source, the population grew. Cities arose and became centers of government and religion. ✓

Three Civilizations

The growth of cities led to **civilizations,** or advanced cultures in which people have developed science and industries. Between A.D. 250 and A.D. 900, the Mayas of Mexico and Central America built temples, pyramids, and palaces. They also developed a system of government and a written language. By studying the stars, the Mayas created an accurate calendar. Around A.D. 900, they mysteriously abandoned their cities.

As Mayan civilization declined, the Aztec civilization was on the rise. The Aztecs built their capital city of Tenochtitlán (tay noch tee TLAHN) on a group of islands in the middle of a large lake. Dozens of temples arose from the sacred city center. Religion dominated the Aztecs' lives, and they practiced human sacrifice to please their gods. After defeating half of Mexico during the 1400s, the Aztecs made people pay high taxes. People turned against them.

In the 1400s, the Incas built the world's largest empire in South America. Many roads linked Cuzco, the Inca capital, to other cities. The Incas made huge stone buildings, as well as canals and bridges suspended over canyons. Inca rulers wore gold and silver jewelry. ✓

Check Your Progress

1. Why was the discovery of farming so important?

___

___

2. List one contribution from each of the three early American civilizations.

___

___

✓ Checkpoint

Name the waterway that now covers the ancient land bridge between Siberia and Alaska.

___

Reading Strategy

Underline the sentence in the bracketed paragraph that tells what caused the Aztecs' control to weaken. Circle the sentence that tells what effect this had.

✓ Checkpoint

List three early American civilizations that developed in Mexico, Central America, and South America.

___

___

Section 1 Notetaking Study Guide

Question to Think About As you read Section 1 in your textbook and take notes, keep this section focus question in mind: **How did early civilizations develop in the Americas?**

▶ Use this chart to record key information from the section. Some information has been filled in to get you started.

The Land Bridge
Why it existed: ______
What body of water covers it now: Bering Strait
Places it linked: ______
When people crossed it: between 20,000 and 30,000 years ago
Why it's important: ______

How Early Civilizations Developed
1. Early people were hunters, following large animals. Eventually they spread across ______ and ______.
2. As ______ became extinct, people changed from hunting to ______ food.
3. About ______ years ago, gatherers in Mexico began cultivating ______ and ______, among other plants.
4. Farmers developed ______, a method to channel ______ from rivers or streams. They also learned how to raise ______.
5. With a dependable food supply, the ______ grew. The Native Americans were soon producing a surplus, or extra food, that could be ______ with others.
6. Some farming communities grew into ______.

Three Great Civilizations

People	Location	Accomplishments
Mayas		
Aztecs		
Incas		

Refer to this page to answer the Chapter 1 Focus Question on page 15.

Section 2

Cultures of North America

Section 2 Focus Question

How did geography influence the development of cultures in North America? To begin answering this question,

- Learn about the earliest peoples of North America.
- Note what Native American groups had in common.
- Explore how geography affected cultures.

Section 2 Summary

The first cultures of North America began in the Southwest and the Mississippi Valley. Many were alike in basic ways.

First Cultures of North America

People in North America developed unique **cultures,** or ways of life. The Mound Builders appeared about 3,000 years ago between the Appalachian Mountains and the Mississippi Valley. They built large mounds to use as burial places and as bases for buildings. One group of Mound Builders, the Mississippians, built the first North American cities, including Cahokia in Illinois.

The Anasazi were located in southern Utah, Colorado, northern Arizona, and New Mexico. They made baskets, pottery, and jewelry. Their homes were cliff dwellings, which they mysteriously left by 1300.

From 300 B.C. to A.D. 1450, the Hohokam people farmed in the deserts of Arizona, digging canals to irrigate their crops. To make jewelry and religious items, they traded for shells with people of the Gulf of California. ✓

Ways of Life

Scholars organize Native Americans into **culture areas,** or regions in which groups of people have a similar way of life. Many culture areas shared some basic traits. For example, women gathered plants while men hunted and fished. People made farming tools from sticks, bones, and shells. Farming areas had more people than nonfarming areas. Native Americans believed that spirits dwelled in nature, and they had a close relationship with the environment. ✓

Key Events

1095	The Pope calls for the crusades to begin.
1200s	The African kingdom of Mali rises.
1400s	The Aztecs conquer most of Mexico.
1500s	The Iroquois League is formed.

✓ Checkpoint

Name three of the first cultures of North America.

____

____

____

✓ Checkpoint

List three items used as farming tools.

____

____

Reading Strategy

Reread the bracketed text about the Southwest. Underline the words that describe the climate. Circle the text that tells how people adjusted to that climate.

Mark the Text

Vocabulary Builder

Use the clues in the underlined sentence to explain what *comprised* means. Then explain what comprised the Iroquois.

✓ Checkpoint

List the seven culture areas of North America.

Native Americans of North America

By A.D. 1500, culture groups of North America lived distinct ways of life.

Native Americans of North America
Far North: Arctic people lived in a mostly ice-covered land. They survived on fish and birds and hunted marine mammals from **kayaks,** small boats made from skins. In the subarctic region, which was also too cold for farming, dense forests provided people with plants and animals
Northwest: From southern Alaska to northern California, abundant game and plants allowed people to live in permanent settlements without farming. High-ranking people practiced the **potlatch,** a ceremony in which hosts gave guests gifts as a show of status.
Far West: Environments ranged from northern forests and grasslands to southern deserts. California offered mild weather and abundant food. Housing included pit houses dug into the ground, cone-shaped houses covered with bark, and houses of wooden planks.
[**Southwest:** This region was dry, except after summer thunderstorms. Southwest groups farmed, and some hunted. People stored water for the dry season. The Hopi, Zuni, and other Pueblo people built towns with homes of **adobe,** or sun-dried brick.]
Great Plains: People in the eastern Plains farmed and lived in earth lodges, or log frames covered with soil. The treeless west was unsuited to farming. People there lived in tepees or dug pits for shelter. Buffalo supplied meat, hides for tepees, and bones for tools.
Eastern Woodlands: People hunted, fished, and foraged for plants in the heavy forests. Some began farming by A.D. 1000. The Algonquian people dominated southern Canada and the Great Lakes. <u>The Iroquois, in what is now New York, comprised five nations.</u> Each nation had **clans,** or groups of families related to one another. Women owned all clan property and chose the clan's **sachem,** or tribal chief.
Southeast: Steamy, hot summers supported farming. The Cherokees and Creeks built cool, dry houses of wooden frames covered with straw mats and mud. The Natchez of the Gulf Coast created a complex society with a ruler, nobles, and commoners.

✓

Check Your Progress

1. Why did culture groups build different kinds of homes?

2. Why did Native Americans value nature so highly?

Section 2 Notetaking Study Guide

Question to Think About As you read Section 2 in your textbook and take notes, keep this section focus question in mind: **How did geography influence the development of cultures in North America?**

▶ Use this chart to record key information from the section. Some information has been filled in to get you started.

First Cultures of North America		
Groups	**Location**	**Accomplishments**
Mound Builders		Constructed mounds for burials and buildings, built the first cities in North America
Anasazi	Southern Utah, Colorado, northern Arizona, New Mexico	
Hohokam		Skilled at farming, dug canals for irrigation, traded for seashells

Native Americans of North America		
Region	**Environment**	**Way of Life, Housing, Food**
Far North	Arctic: harsh, often ice-covered Subarctic:	Arctic: Fished, hunted marine mammals Subarctic: gathered forest plants, hunted caribou, moose, bear
Northwest	Stretches from to	
Far West	Different geographic regions: North: South:	
Southwest		
Great Plains	Vast region between the Mississippi River and the Rocky Mountains Eastern Plains: Western Plains:	Eastern Plains: Western Plains:
Eastern Woodlands		
Southeast	Mostly mild, but summers were	

Refer to this page to answer the Chapter 1 Focus Question on page 15.

Section 3

Trade Networks of Asia and Africa

Key Events

1095	The Pope calls for the crusades to begin.
1200s	The African kingdom of Mali rises.
1400s	The Aztecs conquer most of Mexico.
1500s	The Iroquois League is formed.

Section 3 Focus Question

How did trade link Europe, Africa, and Asia? To begin answering this question,

- Read about the role of Muslims in world trade.
- Find out how trading centers rose in East and West Africa.
- Learn how China controlled the Silk Road, a trade route.

Section 3 Summary

The rise of trade linked people in Asia, Africa, and Europe. Trade networks helped spread the religion of Islam. China controlled trade between East Asia and the Middle East.

The Muslim Link in Trade

By the 1500s, trade linked Europe, Africa, and Asia. A trade network passed through the Arabian Peninsula. Ships from China and India brought spices, silks, and gems to Red Sea ports. The goods were then taken by land to the Middle East.

Trade helped the rise of Islam. This religion emerged in the Arabian Peninsula in the A.D. 600s from the prophet **Muhammad.** He taught that there is one true God. Followers of Islam, called Muslims, believed that the Quran, the sacred book of Islam, held the word of God. Arab armies spread Islam to North Africa and Spain. Muslim merchants also spread the religion far into Africa's interior and to Persia and India, where millions of people converted.

Arab scholars made important contributions to learning and technology. They helped develop algebra and made other advances in math, medicine, and astronomy. They improved ships by introducing large, triangular sails that caught the wind even if it changed direction. ✓

✓ Checkpoint

Name the religion that conquest and trade helped spread to North Africa, Spain, Persia, and India.

____

The African Link in Trade

As early as 3100 B.C., Egyptians set up trade routes around the eastern Mediterranean Sea and the Red Sea to bring home cedar logs, silver, and horses. They also traded for ivory, spices, copper, and cattle from south of Egypt.

Trade centers developed in East Africa about 1000 B.C. By the 1400s, Zimbabwe had become a powerful trade center. Traders paid taxes on goods passing through it. Coastal cities, such as Kilwa, grew wealthy as traders exchanged cloth, pottery, and other goods for gold and ivory from Africa's inland areas. A slave trade also developed between East Africa and Asia across the Indian Ocean.

Desert nomads from the Middle East crossed the Sahara with camel caravans to reach West Africa. Ghana, the first major trade center in West Africa, was affluent because of its location between salt mines and gold fields. War and changing trade routes slowly weakened the kingdom. In the 1200s, Ghana became part of the empire of Mali, ruled by **Mansa Musa.** A Muslim, Mansa Musa turned Mali's great city of Timbuktu into a center of Islamic learning. Mali declined in the 1400s under a series of weak rulers. Timbuktu was captured by the Songhai in 1468. Like Ghana and Mali, Songhai grew rich from salt, gold, and slaves. ☑

The East Asian Link in Trade

China's empire was joined together in 221 B.C. It spread across Asia, linked by highways, canals, and a postal system. China's trade grew from improvements in **navigation,** the science of plotting the course of ships, and inventions like the magnetic compass.

By the 1300s, Chinese traders used sea routes extending from Japan to East Africa. The Chinese explorer **Zheng He** visited 30 nations in Asia and Africa with his fleet of giant ships. A famous trade route on land was the Silk Road. It was not really just one road but a 5,000-mile series of roads extending from Xian, in China, to Persia. Merchants carried silks and pottery across Asia to markets in the Middle East and Europe. ☑

Check Your Progress

1. What bodies of water provided trade routes between Asia, Africa, and Europe?

____

____

____

2. What was the Silk Road?

____

____

Vocabulary Builder

In the underlined sentence, the word *affluent* means "having an abundance of material wealth." List three synonyms for *affluent*.

____

____

____

✓ Checkpoint

Name the major trade centers of East and West Africa.

East Africa: ______________________________

____

West Africa: ______________________________

____

Reading Strategy

Ask and answer a question about China's advanced civilization.

Question: ______________________________

____

Answer: ______________________________

____

✓ Checkpoint

Name the invention that improved China's navigation.

____

Section 3 Notetaking Study Guide

Question to Think About As you read Section 3 in your textbook and take notes, keep this section focus question in mind: **How did trade link Europe, Africa, and Asia?**

▶ Use this chart to record key information from the section. Some information has been filled in to get you started.

Trade Networks
The Muslim Link in Trade
By the 1500s, a complex trade network linked Asia, ______, and ______. Much of this trade passed through the ______ Peninsula in the Middle East. There, the religion of Islam emerged in the A.D. 600s through the prophet ______. Islam spread rapidly through ______ and trade. Arab scholars made remarkable contributions to mathematics, ______, and ______. Ship technology included large, triangular ______.
The African Link in Trade
East Africa The most powerful trade center in eastern Africa in the 1400s was Zimbabwe. The coastal city of ______ exchanged cloth, ______, and manufactured goods for gold, ______, and furs from Africa's interior. The slave trade also developed between East Africa and Asia across the ______.
West Africa Trade linked the ______ and West Africa. Desert nomads guided ______ across the Sahara. ______ was the first major trade center in West Africa. The trade in ______ and ______ made West African rulers rich. Under Mansa Musa, Mali's great city of ______ became a center of learning. The third of the great West African trading empires was ______.
The East Asian Link in Trade
______ had a higher level of technology than any other civilization of the time. The invention of the ______ allowed ships to lose sight of land and still return home safely. The explorer ______ visited ______ nations throughout Asia and Africa. The Silk Road was not one ______, but ______. Goods such as ______, ______, pottery, and ______ flowed west from China to Middle Eastern and ______ markets.

Refer to this page to answer the Chapter 1 Focus Question on page 15.

Section 4
The European Heritage

Section 4 Focus Question

What major influences shaped European civilization? To begin answering this question,

- Consider the importance of the Judeo-Christian tradition.
- Learn how ancient Greece and Rome influenced Europe.
- Read about the crusades and the Renaissance.
- Find out why Europeans looked beyond their borders.

Section 4 Summary

Judaism and Christianity shaped religious beliefs in Europe. Greece and Rome helped shape modern government.

The Judeo-Christian Tradition

Judaism and Christianity shaped European religious and moral beliefs. Judaism arose among the Israelites around 1700 B.C. and was the first major religion to teach **monotheism**, or the idea that there is only one God. Israelites believed that Moses brought them God's laws, including the Ten Commandments, and that all people, even powerful rulers, had to obey them.

Christianity began about 2,000 years ago when a Jewish teacher, **Jesus** of Nazareth, began preaching near the Sea of Galilee. Some saw him as the Messiah, the Savior chosen by God. Others saw him as a political threat and had him crucified. His followers said he rose from the dead. Under Christian teaching, all people have a chance for **salvation**, or everlasting life. The Romans saw the religion as a threat and executed Christians. Later, Roman emperors accepted Christianity, and it became Europe's main religion. ✓

Greek and Roman Traditions

Greek and Roman traditions shaped European political systems, and later influenced the United States. In the 400s B.C., the Greek city-state of Athens was a **direct democracy**, a form of government in which an assembly of ordinary citizens makes decisions. Adult male citizens could participate, but women, slaves, and foreigners could not.

Key Events

1095	The Pope calls for the crusades to begin.
1200s	The African kingdom of Mali rises.
1400s	The Aztecs conquer most of Mexico.
1500s	The Iroquois League is formed.

Reading Strategy

Circle the topic sentence in the bracketed paragraph that tells about the influence of both Judaism and Christianity. Underline the words that give an example of this.

✓ Checkpoint

Name two religions of the Middle East that shaped European religious and moral beliefs.

____

____

✓ Checkpoint

List three groups of people in Athens who could *not* participate in government.

____

____

✓ Checkpoint

Name the events associated with these dates:

476: ______________________

____

1095: ______________________

____

1517: ______________________

____

✓ Checkpoint

Name two navigational instruments Portuguese sailors learned how to use in the 1400s.

____

____

During this time, a few villages in central Italy grew into the city of Rome. In 509 B.C., the Romans set up a **republic**, a form of government in which people choose representatives to govern them. An elected senate and assembly made the laws. Under Rome's code of laws, everyone was equal. A person accused of a crime was considered innocent until proven guilty. ✓

New Horizons

Rome fell to invaders in A.D. 476, and Europe broke up into small states. This began the Middle Ages. By the ninth century, kings and nobles relied on **feudalism**, in which a ruler grants parts of his lands to lords in exchange for knights and money. Daily life revolved around the Catholic Church. In 1095, Pope Urban II declared a crusade, or holy war, to gain control of the Holy Land. The crusades failed, but they resulted in introducing Europeans to Muslim civilization.

In the 1300s, the Renaissance revived interest in ancient Greece and Rome. Art, science, and inventions flourished. Powerful nation-states arose, including Spain, Portugal, France, and England.

In 1517 the German monk **Martin Luther** demanded that the Catholic Church reform itself. Those who joined him in protesting certain practices of the Church were called Protestants. They formed their own churches, which pushed Europe into a series of religious wars. ✓

An Age of Exploration Begins

Prince **Henry the Navigator** expanded Portuguese power and spread Christianity. In the 1400s, he set up a school at Sagres (SAH greesh), where sailors learned to use maps, the magnetic compass, and the astrolabe. With these skills, Portuguese sailors opened the way for exploration. ✓

Check Your Progress

1. How did Judeo-Christian, Greek, and Roman traditions influence Europe?

____

____

____

2. How did the fall of Rome affect Europe?

____

____

Section 4 Notetaking Study Guide

Question to Think About As you read Section 4 in your textbook and take notes, keep this section focus question in mind: **What major influences shaped European civilization?**

▶ Use this chart to record key information from the section. Some information has been filled in to get you started.

Ancient Traditions and Their Influence		
Place	**Religious or Political Tradition**	**Influential Idea**
Middle East	Judaism	______, the idea that there is only one God
______	______	All people have an equal chance for salvation.
Greece	Direct democracy	An assembly of ______ makes decisions.
Rome	• republic • ______	• People can elect ______ to govern them. • An accused person is ______.

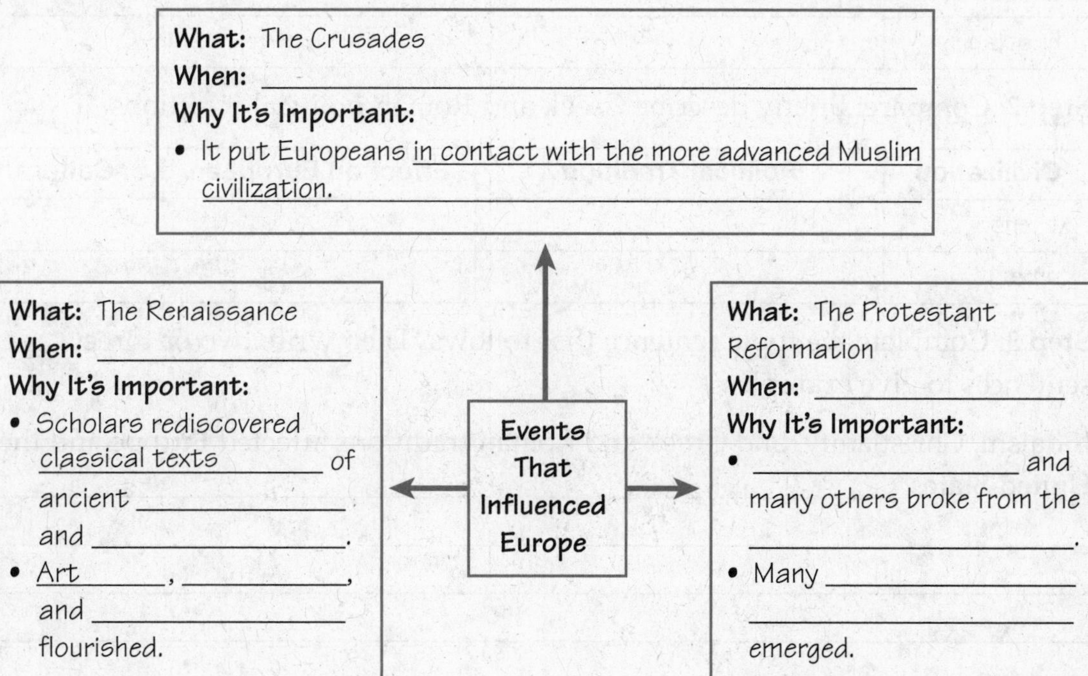

What: The Crusades
When: ______
Why It's Important:
• It put Europeans in contact with the more advanced Muslim civilization.
Events That Influenced Europe
What: The Renaissance
When: ______
Why It's Important:
• Scholars rediscovered classical texts of ancient ______ and ______.
• Art ______, ______, and ______ flourished.
What: The Protestant Reformation
When: ______
Why It's Important:
• ______ and many others broke from the ______.
• Many ______ emerged.

Refer to this page to answer the Chapter 1 Focus Question on page 15.

Chapter 1 Assessment

Directions: Circle the letter of the correct answer.

1. Where was the land bridge over which people first came to the Americas?
- **A** between Siberia and Alaska
- **B** between Mexico and Alaska
- **C** between Alaska and Arizona

2. Which best describes the Hohokam?
- **A** They lived in Cahokia.
- **B** They farmed deserts in Arizona.
- **C** They built cliff dwellings.

3. Which was ***not*** a trade center in Africa?

A Ghana **B** Xian **C** Timbuktu

Directions: Follow the steps to complete this task:

Describe how Judeo-Christian, Greek, and Roman traditions shaped European and U.S. religion and politics.

Step 1: Recall information: List details about two religions of the Middle East.

Religion	Religious Tradition	Effect on European Culture
Judaism		
Christianity		

Step 2: Compare: Briefly describe Greek and Roman political traditions.

Civilization	Political Tradition	Effect on European/U.S. Culture
Athens		
Rome		

Step 3: Complete the topic sentence that follows. Then write two or three sentences to give examples.

Judaism, Christianity, and Greek and Roman traditions affected Europe and the United States ____

Chapter 1 Notetaking Study Guide

Now you are ready to answer the Chapter 1 Focus Question: **How did different cultures and traditions develop around the world?**

▶ Complete the following chart to help you answer this question. Use the notes that you took for each section.

How Early Cultures and Traditions Developed Around the World

The First Americans

A ____________________ once connected Siberia and Alaska. Many scientists think early people crossed into North America here between 20,000 and 30,000 years ago.

Three Civilizations

About 8,000 years ago, the discovery of ____________________ changed life. Three civilizations of the Americas were the Mayas, the ______________, and the ______________.

Native Americans of North America

Culture groups of North America ______________________ to the environment, and based their shared beliefs on a close relationship with ____________________.

Trade Networks of Asia and Africa

By the 1500s, trade linked ____________, ____________, and ____________. Trade and conquest helped spread the religion of ________________, founded by the prophet ____________________. In East Africa, trading centers developed, such as ___________ and ____________. West African trading empires included ____________, ____________, and ____________. Goods from China flowed west along the ________________.

The Judeo-Christian Tradition

Judaism arose in the ________________ around 1700s B.C., and was the first major religion to teach ______________________. Christianity arose about __________ years ago. Initially viewed as a threat, it became the ____________________ of Europe.

Greek and Roman Traditions

Ancient Greek and Roman traditions shaped ________________ through such ideas as direct ______________ and the republic, a form of government in which people choose ____.

New Horizons

In the __________ Ages, daily life revolved around the ______________. In 1095, the ____________________ to the Holy Land put Europeans in contact with ____________ civilization. In the 1300s, the ____________________ revived interest in ____________________. Prince ____________________ set up a center for exploration in Sagres, ________________. Martin Luther began the __________________________ in 1517.

Refer to this page to answer the Unit 1 Focus Question on page 61.

Chapter 2

Europe Looks Outward (1000–1720)

What You Will Learn

In the 1400s, European explorers had their first contact with Native Americans. For the next 300 years, Europeans settled throughout North and South America.

Chapter 2 Focus Question

As you read this chapter, keep this question in mind: **What were the causes and effects of European exploration of the Americas?**

Key Events

1492	Columbus lands in the West Indies.
1539	De Soto begins exploration of what is today the southeastern United States.
1608	The French establish a settlement at Quebec.
1626	New Netherland is settled by the Dutch.

Section 1

The Age of Exploration

Section 1 Focus Question

How did the search for a water route to Asia affect both Europe and the Americas? To begin answering this question,

- Read about the first European contacts with the Americas.
- Learn about the search for water routes to Asia.
- Understand the importance of the Columbian Exchange.

Reading Strategy

On a separate sheet of paper, make a timeline of Columbus's voyages.

Section 1 Summary

The search for a water route to Asia led to the European discovery of two continents and an exchange of resources.

First Visitors From Europe

The first Europeans to visit the Americas were Vikings, a seagoing people from Scandinavia. They explored Newfoundland in 1001. In the 1470s, **Christopher Columbus,** who was from Genoa, Italy, moved to Portugal, Europe's main seafaring nation. He was there to plan a westward voyage to Asia, but Portugal's king would not pay for it. After six years of asking Queen Isabella of Spain, Columbus won Spain's help instead. In August 1492, his crew of 90 set sail on the *Niña,* the *Pinta,* and the *Santa Maria.* On October 12, an island was sighted and Columbus claimed it for Spain. Believing he was in the Asian islands known as the Indies, Columbus called the people he saw Indians. Columbus built a settlement on Hispaniola. He returned to Spain in

January 1493, reporting that the West Indies were rich in gold. In September 1493, he returned to the West Indies as commander of 17 ships. The Spanish wanted to colonize the West Indies and convert the people to Christianity. Columbus built another settlement and enslaved Indians to dig for gold. In 1498, his third expedition reached South America, which he mistook for Asia. He tried to prove this on a fourth voyage in 1502, and died in 1506 in Spain, convinced he had reached Asia. ✓

The Continuing Search for Asia

Other explorers looked for a western route to Asia. Amerigo Vespucci sailed twice to the new lands and believed they were not part of Asia. His descriptions led a mapmaker to label the region "the land of Amerigo," later shortened to "America." In 1510, **Vasco Núñez de Balboa** explored the Caribbean coast of what is now Panama. He hiked westward and became the first European to see the Pacific Ocean.

In 1519, Portuguese explorer **Ferdinand Magellan** searched the South American coast for a **strait**, a narrow passage that connects two large bodies of water, between the Atlantic and Pacific Oceans. He found what is now the Strait of Magellan and from there sailed into the Pacific. In the Philippine Islands, he and several others were killed. Only one ship and 18 men returned to Spain in 1522, making them the first to **circumnavigate**, or travel around, the Earth. ✓

The Columbian Exchange

The Columbian Exchange was a transfer of people, products, and ideas between the Eastern and Western Hemispheres. Europeans introduced hogs, cows, horses, and plants such as oats and wheat. The Americas introduced llamas, turkeys, and food crops. Diseases such as smallpox, chickenpox, and measles killed thousands of Native Americans. ✓

Check Your Progress

1. In what years did Columbus's voyages occur?

____

____

2. What other European explorers sailed to the new lands?

____

____

✓ Checkpoint

Name the country that supported Christopher Columbus's voyages.

____

✓ Checkpoint

Name the first European to see the Pacific Ocean.

____

✓ Checkpoint

List three diseases carried into the Americas from Europe.

____

____

____

Section 1 Notetaking Study Guide

Question to Think About As you read Section 1 in your textbook and take notes, keep this section focus question in mind: **How did the search for a water route to Asia affect both Europe and the Americas?**

▶ Use this chart to record key information from the section.

The Age of Exploration

Explorer	Accomplishments
Leif Erikson	• A Viking who sailed from a colony on ________ in the year ________ • Spent the winter in Newfoundland, which they named ________
Christopher Columbus	• Believed he could reach Asia by ____sailing west____ • Financed by ________ • Voyages: 1492: Landed on a small island, then sailed to ________ and ________ 1493: Discovered other islands, including ________ 1498: Reached the northern coast of ________, but he thought it was the __Asian__ mainland 1502: Attempted to prove his claims in his fourth voyage
Amerigo Vespucci	• Sailed twice to the new lands • Believed that the lands were not part of __Asia__ • A German mapmaker labeled the region ________
Vasco Núñez de Balboa	• Explored the Caribbean coast of ________ • First European to see the ________
Ferdinand Magellan	• Portuguese explorer who set out to find a(n) ________ passage in the year ________ • Spent 38 days sailing through what is today the ________ • Killed in the ________ • 18 remaining men reached ________ in 1522 • First voyage to ________ the Earth

↓

The Columbian Exchange

What it was: ________	
Items brought from Europe to the Americas: • ________ • ________ • ________	Items brought from the Americas to Europe: • ________ • ________

Refer to this page to answer the Chapter 2 Focus Question on page 29.

Section 2

Spain's Empire in the Americas

Section 2 Focus Question

How did Spain establish an empire in the Americas? To begin answering this question,

- Discover how the Spanish defeated the Aztecs and Incas.
- Learn about Spanish explorations in North America.
- Understand Spanish society in the Americas.

Section 2 Summary

Cortés and Pizarro helped establish a Spanish empire in the Americas. Spanish explorers hoped to find cities of gold.

Spanish Conquistadors

Spanish soldier-adventurers called **conquistadors** set out to explore and conquer the new lands. In 1519, **Hernán Cortés** sailed to Mexico with more than 500 soldiers. Conquered earlier by the brutal Aztecs, many Native Americans joined Cortés as he marched on Tenochtitlán. The Aztec leader **Moctezuma** offered gold to get Cortés to leave, but instead he was captured when Cortés claimed Mexico for Spain. In June 1520, the Aztecs forced the Spaniards out. A year later, Cortés returned, destroyed Tenochtitlán, and built Mexico City—the capital of New Spain—in its place.

In 1531, Francisco Pizarro came to seek gold and copied Cortés's methods to defeat the Incas of Peru. In 1532, Pizarro captured the Inca ruler, Atahualpa. The Incas paid a huge ransom to get him back, but Pizarro executed him. By November 1533, Pizarro had defeated the Incas and took their capital city of Cuzco.

The Spanish, with their armor, muskets, cannons, and horses, were easily able to defeat the Aztecs and Incas. In addition, the Native Americans were divided among themselves and did not present a unified force. ✓

Spanish Explorers in North America

In 1513, Juan Ponce de León sailed north from Puerto Rico to *La Florida.* He became the first Spaniard to enter what is now the United States. In 1528, Spaniards landed near the site of St. Petersburg, found no gold, and marched further into Florida. They were attacked by Native Americans and fled by boat. About 80 survivors, led by Álvar Núñez

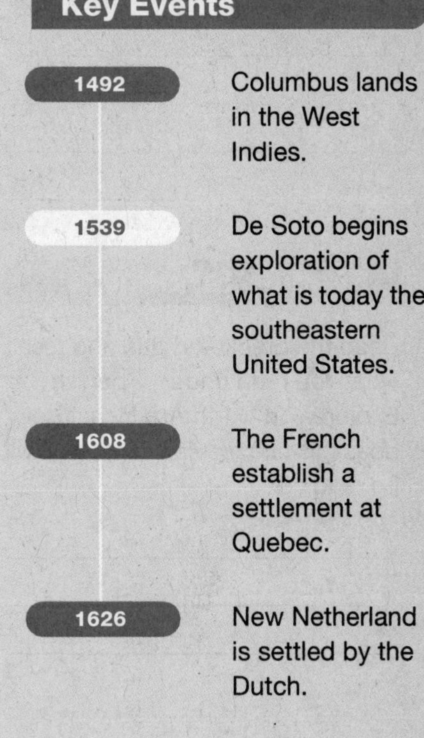

Key Events
1492
Columbus lands in the West Indies.
1539
De Soto begins exploration of what is today the southeastern United States.
1608
The French establish a settlement at Quebec.
1626
New Netherland is settled by the Dutch.

✓ Checkpoint

Name the Aztec and Inca leaders overthrown by the Spanish conquistadors.

____

____

Cabeza de Vaca, landed on the Texas coast. All but 15 died. The rest were enslaved by Native Americans. Cabeza de Vaca, an African named Estevanico, and two others escaped years later, wandering the Southwest. They finally found their way to Mexico City in 1536, telling tales of seven great cities filled with gold. Estevanico led a failed quest for the cities. Francisco Coronado also searched New Mexico, Arizona, Texas, and Kansas in vain. Hernando de Soto found the Mississippi River but no gold. ✓

✓ Checkpoint

Name four explorers who searched in vain for cities of gold.

____

____

____

____

Colonizing Spanish America

At first, Spain let the conquistadors govern the lands they conquered. Later, Spain set up a formal system to rule its new colonies. Government officials gave land to settlers to set up mines, ranches, and **plantations,** or large farms. Land grants called ***encomiendas*** let settlers demand labor or taxes from Native Americans. Forced to work on plantations and in mines, many Native Americans died.

A Spanish priest, **Bartolomé de Las Casas,** tried to improve the *encomienda* system. The Spanish set up Catholic **missions,** or religious settlements, to convert Native Americans to Christianity. As more and more Native Americans died, Spanish colonists began enslaving Africans.

In Spanish colonies, the social system was based on birthplace and blood. At the top were ***peninsulares,*** or colonists born in Spain. Colonists born in America of two Spanish parents were *Creoles.* People of mixed Spanish and Indian parentage, *mestizos,* could prosper but never enter the upper levels of society. *Mulattos,* people of Spanish and African heritage, were held at the bottom of society. ✓

Reading Strategy

Read the bracketed title and recall what you read under "Spanish Explorers in North America." How does this title preview what you will be reading?

____

____

____

✓ Checkpoint

Name the Spanish word for the land grants that allowed settlers to demand labor or taxes from Native Americans.

____

Check Your Progress

1. Who were the conquistadors, and what did they seek?

____

____

2. What were the four levels of Spanish colonial society?

____

____

____

____

Section 2 Notetaking Study Guide

Question to Think About As you read Section 2 in your textbook and take notes, keep this section focus question in mind: **How did Spain establish an empire in the Americas?**

► Use this chart to record key information from the section.

Spain's Empire in the Americas

Spanish Conquistadors: Soldier-adventurers called conquistadors set out to explore and ____________ the Americas. They hoped for riches and ____________ for themselves and ____________.

Hernán Cortés	Francisco Pizarro
1. 1519: Sailed from Cuba to Mexico with more than 500 soldiers	1. Copied methods of Cortés
2. November 8: Marched into the Aztec capital of Tenochtitlán	2. 1531: Landed on the coast of Peru to search for the ____________
3. Native Americans joined him because ____________.	3. September 1532: Led about ________ soldiers into the heart of empire
4. The Aztec leader, ____________, offered Cortés gold to leave.	4. Took the Inca ruler, ____________, prisoner
5. Instead, Cortés ____________.	5. The Inca people paid ____________.
6. 1520: ____________	6. Pizarro instead ____________.
7. A year later, Cortés ____________.	7. By November 1533: ____________

Why Conquistadors Defeated Native Americans:
1. The Indians' weapons were no match for the Spaniards' armor, muskets, and cannons.
2. ____________, which the Native Americans had never before seen.
3. The Native Americans ____________.

The Spanish Social System

Peninsulares: Spanish colonists born in Spain	• Top of the social structure • Most were government officials
Creoles: ____________	Many were ____________.
Mestizos: ____________	Could achieve economic success as ________, ________, and ________, but could not enter ________ of society.
Mulattos: ____________	They were held at bottom of society.

Refer to this page to answer the Chapter 2 Focus Question on page 29.

Section 3

Europeans Compete in North America

Key Events

1492	Columbus lands in the West Indies.
1539	De Soto begins exploration of what is today the southeastern United States.
1608	The French establish a settlement at Quebec.
1626	New Netherland is settled by the Dutch.

Vocabulary Builder

The underlined word *magnitude* comes from the Latin term *magnum,* meaning "great size or significance." Complete these sentences using words with the same root as *magnitude:*

1. A ______________ glass makes objects look bigger.

2. Spain had a vast and ____________ empire.

Reading Strategy

Reread the bracketed text. Underline the causes of King Phillip II's anger.

Mark the Text

Section 3 Focus Question

How did conflicts in Europe spur exploration in North America? To begin answering this question,

- Read about the religious and economic conflicts in Europe.
- Find out about the search for a northwest passage to Asia.

Section 3 Summary

Conflicts in Europe led to struggles in the Americas. Explorers never found a northwest passage.

Conflicts in Europe

The magnitude of the split between Catholics and Protestants became so great that it caused mistrust among European countries. By 1530, rulers had set up Protestant churches in many European states. England's King Henry VIII broke with the Catholic Church because it would not allow him to divorce Catherine of Aragon. Determined to remarry, Henry set up a Protestant church, the Church of England.

European rulers no longer trusted each other. Spain paid for Columbus's voyages in order to get wealth, power, and gold for itself. Spain's king demanded one fifth of all gold found in the Americas. This was part of a system called **mercantilism,** which held that the colonies existed to make the home country wealthy and powerful. European nations needed gold to pay for wars and keep their armies strong.

When King Henry VIII died in 1547, his son Edward ruled for a short time. Henry's daughter Mary ruled next and tried to restore the Catholic Church, but she died in 1558. This put Henry's other daughter Elizabeth I— a Protestant—on the throne. Her reign angered Spain's monarch, King Phillip II, who wanted to make England Catholic again. In addition, the English raided Spanish ships carrying gold from the Americas. In 1588, Phillip assembled 130 warships—the Spanish Armada—to remove Queen Elizabeth from the throne. A fleet of smaller, faster English ships defeated the Armada. The balance of power changed in Europe. With Spain no longer controlling the seas, England and France were able to set up colonies in the Americas. ☑

Asia Continues to Beckon

After Columbus's first voyage to the Americas, Italian explorer **John Cabot** decided a northern route to Asia would be shorter. Only England was interested in supporting his voyage. Cabot left in one ship, in May 1497. On his second voyage in 1498, his ships vanished without a trace. Europeans realized, however, that Cabot had reached a land they had never seen. England, France, and Holland all agreed to pay for voyages to North America to find a **northwest passage,** a sea route from the Atlantic to the Pacific that passed through or around North America. This would mean a shorter route to Asia that would make trade easier.

In 1524, Italian explorer Giovanni da Verrazano searched for a northwest passage for King Francis I of France. He explored the Atlantic coast from North Carolina to Newfoundland. He discovered the mouth of the Hudson River and New York Bay.

French explorer Jacques Cartier made three trips to North America for France. His search led to the St. Lawrence River, which he explored as far as present-day Montreal.

English explorer **Henry Hudson** lost support from the English after two failed voyages in the Arctic Ocean in 1607 and 1608. The Dutch paid for a third voyage in 1609, which led him to New York and the river later named after him. This won English support for a voyage in 1610. After reaching what is now Hudson Bay, however, icy waters halted the voyage. The crew turned against Hudson and set him, his son, and seven loyal crew members adrift. They were never heard from again. ☑

Check Your Progress

1. What happened as a result of England's victory over Spain in 1588?

____

____

____

2. What was the advantage of a northwest passage?

____

____

✓ Checkpoint

Name two reasons that European nations needed gold.

____

____

✓ Checkpoint

Name the "hoped-for" sea route from the Atlantic to the Pacific that would pass through or around North America.

____

____

Section 3 Notetaking Study Guide

Question to Think About As you read Section 3 in your textbook and take notes, keep this section focus question in mind: **How did conflicts in Europe spur exploration in North America?**

► Use this chart to record key information from the section. Some information has been filled in to get you started.

Europeans Compete in North America

Conflicts in Europe:
The split between _____________ and Protestants in Europe heightened religious and economic tensions among European countries.

- King Henry VIII broke with the Catholic Church and set up the _____________.
- Teachings and writings of _____________ influenced Protestant churches in France, Switzerland, _____________, and the Netherlands.
- Mistrustful of Italian and Portuguese traders, Spain supported Columbus's voyages to get _____________, _____________, and _____________.
- _____________ is a system where _____________ exist to make the home country wealthy.
- Queen Mary I tried to restore the _____________ in England, but she died in 1558, and _____________, a Protestant took the throne.
- In 1588, Phillip II assembled _______ warships, a fleet known as the _____________. He wanted to force _____________.

Outcome:
The English _____________, changing the balance of _____________ in Europe. England and France were able to found colonies _____________.

Attempts to Find the Northwest Passage

Explorer	Area of Exploration	How Voyage Ended
John Cabot	_____________, maybe as far south as Chesapeake Bay	His ships vanished without a trace.
Giovanni da Verrazano	_____________	Discovered mouth of the _____________ and _____________
_____________	Discovered the St. Lawrence River	Explored the river as far as _____________
_____________	Arctic Ocean, New York, Hudson Bay	Icy waters halted the voyage. The crew _____________.

Refer to this page to answer the Chapter 2 Focus Question on page 29.

Section 4

France and the Netherlands in North America

Section 4 Focus Question

What impact did the establishment of French and Dutch colonies in North America have on Native Americans? To begin answering this question,

- Read about the French colony by the St. Lawrence River.
- Learn about the Dutch colony along the Hudson River.
- Understand how colonies affected Native Americans.

Section 4 Summary

French colonists depended on the fur trade with Native Americans. The Dutch settled along the Hudson River and also traded with Native Americans. Colonies changed the lives of the native populations.

New France

In 1603, **Samuel Champlain** of France mapped the St. Lawrence River. He set up France's first settlement, a trading post, in Nova Scotia in 1604. Independent traders called *coureurs de bois,* French for "runners of the woods," lived among the Native Americans and went deep into the wilderness to trade for pelts. In 1608, Champlain set up Quebec and explored what is now Lake Champlain. France influenced the area for 150 years. Unlike New Spain, New France grew rich from fish and furs, not precious metals.

In the late 1600s, French colonists began farming as the market for furs weakened. This was due to the Indian wars and the landing of thousands of new French colonists sent by King Louis XIV. In 1673, French missionary **Jacques Marquette** and French Canadian trader Louis Joliet explored the Mississippi River. This gave the French a water route into North America. In 1682, explorer René Robert Cavalier, who was called La Salle, reached the mouth of the Mississippi River at the Gulf of Mexico. He claimed the Mississippi Valley for France and named it Louisiana after King Louis XIV. ✓

New Netherland

In 1610, Dutch traders arrived in the Hudson River valley. Their trade with Native Americans was so good that the Dutch West India Company set up a permanent colony, called New Netherland. In 1624, about 300 settlers from the

Key Events

1492	Columbus lands in the West Indies.
1539	De Soto begins exploration of what is today the southeastern United States.
1608	The French establish a settlement at Quebec.
1626	New Netherland is settled by the Dutch.

✓ Checkpoint

Name the explorer who set up France's first colony in North America.

____

✓ Checkpoint

List the name given to the island at the mouth of the Hudson River that was

(a) purchased in 1626:

____

(b) seized in 1664:

____

Reading Strategy

Reread the bracketed text. Circle phrases that show the positive effects of colonization on Native Americans. Underline the negative effects.

Mark the Text

✓ Checkpoint

List two Native American nations that traded with the French and the Dutch.

____

____

Netherlands moved to Fort Orange, later named Albany. In 1626, another colony and its governor, Peter Minuit, bought the island at the mouth of the Hudson River from Native Americans. They named it New Amsterdam. This Dutch colony made it impossible for English colonies to spread to the west. In 1664 the English took over New Amsterdam. They renamed it New York after England's Duke of York. ✓

The Impact on Native Americans

Because of the rich profits made from furs, the French and Dutch valued Native Americans as trading partners. In exchange for pelts, the traders provided goods such as cloth, iron pots and tools, and guns. In addition, the French and Dutch made **alliances**, or agreements, with Indian nations. Many alliances, however, proved harmful to Native Americans and led to warfare among the tribes. The Huron, for example, allied with the French. The Iroquois had an alliance with the Dutch. Using guns from the Dutch, the Iroquois attacked the Hurons—their longtime enemies—and almost wiped them out.

Diseases caused by contact with Europeans also killed many Native Americans. In addition, the overtrapping of animals weakened the food chain on which Native Americans depended. As fur-bearing animals disappeared, Native Americans were no longer needed by the Europeans. Their land, however, became valuable to the colonists. ✓

Check Your Progress

1. What enabled La Salle to claim the Mississippi River valley for the king of France?

____

____

2. What caused the decline of the fur trade in North America?

____

____

Section 4 Notetaking Study Guide

Question to Think About As you read Section 4 in your textbook and take notes, keep this section focus question in mind: **What impact did the establishment of French and Dutch colonies in North America have on Native Americans?**

▶ Use this chart to record key information from the section. Some information has been filled in to get you started.

France and the Netherlands in North America

New France	New Netherland
Where: St. Lawrence River area	Where: Hudson River valley
Trading posts: • __________ • __________	Traders arrived in the year __________.
Unlike Spain, New France profited from __________ and __________, not precious metals.	Trade was so profitable that New Netherland was made a permanent colony by the __________.
The Spanish forced Native Americans into labor, but the French __________ prized in Europe.	Other colonies: • 1624: Fort Orange (later renamed Albany) • 1626: __________
French colonists began farming as the European __________ declined.	New Netherland was renamed __________ when it was seized by the __________ in 1664.

The Impact on Native Americans

1. In exchange for __________, the French and Dutch provided goods, such as cloth, __________, and __________.
2. The French and Dutch made __________, or agreements, with Native Americans, which often were detrimental to the Indian nations. The Dutch allied with the __________. The French allied with the __________.
3. __________ caused by contact with Europeans killed many Native Americans.
4. The overtrapping of animals __________ on which the Native Americans depended.
5. As __________ disappeared, the Native Americans were no longer valued. Instead, their __________ became more valuable to the colonists.

Refer to this page to answer the Chapter 2 Focus Question on page 29.

Chapter 2 Assessment

Directions: Circle the letter of the correct answer.

1. Which of the following rulers paid for the voyages of Christopher Columbus?
- **A** Queen Isabella of Spain
- **B** King Henry VIII of England
- **C** the king of Portugal

2. For what did Ponce de León, Coronado, and Hernando De Soto search?
- **A** furs for trading
- **B** the northwest passage
- **C** cities of gold

3. What name describes the fleet of ships defeated by the English in 1588?
A the *Santa Maria* **B** *La Florida* **C** the Spanish Armada

Directions: Follow the steps to answer this question:

Why did the Spanish explorers come to the Americas, and how successful were they?

Step 1: Recall information: In the chart, explain why Spanish explorers came to America.

The Spanish explorers, called ________________, came to the Americas for two reasons: to ________________ and to ________________. In this way, they hoped to win ____________ for themselves and ____________ for Spain. European countries such as Spain required gold to ____________ and ____________.

Step 2: Summarize the explorers, where they explored, and their successes and failures.

Conquistador	Area of Exploration	Successes and Failures
Hernán Cortés		
		Defeated Atahualpa and the Incas, captured Cuzco
	La Florida	

Step 3: Complete the topic sentence to summarize the successes or failures of the explorers. Then write two or three more sentences that support your topic sentence.

When the Spanish explorers came to the Americas, they________________________

____

____

Chapter 2 Notetaking Study Guide

Now you are ready to answer the Chapter 2 Focus Question: **What were the causes and effects of European exploration of the Americas?**

► Complete the following chart to help you answer this question. Use the notes that you took for each section.

Europe Looks Outward	
Cause	**Effect**
1. Columbus set out to voyage to Asia.	He arrived in what are now the Americas.
2. Columbus and others reported tales that the new lands were rich in ______.	The Spanish set out to explore and conquer the Americas to win riches for themselves and glory for Spain.
3. The Columbian exchange transferred ______, ______, and ______ between the Eastern and Western Hemispheres.	Good exchanges: Trade items such as cloth, ______ and ______ Negative exchanges: European germs, to which Native Americans had no immunity, brought ______, ______, ______, and other fatal diseases.
4. Hernán Cortés sailed to ______.	He subdued the ______, destroyed Tenochtitlán, built Mexico City, and claimed Mexico for ______.
5. Francisco Pizarro arrived in ______.	He executed ______ and defeated the ______.
6. Spain set up a formal government in New Spain.	A rigid social system took hold, based on ______ and ______. This system helped Spain control its American empire for ______.
7. The split between ______ and ______ heightened tensions among European countries.	
8. England's smaller but faster ships defeated the ______.	The balance of ______ changed in Europe. ______ and ______ founded colonies in the Americas.
9. French traders sought furs and animal skins to sell abroad.	______ weakened the food chain on which Native Americans depended.
10. The fur trade declined.	______ became more valuable to the colonists.

Refer to this page to answer the Unit 1 Focus Question on page 61.

Chapter 3

Colonies Take Root (1587–1752)

What You Will Learn

In the 1600s, England started colonies in America that were influenced by religious beliefs. The Middle Colonies were known for tolerance. Southern Colonies used slave labor.

Chapter 3 Focus Question

As you read this chapter, keep this question in mind: **How did the English start colonies with distinct qualities in North America?**

Key Events

1565	Spain builds the first permanent European settlement in North America.
1607	English start colony at Jamestown, Virginia.
1682	William Penn founds the colony of Pennsylvania.
1732	Georgia is founded by James Oglethorpe.

Section 1

The First English Settlements

Section 1 Focus Question

How did the English set up their first colonies? To begin answering this question,

- Read why the English sought colonies in the Americas.
- Find out why Jamestown barely survived its first year.
- Discover how Jamestown prospered.
- Understand how the Pilgrims set out to govern themselves.

Section 1 Summary

England set up colonies in the Americas. Representative government emerged, as did slavery.

England Seeks Colonies

In the 1500s, England began setting up colonies to provide new markets for its products and to get raw materials for its industries. In the 1580s, two colonies on Roanoke Island failed. The first, set up in 1585, was abandoned. The second, set up in 1587, had vanished by 1590. ✓

✓ Checkpoint

Explain why England established colonies.

____

____

Founding Jamestown

In 1607, a wealthy group formed the Virginia Company of London. King James I gave the company a charter, or document that grants rights, to settle much of the Atlantic coast. In 1607, colonists sailed into Chesapeake Bay and built Jamestown, England's first permanent settlement in North America. There, the swamps spread malaria, a disease that killed many colonists. Colonists seeking gold did little work to grow crops. Chief Powhatan and his people supplied some food, but by 1608, only 38 of the 100 colonists survived.

That year, new leader **John Smith** made tougher rules, including "He who works not, eats not." In 1609, Smith was injured and sent to England. Powhatan tried to drive the colonists away by not giving them food. The winter of 1609–1610 was known as the "starving time." ✓

Jamestown Prospers

Despite hardship, the Virginia Company kept sending new colonists and leaders, and giving free land to the old colonists as an incentive to stay. Farmers began planting tobacco in 1612. They sold all they could grow by the 1620s.

In 1619, colonists met in Virginia's legislature—the House of Burgesses. This marked the start of **representative government** in North America, or government in which voters elect people to make laws for them. Also in 1619, a Dutch ship carried captive Africans to Virginia. Permanent slavery did not begin in Virginia until the late 1600s. ✓

The Plymouth Colony

In the 1500s, people wishing to separate from the Church of England were persecuted. One group of Separatists—the Pilgrims—left for Virginia in 1620. A **pilgrim** is a person who takes a religious journey. In September 1620, they sailed for Virginia on the *Mayflower.* On route to Virginia, storms drove them north to Plymouth, Massachusetts. Before going ashore, 41 men signed the Mayflower Compact, the first document in which colonists claimed self-government. Half the colonists died that winter from hunger or disease. A Native American, **Squanto,** showed them how to plant crops. In 1621 the Pilgrims gave thanks, which is celebrated today as Thanksgiving. ✓

Check Your Progress

1. What happened to the English colony set up in 1587?

____

____

2. What was the name of Virginia's representative body?

____

____

✓ Checkpoint

Name the first permanent English colony in North America.

____

____

Vocabulary Builder

An *incentive* is "something that motivates people to act." What incentive was given to old colonists to stay in Virginia?

____

____

✓ Checkpoint

Name the crop that brought prosperity to Virginia colonists.

____

Reading Strategy

Ask and answer a question about the historical importance of the Mayflower Compact.

Question: ______________________________

Answer: ______________________________

✓ Checkpoint

Name the English Separatists who signed the Mayflower Compact.

____

Section 1 Notetaking Study Guide

Question to Think About As you read Section 1 in your textbook and take notes, keep this question in mind: **How did the English set up their first colonies?**

▶ Use this chart to record key information from the section. Some information has been filled in to get you started.

England Seeks Colonies

In the late 1500s, England began to establish colonies in North America

- to provide ________________
- to get ________________

The first two colonies on ________ Island failed ________.

- 1585: Abandoned a year later
- 1587: ________________

Event or Situation	Why It Was Important
Founding Jamestown	
1607: Virginia Company of London founds Jamestown on Chesapeake Bay.	First permanent English settlement
Many colonists spent their time ________________.	• Not enough ________ • By 1608, only ________
1608: ________ takes charge and draws up tough new rules.	• Most important rule: ________________ • Conditions ________.
1609: John Smith ________	• Conditions ________.
Winter 1609–1610: The "starving time"	• Powhatan ________ • By spring of 1610: ________
Jamestown Prospers	
1612: Colonists planted tobacco, a crop native to the Americas	• Tobacco was a source of ________. • By the 1620s, ________________.
1619: ________ meets for the first time.	• Marked the start of representative government in North America
Summer of 1619: ________	• On board were 20 ________.
The Plymouth Colony	
1607–1609: ________________	• to separate ________ • to practice ________
September 1620: One group of Separatists, the ________, left ________ and landed in ________. Before going ashore, ________________.	• ________________

Refer to this page to answer the Chapter 3 Focus Question on page 46.

Section 2
The New England Colonies

Section 2 Focus Question

How did religious beliefs and dissent influence the New England Colonies? To begin answering this question,

- Learn about the geography of the New England Colonies.
- Read about the Puritan settlement in Massachusetts.
- Understand how religious conflicts led to new colonies.
- Note how the New England Colonies grew and changed.

Section 2 Summary

Although farming was difficult in New England, the forests and fishing grounds were rich resources. The Puritans founded a colony to practice their religion freely. Religious disputes led people to found new colonies. The growing number of colonists led to many changes in New England.

Geography of New England

New England covers the northeastern corner of the United States. Massachusetts, Connecticut, and Rhode Island are in southern New England. New Hampshire, Vermont, and Maine are in the north. Much of the region has hills, low mountains, and forests. Thin, rocky soil made farming difficult, but just off the coast were rich fishing grounds. ✓

Puritans in Massachusetts Bay

The Puritans, a larger group than the Pilgrims, wanted to reform, not separate from, the Church of England. In the 1620s, King Charles I forced hundreds of Puritan ministers to give up their positions. In 1630, about 900 Puritans formed the Massachusetts Bay Company and set sail for Massachusetts and New Hampshire. They were led by landowner and lawyer **John Winthrop.**

The Puritans' main settlement in the Massachusetts Bay Colony was Boston. By the mid-1630s, the colony had an elected assembly, the General Court. Adult male Puritans elected the General Court and the colony's governor each year. The Puritans did not offer others **toleration,** or recognition that people have a right to different opinions. ✓

Key Events

1565	Spain builds the first permanent European settlement in North America.
1607	English start colony at Jamestown, Virginia.
1682	William Penn founds the colony of Pennsylvania.
1732	Georgia is founded by James Oglethorpe.

✓ Checkpoint

Name the present-day states that make up

- Southern New England:

____

____

- Northern New England:

____

____

✓ Checkpoint

Name the ruler who forced Puritan ministers to give up their positions.

____

New Colonies

Religious conflicts led to new colonies. **Roger Williams,** minister of a church in Salem, believed that Puritans should leave the Church of England. He also thought Native American land should be bought, not taken. Forced to leave Massachusetts in 1635, he moved to Rhode Island. In 1644, colonists there received a charter of self-government from the king. People could worship as they chose.

Bostonian **Anne Hutchinson** was put on trial in 1638 for questioning Puritan ideas. Forced out of Massachusetts, she made a settlement in Rhode Island. **Thomas Hooker,** a minister, also left Massachusetts in 1636 and founded Hartford, Connecticut. In 1639, the Fundamental Orders of Connecticut set up an elected legislature and governor. In 1662, Connecticut received a charter of self-government. In 1638, **John Wheelright,** forced out of Massachusetts for agreeing with Hutchinson's views, founded Exeter, New Hampshire. Massachusetts tried to control New Hampshire, but in 1680, the king made it a separate colony. ✓

✓ Checkpoint

List four colonists who had disagreements with some aspects of the Puritan religion.

____

____

____

____

Growth and Change

Puritans believed that towns and churches should govern themselves, and that people should work hard and live in stable families. Each Puritan town set up a **town meeting,** or an assembly of townspeople that decides local issues. New England families earned their living by farming, making leather and other goods, fishing, and shipbuilding. By the 1660s, 300 ships were fishing off the coast or shipping goods.

Reading Strategy

Mark the Text

Underline two beliefs in the bracketed paragraph that affected Puritan society. Then use these details to make a general statement about Puritan society.

____

____

By the 1670s, the number of Native Americans fell to 12,000, due to European diseases. In 1675, the Wampanoag chief, **Metacom** (also called King Philip), fought Puritan expansion. Some Native Americans supported him, but others helped the settlers. The fight, known as King Philip's War, killed thousands. In 1676, Metacom was killed. ✓

✓ Checkpoint

Explain why Metacom declared war on the English.

____

____

Check Your Progress

1. What were Roger Williams's beliefs?

____

____

2. What did the Puritans believe about towns and churches?

____

____

Section 2 Notetaking Study Guide

Question to Think About As you read Section 2 in your textbook and take notes, keep this section focus question in mind: **How did religious beliefs and dissent influence the New England Colonies?**

▶ Use this chart to record key information from the section. Some information has been filled in to get you started.

The New England Colonies	
Geography of New England: • Thin, rocky ________ soil made ________ difficult. • Just off the ________ coastline are some of the ________ ________ in the world. • The long winters and short, warm summers meant that the colonists caught fewer diseases and ________ than colonists in Virginia.	
Puritans in Massachusetts Bay	
Who They Were	**Why They Left England**
People who wanted to ________, not ________ the Church of ________	1620s: King Charles I persecuted them. They believed their way of life ________ ________.
Events	
1630s: 900 Puritans formed the ________ • Led by ________, who was a ________ • Established ________ • Elected an assembly known as the ________ • Only ________ could vote. • By 1634, 20,000 people lived in the Massachusetts Bay Colony.	
New Colonies	
• Disagreements about religion ________. • The Puritans did not believe in ________. • Roger Williams: Believed Puritans should ________ and ________. Founded ________ and decided that the colony would have no ________. • Anne Hutchinson: Questioned some Puritan teachings and was ________ ________. In 1642, she traveled to ________. • Thomas Hooker: Disagreed with ________. Founded ________. In 1639, colonists drew up the ________. • John Wheelright: Shared some of ________ views. Founded ________. In 1680, New Hampshire became a ________.	

Refer to this page to answer the Chapter 3 Focus Question on page 46.

Section 3
The Middle Colonies

Key Events

1565	Spain builds the first permanent European settlement in North America.
1607	English start colony at Jamestown, Virginia.
1682	William Penn founds the colony of Pennsylvania.
1732	Georgia is founded by James Oglethorpe.

✓ Checkpoint

List the four states that made up the Middle Colonies.

____

____

____

____

Section 3 Focus Question

How did the diverse Middle Colonies develop and thrive? To begin answering this question,

- Read about the geography of the Middle Colonies.
- Learn how New York and New Jersey became English.
- Find out how Pennsylvania and Delaware were founded.
- Understand how the Middle Colonies became so diverse.

Section 3 Summary

The Middle Colonies' soil and climate were good for farming. Quakers founded Pennsylvania and Delaware. Europeans from many countries settled the Middle Colonies.

Geography of the Middle Colonies

The Middle Colonies were New York, New Jersey, Pennsylvania, and Delaware. The Hudson River flows south through eastern New York. It empties into the Atlantic Ocean at New York City. New Jersey is mostly lowland along the Atlantic coast. Pennsylvania's largest city, Philadelphia, is located on the Delaware River on lowlands in the southeast. Delaware is located south of New Jersey and also lies along the Atlantic coast.

The warmer, longer growing season and fertile soil made farming easier in the Middle Colonies than in New England. Farmers grew wheat, fruits, and vegetables. ✓

New York and New Jersey

New York was originally called New Netherland and was ruled by the Dutch. By 1660, Dutch farmers, fur traders, and merchants in the Hudson River valley prospered. New Netherland blocked travel between England's northern and southern colonies. In 1664, England's King Charles II gave the Dutch land to his brother James, who conquered it. The colony was renamed New York, after James, the Duke of York. New Amsterdam, its capital, became New York City.

New Jersey was established in 1665, when part of southern New York was split off into a new colony. It began as a **proprietary colony**, or a colony created by a grant of land from a monarch to an individual or family. In 1702, it became a **royal colony,** a colony directly controlled by the English king. New York became a royal colony in 1685. ☑

Pennsylvania and Delaware

In the 1640s and 1650s, new religious groups emerged in England. The Quakers believed that all people are equal, have a direct link with God, and therefore do not need ministers. By the 1660s, thousands of English Quakers refused to pay taxes to support the Church of England. To provide safety from persecution, **William Penn,** a wealthy Quaker leader, used his connections with King Charles II to get a charter for a new colony. In 1681, he received an area nearly as large as England. Penn viewed his colony as a "holy experiment" to see if people from different religions could live peacefully. In 1682, he wrote his Frame of Government for Pennsylvania, which granted an elected assembly and freedom of religion. He did not allow colonists to settle on land until Native Americans sold it to them.

The first European settlers in Delaware were Swedish. Delaware settlers were opposed to sending delegates to a distant Philadelphia. Penn gave the area its own assembly, and in 1704, Delaware became a separate colony. ☑

Growth and Change

Because of its abundant wheat crop, Pennsylvania was called America's breadbasket. Manufacturers produced iron, flour, and paper. Artisans in towns included shoemakers, carpenters, masons, weavers, and coopers, who made barrels to ship and store foods. Pennsylvania's **backcountry,** or the frontier region extending from Pennsylvania to Georgia, was home to Scotch-Irish, and later, Germans. They called themselves *Deutsch* for "German" and became known as the Pennsylvania Dutch. ☑

Check Your Progress

1. Why were Quakers persecuted in England?

____

____

2. How did New Jersey's colonial status change in 1702?

____

____

✓ Checkpoint

Explain why the English wanted Dutch colonial land.

____

____

Reading Strategy

Underline three beliefs that brought Quakers into conflict with the Church of England.

✓ Checkpoint

State how William Penn viewed his colony.

____

✓ Checkpoint

Name five types of artisans in the Middle Colonies.

____

____

____

____

____

Section 3 Notetaking Study Guide

Question to Think About As you read Section 3 in your textbook and take notes, keep this section focus question in mind: **How did the diverse Middle Colonies develop and thrive?**

▶ Use this chart to record key information from the section. Some information has been filled in to get you started.

The Middle Colonies
New York • Began as a Dutch colony named __________ • Economically successful because of farming and the fur trade • Swedish, French, Portuguese, and English settlers were __________ to Dutch rule. • Tension between England and Holland because they were rivals at __________ • New Netherland separated __________ from __________ __________. • In 1664, __________ gave New Netherland to his brother __________. • New Netherland became __________, and New Amsterdam became __________.
New Jersey • Colony was established in __________ when southern New York was split off to form a new colony. • New Jersey began as a __________ colony, but in 1702, __________ __________.
Pennsylvania • Founder: __________ • Granted a charter from __________ in __________ • Offered religious freedom to __________ • Penn's "holy experiment": __________ __________ • In 1682, Penn's Frame of Government for Pennsylvania granted the colony __________ and __________. Economy: • Called America's breadbasket because __________ Diversity: • Many settlers in the backcountry were __________. • Germans described themselves as *Deutsch* and became known as the __________.
Delaware • First European settlers were __________. • Penn's charter included Delaware, but __________. • In 1704, __________.

Refer to this page to answer the Chapter 3 Focus Question on page 46.

Section 4
The Southern Colonies

Section 4 Focus Question

What factors influenced the development of the Southern Colonies? To begin answering this question,

- Read about the geography of the Southern Colonies.
- Learn about the early history of Virginia.
- Note how Maryland, the Carolinas, and Georgia were founded.

Section 4 Summary

A farming region that required many laborers, the Southern Colonies depended on slavery.

Geography of the Southern Colonies

In the 1760s, Charles Mason and Jeremiah Dixon drew the boundary known as the Mason-Dixon line. It became the line between non-slave northern states and southern states where slavery continued. Maryland, Virginia, North Carolina, South Carolina, and Georgia were south of the line. They shared the Tidewater, a coastal lowland with many swamps. The warm, humid climate provided a long growing season for tobacco and rice. Both crops required many field workers, which helped spread slavery. ✓

Virginia Grows

After the 1650s, Virginia's population grew quickly—from 10,000 in 1640 to 40,000 in 1670. Due to disease and violence, the Native American population shrank. Tobacco farmers took Native American land, causing two conflicts in 1622 and 1644. Hundreds of colonists were killed. But Native Americans were defeated and had to accept English rule.

In the 1660s, wealthy Virginia tobacco farmers bought good land near the coast. Poor colonists could neither buy land nor vote. Those who moved inland to farm fought with Native Americans. The governor did not intervene, hoping to avoid war with Native Americans.

In 1675, **Nathaniel Bacon** led 1,000 frontier settlers in attacks on Native Americans. The governor declared Bacon and his men rebels. Bacon burned Jamestown, forcing the governor to flee. Bacon's Rebellion ended when Bacon

Key Events

1565	Spain builds the first permanent European settlement in North America.
1607	English start colony at Jamestown, Virginia.
1682	William Penn founds the colony of Pennsylvania.
1732	Georgia is founded by James Oglethorpe.

✓ Checkpoint

List the five colonies south of the Mason-Dixon line.

____

____

____

____

____

Vocabulary Builder

The word *intervene* comes from the Latin words *inter*, meaning "between" and *venire*, meaning "to come." What is another way to say that the governor did not intervene in this situation?

____

____

✓ Checkpoint

Name the movement in which a colonist led 1,000 settlers in attacks on Native Americans.

____

✓ Checkpoint

Name the law that welcomed all Christians in Maryland.

____

Reading Strategy

Answer *Why?* questions to find causes. Circle the cause that answers this question: Why did the northern part of Carolina develop slowly?

Mark the Text

✓ Checkpoint

Name the founder of Georgia.

____

✓ Checkpoint

State two crops that promoted slavery in the Southern Colonies.

____

____

became ill and died. The governor hanged 23 of his men, but he could not stop settlers from moving inland. ✓

Religious Toleration in Maryland

In 1632, George Calvert set up a colony in Maryland where Catholics could live free from discrimination. When he died, his son Cecil Calvert, **Lord Baltimore,** became owner. Because of tension between Protestants and Catholics, Lord Baltimore supported the Act of Toleration in 1649. It welcomed all Christians and gave adult male Christians the right to vote and hold office. ✓

Colonies in the Carolinas and Georgia

Carolina was founded in 1663. The northern part developed slowly, because it lacked harbors and rivers for ships. Settlers lived on small farms. They produced tobacco and lumber. The southern part grew quickly. Colonists used slave labor to grow sugar and rice. Carolina became two colonies, North Carolina and South Carolina.

Georgia was founded for two reasons. The English feared that Spain was expanding northward from Florida. Also, wealthy Englishmen led by **James Oglethorpe** wanted a colony that would protect **debtors,** or people who owe money, from imprisonment. He banned slavery, but by the 1750s, it was legal. ✓

Change in the Southern Colonies

In the 1700s, the Southern Colonies developed two different ways of life. **Plantations,** or large farms, dominated the economy in the Tidewater region. Tobacco and rice promoted the spread of slavery. The plantation system divided wealthy landowners from poor people who lived in the backcountry. The backcountry was cut off from the coast by poor roads. ✓

Check Your Progress

1. How did Virginia's population change from 1640 to 1670?

____

____

2. For what two reasons was Georgia founded?

____

____

Question to Think About As you read Section 4 in your textbook and take notes, keep this section focus question in mind: **What factors influenced the development of the Southern Colonies?**

▶ Use this chart to record key information from the section. Some information has been filled in to get you started.

The Southern Colonies	
Mason-Dixon Line • States south of the line included ______. • Geography: coastal area called the Tidewater • Why line became important: ______	
Colony	**Important Events and Details**
Virginia	• 1640 to 1670: The number of settlers ______. • 1607 to 1675: The number of Native Americans ______. • Wealthy farmers bought most of the good farmland near the coast. • Poor colonists ______. • Bacon's Rebellion: ______.
Maryland	• 1632: George Calvert set up a colony where ______. • Tensions grew between ______. • 1649: Lord Baltimore helped pass the ______. • It welcomed ______ and gave ______. It was an important step toward ______.
Carolinas	1663: ______ • North Carolina grew slowly because ______. Settlers produced ______ and ______. • South Carolina grew quickly. Settlers produced ______ and ______, crops that depended on ______.
Georgia	Founded because: • England feared Spain was expanding its Florida colony northward. • James Oglethorpe ______.

Change in the Southern Colonies	
1700s: The Southern Colonies developed two distinct ways of life.	
The Tidewater Region • Economy dominated by ______. • A society of ______ and ______. • Divided ______ from ______, who lived in the backcountry.	**The Backcountry** • Cut off from the coast by ______ • Women and girls ______. • People believed that the colonial government ______.

Refer to this page to answer the Chapter 3 Focus Question on page 46.

Section 5

Spanish Colonies on the Borderlands

Key Events

1565	Spain builds the first permanent European settlement in North America.
1607	English start colony at Jamestown, Virginia.
1682	William Penn founds the colony of Pennsylvania.
1732	Georgia is founded by James Oglethorpe.

Section 5 Focus Question

How did the Spanish establish colonies on the borderlands? To begin answering this question,

- Read about Spain's colony in Florida.
- Learn how Spain established settlements across North America.
- Learn about life in the Spanish missions.

Section 5 Summary

Spain set up a colony in Florida long before English settlers arrived in North America. The Spanish Empire controlled much of the country in the 1600s and early 1700s. Missions were set up to convert Native Americans to Christianity and to teach them farming and crafts.

Spanish Florida

Spanish colonies were already hundreds of years old when English colonies were forming along the Atlantic coast. In 1565, Spanish explorers built a fort called St. Augustine to stop France from taking over northern Florida. It was the first permanent European settlement in what is now the United States. Spanish control was threatened when English colonies spread southward. In 1693, the Spanish hoped to weaken the English colonies. They announced that Africans who escaped to Florida would be protected and given land if they defended the colony. Hundreds of enslaved Africans did so in the 1700s. Still, by 1763, there were only three major Spanish settlements in Florida. ✓

✓ Checkpoint

Name the first permanent European settlement in the United States.

____

____

Settling the Spanish Borderlands

The most important Spanish colonies were in Mexico and South America. The purpose of the northern **borderlands,** or lands along a frontier, was to protect Mexico from other European powers. The borderlands began east of Florida and covered much of Texas, New Mexico, Arizona, Colorado, Utah, Nevada, and California.

In 1598, Spanish explorer Juan de Oñate (WAN day ohn YAH tay) went to New Mexico to find gold, to convert Native Americans to Christianity, and to set up a permanent colony. He established Santa Fe. The Spanish used Native Americans to tend their horses, and Native Americans who ran away spread the skill of horseback riding to others. In 1680, Native Americans in New Mexico rebelled and drove out the Spanish, who did not return for ten years.

To convert Native Americans, Father Eusebio Francisco Kino and other missionaries built missions in Texas and Arizona. Missions are religious settlements that aim to spread a religion into a new area. The only early mission that succeeded in Texas was about 150 miles north of the Rio Grande. It converted few Native Americans but did attract colonists. It became the city of San Antonio.

Spain began colonizing California in 1769. **Junípero Serra's** (hoo NEE peh roh SEHR rah) first mission later became the city of San Diego, followed by what are now San Francisco, Los Angeles, and other cities. The Spanish set up almost 20 missions in California between 1769 and 1800. Soldiers built **presidios**, or military posts, to defend the missions. They also set up **pueblos**, or civilian towns, centered around a plaza, or public square. ✓

Life in Spanish Missions

Thousands of Native Americans in Spanish missions farmed, built churches, and learned many crafts. They worked five to eight hours a day five or six days a week, and did not work on Sundays or religious holidays. However, the missionaries punished them if they did not follow mission rules. Many were imprisoned, kept in shackles, or whipped. They often rebelled against the harsh treatment. Thousands died from the poor living conditions and European diseases. ✓

Check Your Progress

1. How did the Spanish try to weaken the English colonies in North America in 1693?

____

____

2. What were presidios, and what was their purpose?

____

____

Reading Strategy

Mark the Text

Underline the sentence in the bracketed paragraph that explains how Native Americans developed skills with horses.

✓ Checkpoint

Name two Spaniards who helped establish missions in Texas and California.

Texas: ____________________

California: ____________________

✓ Checkpoint

Explain why thousands of Native Americans died in the missions.

____

____

Section 5 Notetaking Study Guide

Question to Think About As you read Section 5 in your textbook and take notes, keep this section focus question in mind: **How did the Spanish establish colonies on the borderlands?**

► Use this chart to record key information from the section.

Spanish Colonies on the Borderlands
• The borderlands began in the east with __________. Farther west, they included most of __________. **St. Augustine** • Built in __________ • Why Founded: Spain feared that France might take over the area • Why It's Important: __________ • In 1693: To weaken English colonies, __________. **New Mexico** • Why Founded: Juan de Oñate came to New Mexico to __________. • Why It's Important: __________ became the first permanent settlement in the region. • Oñate used Native Americans to __________. When some Native Americans ran away, they __________. • 1680: __________

Spanish Missions
Texas and Arizona: • Father Eusebio Francisco Kino spread Catholicism and built missions. • The only early mission to take root in Texas was 150 miles north of the __________ and became the city of __________. **California coast:** • Spain began colonizing California in __________. • Missionary __________ led the effort. His first mission eventually became the city of __________. Other missions were in __________ and __________. • Between 1769 and 1800: __________

Life in Spanish Missions	
Positive Aspects	**Negative Aspects**
• Native Americans were not overworked. • They worked __________ and did not work on __________.	• Native Americans did not have __________. • Missionaries __________. • The population fell because of __________.

Refer to this page to answer the Chapter 3 Focus Question on page 46.

Chapter 3 Assessment

Directions: Circle the letter of the correct answer.

1. By the 1670s, how many Native Americans remained in New England?
A 1,200 **B** 12,000 **C** 120,000

2. Which colony was founded by a Quaker?
A Pennsylvania **B** New York **C** New Jersey

3. Which of these divided southern from northern states?
A The Frame of Government
B The Act of Toleration
C The Mason-Dixon Line

Directions: Follow the steps to answer this question:

How did the ability to produce food affect the development of the English colonies?

Step 1: Recall information: In the chart, briefly describe colonists' ability to produce food in the first permanent English settlements in North America.

Jamestown	• • •
Plymouth	• •

Step 2: Provide more details. How did geography affect farming in the English colonies?

New England	• •
Middle Colonies	• •
Southern Colonies	• •

Step 3: Complete the topic sentence that follows. Then write one or two more sentences, giving two examples that support your topic sentence.

The ability of English colonists to sustain themselves in North America depended on such factors as ______________________________

____

____

____

Chapter 3 Notetaking Study Guide

Now you are ready to answer the Chapter 3 Focus Question: **How did the English start colonies with distinct qualities in North America?**

▶ Complete the following chart to help you answer this question. Use the notes that you took for each section.

English Colonies in North America
England established 13 colonies in North America. New England Colonies: ______ Middle Colonies: ______ Southern Colonies: ______
English colonists sought **economic opportunity:** • England wanted to establish colonies to provide new markets for their goods and get raw materials • Because of the thin, rocky soil and long, jagged coastlines, ______. • Because of its abundant wheat, Pennsylvania was called America's breadbasket. • The ______ system of the ______ Colonies helped spread ______.
English colonists showed their **power:** • In 1664, King Charles II granted ______. The colony of ______ became ______. • Even after Bacon's Rebellion collapsed, ______. • As well as offering debtors protection from imprisonment, Georgia was founded to ______.
English colonists exercised freedom of **religion:** • 1620: English Separatists, known today as the ______, landed at ______. • ______ who wanted to reform the Church of England established settlements in what are now ______ and New Hampshire. • Disagreements about religion led to the founding of other colonies, including ______ settlement in Rhode Island, ______ settlement in Connecticut, and ______ settlement in New Hampshire. • ______, who refused to pay taxes to the Church of England, settled in ______ and ______. • George Calvert founded ______ so ______.
English colonists claimed the right to freedom of ***government:*** • 1619: Virginia's ______ marked the start of ______ in North America. • 1620: ______ was the first document in which American colonists claimed the right to govern themselves. • The Puritans believed towns and churches should ______.

Refer to this page to answer the Unit 1 Focus Question on page 61.

Chapter 4

Life in the Colonies (1650–1750)

What You Will Learn

Government and daily life in the American colonies were shaped by English tradition and ideas. By the mid-1700s, however, the colonies had developed traditions and ideas of their own.

Chapter 4 Focus Question

As you read this chapter, keep this question in mind: **How did colonial life take shape?**

Key Events

1730s	The Great Awakening sweeps through the colonies.
1735	The Zenger case marks a step toward freedom of the press.
1750	Georgia becomes the last of the colonies to permit slavery.

Section 1

Governing the Colonies

Section 1 Focus Question

How did English ideas about government and trade affect the colonies? To begin answering this question,

- Learn about key elements of the English political tradition.
- Note how colonies passed laws and who could vote.
- Read about a case that established freedom of the press.
- Find out how the Navigation Acts affected trade.

Section 1 Summary

English ideas about government, individual rights, and trade deeply affected colonial life.

The English Parliamentary Tradition

In 1215, King John signed the Magna Carta, the first document to limit the monarch's power and protect the rights of nobles and other citizens. It also set up Parliament, a two-house **legislature,** or group of people who have the power to make laws. Parliament's greatest power was that the monarch needed its consent to raise taxes. Conflict between King Charles I and Parliament led to the English Civil War in the 1640s. The monarchy fell but was restored in 1660, with Parliament keeping its rights. In 1688 Queen Mary signed the English Bill of Rights. A **bill of rights** is a written list of freedoms that a government promises to protect, including the right to a trial by jury. ✓

✓ Checkpoint

State Parliament's greatest power.

____

____

Reading Strategy

Complete the sentences below with two signal words from the bracketed text.

__________ shows a cause-and-effect relationship.

__________ shows a contrasting relationship.

✓ Checkpoint

List three groups of people who could not vote in the American colonies.

____

____

____

✓ Checkpoint

Name the publisher whose case helped establish freedom of the press.

____

✓ Checkpoint

Explain why Parliament passed the Navigation Acts.

____

____

Colonial Self-Government

Colonists expected to have the same rights they had under Parliamentary law. Therefore, they set up legislatures in many colonies, such as the House of Burgesses in Jamestown and the General Court in Massachusetts. However, the British government gave William Penn full ownership of Pennsylvania. In 1701, colonists in Pennsylvania forced Penn to change the legal system. They created the General Assembly to make laws. By 1760, every colony had a legislature. More white males could vote in the American colonies than in England. However, many groups could not vote, including women, Native Americans, or Africans. ✓

Freedom of the Press

The Zenger trial of 1735 helped to establish **freedom of the press,** or the right of journalists to publish the truth without penalty. Publisher John Peter Zenger was arrested for printing articles that criticized New York's governor. Zenger was accused of **libel,** the publishing of statements that damage a person's reputation. The jury found him not guilty because the articles were based on fact. ✓

Regulating Trade

Under mercantilism, colonies existed to serve the economic needs of their parent country. In 1651, Parliament passed the first of several Navigation Acts to support mercantilism. The laws required that any shipments bound for the colonies had to stop in England first. Any colonial shipments to England had to travel in British-owned ships. Colonies could sell tobacco, sugar, and other key products only to England. These laws gave the colonies a steady market, yet many colonists resented the laws. They felt the laws favored England and limited the colonists' chances to make money by not being able to sell goods to foreign markets. ✓

Check Your Progress

1. What was the significance of the Magna Carta?

____

____

2. Why did some colonists resent the Navigation Acts?

____

____

Section 1 Notetaking Study Guide

Question to Think About As you read Section 1 in your textbook and take notes, keep this section focus question in mind: **How did English ideas about government and trade affect the colonies?**

► Use this chart to record key information from the section. Some information has been filled in to get you started.

The English Parliamentary Tradition

In 1215, English nobles forced King John to sign the ______________.
This was the first document to place restrictions on ______________
and limited the monarch's right to ______________.
It also protected the right to own private property and guaranteed the right to ______________.

In ______, William and Mary signed the ______________
that upheld these rights: ______________
______________.

Colonial Self-Government

In the Jamestown colony, laws were made by the House of Burgesses.
In Massachusetts, laws were made by the ______________.
The British government gave full ownership of ______________ to William Penn.
However, the colonists forced Penn to agree that only the ______________
______________.

By ______, every British colony in America had some form of ______________.

Freedom of the Press

John Peter Zenger was put on trial because he published articles criticizing the governor.
He was charged with ______________. The jury found that Zenger was ______.
This case helped to establish the principle of freedom of the press, which ensures that
______________.

Regulating Trade

Three laws of the Navigation Acts:

- Ships from Europe to English colonies had to ______________
______________.
- Imports to England from the colonies had to ______________
______________.
- The colonies could sell ______________
______________.

The Navigation Acts benefited colonies because ______________
______________. However, many colonists resented the
Navigation Acts because ______________
______________.

Refer to this page to answer the Chapter 4 Focus Question on page 60.

Section 2

Colonial Society

Key Events

1730s	The Great Awakening sweeps through the colonies.
1735	The Zenger case marks a step toward freedom of the press.
1750	Georgia becomes the last of the colonies to permit slavery.

✓ Checkpoint

Explain why extended families were useful on colonial farms.

____

____

Vocabulary Builder

The word *assess* is the verb form of the related noun, *assessment.* You might know that an assessment is a test. Use this fact and clues in the underlined sentence to define the word *assess.*

____

____

Section 2 Focus Question

What were the characteristics of colonial society? To begin answering this question,

- Understand family structure in colonial times.
- Read about the roles held by men, women, and children.
- Learn about the main social classes in colonial society.

Section 2 Summary

Although colonists had differences, they were united by a common culture and faced many of the same challenges.

The Family in Colonial Times

Many colonists lived with their **extended families,** groups that include parents, children and other family members such as grandparents, aunts, uncles, and cousins. Most colonists lived on farms, where large families were helpful because there was so much work. Farms were usually far apart, so each family had to be independent. Farmhouses were not very comfortable. During cold winters, families might sleep near the only source of heat, the fireplace.

There were few towns in the colonies. Single people found it easier to find jobs in towns than on farms. In Puritan New England, single men and women were expected to live with a family as a servant or boarder. ✓

Men, Women, and Children

In colonial society, men, women, and children had clear roles. Men controlled the family income and property, and they represented the family in public life. <u>Women were expected to marry men chosen by their parents, who would first assess a man's property, religion, and interests</u>. A woman's property and income became her husband's when she married. Women took care of the children and household duties such as cooking, cleaning, and spinning yarn for cloth. Women also milked cows, tended chickens, and preserved food. In wealthy families, a wife might have help from a servant. Women could not hold office or vote.

Until the age of seven, children could spend their time playing. By the age of seven, children were expected to work, helping with household and farm work. Poor children might become servants for other families. Older children had even greater responsibilities. Boys worked in the fields, and girls helped their mothers. Some boys became **apprentices,** or someone who learns a trade by working for a person in that trade for a certain period of time. ✓

Social Classes

Many colonists came to America hoping to own land and build a better life. In England, land meant wealth, but most of the land was already owned by the upper classes. Those born poor in England had little chance to improve their status. In the colonies, however, land was available. There was also greater social equality in colonial America, although class roles still existed.

Colonial Class Distinctions
The **gentry** was the upper class of colonial society and included merchants, owners of large farms, royal officials, and lawyers. The gentry had great power and could often live in luxury.
The **middle class,** neither very rich nor very poor, included the great majority of colonists. These were the small planters, independent farmers, and artisans. Middle-class men could vote, and some held office. Most of the middle class were white, although a small percentage were of African descent. Unlike in England, the poor could move upward socially and enter the middle class.
Indentured servants were people who signed a contract to work in the colonies for anywhere from 4 to 10 years. The contract holder paid for a servant's ocean passage to America. Indentured servants had few rights while in service, but once the contract expired, the servant was freed. A few became landowners or artisans. Others returned home or lived in poverty.
Free African Americans were not a large part of the colonial population. They could own property (including slaves), but most could not vote or sit on juries.

✓

Check Your Progress

1. Describe the roles that women had in colonial society.

____

____

2. How could people move up in class in colonial society?

____

____

✓ Checkpoint

Name one way in which life changed for colonial children at the age of seven.

____

____

Reading Strategy

Ask and answer a question about the differences between social classes in England and the colonies.

Question: ______________________________

____

Answer: ______________________________

____

✓ Checkpoint

List two differences between the middle class and the gentry.

____

____

____

____

Section 2 Notetaking Study Guide

Question to Think About As you read Section 2 in your textbook and take notes, keep this section focus question in mind: **What were the characteristics of colonial society?**

▶ Use this chart to record key information from the section. Some information has been filled in to get you started.

<table>
<tr><th colspan="2">Colonial Society</th></tr>
<tr>
<td>

I. The Family in Colonial Times
Most colonists lived on farms.
Homes were far apart, so families needed to be ________________.
It was easier for ________________ to support themselves in towns than on farms.

II. Men, Women, and Children
The key roles that men had:
• fulfill home duties
• ________________
• ________________

The key roles that women had:
• childcare
• Domestic responsibilities: ________________
• Outdoor responsibilities: ________________

The key roles that children had:
• Until about the age of seven, children ________________.
• By the age of seven, children ________________.
• An apprentice was ________________.

</td>
<td>

III. Social Classes
Social class in England was very rigid.
People could not easily move from a lower class to a higher class.

Classes in Colonial America
The Gentry
The gentry were the upper class of colonial society.
People in this class included ________________.

The Middle Class
This class included the great majority of colonists.
People in this class included ________________.
The poor could become part of this class by ________________.

Indentured Servants
An indentured servant signed a ________ agreeing to work for someone for 4 to 10 years in exchange for ________________. When the contract was over, the signer was ________________.

Free African Americans
Free African Americans could own ________________. They could not ________ or ________.

</td>
</tr>
</table>

Refer to this page to answer the Chapter 4 Focus Question on page 60.

Section 3
Slavery in the Colonies

Section 3 Focus Question

How did slavery develop in the colonies and affect colonial life? To begin answering this question,

- Read how the slave trade brought Africans to the colonies.
- Learn why slavery developed and how it was maintained.
- Understand African cultural traditions in America.

Section 3 Summary

Captive Africans were brought to the colonies and enslaved on farms and plantations as a source of steady labor.

The Atlantic Slave Trade

Between the 1500s and the 1800s, more than 10 million Africans were enslaved and brought to the Americas. The first Africans were brought to the Americas by the Spanish and the Portuguese. In time, the British, Dutch, and French also entered the slave trade. Slave traders in Africa bought captives from the interior. Many captives died during the long journey to the coast.

Enslaved Africans were traded for guns and other goods. They then traveled the Middle Passage, a voyage across the Atlantic Ocean. It was so brutal that 15 to 20 percent of the captives died or committed suicide on the way over. In the Americas, the captives were sold at auction. Most worked on plantations in New Spain, Brazil, or the Caribbean.

Slave traders followed a routine known as the **triangular trade.** It was a three-way trade between the colonies, the West Indies (islands of the Caribbean), and Africa:

- Ships from New England carried fish, lumber, and other goods to the West Indies. They returned with sugar and molasses, a syrup used to make rum.
- Ships from New England carried rum, guns, and goods to West Africa. These were traded for enslaved Africans.
- Ships from West Africa carried the slaves to the West Indies, where they were sold. With the profits, traders bought more molasses. ✓

Key Events

1730s	The Great Awakening sweeps through the colonies.
1735	The Zenger case marks a step toward freedom of the press.
1750	Georgia becomes the last of the colonies to permit slavery.

✓ Checkpoint

List the three regions connected by the triangular trade.

____

____

____

Reading Strategy

Reread the bracketed paragraph. Underline two details that answer this question: Why were there more slaves than indentured servants?

Mark the Text

Vocabulary Builder

Be alert for words with more than one meaning. The word *episodes* can refer to programs in a TV series. Define the word as it is used in the underlined sentence.

____

____

✓ Checkpoint

Explain why the plantation system encouraged the growth of slavery.

____

____

____

✓ Checkpoint

Name three African cultural traditions maintained in America.

____

____

____

Slavery in the Colonies

A harsh and permanent system of slavery developed in the colonies. The plantation system contributed to the rise of slavery. Planters used thousands of enslaved Africans to grow tobacco and rice. Slaves were preferable to indentured servants for several reasons. Indentured servants were temporary, and their number decreased as conditions improved in England. Africans could be enslaved for life. A 1639 Maryland law prevented slaves from becoming free by declaring that baptism did not lead to freedom. A 1663 Virginia court decision declared that the child of a slave was also a slave. When Georgia lifted its ban on slavery in the 1750s, slavery became legal in all of the colonies.

Though not every African in America was a slave, only people of African descent were slaves. Because of this, slavery in America was linked to **racism**, the belief that one race is superior or inferior to another.

The first serious slave revolt took place in Gloucester, Virginia, in 1663. The uprising failed. Fearing similar episodes, colonists wrote **slave codes**, or strict laws that restricted the rights and activities of slaves. Slaves could not gather in large groups, own weapons, or leave a plantation without permission. It became illegal to teach slaves to read or write. Masters who killed slaves could not be tried for murder. Revolts continued until slavery ended in 1865. ✓

African Cultural Influences

About 10 percent of enslaved Africans lived north of Maryland. They worked as blacksmiths, house servants, or farm workers. On isolated rice plantations in South Carolina, slaves kept many West African customs, such as speaking Gullah, a dialect that blended English and several African languages. Although other Africans in the South were less isolated, African craft styles were still continued. African drum rhythms became part of American music. ✓

Check Your Progress

1. What work was done by most enslaved Africans?

____

____

2. What racist ideas did the slave codes reinforce?

____

____

Section 3 Notetaking Study Guide

Question to Think About As you read Section 3 in your textbook and take notes, keep this section focus question in mind: **How did slavery develop in the colonies and affect colonial life?**

► Use this chart to record key information from the section. Some information has been filled in to get you started.

The Atlantic Slave Trade
• The first enslaved Africans were brought to the Americas by the Spanish and ________. Later, the ________, ________, and ________ also entered the slave trade. • Most slaves were captured in the African interior and then sold to traders along the ________ coast. • The Middle Passage was ________. Between ________ and ________ percent of captives died during this journey.

Three Parts of the Triangular Trade		
1. Ships from New England carried ________ to the West Indies. They returned with ________.	2. Ships from New England carried rum and guns to ________. There, merchants traded these goods for ________.	3. Ships sailed from ________ to the ________, where they sold ________ and bought molasses.

Slavery in the Colonies
The plantation system helped slavery take root in America because ________. Early attempts to stop slavery were not successful and did not last long. In 1663 in Gloucester, Virginia, ________, but failed. In 1739 an enslaved African named Jemmy ________. Slave codes were written to ________.

African Cultural Influences
________ percent of enslaved Africans lived north of Maryland. Slaves on rice plantations in South Carolina kept many customs of West Africa because ________. Gullah is ________. Other examples of West African culture in the Americas: • crafts such as ________ • rhythms of ________ and musical instruments such as ________ • ________

Refer to this page to answer the Chapter 4 Focus Question on page 60.

Section 4

The Spread of New Ideas

Key Events

1730s	The Great Awakening sweeps through the colonies.
1735	The Zenger case marks a step toward freedom of the press.
1750	Georgia becomes the last of the colonies to permit slavery.

✓ Checkpoint

List four subjects that were taught in colonial schools.

____

____

____

____

Vocabulary Builder

An *academy* is a school. Use this clue and the underlined sentence to explain what an academic writing style might be like.

____

____

Section 4 Focus Question

How did ideas about religion and government influence colonial life? To begin answering this question,

- Learn about colonial schools.
- Find out about three early American writers.
- Discover the impact of the Great Awakening.
- Read about Enlightenment ideas that influenced America.

Section 4 Summary

Puritan ideas influenced colonial education, and American literature began to be written. The Great Awakening and the Enlightenment influenced American thought.

The Importance of Education

Puritans in New England combined education with religion. They made laws requiring towns to provide schools. **Public schools** are supported by taxes. Puritan schools were supported by both public and private money. Colonial schools taught religion, reading, writing, and arithmetic. Most schools were in the north, where people lived closely together. In the South, members of the gentry hired private teachers. Children of poor families often had no education.

Only some schools admitted girls. **Dame schools** were opened by women to teach girls and boys to read. Schools did not admit enslaved Africans. Some Quaker and Anglican missionaries taught slaves to read.

After elementary school, some boys went to grammar school. The first American colleges were founded mainly to educate men to become ministers. ✓

Roots of American Literature

The first American literature was sermons and histories. America's first published poet was **Anne Bradstreet.** Her poems described the joys and hardships of life in Puritan New England. **Phyllis Wheatley** was an enslaved African in Boston. Her first poem was published in the 1760s when she was about 14. <u>She wrote in an academic style</u>.

Benjamin Franklin started writing the *Pennsylvania Gazette* when he was 17. His most popular work, *Poor Richard's Almanack,* was published yearly from 1733 to 1753. He was also a scientist, businessman, and diplomat. ✓

The Great Awakening

Religion was always a part of colonial life. By the 1700s, rules on religion had become less strict in many of the colonies. As a result, a strong Christian movement called the Great Awakening arose in the 1730s and 1740s. **Jonathan Edwards,** a Massachusetts preacher, called on people to commit themselves to God. Other preachers spread the movement on sermon tours. New churches grew, including Methodists and Baptists. Other churches split into two groups: those who followed the Great Awakening and those who did not. New churches led to more tolerance of various religions and reinforced democratic ideas. ✓

The Enlightenment

Enlightenment thinkers believed that all problems could be solved by reason. They looked for "natural laws" governing politics, society, and economics. Englishman John Locke contributed some of the movement's key ideas. He thought that people have **natural rights,** or rights that belong to every human from birth and cannot be taken away. Locke argued that government exists to protect these rights. If a monarch violates these rights, citizens should overthrow the monarch. His ideas shaped the founding of the United States.

Frenchman Baron de Montesquieu also influenced American ideas. He favored **separation of powers,** or a division of the power of government into separate branches. This would prevent any one group from gaining too much power. He suggested a legislative branch to make laws, an executive branch to enforce laws, and a judicial branch to make judgments based on law. ✓

Check Your Progress

1. What was the focus of the Great Awakening?

____

____

2. What were two ideas held by Enlightenment thinkers?

____

____

✓ Checkpoint

Describe the topic of Anne Bradstreet's poems.

____

____

✓ Checkpoint

Identify the trend to which the Great Awakening reacted.

____

____

Reading Strategy

Underline a cause in the bracketed paragraph. Then circle the effect of that cause.

✓ Checkpoint

Explain the concept of natural rights.

____

____

Section 4 Notetaking Study Guide

Question to Think About As you read Section 4 in your textbook and take notes, keep this section focus question in mind: **How did ideas about religion and government influence colonial life?**

▶ Use this chart to record key information from the section.

The Importance of Education
Massachusetts' laws requiring schools were the beginning of public schools in America. Colonial elementary schools taught ________, ________, ________, and ________. Dame schools were ________________________.

Roots of American Literature	
Poetry	• Anne Bradstreet was America's first published poet. Her poetry described ________________. • Phyllis Wheatley was ________________.
Ben Franklin	• At age 17, Benjamin Franklin started the newspaper ________. • ________________ was his most popular work.

The Great Awakening

Cause		Effect
Religion played a key role in the 13 colonies, but by the 1700s rules on religion had become less strict.	→	The Great Awakening was a reaction against this trend. It was ________________.
The Great Awakening led to the rise of ________________.	→	As a result, ________________.

The Enlightenment	
John Locke	• Defined natural rights: rights that belong to every human from birth and cannot be taken away. • Justified the overthrow of a monarch if ________________.
Montesquieu	• Separation of powers: division of government into separate branches • Government should be divided into three branches: ________, ________, and ________.

Refer to this page to answer the Chapter 4 Focus Question on page 60.

Chapter 4 Assessment

Directions: Circle the letter of the correct answer.

1. What was one key idea behind the Navigation Acts?
   A Religious freedom must be protected.
   B The slave trade is profitable.
   C Colonists must trade with England only.

2. Where did most colonists live?
   A on farms
   B in Massachusetts
   C in small towns

3. What was the goal of the Great Awakening?
   A to end slavery
   B religious commitment
   C the separation of powers

Directions: Follow the steps to answer this question:

What was the main reason that slavery took root in the colonies?

Step 1: Recall information: Note how three factors below affected the growth of slavery.

Factors Leading to Slavery
Plantation System: ______________________________
Indentured Servants: ______________________________
Racism: ______________________________

Step 2: Evaluate: Rank the three factors from most to least important. Give two reasons why you chose the element you ranked as most important.

_____ Plantation System _____ Indentured Servants _____ Racism
• Reason 1: ______________________________
• Reason 2: ______________________________

Step 3: Complete the topic sentence that follows. Then write two or three more sentences that support your topic sentence.

The main reason that slavery took root in the colonies was

____

____

____

Chapter 4 Notetaking Study Guide

Now you are ready to answer the Chapter 4 Focus Question: **How did colonial life take shape?**

► Complete the following chart to help you answer this question.

Ideas That Shaped the Colonies	
Rights	• As English subjects, colonists believed that they had political rights. • In America, ______ had the right to vote. Colonial ______ made laws. • The Zenger Trial helped establish the ______. • Enlightenment thinkers believed that ______.
Education	Colonies developed public schools to teach religion and ______, ______, and ______. The first college in the colonies was ______, which opened in the year 1638.
Religion	The Great Awakening was a ______ movement that ______.
Racism	Racism in the colonies encouraged the development of ______.
Laws That Shaped the Colonies	
Navigation Acts	First passed in 1651, these laws were designed to ______.
Slave Codes	These laws were passed in order to ______.
Economic Systems That Shaped the Colonies	
Plantations	The plantation system led to slavery because plantations needed ______.
Triangular Trade	This three-way trade between ______, ______, and ______ resulted in ______.
Roles That Shaped the Colonies	
Family Roles	Men: ______ Women: ______ Children: ______
Social Classes	The major social classes in the colonies were ______.

Refer to this page to answer the Unit 1 Focus Question on page 61.

Unit 1 Pulling It Together Activity

What You Have Learned

Chapter 1 Early people spread across the Americas as different cultures were developing in Africa, Asia, and Europe. European traditions that influenced the United States included Judaism, Christianity, and Greek democracy.

Chapter 2 During the 1400s, European explorers came into contact with Native Americans. Europeans competed to build settlements in the Americas.

Chapter 3 The English set up colonies in North America. Puritans influenced the New England Colonies, the Middle Colonies became known for religious tolerance, and the Southern Colonies developed plantations based on slavery.

Chapter 4 Although life in the English colonies was influenced by European ideas, the colonies developed their own distinct ideas and traditions. The Enlightenment influenced scientific and political thought.

Think Like a Historian

Read the Unit 1 Focus Question: **How did the colonists, with strong roots in the past, develop their own way of life?**

► Use the organizers on this page and the next to collect information to answer this question. How did colonists develop their own way of life? Some details are listed in the chart below and on the next page. Review your section and chapter notes. Then complete the organizer.

How Colonists Developed Their Own Way of Life	
Government Colonial legislatures: • • Colonial documents: • •	**Religion** Religions that came to the colonies: • • • • Colonies that offered religious tolerance: • •

How Colonists Developed Their Own Way of Life (*Continued*)	
New Colonies • New England Colonies: • Middle Colonies: • Southern Colonies:	**Economic Developments in:** • New England Colonies: • Middle Colonies: • Southern Colonies:

Look at the other part of the Unit 1 Focus Question: **How was the colonists' way of life rooted in the past?** The organizer below gives you a part of the answer. Review your section and chapter notes. Then fill in the rest of the organizer.

How the Colonists' Way of Life Was Rooted in England's Past	
England's Political Traditions • Monarchy • • •	**England's Religion** • • Persecution of
England's Economic Control • Mercantilism: Colonies expected to • Navigation Acts: • •	

Unit 2

Forming A New Nation

What You Will Learn

Chapter 5 The American colonists, although united with Britain throughout the French and Indian War, grew rebellious over Britain's effort to control them. As tensions increased, rebellion turned into a call for independence.

Chapter 6 In 1776, the colonists officially announced their Declaration of Independence. A difficult war followed. The American Revolution ended in 1783 with a treaty declaring American independence from British rule.

Chapter 7 The new United States set up its first national government. Weaknesses in the Articles of Confederation, however, led to the drafting of a new constitution for the nation. A bill of rights was soon added.

Citizenship Handbook To be an active citizen, it is important to understand the ideas behind the U.S. Constitution.

Focus Your Learning As you study this unit and take notes, you will find the information to answer the questions below. Answering the Chapter Focus Questions will help build your answer to the Unit Focus Question.

Chapter 5 Focus Question
How did the relationship between Britain and the colonies fall apart?
(page 64)

Chapter 6 Focus Question
How did the American colonists gain their independence?
(page 78)

Unit 2 Focus Question
How did the colonists break away from Britain and create a republican form of government?
(page 119)

Chapter 7 Focus Question
What were major successes and failures of the government under the Articles of Confederation?
(page 92)

Chapter 5

The Road to Revolution 1745–1776

What You Will Learn

Britain and the colonists win the French and Indian War. When Britain tries to use greater control over the colonies, tensions mount and finally erupt into a war of revolution.

Chapter 5 Focus Question

As you read this chapter, keep this question in mind: **How did the relationship between Britain and the colonies fall apart?**

Key Events

1754	French and Indian War begins.
1765	Stamp Act is passed.
1775	Fighting at Lexington and Concord marks the beginning of the American Revolution.

Section 1

Trouble on the Frontier

Section 1 Focus Question

How did the British gain French territory in North America? To begin answering this question,

- Understand what caused war between Britain and France.
- Find out why British generals suffered early defeats.
- Learn about the Battle of Quebec and the Treaty of Paris.

Section 1 Summary

Britain and France fought over American territory. After several defeats, the British won the key battle of Quebec. The French gave their American territories to Britain and Spain.

Competing Empires

In 1753, the French began building forts to protect their claim to the Ohio River valley. The Virginia Colony claimed the land, too. The governor of Virginia sent soldiers, led by young **George Washington,** to build a fort where the Ohio River forms. But the French were already building Fort Duquesne (du KANE) at the spot. A large French army forced Washington and his men to return to Virginia.

In Albany, New York, colonial leaders discussed war with France and a possible **alliance,** or agreement, with the Iroquois. The Iroquois, believing the French had the stronger military advantage, chose not to ally with the British. At the meeting,

Vocabulary Builder

Reread the underlined sentence. If an *alliance* is an agreement between two nations to help each other, what does it mean to *ally* with someone?

____

____

Benjamin Franklin presented his Albany Plan of Union. Under this plan, colonial assemblies would elect a council that had authority over western settlements, as well as the power to organize armies and collect taxes to pay war expenses. The Albany Congress agreed to the plan, but the colonial assemblies, fearful of losing control of their taxes and armies, rejected it. ✓

Early British Defeats

In 1755, the British government sent General Edward Braddock to push the French from the Ohio River valley. Braddock did not know the fighting styles of Native Americans. As Braddock's troops and Virginia militia neared Fort Duquesne, the French and their Native American allies launched an ambush. Braddock and more than half his men were killed. Also in 1755, the colonials were defeated at Fort Niagara and Lake George.

In May 1756, Britain declared war on France—the official beginning of the Seven Years' War. Shortly after, the French captured two more British forts. ✓

The British Turn the Tide

William Pitt became Britain's prime minister in 1757. He appointed generals whose talents were equal to the French challenge. In 1758, Britain captured the fort at Louisbourg and then Fort Duquesne. These two victories, followed by others, convinced the Iroquois to ally with the British. With growing confidence, Britain prepared to attack the city of Quebec, the capital of New France.

The Battle of Quebec took place in September 1759. General James Wolfe led the British to victory over General Montcalm. Without Quebec, France could not defend the rest of its territories. In 1763, the two countries signed the Treaty of Paris. France **ceded,** or surrendered, almost all of its North American possessions to Britain and Spain. ✓

Check Your Progress

1. What were the provisions of the Albany Plan of Union?

___

___

2. What two military changes helped the British win?

___

___

✓ Checkpoint

State the cause of the initial clash between the British and the French.

___

___

Reading Strategy

The word *ambush* has its origins in ancient Latin and French words: *imboscare*, where *boscus* means "woods," and *busk* means "bush." How does knowing this help you to confirm the meaning of *ambush*?

___

___

✓ Checkpoint

Explain why Braddock's well-trained troops suffered defeat at Fort Duquesne.

___

___

✓ Checkpoint

Name two victories that convinced the Iroquois to ally with the British.

___

___

Section 1 Notetaking Study Guide

Question to Think About As you read Section 1 in your textbook and take notes, keep this section focus question in mind: **How did the British gain French territory in North America?**

▶ Use this chart to record key information from the section. Some information has been filled in to get you started.

Competing Empires
The French and Indian War begins • By the 1750s, the British and French were in conflict over the Ohio River valley. • To protect Britain's claim to the valley, ________ built Fort Necessity south of France's Fort Duquesne. • A large French army forced Washington to ________.
The Albany Congress • During a meeting in Albany, New York, colonial leaders discussed how to win the war and forming an alliance with the Iroquois, who refused to ally with the British. • ________ drew up the Albany Plan of Union. • Provisions of the Plan: 1. A council would have authority over ________ and relations with ________. 2. The council could organize armies and collect ________. • Colonial assemblies ________ the plan.
Early British Defeats
• British General ________ was defeated at Fort Duquesne when he ignored warnings about the dangers of ambushes. • In May 1756, Britain declared war on France, the official beginning of the ________. • French General Montcalm captured ________ on Lake Ontario and Fort William Henry on Lake George.
The British Turn the Tide
• British Prime Minister ________ sent top generals to command the British. • In the fall of 1758, the British took ________. • In 1759, the British captured ________, the capital of New France. The other major French city, ________, fell in 1760.
Terms of the Treaty of Paris, 1763 • Britain's new territories: ________ • Spain's new territories: ________

Refer to this page to answer the Chapter 5 Focus Question on page 77.

Section 2

The Colonists Resist Tighter Control

Section 2 Focus Question

How did the French and Indian War draw the colonists closer together but increase friction with Britain? To begin answering this question,

- Find out why Britain prevented colonists from settling beyond the Appalachian Mountains.
- Learn why Britain tried to increase the colonists' taxes.
- Find out how the colonists reacted to the Stamp Act.
- Understand why the Townshend Acts led to protests.

Section 2 Summary

To pay its war debts, Britain levied new taxes and controls on the American colonists. Each new act caused greater disunity between the British government and the colonies.

Conflict With Native Americans

By 1763, Britain controlled most of North America east of the Mississippi River. Native Americans within this region feared the encroachment of British settlers onto their lands. In May 1763, the Ottawa leader, Pontiac, attacked British settlements. Many settlers were killed, and Britain struck back. By August, Pontiac's forces were defeated. Pontiac fought for another year, but by fall 1764, the war was over.

To avoid more conflicts, Britain issued the Proclamation of 1763. It banned colonial settlements west of the Appalachian Mountains. Many colonists felt the ban went against their right to live where they pleased. ✓

British Rule Leads to Conflict

The colonists were proud of helping to win the French and Indian War. Most colonists felt some independence from Britain, but they were still loyal British subjects. That loyalty began to erode when Britain, now deeply in debt from the French and Indian War, began to pass new taxes.

In 1764, Parliament passed the Sugar Act, which put a **duty,** or import tax, on several products, including molasses. Colonial merchants protested. A year later, Parliament tried to save money with the Quartering Act. This law made

Key Events

1754	French and Indian War begins.
1765	Stamp Act is passed.
1775	Fighting at Lexington and Concord marks the beginning of the American Revolution.

Vocabulary Builder

Reread the underlined sentence. To *encroach* means "to intrude gradually." Why did Native Americans fear the encroachment of settlers?

____

____

✓ Checkpoint

Explain why Britain banned the colonists from settling west of the Appalachian Mountains.

____

____

✓ Checkpoint

Describe what the Quartering Act required colonists to do.

____

____

colonists provide housing and food to British troops stationed in the colonies. The colonists angrily complained that the Quartering Act violated their rights. ✓

The Stamp Act

In 1765, Parliament passed the Stamp Act. It made colonists buy special tax stamps to put on products, newspapers, and legal documents. In protest, some colonies passed a resolution declaring that only the colonial governments had the right to tax the colonists. Merchants in major cities **boycotted,** or refused to buy, British goods.

✓ Checkpoint

State how colonial merchants protested the Stamp Act.

____

____

Finally, colonial delegates sent a **petition,** a written request to the government, demanding an end to the Sugar Act and the Stamp Act. Parliament repealed the Stamp Act. At the same time, it passed the Declaratory Act, which said that Parliament had full authority over the colonies. ✓

Protests Spread

In 1767, Parliament passed the Townshend Acts, which taxed products imported into the colonies. To enforce these taxes, and to find smuggled goods, officers used **writs of assistance.** These legal documents allowed customs officers to make searches without saying what they were looking for.

Reading Strategy

The Townshend Acts resulted in problems both in the colonies and back in Britain. In the bracketed paragraph, underline the cause of problems in Britain. Circle the effects.

Mark the Text

Colonists boycotted British goods to protest this violation of their rights. Merchants in Britain suffered from the boycott. They pressured Parliament to repeal the Townshend duties, which it did—except for the tax on tea.

Then, on March 5, 1770, soldiers in Boston fired into an angry crowd, killing five. After this Boston Massacre, **Samuel Adams** established a Committee of Correspondence in Massachusetts. Soon other colonies set up similar committees. They wrote letters and pamphlets to keep colonists informed of British actions. This helped to unite the colonies. ✓

✓ Checkpoint

Name the informational organization set up by Samuel Adams.

____

____

Check Your Progress

1. Why did Britain pass the Sugar Act and Quartering Act?

____

____

2. How did the Committee of Correspondence unite the colonists?

____

____

Section 2 Notetaking Study Guide

Question to Think About As you read Section 2 in your textbook and take notes, keep this section focus question in mind: **How did the French and Indian War draw the colonists closer together but increase friction with Britain?**

▶ Use this chart to record key information from the section. Some information has been filled in to get you started.

The Colonists Unite to Resist British Control	
1754–1763	Colonists fought alongside the British to win the French and Indian War, expecting gratitude for their service. But the war put Britain deeply in debt.
1763	Britain issued the ______________, banning settlement west of the Appalachian Mountains. The British hoped to avoid more wars with Native Americans, but the colonists largely ______________ the ban.
1764	Colonists protested the Sugar Act, which put a ______________ on several products, including molasses, and called for harsh punishment of ______________.
1765	Colonists protested the ______________, which required them to provide homes and food for British soldiers. Colonists also protested the ______________, which put a tax on items such as newspapers and legal documents. Colonial governments declared that only they could levy taxes. Patrick Henry made an emotional speech that bordered on ______________. Colonial merchants ______________ British goods.
1766	Parliament repealed the ______________, but passed the ______________, which claimed that Parliament had total authority over the colonies.
1767	The ______________ set up a system to enforce new import duties. Colonists protested court orders called writs of assistance, which were used to search for illegal goods. Once again, the colonists boycotted.
1770	Parliament repealed all the Townshend duties, except the one on ______________. That tax was left in force to demonstrate ______________. On March 5, the ______________ occurred, in which five Boston citizens were killed and six were injured. The colonies set up ______________ to keep colonists informed of British actions.

Refer to this page to answer the Chapter 5 Focus Question on page 77.

Section 3

From Protest to Rebellion

Key Events

1754	French and Indian War begins.
1765	Stamp Act is passed.
1775	Fighting at Lexington and Concord marks the beginning of the American Revolution.

Section 3 Focus Question

How did British tax policies move the colonists closer to rebellion? To begin answering this question,

- Understand why the colonists resented the Tea Act.
- Learn how Britain responded to the Boston Tea Party.
- Read about the battle that began the Revolution.

Section 3 Summary

The colonists' protests over British policies continued to rise until the British sent in troops to control the situation. This caused a confrontation that started the American Revolution.

A Dispute Over Tea

Although most of the Townshend duties had been repealed, the tax on tea remained. Then in 1773, Parliament passed the Tea Act. It gave the British East India Company a **monopoly** on British tea. This meant that the company had total control over all tea sold in the colonies. The Tea Act actually lowered the price of tea, but it also kept colonial merchants from selling Dutch tea at competitive prices.

The colonists resented the tea tax and the way it limited competitive commerce. To protest the Tea Act, the Sons of Liberty prevented the unloading of tea from the East India Company at many of the colonial ports. However, in Boston, Governor Thomas Hutchinson decided not to allow the tea ships to leave port until they were unloaded.

On the night of December 16, 1773, a large group of men disguised as Native Americans boarded the tea ship waiting in Boston harbor. The ship's cargo of tea, worth thousands of dollars, was tossed into Boston harbor. This event became known as the Boston Tea Party. ✓

✓ Checkpoint

Explain why colonial merchants resented the Tea Act.

____

____

The Intolerable Acts

In response to the Boston Tea Party, the angry British government passed harsh laws. The colonists called them the Intolerable Acts. The laws closed the port of Boston, increased the powers of the royal governor, decreased the power of colonial self-government, and strengthened the

Quartering Act. Parliament also passed the Quebec Act. This set up new Canadian boundaries that blocked colonists from moving west.

As citizens in all the colonies sent food and supplies to help Boston through the embargo, the Committee of Correspondence held a meeting to discuss what to do next. This meeting, known as the First Continental Congress, took place in Philadelphia in 1774. Delegates from all the colonies except Georgia took part. The Congress demanded that Parliament **repeal,** or officially end, the Intolerable Acts. It also declared that the colonists had a right to tax and govern themselves. The Congress made training militias a priority, and the delegates called for a new boycott against British goods. Finally, the Congress voted to meet again in May 1775 if their demands weren't met. ☑

The Shot Heard Round the World

Britain rejected the demands of the First Continental Congress. It decided to restore its authority in the colonies by force. The colonists formed militia units called **minutemen.** These were citizen soldiers who could be ready to fight in a minute.

In April, the governor of Massachusetts sent troops to seize the colonists' weapons stored at Concord, Massachusetts, and capture important colonial leaders. On April 18, 1775, Paul Revere and William Dawes rode all night to warn the minutemen that the British were on the march. The British soldiers and the minutemen had their first confrontation in the town of Lexington, Massachusetts. A shot now known as "the shot heard round the world" was fired, setting off gunfire between the soldiers and the minutemen. In nearby Concord, another battle was taking place. The American Revolution had begun. ☑

Check Your Progress

1. What prompted the British to pass the Intolerable Acts?

____

____

2. What did the First Continental Congress accomplish?

____

____

Vocabulary Builder

An *embargo* is an order to close a seaport to block import and export trade. What smaller word within *embargo* means "to block"?

____

✓ Checkpoint

List the provisions of the Intolerable Acts.

____

____

____

____

Reading Strategy

The bracketed paragraph states five events that marked the start of the American Revolution. Place the numbers 1 to 5 beside each event in the paragraph to show the sequence of events.

✓ Checkpoint

Name the location of the "shot heard round the world."

____

____

Section 3 Notetaking Study Guide

Question to Think About As you read Section 3 in your textbook and take notes, keep this section focus question in mind: **How did British tax policies move the colonists closer to rebellion?**

▶ Use this chart to record key information from the section. Some information has been filled in to get you started.

Escalating Toward Rebellion	
Tea Act	What it did: • It lowered the __price of tea__, but kept __the tea tax__. • It gave the East India Tea Company __a British tea monopoly__. • It prevented colonial merchants from ________. Colonial reaction: • They stopped East India ships from ________. • They dumped ________
The Intolerable Acts	What prompted their enactment: • They were Britain's response to ________. What they did: • ________ • ________ • ________ • ________ • __strengthened the Quartering Act__ The Quebec Act • Took away ________ • Blocked ________
First Continental Congress	What it was: • a meeting in ________ in September and October of ________ to decide what to do next What it did: • ________ • ________ • ________ • ________ Britain's reaction Britain chose to use __force__.
Battles of Concord and Lexington	On the night of April 18, 1776, ________ and William Dawes rode to warn the ________ that the British were on their way. The first shot was fired at ________. By the time the British retreated to Boston, almost ________ British soldiers had been killed or wounded.

Refer to this page to answer the Chapter 5 Focus Question on page 77.

Section 4
The War Begins

Section 4 Focus Question

How did the American Revolution begin? To begin answering this question,

- Read how the Second Continental Congress started to act like a government and began to prepare for war.
- Understand why the Battle of Bunker Hill was such an important conflict for the colonists.

Section 4 Summary

The Second Continental Congress prepared for war with Britain. Parliament sent a large army to end the revolt. Early battles between the British and the colonists indicated that the colonists could and would fight for their freedom.

The Second Continental Congress

In May 1775, the Second Continental Congress met in Philadelphia. Some delegates wanted to declare independence from Britain. Others wanted to work for peace. Nearly all realized that they had to prepare for war. They formed the Continental army, made George Washington the commander, and printed paper money to pay for war expenses.

Like the delegates, the American people themselves were split in their loyalties. Farmers, workers, and many merchants who were affected by the new tax laws were willing to fight for independence. They were called Patriots. Those who owned property and held government positions were Loyalists. They remained loyal to the British monarchy in order to keep their lands and positions. Also siding with the British were many enslaved African Americans who hoped to win their freedom, and Native Americans who feared losing their lands if the colonists won the war.

As the Second Continental Congress began, Patriot Ethan Allen and his Green Mountain Boys captured Fort Ticonderoga, a British fort near Lake Champlain. This victory provided the colonists with much-needed weapons, especially cannons.

In July 1775, the Second Continental Congress sent two petitions to the King. The first one, called the Olive Branch Petition, stated that the colonists were the King's loyal

Key Events

1754	French and Indian War begins.
1765	Stamp Act is passed.
1775	Fighting at Lexington and Concord marks the beginning of the American Revolution.

Reading Strategy

Ask and answer a question about Loyalists.

Question: ______________________

____

Answer: ______________________

____

✓ Checkpoint

Name the opposing sides of Americans during the Revolutionary War.

____

____

subjects. The second stated that the colonists were ready to fight for their freedom. The British Parliament ignored the Olive Branch Petition and voted to send 20,000 soldiers to the colonies to end the revolt. ✓

Early Battles

By June 1775, there were 6,500 British troops camped in Boston, while about 10,000 Americans surrounded the city. Nearly 1,600 of the colonial militia were atop Breed's Hill, which overlooked the city. More were on nearby Bunker Hill. These colonial troops were farmers and workers, not trained soldiers. British General William Howe decided to attack straight up the hill. His first and second attacks failed, and many of his men were killed. His third attack succeeded, but only because the Americans ran out of ammunition. The British won this battle, known as the Battle of Bunker Hill, but it proved that the Americans could successfully fight.

In July 1775, George Washington took charge of the army surrounding Boston. He had the cannons seized earlier at Fort Ticonderoga moved to high ground overlooking Boston. This made it impossible for the British to defend the city. On March 17, 1776, the British withdrew from Boston. Although the Americans won this battle, Britain still held most of the advantages. Its navy **blockaded,** or shut off, American ports. The British also strengthened their ranks with hired **mercenaries,** soldiers who serve another country for money.

While Washington trained one army outside Boston, two other armies tried to invade Canada and take Quebec. One was led by Richard Montgomery; the other by Benedict Arnold. Due to severe winter weather, sickness, and hunger, the attack failed. The Americans withdrew, leaving Canada to the British. ✓

✓ Checkpoint

Explain what finally drove the British from Boston.

____

____

Check Your Progress

1. What did the Continental Congress do to prepare for war?

____

____

2. Why was the Battle of Bunker Hill so important?

____

____

Section 4 Notetaking Study Guide

Question to Think About As you read Section 4 in your textbook and take notes, keep this section focus question in mind: **How did the American Revolution begin?**

▶ Use this chart to record key information from the section. Some information has been filled in to get you started.

Preparing for War

Second Continental Congress

Date: May 1775

New delegates: Thomas Jefferson, ______, and ______

Steps taken:

- ______
- ______
- ______

Colonists Divided

- Colonists who wanted independence were called ______.
- Colonists who were loyal to the British Crown were called ______.

Fort Ticonderoga

On May 10, 1775, ______ and 83 men, called the ______ captured Fort Ticonderoga. The men seized weapons, including ______, which were later moved to Boston.

Petitions to Britain

These two resolutions showed the uncertainty among the colonists:

- The Olive Branch Petition stated that ______.
- The Declaration of the Causes and Necessities of Taking Up Arms stated that the colonists were ready to die for freedom.

Early Battles

Bunker Hill

The British won the Battle of Bunker Hill after the third attack because the American militia ran out of ______. This battle proved that the Americans could ______.

Canada

In December 1775, one army led by ______ and another led by ______ invaded Canada and attacked the city of ______. The attack failed.

Refer to this page to answer the Chapter 5 Focus Question on page 77.

Chapter 5 Assessment

Directions: Circle the letter of the correct answer.

1. Over which area did Britain and France go to war?
   - **A** the city of Quebec
   - **B** land east of the Appalachian Mountains
   - **C** the Ohio River valley

2. Why did Britain increase the colonists' taxes?
   - **A** to pay for war debts
   - **B** to exert control over the colonies
   - **C** to pay for the costs of imports

3. What did the colonists resent most about the Tea Act?
   - **A** It raised the price of tea.
   - **B** It strengthened the law against smuggling.
   - **C** It gave Britain a tea monopoly.

Directions: Follow the steps to answer this question:

How united were the colonists against Britain?

Step 1: Recall information: Identify the colonists who supported independence from Britain and those who did not.

Who Supported America's Independence?	Who Did Not Support America's Independence?

Step 2: Compare and contrast: Briefly describe the differences between the two sides.

Those Who Supported American Independence	Those Who Did Not Support American Independence

Step 3: Draw conclusions: Complete the topic sentence that follows. Then write two or three more sentences that support your topic.

The colonies' conflict with Britain also caused a conflict between ____________

____

____

____

Chapter 5 Notetaking Study Guide

Now you are ready to answer the Chapter 5 Focus Question: **How did the relationship between Britain and the colonies fall apart?**

▶ Complete the charts to help you answer this question. Use the notes that you took for each section.

The Path to Revolution

Result of the French and Indian War

- Although the Treaty of Paris gave Britain more North American territory, Britain banned settlement west of the __________. Britain hoped this would avoid more costly wars with Native Americans.
- Because the French and Indian War left Britain in debt, Parliament increased the colonists' __________ to raise money, and expected the colonists to house and feed __________ to save money.
- Expecting gratitude for their role in winning the war, the colonists became outraged. The colonists organized __________ against British goods.

↓

Cause and Effects of the Tea Act

- Colonists protested the Tea Act by __________.
- The British retaliated by __________.
- The First Continental Congress called for a trained militia.
- The "shot heard round the world" occurred in __________.

↓

Preparing for War

- The Second Continental Congress established the __________ with __________ as its commander.
- Ethan Allen and his men captured Fort __________.
- The Second Continental Congress sent Britain a declaration stating that they were willing to die fighting for freedom.

↓

Results of Early Battles

- The Americans lost the Battle of Bunker Hill because they ran out of __________.
- The British finally left Boston, but their navy was able to __________ American ports, and their army was strengthened because they hired __________.
- After an American attack on Quebec failed, Canada was left for the __________.

Refer to this page to answer the Unit 2 Focus Question on page 119.

Chapter 6

The American Revolution (1776–1783)

What You Will Learn

In 1776, the colonies declared their independence from Britain. Then they fought a difficult war for their freedom. The American Revolution ended in 1783 with a peace treaty declaring American independence from British rule.

Chapter 6 Focus Question

As you read this chapter, keep this question in mind: **How did the American colonists gain their independence?**

Key Events

1776 The Continental Congress issues the Declaration of Independence.

1777 The American victory at Saratoga marks the turning point in the war.

1781 British troops surrender to the Americans at the Battle of Yorktown.

Section 1

A Nation Declares Independence

Section 1 Focus Question

Why did many colonists favor declaring independence? To begin answering this question,

- Find out how the call for independence gained support.
- Learn how the Declaration of Independence explained the colonists' reasons for breaking away from British rule.
- Read about the final steps the colonists took to declare their freedom from Britain.

Section 1 Summary

The first half of the year 1776 saw a change in the colonists' thinking about their relationship with Britain. These months were also filled with actions by Patriots and Congress. These actions led to a formal statement of independence.

A Call for Independence

In early 1776, few colonists supported a struggle for independence. The publication of **Thomas Paine**'s *Common Sense,* however, marked the beginning of a shift in people's thinking. In May 1776, **Richard Henry Lee** presented to Congress a **resolution,** or formal statement of opinion, on the right of the colonies to be free. Congress then asked Thomas Jefferson to draft a document listing reasons why the colonies should separate from Britain. ✓

Reading Strategy

The bracketed paragraph tells about a series of events. Underline the words in the paragraph that are clues to the sequence.

Mark the Text

✓ Checkpoint

Name the publication that shifted the colonists toward independence.

____

The Declaration of Independence

Jefferson's brilliance as a writer is evident in the Declaration of Independence. The document has a logical flow through an introduction and three distinct sections.

Preamble: This introduction explains why the document is being written.

General Ideas About Society and Government: This section states the colonists' basic beliefs:
- All people have natural rights.
- Government should protect those rights.
- When government fails to protect people's rights, the people should abolish the government.

*List of **Grievances***: This section states the formal complaints against King George III of England. He is accused of failing to protect the colonists' rights. Beyond that, the King is accused of actually violating their rights.

Conclusion: This section puts together the colonists' beliefs and grievances to show that the only course left to the colonists is to dissolve all political ties with Britain. An ending pledge demonstrates the seriousness of the colonists' declaration of independence.

Impact of the Declaration

Congress met in July 1776 to decide whether to adopt Lee's resolution and approve the Declaration of Independence. On July 4, 1776, the approval was announced. The Declaration was signed by the delegates on August 2. From that time forward, the Patriots were fighting to become an independent nation. ✓

Check Your Progress

1. What two things happened to bring the colonists and the Congress closer to a formal call for independence?

____

____

2. What did the signing of the Declaration of Independence mean for the colonists?

____

____

Vocabulary Builder

If the noun *logic* means "careful thought," what does the adjective *logical* mean? Write a definition from context clues in the underlined sentence.

____

____

✓ Checkpoint

State the purpose of the Preamble.

____

____

✓ Checkpoint

Describe the event that occurred on August 2, 1776.

____

____

Section 1 Notetaking Study Guide

Question to Think About As you read Section 1 in your textbook and take notes, keep this section focus question in mind: **Why did many colonists favor declaring independence?**

▶ Use these charts to record key information from the section. Also refer to the Declaration of Independence on pages 174–178 of your textbook. Some information has been filled in to get you started.

A Call for Independence		
Date	**Event**	**Results**
January 1776	Publication of *Common Sense* Description: a pamphlet by ____ explaining ____	• People inspired by words • 500,000 copies distributed • ____
May 1776	Introduction of Virginia resolution to Congress Description: ____	• ____ • ____

The Declaration of Independence	
Sections	**Important Points to Remember**
Preamble	• States why the document was written: to explain the need for independence
Declaration of Natural Rights	• ____ • ____ • ____
List of Grievances	• ____ • ____ • ____
Resolution of Independence	• The colonists say they are free • ____ • ____
Declaration written by: ____ Date approved: ____ Date signed: ____ Immediate result: ____ Lasting result: People remain inspired by the notion that "all men are created equal."	

Refer to this page to answer the Chapter 6 Focus Question on page 91.

Section 2

A Critical Time

Section 2 Focus Question

How were the early years of the war a critical time? To begin answering this question,

- Read about the military setbacks for the Continental army.
- Learn how the Continental soldiers' spirits were raised.
- Read why the Battle of Saratoga was a turning point.
- Note how Europeans helped Americans in their fight.
- Describe the Continental army's struggles at Valley Forge.

Key Events

1776	The Continental Congress issues the Declaration of Independence.
1777	The American victory at Saratoga marks the turning point in the war.
1781	British troops surrender to the Americans at the Battle of Yorktown.

Section 2 Summary

The early years of the war included losses as well as victories for the Continental army. Help came in surprising ways to cause the tide to turn in favor of the Americans.

Retreat From New York

By mid-1776, the war shifted from Boston and New England to the Middle States. In New York, the Continental army did not fight well against the British. Sir William Howe led 34,000 British troops and 10,000 sailors. They attacked the smaller, less experienced American forces on Long Island. Washington and his troops had to retreat several times. **Nathan Hale** emerged as an American hero. He volunteered to spy on the British at Long Island. He was caught and hanged. His famous last words were, "I only regret that I have but one life to lose for my country." ✓

✓ Checkpoint

List two reasons the Continental army had to keep retreating from General Howe's attacks.

____

____

Surprises for the British

By December 1776, the Continental army had retreated all the way into Pennsylvania. The soldiers' spirits plunged as they failed to achieve any victories. Some soldiers even began to desert the army. Thomas Paine wrote *The Crisis* to inspire soldiers to remain committed to freedom.

On Christmas night, Washington led his soldiers across the Delaware River for a surprise attack on Trenton from two sides. The defeated troops were Hessian **mercenaries,** or soldiers who are paid to fight for a country other than their own. Another American attack near Princeton boosted spirits throughout the army. ✓

✓ Checkpoint

Explain why Thomas Paine wrote *The Crisis.*

____

____

Reading Strategy

Reread the bracketed paragraph. Write the main idea of this paragraph in your own words.

____

____

____

✓ Checkpoint

Name two generals at the Battle of Saratoga.

____

____

✓ Checkpoint

List three improvements Baron von Steuben made to American recruits.

____

____

____

✓ Checkpoint

Name four things that soldiers at Valley Forge desperately needed.

____

____

Saratoga: A Turning Point

British General John Burgoyne came up with a plan to defeat the Americans. He designed a three-pronged attack to cut off New England from the other states. The Americans were successful in blocking British movements, however. On October 17, 1777, American General Horatio Gates and his troops forced Burgoyne to surrender in Saratoga, New York. This victory secured the New England states for the Americans and lifted the Patriots' spirits. It also showed Europe that the Continental army might win the war. ✓

Help From Overseas

In 1778, France became the first foreign country to sign a treaty with the United States. France and two of its allies, Spain and the Netherlands, then joined the war against Britain. This caused the British to fight in several areas besides North America, which helped the American cause.

Individual Europeans also aided the Americans. **Marquis de Lafayette**, a French noble, became a good friend of Washington's as they led troops together. Casimir Pulaski from Poland trained the Patriot **cavalry**, or units of troops on horseback. **Baron Friedrich von Steuben**, a masterful German commander, was especially helpful. He taught American recruits how to march, aim, and attack with bayonets. ✓

Valley Forge

Through the bitter winter of 1777–1778, Washington and his troops suffered terribly at Valley Forge, Pennsylvania. The army faced shortages in food, clothing, and medicine. Drafty huts could not keep out the chill. About one fourth of the soldiers were sick at any given time. Nevertheless, the soldiers gathered their strength and sharpened their skills for the battles to come. ✓

Check Your Progress

1. What were the effects of the Battle of Saratoga?

____

____

2. How did European countries and individuals help the Americans?

____

____

Section 2 Notetaking Study Guide

Question to Think About As you read Section 2 in your textbook and take notes, keep this section focus question in mind: **How were the early years of the war a critical time?**

▶ Use these charts to record key information from the section.

Important Battles and Places

Where	When	What Happened	Why Important
New York State		American forces had to keep retreating.	
Trenton			
Saratoga			
Valley Forge	Winter of 1777–1778		The army gathered its strength for the coming battles.

Important People

Who	What They Did and Why It Was Important
Sir William Howe	• • led British during the worst days of the war for the Patriots
Nathan Hale	• • showed the highest level of commitment to freedom
Thomas Paine	• •
George Washington	• • great military leader and an inspiring hero
John Burgoyne	• British general who planned to cut off New England •
Horatio Gates	• •
Marquis de Lafayette	• • helped Washington win key battles
Thaddeus Kosciusko	•
Casimir Pulaski	•
Baron von Steuben	• helped train the Continental army •

Refer to this page to answer the Chapter 6 Focus Question on page 91.

Section 3
The War Widens

Section 3 Focus Question

How did the effects of the war widen? To begin answering this question,

- Learn why African Americans joined the war effort.
- Read about the role of American women in wartime, and financial difficulties created by the war.
- Find out how the war reached into the western frontier.
- Understand the importance of skirmishes at sea.

Key Events

1776	The Continental Congress issues the Declaration of Independence.
1777	The American victory at Saratoga marks the turning point in the war.
1781	British troops surrender to the Americans at the Battle of Yorktown.

Section 3 Summary

The American Revolution was mostly centered in the colonies and fought by free men. All peoples and areas of the country were affected by the war, however.

African Americans in the War

Both free and enslaved African Americans were soldiers from the beginning of the war. The British offered freedom to all enslaved people who would serve on their side. Americans at first blocked African Americans from service in the army. Washington changed this policy after many African Americans joined the British side. By the end of the war, some 7,000 African Americans had joined the American forces. Most southern states still kept African Americans out of state armies, fearing slave revolts. Several northern states moved to end slavery during the Revolutionary War. ✓

✓ Checkpoint

Explain why Washington decided to accept African American soldiers.

____

____

The War at Home

Difficult times during the war were not limited to soldiers. <u>Civilians, or people not in the military, also had to deal with problems</u>. These included food shortages, enemy attacks, and increased responsibilities in areas in which they usually had little involvement. Women especially experienced huge changes. With these changes came many new opportunities, however. Women successfully took on the roles traditionally held by their husbands, fathers, and brothers.

Reading Strategy

Reread the bracketed text. The main idea is underlined. Circle three details that support this main idea.

Mark the Text

Hardships also occurred because of the monetary costs of fighting a war. Soldiers had to be paid and supplied. Without the power to tax, Congress had to beg the states for money. Congress began to print money, known as **continentals.** As they printed more and more money, it eventually became practically worthless. ✓

Fighting in the West

As the war pushed into the western frontier, most Native Americans sided with the British. They feared that an American victory would result in more takeovers of their lands. In 1778, **George Rogers Clark** was sent by Virginia to try to capture British forts west of the Appalachian Mountains. During that year and the next, Clark and his forces took three important posts in the Ohio Valley area from the British and their Native American allies.

Spain also helped the Americans in the west. **Bernardo de Gálvez,** the governor of Louisiana, provided money and weapons for Clark. He offered American ships safe harbor in New Orleans. From 1779 to 1781, Gálvez played a key role in capturing British forts on the Mississippi River and the Gulf of Mexico. Wealthy Spanish women in Cuba, known as "Havana's Ladies," also joined together to give millions of dollars to the Americans at a time when money was desperately needed. ✓

The War at Sea

The American navy was tiny compared to the British fleet. Americans became skilled at hit-and-run attacks, however. One famous American sea victory came under the command of **John Paul Jones.** His ship, the *Bonhomme Richard*, defeated the British warship *Serapis* off the coast of England in a ferocious 1779 battle. The American navy was also assisted by hundreds of **privateers.** These ships were not part of any navy, but they were allowed by their governments to attack and loot enemy ships. ✓

Check Your Progress

1. What positive change happened for American women during the Revolution?

____

____

2. What role did George Rogers Clark play in the battle on the western frontier?

____

____

✓ Checkpoint

Name one thing Congress did to try to pay for the costs of the war.

____

____

✓ Checkpoint

Describe how Spain and Cuba helped the American war effort.

____

____

____

____

✓ Checkpoint

Name the person whose heroic naval efforts are still remembered today.

____

Section 3 Notetaking Study Guide

Question to Think About As you read Section 3 in your textbook and take notes, keep this section focus question in mind: **How did the effects of the war widen?**

▶ Use these cause-and-effect diagrams to record key information from the section. Some information has been filled in to get you started.

African Americans in the War		
The British offered enslaved African Americans freedom in exchange for fighting on their side. →	Many African Americans join the British effort. →	Washington decides ______________________.
The War at Home		
Many men enlist in the army. Women take over traditional male roles. →	• Women on farms ______________________. • Women in towns take over their husbands' businesses. • Women in military camps ______________________. →	Women have new confidence and opportunities open to them.
Congress has little money to pay for war. →	• States ______________________. • Congress ______________________. →	Printed money ______________________.
Fighting in the West		
Most Native Americans choose to join the British side. →	George Rogers Clark is sent ______________________. He captures ______________________.	
Spain joins the American side. →	Bernardo de Gálvez ______________________. Havana's Ladies ______________________.	
The War at Sea		
Huge British navy blockades American ports. →	• Small American navy uses hit-and-run attacks • Famous navel battle between American ship ______________ and the British warship ______________ • Captain ______________ refuses to give up. • American navy has help from some 800 ______________.	

Refer to this page to answer the Chapter 6 Focus Question on page 91.

Section 4

Winning Independence

Section 4 Focus Question

How did the Americans win the war and make peace? To begin answering this question,

- Read about the battles in the southern states and the final victory by the Americans in Virginia.
- Learn about the terms for peace in the Treaty of Paris.
- Find out why Americans won the war.
- Understand the lasting effects of the American Revolution.

Section 4 Summary

The British shifted their battle plans to southern states in what they thought would be a sure way to achieve victory. The strategy did not work. American troops took bold actions that resulted in a final American victory.

Fighting Moves South

In late 1778, the British began to focus their efforts on the South. Taking key cities, they moved from Florida all the way into North Carolina under Commander **Charles Cornwallis.** To slow the British advance, the Americans used **guerrilla** tactics, working in small groups to perform surprise hit-and-run attacks against the British. **Francis Marion**, also called the Swamp Fox, was the most famous leader of these attacks. Meanwhile, Loyalist bands burned, plundered, and killed men, women, and children throughout the South. In addition, a high-ranking American named Benedict Arnold, perhaps the most infamous **traitor** in American history, switched to the British side and led other Loyalists in successful attacks.

Things seemed very grim for the Patriots. By the fall of 1780, however, American fortunes began to improve. Patriots won key victories in South Carolina. General **Nathanael Greene** led American troops well. They began to push the British out of the Deep South. At this point, Cornwallis made a <u>strategic</u> blunder. He moved his troops to the Yorktown peninsula in Virginia, where he hoped to get help from the British fleet. However, French ships soon pushed out the British navy, and Washington's American and

Key Events

1776 The Continental Congress issues the Declaration of Independence.

1777 The American victory at Saratoga marks the turning point in the war.

1781 British troops surrender to the Americans at the Battle of Yorktown.

Vocabulary Builder

The underlined word *strategic* is a form of the word *strategy,* which refers to moving troops into the best position for fighting.

✓ Checkpoint

Describe the key strategic blunder made by the British near the end of the war.

____

____

✓ Checkpoint

Name the treaty that ended the Revolutionary War.

____

✓ Checkpoint

List four factors that helped the Americans win the Revolutionary War.

____

____

____

____

✓ Checkpoint

List two important ideas for which Americans fought.

____

____

French troops surrounded Cornwallis on land. Cornwallis was forced to surrender. Yorktown was the last major battle of the war. ✓

Making Peace With Britain

Following the surrender at Yorktown, the British Parliament decided it was time to make peace. The process began in Paris in 1782. Britain recognized the United States as independent. Borders were established for the new country—Canada to the north, the Atlantic Ocean on the east, Florida to the south, and the Mississippi River on the west. On April 15, 1783, Congress approved the Treaty of Paris, officially ending the war. General Washington bade farewell to his officers and returned to his plantation life. ✓

Why Did the Americans Win?

Four things worked in favor of the Americans during the Revolutionary War. First, the Americans knew the geography of the country and had local supply lines. Second, patriotism kept the troops fighting hard. Third, help from allies was a major part of American success. French military and naval assistance as well as money and privateers from Spain and the Netherlands were extremely important. Finally, the Americans had great leaders. George Washington's courage and knowledge made him the nation's most admired hero. ✓

Impact of the Revolution

After winning the war, the United States was finally an independent nation with 13 states. Equality and liberty were ideas that appealed to the rest of the world, too. Over the next few decades, independence movements occurred in France and Latin America. They modeled many of their efforts after the successful American Revolution. ✓

Check Your Progress

1. Describe the British plan of attack and its successes during late 1778 and early 1779.

____

____

2. What effect did the American Revolution have on the rest of the world?

____

____

Section 4 Notetaking Study Guide

Question to Think About As you read Section 4 in your textbook and take notes, keep this section focus question in mind: **How did the Americans win the war and make peace?**

▶ Use these charts to record key information from the section. Some information has been filled in to get you started.

The End of the War

The British march north under Cornwallis and important cities are captured:
In Georgia: Savannah
In South Carolina: ______
Loyalists also play a part: Bands of Loyalists roamed the South, burning, plundering, and massacring; Traitor Benedict Arnold also led Loyalist attacks on Virginia

The Americans Fight Back
1. Guerrilla attacks
What they were: ______
Important leader: ______
2. Frontier fighters
When: ______ Where: ______
What happened:
3. Nathanael Greene's Plan: ______
What resulted: ______

Weakened, the British go to Virginia.
Where: ______
Why: Cornwallis expected help from the British fleet
What happened: ______

The Peace Process

Peace Talks
Where: ______ When: ______
Terms of the Treaty of Paris:
Britain agreed ______
The United States agreed ______
Congress approved treaty on ______

Why the Americans Won

1. They fought on land they knew, and they had local supply lines.
2.
3.
4.

Refer to this page to answer the Chapter 6 Focus Question on page 91.

Chapter 6 Assessment

Directions: Circle the letter of the correct answer.

1. How did the Declaration of Independence end?
  A with a list of grievances against King George III
  B with an overview of colonial beliefs
  C with a solemn pledge by Congress to uphold the ideas stated

2. Which battle was an early turning point in the war?
  A Saratoga **B** Savannah **C** Valley Forge

3. For what is John Paul Jones remembered?
  A showing heroism during a sea battle
  B serving as an American spy
  C turning into an American traitor

Directions: Follow the steps to answer this question:

How can we see evidence of the power of the written word during the American Revolution?

Step 1: Recall information: List all the important pieces of writing you have read about that were part of American history from 1776 to 1783.

-
-
-
-
-

Step 2: Description: For each piece of writing, describe why it was written. Explain the powerful effect it produced.

Writing	Why It Was Written	Effect

Step 3: Complete the topic sentence that follows. Then write two or three more sentences that support your topic sentence.

During the American Revolution, the written word was used ____________

____

____

Chapter 6 Notetaking Study Guide

Now you are ready to answer the Chapter 6 Focus Question: **How did the American colonists gain their independence?**

▶ Fill in the chart to help you answer this question. Use the notes you took for each section.

The American Revolution

The colonists gathered support for independence.
In 1776, two Patriots took actions that made people more interested in independence:
Thomas Paine published *Common Sense*.
Richard Henry Lee ______________________.

The colonists declared their freedom.
In 1776, the Continental Congress decided to ______________________.
The delegates chose ______________________ for this job. The result was the Declaration of Independence. It included these sections:

Section	Purpose
1.	
2.	
3.	
4. Resolution of Independence	Stated that the colonists declared independence from Britain

The colonists fought and won the war for freedom.
Major battles were fought from 1776 to 1781. Early battles were centered in the Middle States. A turning point for the Americans occurred in __________ at __________. Following this victory, Americans received help from __________, __________, and __________. Foreigners such as Frenchman __________ and German __________ were vital to the war effort. When the British focused on the South, Americans fought back with __________ tactics and frontier fighters such as Francis Marion, known as __________, and __________, the commander of the Continental army in the South. The final American victory came in __________ at __________.

The British agreed that the colonists were free and independent.
Peace talks began in 1782 in Paris. According to the Treaty of Paris:

- Britain declared the independence of the United States
-
-

Congress approved the treaty on ______________________.

Refer to this page to answer the Unit 2 Focus Question on page 119.

Chapter 7

Creating the Constitution (1776–1790)

What You Will Learn

Weaknesses in the Articles of Confederation led to the drafting of a new constitution for the nation. After much debate, the states approved the Constitution, but many insisted that a bill of rights be added.

Chapter 7 Focus Question

As you read through this chapter, keep this question in mind: **How did the U.S. Constitution overcome the weaknesses of the Articles of Confederation and provide for the organization of the new government?**

Key Events

1776	Many new American states write constitutions.
1787	Constitutional Convention creates a new plan of government.
1791	After three fourths of the states approve it, the Bill of Rights goes into effect.

Section 1

Governing a New Nation

Section 1 Focus Question

What were major successes and failures of the government under the Articles of Confederation? To begin answering this question,

- Learn about the new state constitutions.
- Learn about the Articles of Confederation.
- Find out about laws for settling new lands in the west.
- Understand the problems of the Articles of Confederation.

Section 1 Summary

Americans created new state and national governments based on the principles of the American Revolution. Problems with the Articles of Confederation led to calls for a stronger national government.

Government by the States

Most of the 13 states wrote new constitutions. A document stating the rules under which government will operate is a **constitution**. Most states minimized the power of state governors and gave state legislatures the most power. A legislature is the part of the government that makes laws. Its members are elected by the people.

Vocabulary Builder

The verb *minimize* is related in meaning to the noun *minimum*, which means "the smallest quantity or amount." Using what you know about the meaning of *minimum*, what do you think *minimize* means?

____

____

New state constitutions allowed more people to vote than in colonial times. Still, in most states only white men who owned some property could vote. Virginia's constitution was the first to have a bill of rights, which is a list of key freedoms that the government is required to respect. ✓

The Articles of Confederation

The Continental Congress created the Articles of Confederation in 1777. The Articles set up a new national government. It limited the powers of the government, which consisted of a one-house legislature called Congress. All states were equal, and most power remained with the states. ✓

Settling the Western Lands

One of the national government's most important tasks was to create a way to sell national lands to the public. The Land Ordinance of 1785 was the system it created. It divided western lands into square townships.

A law called the Northwest Ordinance of 1787 applied to the territory north of the Ohio River. It guaranteed basic rights to settlers, outlawed slavery, and established a way to create new states. ✓

Growing Problems

Under the Articles of Confederation, the United States won its independence, signed a peace treaty with Britain, and created rules for settling territories. There were also problems: Trade and tax issues between states hurt the economy, the national government could not stop public unrest, and it had little money because it could not collect taxes.

In the mid-1780s, there was an **economic depression**, or period of slow economic growth. In Massachusetts, many farmers lost their land because they could not pay their taxes. In Shays' Rebellion, farmers rose up against the state. This added to calls for a stronger national government. ✓

Check Your Progress

1. Why were the state and national governments' powers limited?

____

____

2. List two problems with the national government under the Articles of Confederation.

____

____

✓ Checkpoint

List one characteristic of the new state governments.

____

____

____

✓ Checkpoint

List two features of the national government created by the Articles of Confederation.

____

____

✓ Checkpoint

Name two laws that related to the settling of western lands.

____

____

✓ Checkpoint

List two successes of the national government created by the Articles of Confederation.

____

____

____

Section 1 Notetaking Study Guide

Question to Think About As you read Section 1 in your textbook and take notes, keep this section focus question in mind: **What were major successes and failures of the government under the Articles of Confederation?**

▶ Use these charts to record key information from the section. Some of the information has been filled in to get you started.

Government by the States

Problems the Colonists had with Colonial Government		Main Characteristics of the State Governments
Colonial governors: Most colonists were unhappy with the governors appointed by the British Crown.	Changed in new constitutions →	**State governors:** had __limited__ power
		Voting: ________ people were allowed to vote
Parliament: Parliament, which was part of the __central__ government, exerted power over the elected ________ legislatures.		**Individual rights:** protected in several states' ________ of ________

National Government Under the Articles of Confederation

Main Characteristics

- No __executive__ or ________ branch of government
- One legislative branch, called ________, with each state having one vote
- ________ out of 13 states had to approve laws
- Legislative power limited to:
  - dealing with foreign nations and Native Americans
  -
  -
  -
  -

Strengths

- Won ________ from Britain and negotiated peace treaty
- The ________ and the ________ established rules for settling new lands and creating new states.

Weaknesses

- No authority to regulate ________ or collect ________
- Could not protect land from foreign occupation
- Could not stop public unrest as shown in ________

Refer to this page to answer the Chapter 7 Focus Question on page 102.

Section 2
The Constitutional Convention

Section 2 Focus Question

What role did compromise play in the creation of the U.S. Constitution? To begin answering this question,

- Learn how the Constitutional Convention began.
- Read about the proposals in the Virginia Plan.
- Find out about the terms of the Great Compromise.
- Learn how slavery issues influenced the Constitution.
- Discover the source of the new Constitution's authority.

Section 2 Summary

By its end, the Constitutional Convention of 1787 had replaced the Articles of Confederation. The new U.S. Constitution created a stronger central government based on the authority of the people instead of the states.

The Constitutional Convention Begins

The Constitutional Convention met in Philadelphia in 1787. At the start, it was decided to hold discussions in secret so that there would be less public pressure. The convention's purpose at first was to change the Articles, but soon its members agreed to organize a totally new framework of government. ✓

The Virginia Plan

The Virginia Plan was authored by **James Madison**. It called for a strong central government with three branches instead of just one. A **judicial branch** would consist of a system of courts to settle disputes involving national issues. An executive branch would carry out the laws. The executive branch would have one chief executive, or the President.

Congress would make up the legislative branch. But the Virginia Plan wanted to change Congress in two ways. First, it added a second house to Congress. Second, each state was represented based on the size of its population. ✓

The Great Compromise

States with a small population opposed the changes in the legislative branch. They offered their own plan, called the New Jersey Plan, which called for a single house with equal representation for each state.

Key Events

1776	Many new American states write constitutions.
1787	Constitutional Convention creates a new plan of government.
1791	After three fourths of the states approve it, the Bill of Rights goes into effect.

✓ Checkpoint

Name the location of the Constitutional Convention of 1787.

____

Reading Strategy

Reread the bracketed text. The main idea is included in the underlined sentence. Circle three details that support this main idea.

Mark the Text

✓ Checkpoint

List the three branches of government proposed in the Virginia Plan.

____

____

____

✓ Checkpoint

List the two houses of Congress that the Great Compromise proposed.

____

____

The Great Compromise settled the disagreement between the large and small states. A **compromise** is an agreement in which each side gives up part of what it wants. To please the large states, the House of Representatives was developed. Each state's representation in the House was based on population. Its members would serve two-year terms. The Senate was formed to please the small states. Each state would have two senators serving six-year terms. The Great Compromise was a vital step in creating a new Constitution. Now, small-state delegates were willing to support a strong central government. ✓

Debates Over Slavery

✓ Checkpoint

Name two main issues about slavery that divided the northern and southern states during the Constitutional Convention.

____

____

____

____

Slavery also divided the convention. The southern states wanted slaves to count toward representation in the House. Northerners argued that slaves, who were not allowed to vote, should not be counted. It was decided to count each slave as three fifths of a person, which was called the Three-Fifths Compromise.

A second dispute arose when northern delegates called for a total ban on the buying and selling of slaves. A compromise was reached whereby the import of slaves from other countries could be banned in 20 years. However, there were no restrictions on the slave trade within the United States. ✓

A New Constitution

✓ Checkpoint

Name the author of the Preamble to the U.S. Constitution.

____

A "Committee of Style" was created to draw up the Constitution's final wording. **Gouverneur Morris** wrote most of the Preamble, or introduction, to the Constitution. It began with, "We the People of the United States," making it clear that the Constitution got its authority from the people instead of the states. ✓

Check Your Progress

1. What was the initial purpose of the Constitutional Convention of 1787?

____

____

2. What was important about the first words of the Preamble to the new U.S. Constitution?

____

____

Section 2 Notetaking Study Guide

Question to Think About As you read Section 2 in your textbook and take notes, keep this section focus question in mind: **What role did compromise play in the creation of the U.S. Constitution?**

▶ Use these organizers to record key information from the section. Some of the information has been filled in to get you started.

The Constitutional Convention

Issue: How to encourage debate during the convention without public pressure
Solution: Convention delegates voted to hold discussions in secret.

↓

Issue: How to create a stronger national government with more powers than under the Articles of Confederation
Solution Provided by the Virginia Plan: Create a government with ________________ branches, and separate ________________ into two houses. James Madison authored the plan.

↓

Issue: How many people should lead the executive branch
Solution Reached After a Vote: ______________________

↓

Issue: How to elect representatives to the two houses of the legislative branch
Solution Proposed by the Virginia Plan: Elect representatives to both houses according to ________________________________. **Solution Proposed by the New Jersey Plan:** Give each state _____________ vote(s), regardless of its population. **Solution Reached by the Great Compromise:** House of ________________ would be based on ______________________, and states would be represented equally in the ________________. ________________ suggested The Great Compromise.

↓

Issue: How to show that the Constitution derived its authority from the people
Solution: Add a preamble that says, "We the ____________________________..." Gouverneur Morris wrote the Preamble.

Refer to this page to answer the Chapter 7 Focus Question on page 102.

Section 3

Debating the Constitution

Key Events

1776	Many new American states write constitutions.
1787	Constitutional Convention creates a new plan of government.
1791	After three fourths of the states approve it, the Bill of Rights goes into effect.

Reading Strategy

Reread the bracketed paragraphs. What is one point the Federalists and Antifederalists agreed on?

✓ Checkpoint

Name the Federalists' main argument in favor of the Constitution.

Section 3 Focus Question

How did those in favor of the Constitution achieve its ratification? To begin answering this question,

- Read about the arguments for and against the Constitution.
- Learn about the debate over ratification of the Constitution.
- Find out why the Bill of Rights was added to the Constitution.

Section 3 Summary

The Constitution was sent to the states for approval. After energetic debates, and after the Bill of Rights was added, all the states approved the Constitution.

Federalists Versus Antifederalists

The Federalists wanted a strong federal, or national, government. **John Jay, Alexander Hamilton,** and James Madison were Federalists who wrote a series of 85 newspaper essays called the *Federalist Papers*. They argued that the country needed a stronger central government. They wrote that if the Union was to survive, the national government needed the power to enforce laws.

Opponents of the Constitution were called Antifederalists. Many Antifederalists, such as **George Mason** and Patrick Henry, agreed that changes were needed in the organization of the national government. However, they felt that the Constitutional Convention had gone too far.

	Antifederalist Arguments Against the Constitution
1	The Constitution weakened the state governments by giving too much power to the national government.
2	The Constitution also did not include a bill of rights to protect basic freedoms.
3	The President could become like a king by being repeatedly reelected.

The Ratification Debate

At least nine states had to **ratify**, or approve, the Constitution before it took effect. Delaware was the first state to ratify it. Its convention approved the Constitution in December 1787. Pennsylvania, New Jersey, Georgia, and Connecticut followed close behind.

The Federalists' strong efforts in Massachusetts led to approval there, even though there was opposition in rural areas from which Shays' Rebellion had drawn its strength. By then, Maryland and South Carolina had ratified, which made a total of eight ratifications. Then in June 1788, New Hampshire became the ninth state to ratify the Constitution. This meant it could now go into effect. The other states eventually approved the Constitution, with Rhode Island being the final state to do so in May 1790. ✓

✓ Checkpoint

Name the first and last states to ratify the Constitution.

First: ______________________

Last: ______________________

The Bill of Rights

After nine states ratified the Constitution, Congress took steps to prepare for a presidential election. George Washington was elected the first President. John Adams was elected Vice President.

During the debate on the Constitution, many states had insisted that a bill of rights be added. This became one of the first tasks of the new Congress that met in March 1789.

In 1789, Congress passed a series of amendments, or changes to a document. By December 1791, three fourths of the states had ratified 10 amendments. These amendments are called the Bill of Rights.

The Bill of Rights protects citizens against unfair use of government power. The First Amendment protects freedom of religion, speech, and the press. The next three amendments were a response to Britain's abuses during the colonial era. The Fifth through Eighth Amendments mainly protect those accused of crimes. The last two amendments limit the powers of the national government to those mentioned in the Constitution. ✓

✓ Checkpoint

List three freedoms the First Amendment protects.

____

____

____

Check Your Progress

1. Why did the Antifederalists object to the Constitution?

____

____

2. What role does the Bill of Rights play?

____

____

Section 3 Notetaking Study Guide

Question to Think About As you read Section 3 in your textbook and take notes, keep this section focus question in mind: **How did those in favor of the Constitution achieve its ratification?**

▶ Use these charts to record key information from the section. Some of the information has been filled in to get you started.

Federalists Versus Antifederalists

Federalists
Leaders: 1. John Jay, 2. ____________, 3. ____________
Position on the new Constitution: ____________
Main argument for position: need for a ____________ central government

Antifederalists
Leaders: 1. Patrick Henry, 2. ____________
Position on the new Constitution: ____________
Arguments for position:
1. ____________
2. ____________
3. The President could become like a king by being repeatedly reelected.

The Ratification Debate

- Approval needed from ____________ states before the Constitution could go into effect.
- Importance of Massachusetts: Antifederalists hoped it would reject the Constitution because opposition was strong where Shays' Rebellion had occurred. It was approved after a major campaign by the Federalists.
- Importance of Virginia: Virginia was ____________ and ____________. If it rejected the Constitution, ____________ and other states might do so, too.

The Bill of Rights

Many states believed that a bill of rights was essential to protect basic <u>liberties</u> and to protect against abuses by the ____________.

- First Amendment: guarantees freedom of ____________, ____________, and ____________.
- Second Amendment: deals with the right to ____________
- Third Amendment: bars Congress from ____________.
- Fourth Amendment: protects citizens from ____________ or ____________.
- Fifth through Eighth Amendments: protect citizens who are ____________ ____________.
- Ninth and Tenth Amendments: limit the powers of the ____________ to those granted in the ____________.

Refer to this page to answer the Chapter 7 Focus Question on page 102.

Chapter 7 Assessment

Directions: Circle the letter of the correct answer.

1. Who had the most political power under the Articles of Confederation?
- **A** the President
- **B** the state governments
- **C** the Continental Congress

2. What was a result of the Great Compromise during the Constitutional Convention?
- **A** the immediate end to the slave trade
- **B** adding the Bill of Rights to the Constitution
- **C** the creation of a legislative branch with two houses

3. One reason that some of the Antifederalists opposed the Constitution was
- **A** they believed the Constitution should include a bill of rights.
- **B** they believed it gave too much power to the states.
- **C** they believed they had a better plan for the national government.

Directions: Follow the steps to answer this question:

What do the successes and failures of the government under the Articles of Confederation tell you about it?

Step 1: Recall information: List two successes and two failures of the government under the Articles of Confederation.

Successes	Failures
1. 2.	1. 2.

Step 2: Compare: What do the successes of the government tell you about it? What do the failures of the government tell you about it?

What the Successes Tell You	What the Failures Tell You

Step 3: Complete the topic sentence that follows. Then write two or three more sentences that discuss the strengths and weaknesses of the Articles of Confederation.

Under the Articles of Confederation, the United States ____________________

____

____

____

____

Chapter 7 Notetaking Study Guide

Now you are ready to answer the Chapter 7 Focus Question: **How did the U.S. Constitution overcome the weaknesses of the Articles of Confederation and provide for the organization of the new government?**

► Complete the following charts to help you answer this question. Use the notes that you took for each section.

Articles of Confederation	
Form of government	• single branch: a one-house legislature called Congress • each state had __one__ vote(s) • _____ states had to agree before a law could go into effect
Limited government	• limited __________ government; most power held by the __________ • __________ could not enforce laws

Constitutional Convention of 1787	

Virginia Plan	• strong central government
	• three branches of government:
	  • executive
	  •
	  •
	• legislature divided into __________ houses
	• representation based on __________
	• Small states objected to the plan because the more __________ a state had, the more __________ it would have.

New Jersey Plan	• __________ house(s) in Congress • __equal__ representation for each state • expanded powers of Congress to __________ and __________

The Great Compromise	Two houses of Congress
	• lower house: __________
	  • representation based on __________
	• upper house: __________
	  • each state had ______ seats

The Three-Fifths Compromise	• Southerners said that enslaved people should be counted in calculating how many __________ a state should have in Congress. Northerners objected because enslaved people were not allowed to __________. • As a compromise each enslaved person was counted as three fifths of a __________ .

Refer to this page to answer the Unit 2 Focus Question on page 119.

Constitution Notetaking Study Guide

Question to Think About As you read the Constitution in your textbook and take notes, keep this question in mind: **How do the amendments affect life in the United States today?**

▶ Use the charts on this page and the next to record key information about amendments to the U.S. Constitution. Some of the information has been filled in to get you started.

AMENDMENTS 11–18 TO THE U.S. CONSTITUTION				
Amendment	**Year Ratified**	**Subject**	**Does the amendment allow…**	**Yes or No**
Eleventh	1795	suits against states	a citizen of one state to sue the government of another state in federal court?	no
Twelfth			electors to cast one ballot for President and Vice President?	
Thirteenth			slavery to exist in the United States?	no
Fourteenth			states to make laws that limit the rights of citizens?	
Fifteenth		right to vote—race, color, servitude	the federal government or states to limit the right to vote based on race?	
Sixteenth			Congress to tax people on their income?	
Seventeenth			state legislatures to choose senators?	
Eighteenth	1919		people to make, sell, or transport alcohol?	

▶ Complete this chart to record information about the last nine amendments to the U.S. Constitution.

AMENDMENTS 19–27 TO THE U.S. CONSTITUTION				
Amendment	**Year Ratified**	**Subject(s)**	**Does the amendment allow…**	**Yes or No**
Nineteenth	1920	women's suffrage	women to vote in state and federal elections?	yes
Twentieth			the Vice-President-elect to become President if the President-elect dies before taking office?	
Twenty-first			people to make, sell, or transport alcohol?	
Twenty-second		presidential tenure	a person to serve as President for more than two terms?	
Twenty-third			the people living in the District of Columbia to vote for President?	
Twenty-fourth	1964		U.S. citizens to be required to pay a tax before voting in federal elections?	
Twenty-fifth			the Vice President to take over the duties of President if the President declares that he or she is unable to carry them out?	
Twenty-sixth			citizens eighteen or older to vote?	yes
Twenty-seventh			members of Congress to receive right away a pay increase they voted for themselves?	

Refer to these charts to answer the Unit 2 Focus Question on page 119.

Citizenship Handbook

What You Will Learn

The U.S. Constitution is the supreme law of the United States. It determines the structure of the federal government. Government also operates at the state and local levels.

Citizenship Handbook Focus Question

As you read this handbook, keep this question in mind: **How did the Constitution create a strong government with roots in history that allowed for change and met the needs of the people?**

Summary 1

Summary 1 Focus Questions

- What were the ideas behind the Constitution?
- What is the structure of the Constitution?
- What are the basic principles of the Constitution?

Summary

In drafting the Constitution, the Framers used ideas and principles from historical documents and thinkers.

Ideas Behind the Constitution

The writers of the Constitution looked to the Roman Republic as a model. A **republic** is a government in which citizens rule themselves through elected representatives.

The following principles from the Magna Carta and the English Bill of Rights also influenced the Constitution:

- Citizens have rights, which the government must protect.
- Even the head of the government must obey the law.
- Taxes cannot be raised without the consent of the people.
- Elections should be held frequently.
- People accused of crimes have two rights: trial by jury and **habeas corpus.** This means that individuals cannot be held in prison unless they are charged with a crime.
- People have the right to **private property,** or property owned by an individual.

Enlightenment thinkers John Locke and Baron de Montesquieu were also key influences. Locke declared that every

Reading Strategy

In a republic, elected representatives make decisions and policies that carry out the will of citizens.

Underline the principle intended to make sure that representatives really follow the wishes of the people.

✓ Checkpoint

Name two documents from British history that influenced the U.S. Constitution.

____

____

person has a natural right to life, liberty, and property. Montesquieu introduced the idea of **separation of powers.** This states that the powers of government must be clearly divided into legislative, executive, and judicial branches.

Each colonial charter identified the power and limits of government by the king of England. In writing the Constitution, the Founders wanted to prevent the abuses of George III listed in the Declaration of Independence. ✓

✓ Checkpoint

List two issues dealt with in Article 4 of the Constitution.

____

____

____

____

Structure of the Constitution

The Preamble, or opening statement, of the Constitution outlines the goals of the document. Seven sections called the articles make up the Constitution's main body. The first three articles describe the branches of government: legislative, executive, and judicial. Article 4 requires states to honor one another's laws and sets up a system for admitting new states. Article 5 provides a process for amending the Constitution. Article 6 declares the Constitution as the "supreme law of the land." Article 7 sets up the way for the states to ratify the Constitution. ✓

✓ Checkpoint

List three of the basic principles embodied in the Constitution.

____

____

____

Principles of the Constitution

The Constitution rests on seven basic principles.

- **Popular sovereignty** states that the people are the main source of the government's power.
- **Limited government** means the government only has powers given to it by the Constitution.
- Separation of powers divides the government into three branches. Each branch has its own duties.
- **Checks and balances** is a system by which each branch of government can limit the actions of the other two.
- **Federalism** is the division of power between the federal government and the states.
- Republicanism provides for a government in which people elect representatives to carry out their will.
- The principle of individual rights means the Constitution protects rights such as freedom of speech. ✓

Check Your Progress

1. What was Montesquieu's idea of the separation of powers?

____

____

2. What is described in the first three articles of the Constitution?

____

Constitution Notetaking Study Guide

Keep in mind the Summary 1 Focus Questions as you read about the Constitution in your textbook and take notes.

▶ Use these charts to help you record key Constitution facts. Some information has been filled in to get you started.

Ideas Behind the Constitution
Ideas from Rome and England *The Example of Rome:* The government of early Rome was a republic in which citizens ruled through ________________. However, this form of government collapsed and was replaced with a ________. *Documents from England:* The ____________ and the English ____________ placed limits on the power of rulers and protected the ________ of citizens.
Ideas from the Enlightenment *John Locke:* 1. 2. 3. People have a right to rebel if a ruler violates the people's natural rights. *Baron de Montesquieu:* Separation of powers: ________________________

Articles of the Constitution

Article	Subject of the Article
Article 1	
Article 2	establishes the powers of and limits on the President
Article 3	establishes the powers of and limits on the Courts
Article 4	
Article 5	
Article 6	
Article 7	

Seven Principles of the Constitution

Principle	Meaning
Popular Sovereignty	The people are the primary source of the government's power.
Limited Government	
Separation of Powers	
Checks and Balances	Each branch of government limits the actions of the others.
Federalism	
Republicanism	
Individual Rights	

Refer to this page to answer the Citizenship Handbook Focus Question on page 118.

Summary 2

Summary 2 Focus Question

What are the powers of each branch of government?

Summary

The federal government consists of three branches, each of which has its own unique powers and responsibilities.

How the Federal Government Works: The Legislative Branch

The first article of the Constitution sets up the Congress to make the nation's laws. Congress is made up of two bodies: the Senate and the House of Representatives.

The Senate is based on equal representation and has two senators from each state. Each serves a six-year term. The Vice President is also the president of the Senate.

The House of Representatives is the larger of the two bodies. Representation in the House is based on a state's population. People elect their representatives for two-year terms. The leader of the House, the Speaker, manages debates and agendas in the House.

Congress's most important power is to make laws. Most laws start as **bills**, or proposals, that are introduced in the House or the Senate. Congress can also collect taxes, coin money, establish post offices, fix standard weights and measures, and declare war. ✓

How the Federal Government Works: The Executive Branch

Article 2 of the Constitution sets up the executive branch to carry out laws and to run the affairs of the national government. The President is the head of the executive branch. The branch also includes the Vice President, the Cabinet, and the many governmental departments and agencies. The Constitution says little about the powers of the President. Today, the President can veto bills, propose laws, grant pardons, appoint high officials, and negotiate treaties. The President also serves as commander in chief of the armed forces.

The President serves a four-year term and cannot serve more than two terms. The President is elected through a system called the electoral college. Americans do not directly elect the President but rather they vote for a group of electors. The number of electors depends on each state's

Vocabulary Builder

Read the bracketed text. Based on context clues, write a definition of *agenda*.

____

____

✓ Checkpoint

Name the two bodies of the legislative branch.

____

____

number of senators and representatives. In most states, the candidate with the majority of popular votes receives that state's electoral votes. The candidate who gets the most electoral votes becomes President. ✓

How the Federal Government Works: The Judicial Branch

The Constitution also creates a Supreme Court. It also authorizes Congress to establish other courts as needed.

Most federal cases begin in district courts, where evidence is presented and a judge or a jury decides the facts of a case. If a party disagrees with the decision of the judge or jury, it may appeal. An **appeal** asks that the decision be reviewed by a higher court. A judge in an appellate court, or court of appeals, reviews the decision to determine if the lower court interpreted and applied the law correctly.

Court cases can be filed under federal or state jurisdiction. A **jurisdiction** is the power to hear and decide cases. Most cases are tried under state jurisdiction because they involve state laws. A case may be placed under federal jurisdiction if:

- The United States is either suing another party or being sued by another party.
- The case is based on the Constitution or on a federal law.
- The case involves disputes between different states.

The Supreme Court is at the top of the judicial branch and consists of a chief justice and eight associate justices. Judges are nominated by the President and approved by Congress. The Supreme Court is the final court of appeal. Decisions rest on a majority of at least five of the justices.

The most important power of the Supreme Court is the power to decide what the Constitution means. The Court can declare whether the acts of the President or laws passed by Congress are unconstitutional. **Unconstitutional** means that an act or law is not allowed by the Constitution. ✓

Check Your Progress

1. Who and what makes up the executive branch?

____

____

2. Describe the process by which a justice is added to the Supreme Court.

____

____

✓ Checkpoint

Name the system by which the President is elected.

____

Reading Strategy

Do most court cases fall under state or federal jurisdiction? Underline the sentence that tells you this.

Mark the Text

✓ Checkpoint

List the two things that the Supreme Court can declare unconstitutional.

____

____

Branches of Government Notetaking Study Guide

Keep in mind the Summary 2 Focus Question as you read about the structure of the U.S. government in your textbook and take notes.

▶ Use these charts to help you record key facts about the branches of government. Some information has been filled in to get you started.

The Legislative Branch	
The Senate Number of members for each state: two per state Length of term: ______ President of the Senate: ______	**House of Representatives** Number of members for each state: based on population Current number of members: ______ Representatives elected by: ______ Length of term: ______
Powers of Congress: 1. make nation's laws, 2. collect ______, 3. coin ______, 4. establish post offices, 5. fix standard ______ and ______, 6. declare ______	

The Executive Branch
Duties: Carry out the ______ and run the affairs of ______ Head executive: President Other members: Vice President, Cabinet, ______, ______ Length of President's term: ______, but no more than two terms System by which President is elected: ______

The Judicial Branch
Lower Courts 1. In district courts, ______ is presented during trials, and a ______ or a ______ decides the facts of the case. 2. A party that disagrees with a decision may appeal to a higher court. 3. Appellate court judges review the decisions of district courts to ______. 4. Jurisdiction is ______.
The Supreme Court Court consists of: ______ Justices appointed by: President Appointments must be approved by: ______ Length of Justices' service: ______ Main job: ______ Number of cases heard per year: ______ Most important power: ______ What the court can declare as unconstitutional: ______

Refer to this page to answer the Citizenship Handbook Focus Question on page 118.

Summary 3

Summary 3 Focus Question

How can the Constitution be amended to meet changing needs?

Summary

The Founders created a Constitution that allowed for change. The first ten changes made to the Constitution concerned the rights of the American people.

Amending the Constitution

The Constitution originally said nothing about the rights of the American people. This omission was fixed with the addition of the Bill of Rights, the first ten amendments to the Constitution. Such an addition was possible because of Article 5, which laid out the method of amending the Constitution. **Amending** is another word for changing.

There are two ways of proposing an amendment. First, Congress can propose an amendment. Second, a national convention can formally propose an amendment.

An amendment can be ratified or approved through actions of the state legislatures. It can also be ratified through the actions of state conventions. Conventions are special meetings to address a specific issue.

The Bill of Rights addresses the freedoms of all citizens.

The Bill of Rights

Amendment	Subject Addressed
First	freedom of religion, speech, and the press; right of petition and assembly
Second	right to bear arms
Third	government cannot force people to quarter troops in their homes
Fourth	protects against unreasonable search and seizure
Fifth	rights of people accused of crimes
Sixth	right to trial by jury in criminal cases
Seventh	right to trial by jury in civil cases
Eighth	forbids excessive bail and cruel or unusual punishment
Ninth	people's rights are not limited to those listed in the Constitution
Tenth	states or people have all powers not denied or given to federal government by the Constitution

Vocabulary Builder

Omission is a noun meaning "something left out." Based on this, what does the verb *omit* mean?

____

____

✓ Checkpoint

What are the first ten amendments called?

____

Reading Strategy

Underline the topic sentence of the section under the heading "The First Amendment." Then draw arrows to two sentences that explain specific ways the Framers were reacting to events of the colonial period.

Mark the Text

✓ Checkpoint

List the five freedoms covered by the First Amendment.

____

____

____

____

____

The First Amendment

The colonial experience inspired the First Amendment. Religious groups had all come to North America in the 1600s because they wanted to practice their religion freely. Yet, some religious leaders were driven from their communities after disputes with leaders over religious issues. The Framers drafted the First Amendment because they wanted to end such disputes. Thus, the First Amendment makes freedom of religion a basic right. Americans can choose to follow any religion, or no religion.

The part of the First Amendment that dealt with religion used ideas that came from the Virginia Statute on Religious Freedom. Thomas Jefferson, the author of the Virginia document, later spoke of a "wall of separation between Church and State." However, not everyone agrees on how religion and government should be separated. Some people believe that the First Amendment means that religion should play no role in government. Others argue that the Amendment says only that Congress cannot establish an official church or limit people's freedom of worship.

The First Amendment also protects the right to speak and protects the press from government censorship. **Censorship** is the power to review, change, or prevent the publication of news.

The Framers remembered that King George III and Parliament had ignored colonists' petitions protesting the Stamp Act. Such experiences had a powerful effect on the people who wrote the Bill of Rights. The First Amendment thus guarantees the right of Americans to assemble in peaceful protest. It also protects Americans' right to petition the government for a change in policy. ✓

Check Your Progress

1. Explain the two ways by which an amendment to the Constitution can be ratified.

____

____

2. What colonial experience led American leaders to specifically protect the right of citizens to follow any religion or no religion?

____

____

____

Amending the Constitution Notetaking Study Guide

Keep in mind the Summary 3 Focus Question as you read about changing the Constitution in your textbook and take notes.

▶ Use these charts to help you record key facts. Some information has been filled in to get you started.

Amendment Process	
Proposing Amendments 1. 2. State legislatures call for a national convention to formally propose an amendment.	Ratifying Amendments 1. 2. Action of state conventions

The Bill of Rights

Amendment	Rights and Protections
First Amendment	• Protects freedom of religion, freedom of ________, and freedom of the ________ • Also protects the right of petition and peaceful ________
Second Amendment	Right to ________
Third Amendment	Protects against the ________ of ________ in people's homes
Fourth Amendment	Protects against unreasonable search and ________
Fifth Amendment	Protects the rights of people accused of ________
Sixth Amendment	Right to a ________ by jury in criminal cases
Seventh Amendment	Right to a ________ by ________ in ________ cases
Eighth Amendment	Forbids ________ and cruel or unusual ________
Ninth Amendment	People's rights are not limited to ________
Tenth Amendment	States or people have all ________ not denied or ________ by the Constitution

Refer to this page to answer the Citizenship Handbook Focus Question on page 118.

Summary 4

Summary 4 Focus Questions

- What are the powers of state and local governments?
- What are the rights and responsibilities of citizens?

Summary

Not only do state and local governments have many important responsibilities, but individual citizens have many important responsibilities as well.

State and Local Government

The Constitution divides powers between the federal government and state governments. The states concern themselves with local needs.

State governments are like the federal government. Each state has its own constitution that can be amended. States have the same three branches of government as the federal government. Each state has a legislature, a governor who serves as the chief executive, and a judiciary. There are some differences between federal and state governments. Nebraska, for instance, is the only state in the Union with a one-house legislature.

State governments have the power to create corporate law, regulate trade within the state, maintain public schools, and establish local governments. States also make laws about marriage and divorce, conduct elections, and provide for public safety.

The Constitution identifies the powers of the federal and state government. However, it says nothing about local governments. Local government consists of smaller units such as counties, cities, and towns.

Local governments spend most of their budgets on education. Cities, towns, and school districts hire teachers, buy books, and maintain school buildings. Local governments control the school system. However they must meet the state's education standards.

Local governments play a more direct role in people's lives than state government does. For instance, local governments hire firefighters, police officers, and garbage collectors. They also maintain local roads and hospitals, provide public services, run libraries, oversee parks and recreational facilities, and inspect buildings for safety. ✓

✓ Checkpoint

Name three units of local government.

____

____

____

Rights and Responsibilities of Citizenship

A **citizen** is someone who is entitled to all the rights and privileges of a nation. A person must be born in the United States, have a parent who is a United States citizen, be naturalized, or be 18 years old or younger when his or her parents are naturalized. **Naturalization** is the legal process of becoming a citizen. To be naturalized, a person must live in the United States for five years, then apply for citizenship, take a citizenship exam, undergo interviews, and then take the citizenship oath.

Many of American citizens' rights are spelled out in the Bill of Rights. But the Ninth Amendment states that citizens' rights are not limited to the ones listed in the Constitution. Over the years, federal and state laws have identified other rights. For example, the Constitution does not mention education. But today, laws in every state guarantee that children have the right to an education.

The law holds citizens to certain responsibilities. For example, every citizen must obey the law and pay taxes. If they do not, they face legal punishment. Good citizens meet other responsibilities as well. These are not required by law, but they are important. These responsibilities include learning about important issues and voting.

Some people participate in the political process through interest groups. An **interest group** is an organization that represents the concerns of a particular group. They work to influence lawmakers. Examples of interest groups are the National Rifle Association and the Sierra Club.

Young people, too, can get involved in the political process. For example, students in one community in California needed assistance paying for public transportation. They organized to solve this problem. Using their First Amendment rights, they collected signatures on petitions and held peaceful public rallies. Finally, local transportation officials came up with a plan to solve the problem. ✓

Check Your Progress

1. Which level or levels of government are responsible for education?

____

2. Which amendment states that citizens have rights not mentioned in the Constitution?

____

Reading Strategy

The underlined sentence is a specific example. Draw an arrow to the general statement it supports.

Vocabulary Builder

Political comes from the Greek word *polis*, meaning "city." The word *police* shares the same root.

✓ Checkpoint

Name two examples of interest groups.

____

____

Governments and Citizens Notetaking Study Guide

Keep in mind the Summary 4 Focus Questions as you read about the powers of state and local governments and the responsibilities of citizens in your textbook and take notes.

▶ Use these charts to help you record key facts. Some information has been filled in to get you started.

State Government	
Each state has its own <u>constitution</u>. State governments made up of: • executive (headed by ______________) • •	Powers of State Government: • create corporate law • • • • • •

Local Government
Includes <u>county</u>, ______________, and ______________ Most of local budgets are spent on ______________. Local governments hire ______________, ______________, and ______________. Local governments maintain ______________ and ______________ and provide public services.

Citizenship
• A ______________ is entitled to all the rights and privileges of a particular nation. • To be a citizen of the United States, a person must be one of the following: 1. 2. have a parent who is a citizen 3. • ______________ is the official legal process of becoming a citizen. Steps in process: 1. 2. apply for citizenship 3. 4. 5. • Some responsibilities of citizens are required by ______________. • Other responsibilities are not required by law. These include serving the <u>community</u>, staying well informed, ______________ in elections, and helping to create a just ______________.

Refer to this page to answer the Citizenship Handbook Focus Question on page 118.

Citizenship Handbook Assessment

Directions: Circle the letter of the correct answer.

1. The electoral college is the system used to determine who becomes
   A chief justice. **B** President. **C** senator.

2. In what way are the state governments like the federal government?
   A Both levels of government are divided into three branches.
   B All states have two-house legislatures, as does the federal government.
   C Both levels of government have the power to coin money.

3. Which of the following principles of the U.S. Constitution introduces the idea that government authority comes from the people?
   A limited government
   B popular sovereignty
   C checks and balances

Directions: Follow the steps to answer this question:

How does the structure of the federal government reflect the Framers' belief that power should rest in the hands of citizens?

Step 1: Recall details about each branch of the federal government.

	Branch		
	Executive	**Legislative**	**Judicial**
Highest office or level		Congress	
How officeholders are selected:	nationwide election through electoral college system		

Step 2: Compare: In which of the three branches are the top officeholders most directly selected by voters?

____

Step 3: Complete the topic sentence that follows. Then write two or three more sentences that support your topic sentences.

The Framers of the Constitution felt that power should rest in the hands of the citizens because ______________________________

____

____

____

Citizenship Handbook Notetaking Study Guide

Now you are ready to answer the Citizenship Handbook Focus Question: **How did the Constitution create a strong government with roots in history that allowed for change and met the needs of the people?**

▶ Complete the following chart to help you answer this question. Use the notes that you took for each section.

The Foundation of Strong Government

Ideas Behind the Constitution

American leaders looked to Rome as an example of a __________, or government in which citizens rule themselves through elected representatives.

The ____________________ and the English ____________________ placed limits on the ruler and protected the rights of citizens.

The ideas of the European Enlightenment thinkers ____________________ and ____________________ were very influential.

Structure of the Constitution

The ____________, or opening statement, of the Constitution outlines six main goals.	The first three Articles describe the branches of government: ____________, ____________ and ____________.

The Constitution rests on seven basic principles: popular sovereignty, ____________________, ____________, ____________________, ____________________, federalism, and ____________________.

Amendments to the Constitution

An amendment can be ratified or approved by three fourths of ____________________ or ____________________.

The first ten amendments are known as ____________________.

They address ____________________.

The Ninth Amendment states that Americans are entitled to many rights, not just those spelled out in the Constitution.

State and Local Government

Like the federal government, each state has a ____________________ and three ____________________.

Some of the many duties of state government include regulating trade within the state, making laws about ____________ and divorce, conducting ____________, and providing for public ____________.

____________ government plays the most direct role in people's lives.

Refer to this page to answer the Unit 2 Focus Question on page 119.

Unit 2 Pulling It Together Activity

What You Have Learned

Chapter 5 After the French and Indian War, the American colonists grew rebellious over Britain's effort to control them. As tensions increased, the spirit of rebellion turned into a call for independence and war.

Chapter 6 In 1776, the colonists officially announced their Declaration of Independence. A difficult war followed. The American Revolution ended in 1783 with the signing of a treaty declaring that the United States was its own nation.

Chapter 7 Delegates from each state met in Philadelphia in 1787 to revise the Articles of Confederation. The delegates decided that the nation needed a stronger federal government.

Citizenship Handbook To be an active citizen, it is important to understand the ideas behind the U.S. Constitution.

Think Like a Historian

Read the Unit 2 Focus Question: **What are the roles and responsibilities of governments and citizens?**

▶ Use the organizers on this page and the next to collect information to answer this question.

What are the responsibilities of citizens? Some of them are listed in this organizer. Review your section and chapter notes. Then complete the organizer.

Rights and Responsibilities of Citizens

From the Bill of Rights	Civic Responsibilities
• freedom of religion, speech, and the press	• voting
• trial by jury and equal treatment before the law	•
•	•
•	

Look at the other part of the Unit Focus Question. It asks about responsibilities of government. The organizer below gives you a part of the answer. Review your section and chapter notes. Then fill in the rest of the organizer.

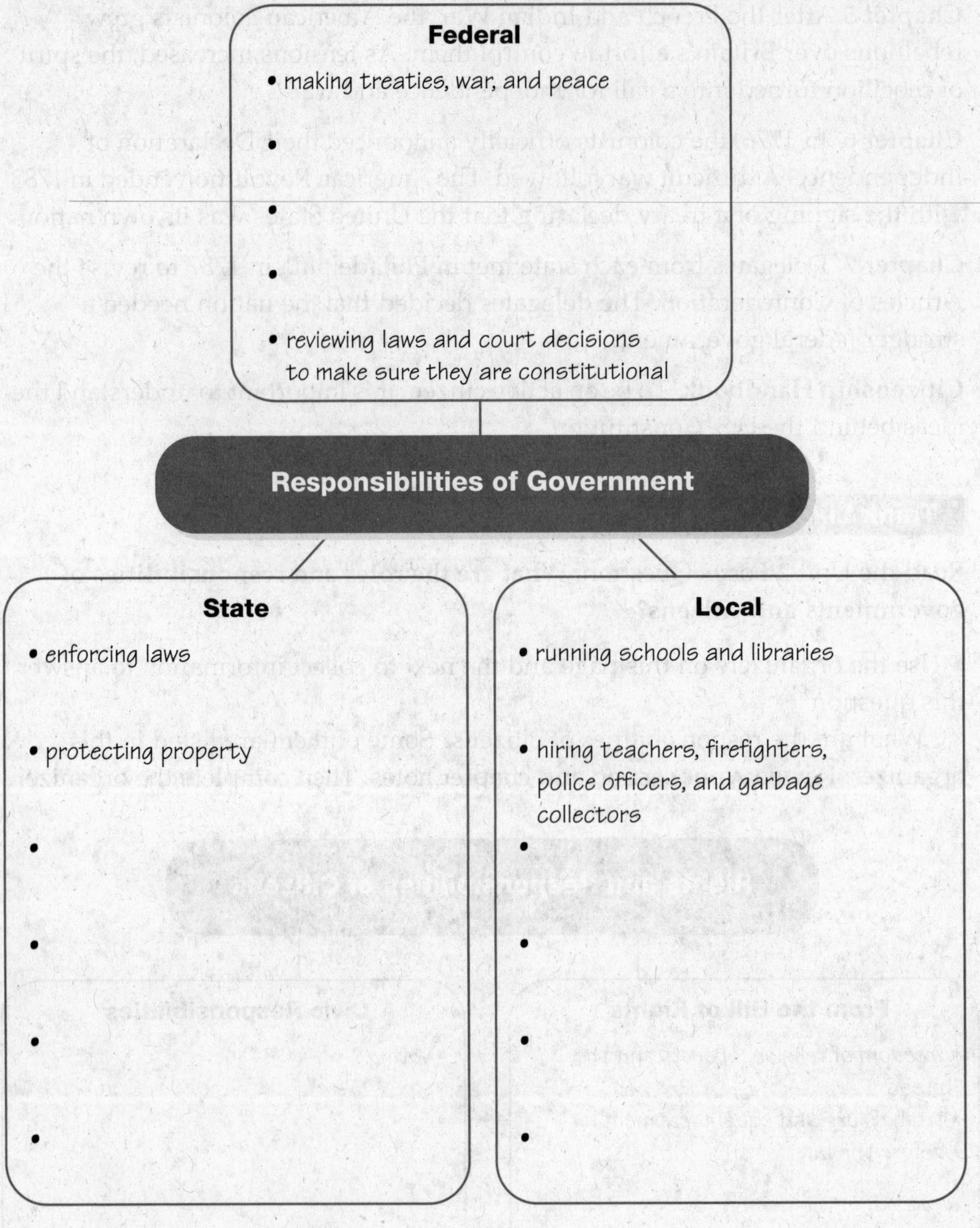

Federal
• making treaties, war, and peace
•
•
•
• reviewing laws and court decisions to make sure they are constitutional
Responsibilities of Government
State
• enforcing laws
• protecting property
•
•
•
•
Local
• running schools and libraries
• hiring teachers, firefighters, police officers, and garbage collectors
•
•
•
•

Unit 3

The New Republic

What You Will Learn

Chapter 8 As the nation's first President, George Washington established the U.S. government's authority in domestic as well as foreign affairs. Political divisions and strife with France rocked John Adams's presidency.

Chapter 9 The Louisiana Purchase of 1803 doubled the size of the United States. At the same time, the United States struggled to remain neutral in its foreign policy. British support of Native Americans led to the War of 1812.

Chapter 10 During the early 1800s, the federal government increased its authority. At the same time, the Monroe Doctrine expanded U.S. influence in Latin America. More people earned the right to vote during Andrew Jackson's presidency, yet Jackson forced Native Americans in the South to move west.

Focus Your Learning As you study this unit and take notes, you will find the information to answer the questions below. Answering the Chapter Focus Questions will help build your answer to the Unit Focus Question.

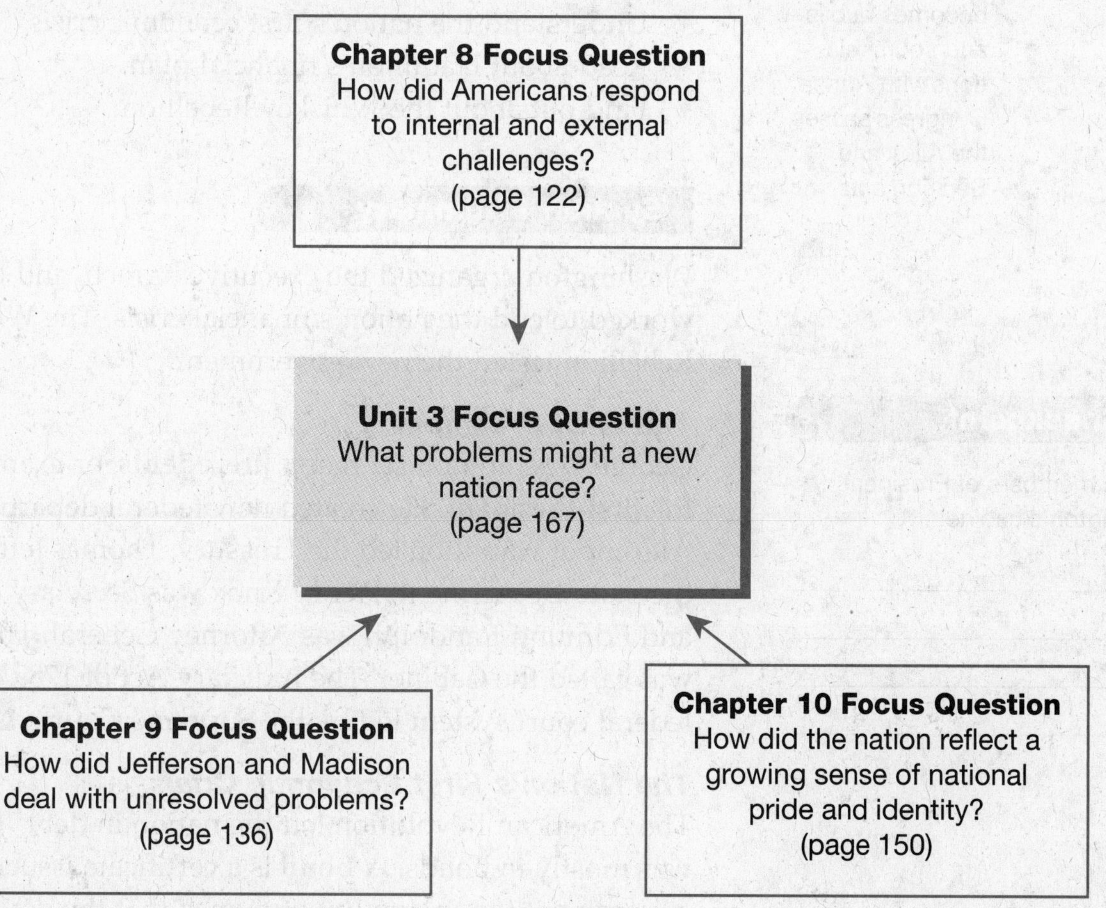

Chapter 8 Focus Question
How did Americans respond to internal and external challenges?
(page 122)
Unit 3 Focus Question
What problems might a new nation face?
(page 167)
Chapter 9 Focus Question
How did Jefferson and Madison deal with unresolved problems?
(page 136)
Chapter 10 Focus Question
How did the nation reflect a growing sense of national pride and identity?
(page 150)

Chapter 8

Launching a New Nation (1789–1800)

What You Will Learn

The new federal government dealt with challenges at home and abroad. During John Adams's presidency, disagreements increased between the parties.

Chapter 8 Focus Question

As you read this chapter, keep this question in mind: **How did Americans respond to internal and external challenges?**

Key Events

1789	Washington organizes new government departments and appoints heads.
1795	Senate approves Jay's Treaty with Britain.
1798	"XYZ Affair" becomes public and sours relations with France. Congress passes the Alien and Sedition acts.

Section 1

Washington Takes Office

Section 1 Focus Question

How did President Washington set the course for the new nation? To begin answering this question,

- Learn about the first President, George Washington.
- Understand the nation's first economic crisis.
- Read about Hamilton's financial plan.
- Find out about the Whiskey Rebellion.

Section 1 Summary

Washington organized the executive branch, and Hamilton worked to end the nation's financial crisis. The Whiskey Rebellion tested the new government.

✓ Checkpoint

List the members of President Washington's cabinet.

____

____

____

____

The First President

George Washington set many **precedents,** or examples, as the first President. He created new federal departments. Alexander Hamilton led the Treasury, Thomas Jefferson led the State Department, Henry Knox was Secretary of War, and Edmund Randolph was Attorney General. The group was called the Cabinet. The Judiciary Act of 1789 created a federal court system led by the Supreme Court. ✓

The Nation's First Economic Crisis

The American Revolution left the nation in debt. The debt was mostly in bonds. A **bond** is a certificate issued by a government for an amount of money that the government promises to pay back with interest. **Speculators,** or people who invest in a risky venture in the hope of making a large profit, bought bonds for less than they were worth. Many believed it was unfair to pay speculators in full. ✓

Hamilton's Financial Plan

Hamilton developed a plan to solve the country's financial crisis. The first part of the plan was for the government to pay back all federal and state debts. Many southern states did not want the federal government to pay state debts because they had already paid theirs on their own. Eventually the South agreed to this part of the plan. In return, the government agreed to build its capital in the South.

The second part of Hamilton's plan was to charter a national bank. Jefferson argued that a national bank was **unconstitutional**—contrary to what is permitted by the Constitution. He called for a "strict" interpretation, or reading, of the Constitution. Hamilton, on the other hand, called for a "loose" interpretation. He believed that the Constitution gave Congress the power to do things not directly allowed. <u>A national bank was created, but interpretation of the Constitution still provokes disagreement today.</u>

Southerners also opposed Hamilton's idea for a national **tariff,** or a tax on imported goods. The tariff raised federal funds and also protected United States' manufacturers. This helped northern industries because it protected them from lower priced foreign goods. Since southerners had little industry, the tariff hurt them by raising prices. Congress did not pass the tariff. ✓

The Whiskey Rebellion

Congress put a tax on all whiskey made and sold in the country. Some Pennsylvania farmers who were against the tax started a violent protest. Washington sent federal troops to Pennsylvania, showing that armed rebellion would not be accepted. ✓

Check Your Progress

1. What two crises occurred during the early part of President George Washington's administration?

____

____

2. What were the three parts to Hamilton's financial plan?

____

____

✓ Checkpoint

After the American Revolution, the nation's debt was mostly in what form?

____

Vocabulary Builder

Provoke comes from the Latin verb *provocare*, which means "to call out." What is being "called out" in the underlined sentence?

____

✓ Checkpoint

Name the two types of constitutional interpretation used during the debate about the national bank.

____

____

✓ Checkpoint

What caused the Whiskey Rebellion?

____

Section 1 Notetaking Study Guide

Question to Think About As you read Section 1, keep this question in mind: **How did President Washington set the course for the new nation?**

► Use this chart to record key information from the section.

Washington Takes Office

The first job of the President and Congress: to put a working government in place

Executive Branch

- Congress passed laws to set up three executive departments: ________ ________________
- The President appointed a secretary to head each department. He also appointed an ________________ to advise him on legal matters.
- This group of people became known as the ____________.

Judicial Branch

- The Constitution called for a judiciary, or a court system.
- The ________________ provided for a Supreme Court of 6 justices, ___ circuit courts, and 13 ________ courts.
- Main job of federal courts: ________ ________________ ________________

Hamilton's Financial Plan

The American Revolution had left the national government and states deeply in debt, which was mainly in the form of ______.

Part 1: Paying the Debt

- Hamilton wanted the United States to honor its ______.
- Many southerners opposed the plan to repay ______ debts.
- The agreement: ______ ________________ ________________ ________________ ________________

Part 2: ____________

- The debate over the bank focused on the powers of the ____________ under the ____________.
- Some had a ________ interpretation of the Constitution. Others had a ________ interpretation.
- The bank was ________.

Part 3: High Tariff

- Hamilton wanted a high tariff to ______ for the federal government and to protect U.S. manufacturers from ________________.
- Southerners argued the tariff would help the ______ but ______ the South.
- Congress ______ it.

The Whiskey Rebellion

- To raise money, Congress __________ all whiskey made and sold in the United States.
- It led to an armed revolt that tested the __________ of the new government.
- Washington sent the __________ as a sign that armed revolt was unacceptable.

Refer to this page to answer the Chapter 8 Focus Question on page 135.

Section 2

The Birth of Political Parties

Section 2 Focus Question

How did two political parties emerge? To begin answering this question,

- Learn why political parties emerged.
- Learn about the differences between Republicans and Federalists.
- Find out about how the election of 1796 increased tension between the parties.

Section 2 Summary

The Framers did not expect political parties to develop. But differences over issues led to the creation of parties. After the 1796 election, tensions increased between the parties.

Political Parties Emerge

The Framers of the Constitution did not expect political parties to develop in the United States. Instead, they thought that government leaders would work together for the sake of the whole nation.

In those days, people spoke of *factions* rather than *political parties*. A **faction** was an organized political group, and the word was not complimentary. **James Madison** thought factions were selfish groups that ignored the well-being of the whole nation. President Washington tried to discourage the growth of factions, but by the early 1790s, they began to form anyway. ✓

Republicans Against Federalists

The two parties that formed were the Republicans and the Federalists. The Republicans developed out of Democratic-Republican clubs that accused the federal government of growing too strong. They wanted to keep most power at the state or local level. The Federalists took their name from the people who had supported the adoption of the Constitution. They believed the United States needed a strong federal government to hold the country together.

At the time that both parties were organizing, the Federalists had an advantage. President Washington usually supported **Alexander Hamilton** and his policies. **Thomas Jefferson** resigned as secretary of state because of the federal government's support of Federalist policies.

Key Events

1789	Washington organizes new government departments and appoints heads.
1795	Senate approves Jay's Treaty with Britain.
1798	"XYZ Affair" becomes public and sours relations with France. Congress passes the Alien and Sedition acts.

✓ Checkpoint

Name the term that people used instead of the term *political parties*.

____

Reading Strategy

Ask and answer a question about a difference between the Republican Party and the Federalist Party.

Question: _______________________

Answer: _______________________

Republicans	Federalists
• **Main Supporters:** southern planters and northern artisans and farmers • **Main Leaders:** Thomas Jefferson and James Madison • Supported strong state government • Opposed a national bank • Opposed a tariff on imported goods • Supported France because it had recently overthrown its king • Strictly interpreted the Constitution	• **Main Supporters:** merchants, other property owners, and workers in trade and manufacturing • **Main Leader:** Alexander Hamilton • Supported a strong national government • Supported a national bank • Supported a tariff on imported goods • Were pro-British • Loosely interpreted the Constitution

✓

✓ Checkpoint

List the main supporters of the Republicans and Federalists.

Republicans: ____________________

____

Federalists: ____________________

____

The Election of 1796

In 1796, George Washington announced that he would not run for a third term as President. His action set an important precedent. Not until Franklin Roosevelt ran for and won a third term in 1940 would any President seek more than two terms. In 1951, the Twenty-second Amendment to the Constitution limited Presidents to two terms.

Today, the President and Vice President run together on the same ticket. However, at the time of the 1796 election, the President and the Vice President were not elected as a ticket. The candidate with the most votes became President. The candidate who came in second place was elected Vice President. In the 1796 election, a Federalist, **John Adams**, became President, but the Republican candidate, Thomas Jefferson, became Vice President. This led to serious tensions during the next four years. ✓

Vocabulary Builder

A *precedent* is an action or decision that is used as an example for a later one.

✓ Checkpoint

Name the person elected president in 1796.

____

Check Your Progress

1. Why did the Framers of the Constitution not expect political parties?

____

____

____

2. What were the two political parties' positions on the power of the national government?

____

____

____

Section 2 Notetaking Study Guide

Question to Think About As you read Section 2 in your textbook and take notes, keep this question in mind: **How did two political parties emerge?**

► Use these charts to record key information from the section. Some information has been filled in to get you started.

The Birth of Political Parties
At first, political parties did not exist because people felt a leader should represent ____________________.
President Washington tried to discourage the growth of political parties, which were originally called ____________________.

The Two Parties		
	Federalists	**Republicans**
Origin	Took name from early supporters of the Constitution	Democratic-Republican clubs
Leaders	•	• James Madison •
Supporters	• merchants • •	• • northern farmers and artisans
Position on state vs. federal power	•	•
Positions on other issues	Favored: • loose interpretation of Constitution • • • close ties with ____________	Favored: • • close ties with ____________ Opposed: • •
Presidential candidate in 1796	•	• Thomas Jefferson

Results of the 1796 Election
President: ____________________ Vice President: ____________________

Refer to this page to answer the Chapter 8 Focus Question on page 135.

Section 3

Troubles at Home and Abroad

Key Events

1789 Washington organizes new government departments and appoints heads.

1795 Senate approves Jay's Treaty with Britain.

1798 "XYZ Affair" becomes public and sours relations with France. Congress passes the Alien and Sedition acts.

Section 3 Focus Question

How did the actions of Britain and France affect the United States? To begin answering this question,

- Find out about conflicts in the Northwest Territory.
- Learn about the French Revolution and how Americans reacted to it.
- Note President Washington's accomplishments and advice.

Section 3 Summary

President Washington faced conflict with Native Americans and foreign threats to American shipping. He advised Americans to avoid political divisions and involvement in European affairs.

Conflicts in the Northwest Territory

The Northwest Territory was the land north and west of the Ohio River to the Mississippi River. The United States won the territory from Britain as part of the terms of the treaty that ended the American Revolution.

Britain had promised to withdraw its forts from the region. Ten years later the forts were still there. The British were also supplying Native Americans with guns and ammunition. The British hoped that this would limit American settlement in the Northwest Territory.

During the 1780s, many American settlers moved into the Northwest Territory. Native Americans were worried about losing their lands. Several Native American groups joined together to oppose American settlement.

By 1790, the federal government had bought much of the Native Americans' lands south of the Ohio River. However, Native Americans in the Northwest Territory refused to sell and they attacked settlers.

Washington sent troops to the Northwest Territory. Three battles occurred between American troops and Native Americans. The Native Americans won the first two battles.

In 1794, General **Anthony Wayne** defeated the Native Americans at the Battle of Fallen Timbers. In the 1795 Treaty of Greenville, Native Americans gave up much of their land in the Northwest Territory. ✓

Reading Strategy

Circle the sentence that tells you about the Native Americans' worry. Draw an arrow to the sentence in which their worry comes true.

Mark the Text

✓ Checkpoint

Name the battle and the treaty that ended conflict between settlers and Native Americans in the Northwest Territory.

____

____

The French Revolution

When the French Revolution began in 1789, Americans supported the French effort to overthrow the king. Growing violence in France led Federalists to oppose the revolution. Republicans continued to support it. They argued that some violence could be expected in a fight for freedom.

By 1793, Britain and France were at war. Republicans backed France. Federalists backed Britain. President Washington issued a proclamation that said the United States would remain **neutral,** not favoring either side of the dispute. In response, both France and Britain started seizing American ships. Britain made matters worse by the **impressment** of American sailors. This means it seized the sailors and forced them to serve in the British navy.

Washington sent **John Jay** to discuss a treaty with Britain. In a 1795 treaty, the United States agreed to pay debts owed to British merchants. Britain agreed to pay for the ships it had seized and to withdraw its troops from the Northwest Territory. However, it refused to stop impressing sailors. The British also refused to recognize the U.S. right to trade with France. Republicans opposed the treaty, arguing that it gave away too much. But with Federalist support, the Senate approved the treaty to keep peace with Britain. ✓

Washington Retires From Public Life

At the end of his second term in 1796, Washington published his Farewell Address. He warned against the dangers of political divisions at home. He also advised that the United States stay out of European affairs. Washington's main accomplishments as President were establishing a federal government, ending the country's economic crisis, getting the British to leave the Northwest Territory, and keeping the country out of war. ✓

Check Your Progress

1. What role did Britain play in the Northwest Territory?

2. How did public support in the United States for the French Revolution change over time?

Vocabulary Builder

Reread the underlined sentence. If to proclaim something means to announce it, what is a *proclamation*?

✓ Checkpoint

What led the Federalists to oppose the French Revolution?

✓ Checkpoint

List the two things that Washington recommended in his Farewell Address.

Section 3 Notetaking Study Guide

Question to Think About As you read Section 3 in your textbook and take notes, keep this question in mind: **How did the actions of Britain and France affect the United States?**

▶ Use this chart to record key information from the section. Some information has been filled in to get you started.

I. Conflicts in the Northwest Territory	
Conflict with Britain	• A decade after the ____________, British troops still occupied forts in the Northwest Territory. • The British were also supplying Native Americans with ________ and ________ to help limit American ____________.
Conflict with Native Americans	• Americans tried to ________ Native Americans to sell their lands in the Northwest Territory. • Native Americans sold some land but refused to sell other lands. • After an American victory at the ____________, the leaders of defeated Native American nations gave up most of their land in the 1795 ____________.

II. The French Revolution
• At first, Americans ________ the revolutionaries. • Reasons the French Revolution became controversial 1. Violence peaked in a period called the ________. ________ denounced the violence, but Republicans said some violence should be expected. 2. Both Britain and ________, which were at war, began stopping American ships and ________ their cargoes. The British made matters worse by the ________ of the ships' sailors. • Terms of Jay's Treaty What the Americans agreed to: ____________ What the British agreed to: ____________ ____________ What the British did not agree to: ____________ ____________

III. Washington Retires	
Farewell Address Advice	• warned about political divisions at home •
Washington's Accomplishments	• established federal government • • •

Refer to this page to answer the Chapter 8 Focus Question on page 135.

Section 4

The Presidency of John Adams

Section 4 Focus Question

How did problems with France intensify the split between the Federalists and Republicans? To begin answering this question,

- Find out about America's troubles with France.
- Read about the impact of the Alien and Sedition acts.
- Learn about the idea of states' rights.

Section 4 Summary

Events in Europe intensified the split between Federalists and Republicans. Tensions increased further with the passage of the Alien and Sedition acts.

Troubles With France

The decision of the United States to stay neutral during the war between France and Britain angered France. The French had supported America during the American Revolution. They thought the support should be returned. Also, Jay's Treaty made it look as if the United States favored Britain. As a result, the French refused to meet with an American diplomat, and they continued to seize American ships.

In 1797, Adams sent three diplomats to France. Agents of the French foreign minister demanded a bribe from the Americans. The so-called XYZ Affair outraged many Americans, especially Federalists. (XYZ refers to the three French agents whose real names were kept secret.) The affair led to an undeclared naval war with France. Adams and Congress increased the army and rebuilt the navy.

Adams opposed war with France. He sent another group of diplomats to France. In 1800, a treaty was signed. France agreed to stop seizing American ships. War was avoided. The treaty angered many of Adams's fellow Federalists who wanted war with France. ✓

The Alien and Sedition Acts

The undeclared war with France increased distrust between Federalists and Republicans. Federalists feared that European immigrants would spread dangerous ideas. They feared that immigrants would support the Republicans when they became citizens.

Key Events

1789	Washington organizes new government departments and appoints heads.
1795	Senate approves Jay's Treaty with Britain.
1798	"XYZ Affair" becomes public and sours relations with France. Congress passes the Alien and Sedition acts.

Reading Strategy

Read the bracketed paragraph. Underline the cause and the effects of France's anger. Draw an arrow from the cause to the effect.

✓ Checkpoint

To what did the XYZ Affair lead?

____

As a result of their fears, the Federalist-controlled Congress passed several laws. The first law it passed was the Alien Act. This law increased the time from 5 to 14 years that it took for an **alien**, or outsider or someone from another country, to become a citizen. It also allowed the President to jail or deport aliens he considered dangerous. Congress also passed the Sedition Act. **Sedition** is an activity aimed at overthrowing a government. This act made it a crime to say or write anything insulting or false about the government. The Sedition Act placed the harshest limits on free speech in America's history. People who were convicted of breaking this law were either jailed or fined. ✓

✓ Checkpoint

Name the act that targeted Republicans.

____

States' Rights

Republicans opposed the Alien and Sedition acts. They said that the Sedition Act violated the First Amendment right to free speech.

James Madison and Thomas Jefferson wrote <u>resolutions</u> for the Virginia and Kentucky legislatures. They stated that the Alien and Sedition acts were unconstitutional. They also argued that the states had the right to declare federal laws unconstitutional.

The Virginia and Kentucky resolutions had little short-term impact. By 1802, the Alien and Sedition acts had expired. Congress restored the waiting period for citizenship to five years.

Vocabulary Builder

The word *resolution* has different meanings depending on its context. Which definition is most like that in the bracketed text?

A. A statement of a group's opinion

B. The solving of a problem

The resolutions were more important over the long run. They established the ideas of states' rights and nullification. **States' rights** is the idea that the union binding "these United States" is an agreement between the states. Therefore, they can overrule federal law. Nullification is the related idea that states have the power to **nullify**, or deprive of legal force, a federal law. The ideas increased in importance when the southern states began defending slavery. ✓

✓ Checkpoint

Name the two men who wrote resolutions for Virginia and Kentucky.

____

____

Check Your Progress

1. How did John Adams deal with problems with France?

____

____

2. What two principles did the Virginia and Kentucky resolutions help to establish?

____

____

Section 4 Notetaking Study Guide

Question to Think About As you read Section 4 in your textbook and take notes, keep this question in mind: **How did problems with France intensify the split between the Federalists and Republicans?**

▶ Use this chart to record key information from the section. Some information has been filled in to get you started.

The Presidency of John Adams

Troubles with France

- France was angry that the United States remained ____________ in the war between France and Britain. The French also felt that Jay's Treaty favored Britain.
- France ____________ an American diplomat and continued to seize ____________.
- XYZ Affair
  - French officials demanded a ____________ from three American ____________.
  - Many Americans, especially ____________, were outraged.
- American anger over the XYZ Affair led to an ____________. Adams increased the size of the ____________ and established a ____________.
- In 1800, France and the United States signed a treaty. France agreed to ____________, and the United States ____________.
- The treaty angered many Federalists, which ____________ President Adams's political power.

The Alien and Sedition Acts

- Reasons Federalists opposed European immigration
  -
  -
- The Alien Act increased the time it took for an alien to ____________. It also allowed the President to jail or ____________ an alien he considered dangerous.
- The Sedition Act made it a crime to ____________ about the government. This was a limit on ____________.

States' Rights

- The legislatures of Virginia and ____________ passed resolutions stating that the Alien and Sedition acts were unconstitutional and that states had the right to ____________.
- The long-term effect was to establish the principles of states' rights and ____________, or the idea that states have the power to deprive a federal law of legal force.

Refer to this page to answer the Chapter 8 Focus Question on page 135.

Chapter 8 Assessment

Directions: Circle the letter of the correct answer.

1. Which was a crisis faced by President George Washington?
  A Shays' Rebellion
  B repaying war debt
  C fighting a war with France

2. Which best describes the Republican Party?
  A It supported Britain over France.
  B Its leader was Alexander Hamilton.
  C It opposed a national bank.

3. Which was a result of the Virginia and Kentucky resolutions?
  A idea of nullification
  B freedom of religion
  C individual rights

Directions: Follow the steps to answer this question:

How did the advice Washington gave in his Farewell Address reflect or not reflect his accomplishments as President?

Step 1: Recall information: List Washington's advice and accomplishments.

Washington's Advice	Washington's Accomplishments
1.	1.
	2.
2.	3.
	4.

Step 2: Identify similarities and differences between Washington's advice and his accomplishments.

____

____

____

Step 3: Complete the topic sentence that follows. Then write two or three sentences explaining how Washington's accomplishments did or did not reflect his advice.

Washington's accomplishments as President ____________________

____

____

____

Chapter 8 Notetaking Study Guide

Now you are ready to answer the Chapter 8 Focus Question: **How did Americans respond to internal and external challenges?**

▶ Complete the following chart to help you answer this question. Use the notes that you took for each section.

Challenges Facing the New Government	
Internal Challenges	**External Challenges**
Organizing the Government • Congress passed laws to set up three departments in the executive branch: ______, ______, and ______ • Judicial branch: Judiciary Act of 1789	**The French Revolution** • Federalist reaction: denounced the violence of the revolution • Republican reaction: ______
The Nation's First Economic Crisis • Problem: nation and states in debt • Solution: Alexander Hamilton proposed a ______ plan. Congress agreed to 1. ______ 2. ______	**France and Britain at War** • U.S. position: remained neutral • Effect of position: ______
The Whiskey Rebellion • To raise money, Congress imposed a ______ that led to a revolt. • Washington sent in the militia, which confirmed ______.	**Troubles with Britain** Jay's Treaty: • Americans agreed to: ______ British agreed to: pay for ships it seized, remove its troops from Northwest Territory, stop aiding Native Americans • British did not agree to: ______
Political Disagreements • Two parties formed: ______, ______.	
Conflicts in the Northwest Territory • Reasons U.S. upset with Britain: ______ • Source of conflict with Native Americans: Native Americans did not want to sell their land to Americans for settlement • Terms of the Treaty of Greenville: ______	**Troubles with France** • Jay's Treaty and XYZ Affair led to an ______ • U.S. agreement with France: ______
	Alien and Sedition Acts Increasing tensions with France prompted the Federalist-led government to pass laws that made it harder to gain ______ and restricted ______.

Refer to this page to answer the Unit 3 Focus Question on page 167.

Chapter 9

The Era of Thomas Jefferson (1800–1815)

What You Will Learn

During Thomas Jefferson's presidency, the United States acquired a vast expanse of western territory. Conflicts with the British and Native Americans soon led to the War of 1812.

Chapter 9 Focus Question

As you read this chapter, keep this question in mind: **How did Jefferson and Madison deal with unresolved problems?**

Key Events

1803	The United States purchases Louisiana from France.
1811	Americans defeat Native Americans at Battle of Tippecanoe.
1812	United States declares war on Britain.

Section 1

Jefferson Takes Office

Section 1 Focus Question

How did Jefferson chart a new course for the government? To begin answering this question,

- Learn about the Republican victory in the election of 1800.
- Find out about Jefferson's new course for government.
- Learn about judicial review.

Section 1 Summary

After a bitter campaign, Thomas Jefferson became President. Jefferson tried to reduce the power of the federal government. Meanwhile, judicial review increased the Supreme Court's power.

Republicans Take Charge

The presidential campaign of 1800 was a bitter contest between the Federalists and the Republicans. The Republican candidate, **Thomas Jefferson,** defeated John Adams, the Federalist candidate. However, he received the same number of electoral votes as his running mate, **Aaron Burr**. It was up to the House of Representatives to break the tie. The House chose Jefferson. To avoid this situation in the future, the Twelfth Amendment to the Constitution established separate votes for President and Vice President. ✓

✓ Checkpoint

Name the body that decided the election of 1800.

____

Jefferson Charts a New Course

Jefferson's first goal was to reduce the federal government's power over states and citizens. He believed in an idea known as **laissez faire,** which means that the government should not interfere with the economy.

Jefferson's Main Policy Changes
• Reduced the number of people in government • Cut military spending • Eliminated federal taxes in the country, except tariffs • Released those jailed under the Sedition Act

Jefferson did not reverse all Federalist policies, however. For example, he believed that the nation should keep repaying its debt. ✓

The Supreme Court and Judicial Review

John Adams appointed several judges in the last hours of his term. Jefferson opposed these appointments. He felt that Adams was trying to maintain Federalist power. Jefferson ordered his secretary of state, James Madison, to stop work on the appointments. William Marbury, one of Adams's appointees, sued Madison to receive his commission. Marbury argued that the Judiciary Act of 1789 gave the Supreme Court the power to review cases brought against a federal official.

The Supreme Court declared the Judiciary Act unconstitutional. Chief Justice **John Marshall** wrote that the Court's authority came from the Constitution, not Congress. So, Congress could not pass laws giving the Court new powers. *Marbury* v. *Madison* established **judicial review,** or the authority of the Supreme Court to strike down unconstitutional laws. This ruling increased the Court's power. ✓

Check Your Progress

1. How did the election of 1800 affect future elections?

____

____

2. What power does judicial review give the Supreme Court?

____

____

✓ Checkpoint

List a Federalist policy that Jefferson kept.

____

Vocabulary Builder

Reread the bracketed paragraph. The text says Marbury was one of Adams's appointees. Using context clues in the paragraph, write a definition of *appointee* on the lines below.

____

____

Reading Strategy

Underline the definition of *judicial review*. Then circle the sentence that describes an effect of judicial review.

✓ Checkpoint

Name the justice who wrote the opinion for *Marbury* v. *Madison*.

____

Section 1 Notetaking Study Guide

Question to Think About As you read Section 1 in your textbook and take notes, keep this section focus question in mind: **How did Jefferson chart a new course for the government?**

▶ Use these charts to record key information from the section. Some information has been filled in to get you started.

The Election of 1800

- **The presidential candidates**
  1. Federalist: John Adams
  2. Republican: Thomas Jefferson
- The tie between Jefferson and Burr occurred because ______
- Deadlock resolved by ______
- Amendment passed as a result of the tie: ______
- Amendment established ______

Jefferson Charts a New Course

- Jefferson's first goal as president: ______
- The reforms Jefferson made to meet his goal:
  - cut the number of government employees
  -
  -
  -
  -
- Federalist policies Jefferson did not reverse:
  -
  -

The Supreme Court and Judicial Review

- In ______ v. ______, the Supreme Court ruled the ______ unconstitutional because ______
- This decision established judicial review, or the authority of the Supreme Court to strike down ______ laws.

Refer to this page to answer the Chapter 9 Focus Question on page 149.

Section 2

The Louisiana Purchase

Section 2 Focus Question

What was the importance of the purchase and exploration of the Louisiana Territory? To begin answering this question,

- Learn about the nation's westward expansion.
- Find out about the Louisiana Purchase.
- Learn about Lewis and Clark's western expedition.

Section 2 Summary

The Louisiana Purchase almost doubled the size of the United States, and the Lewis and Clark expedition provided Americans with new knowledge of the West.

The Nation Looks West

By 1800, more than one million settlers lived between the Appalachian Mountains and the Mississippi River. There were few roads in the West, so most farmers shipped their crops down the Mississippi to New Orleans. From there, goods were shipped to markets in the East. Spain controlled the Mississippi and New Orleans. In 1795, the United States negotiated the Pinckney Treaty with Spain. It guaranteed Americans the right to ship goods down the Mississippi to New Orleans.

In 1801, Jefferson discovered that Spain had secretly transferred New Orleans and the rest of its Louisiana territory to France. Jefferson feared that Napoleon Bonaparte, the French leader, intended to expand France's control in America. This would block U.S. expansion. ✓

Buying Louisiana

Shortly before it handed over Louisiana to France, Spain withdrew Americans' rights to ship their goods through New Orleans. Westerners demanded that Jefferson go to war to win back their rights. Instead Jefferson sent James Monroe to Paris to offer to buy New Orleans and a territory to the east called West Florida from the French.

Around this time, a revolution had driven the French from their Caribbean colony of Haiti. At the same time, tensions between France and Britain were headed toward war. Napoleon needed money to pay for the war. As a result, France offered to sell the entire Louisiana Territory to

Key Events

1803	The United States purchases Louisiana from France.
1811	Americans defeat Native Americans at Battle of Tippecanoe.
1812	United States declares war on Britain.

✓ Checkpoint

Describe the route by which Western farm products reached markets in the East.

____

____

____

Reading Strategy

Identify a cause and an effect in the bracketed paragraph. Underline the cause and circle the effect.

✓ Checkpoint

List the four boundaries of Louisiana Territory.

Vocabulary Builder

An early definition of *expedition* was "helping forward or accomplishing." How can this definition still explain the word *expedition*?

✓ Checkpoint

Name the Native American woman who served as a translator for Lewis and Clark.

the United States. The territory stretched from the Gulf of Mexico to Canada and from the Mississippi River to the Rocky Mountains. This doubled the size of the country and gave the United States control of the Mississippi.

Jefferson had a problem, though. The Constitution did not give the President the power to buy land from a foreign country. However, the Constitution did give the President the power to make treaties. Jefferson decided this allowed him to buy Louisiana. The Senate approved the treaty, and Congress quickly voted to pay for the land. ✓

Lewis and Clark Explore the West

Jefferson called for a western **expedition,** or long and carefully organized journey. Army officers **Meriwether Lewis** and **William Clark** were its leaders.

Lewis and Clark's mission had three goals. First, they were to report on the geography, plants, animals, and other natural features of the region. Second, they were to make contact with Native Americans. Third, they were to find out if a waterway connected the Mississippi River to the Pacific Ocean.

Lewis and Clark left St. Louis in 1804 with about 40 men. Along the way, a Native American woman named Sacagawea joined them as a translator. During their trip, they reached the Continental Divide. A **continental divide** is the place on a continent that separates river systems flowing in opposite directions. Later, they reached the Columbia River, which carried them to the Pacific Ocean. When they returned east, they brought a new awareness of a rich and beautiful part of the continent.

Zebulon Pike led another expedition through the southern part of the Louisiana Territory. On his return, he traveled through Spanish New Mexico, where he and his men were arrested as spies. After several months, the men were released. Pike's reports about the Spanish borderlands created great American interest in the region. ✓

Check Your Progress

1. Why was the Louisiana Purchase important?

2. What was one purpose of the Lewis and Clark expedition?

Section 2 Notetaking Study Guide

Question to Think About As you read Section 2 in your textbook and take notes, keep this section focus question in mind: **What was the importance of the purchase and exploration of the Louisiana Territory?**

▶ Use these charts to record key information from the section. Some information has been filled in to get you started.

Westward Expansion
Importance of access to the Mississippi River: few roads; farmers depended on the river to move their farm products to the East
Importance of Pinckney's Treaty:
Jefferson's fear about the transfer of Louisiana to France:

Buying Louisiana
Jefferson's proposed deal: purchase New Orleans and West Florida from France
Situation in France at the time: • •
France's offer:
Jefferson's dilemma:
Resolution to the dilemma:

Exploring the West
Reasons for Lewis and Clark's expedition: • learn about geography, plants, animals, and natural features of the region • •
• **Route to Pacific:**
• **Result:**
• **Route of Pike's Expedition:**
• **Result:**

Refer to this page to answer the Chapter 9 Focus Question on page 149.

Section 3
A Time of Conflict

Key Events

1803	The United States purchases Louisiana from France.
1811	Americans defeat Native Americans at Battle of Tippecanoe.
1812	United States declares war on Britain.

Section 3 Focus Question

How did Jefferson respond to threats to the security of the nation? To begin answering this question,

- Learn about the defeat of the Barbary States.
- Find out about threats to American neutrality.
- Read about the trade embargo Jefferson imposed.
- Explore the efforts of Tecumseh and the Prophet to preserve Native American lands and ways of life.

Section 3 Summary

Jefferson faced threats to the nation's security and economy, including piracy, seizure of American ships by Britain and France, and unrest among Native Americans.

Defeating the Barbary States

Trade with Europe was important to the U.S. economy. Americans sold goods to Europeans. They also bought goods made in Europe. After the American Revolution, pirates began attacking American ships in the Mediterranean Sea. The pirates came from four North African countries—Morocco, Algiers, Tunisia, and Tripoli—known as the Barbary States. European nations paid the Barbary States **tribute**, or money paid by one country to another in return for protection. In exchange, pirates left their ships alone.

For a time, the United States also paid tribute, but Jefferson put an end to the practice. He sent warships to the Mediterranean to protect American merchant ships. At first these military patrols went badly, but later, a small force of American marines captured Tripoli. The victory made the United States confident that it could deal with threats from foreign powers. ✓

✓ Checkpoint

List the four Barbary States.

____

____

____

____

American Neutrality Is Challenged

By 1803 Britain and France were once again at war. The United States remained neutral and traded with both countries. Britain and France wanted to weaken each other by cutting off the other's foreign trade, so they began seizing, or taking control, of American ships. Between 1803 and 1807, Britain seized more than 1,000 American ships. Britain also impressed, or forced, thousands of American sailors to serve in the British navy. ✓

✓ Checkpoint

Name the countries that challenged the United States' neutrality.

____

____

Jefferson Responds With an Embargo

In response to attacks on American ships, Jefferson issued an **embargo.** This is a government order that forbids foreign trade. In 1807 Congress passed the Embargo Act. Jefferson predicted that France and Britain would soon stop attacking American ships. However, the results of the Embargo Act were not what Jefferson expected. The big loser was the American economy. Crop prices fell, and tens of thousands of Americans lost their jobs. The embargo was especially unpopular in New England, where merchants depended heavily on foreign trade. Many Americans began smuggling goods to get around the embargo. **Smuggling** is the act of illegally buying and selling goods.

Congress repealed the Embargo Act in 1809. It then passed a law that reopened trade with all countries except Britain and France. The law stated that trade with Britain and France would resume when they started respecting America's trading rights as a neutral nation. ✓

Tecumseh and the Prophet

After the Battle of Fallen Timbers, tens of thousands of settlers moved westward. The settlement had a terrible impact on Native Americans. It exposed Native Americans to disease, threatened Native Americans' hunting grounds, and drove away game. The Native American population declined, and so did the power of their traditional leaders.

Two Shawnee brothers, **Tecumseh** and Tenskwatawa, or the Prophet, began urging Native American resistance. American officials were concerned by these activities. **William Henry Harrison,** the governor of the Indiana Territory, led an attack on Shawnee villages on the Tippecanoe River. Harrison's troops defeated the Native Americans. The Battle of Tippecanoe marked the high point of Native American resistance to settlement. Still, Tecumseh and his warriors continued their struggle for several more years. ✓

Check Your Progress

1. What were the main threats to American trade?

____

____

2. How did westward expansion affect Native Americans?

____

____

Reading Strategy

Read this title and think about what you read under "American Neutrality Is Challenged." How does this title preview what you will be reading?

____

____

✓ Checkpoint

List two effects of the Embargo Act on the United States' economy.

____

____

✓ Checkpoint

Name the two Native American leaders who fought back against American settlement in the West.

____

____

Section 3 Notetaking Study Guide

Question to Think About As you read Section 3 in your textbook and take notes, keep this section focus question in mind: **How did Jefferson respond to threats to the security of the nation?**

▶ Use this organizer to record key information from the section. Some information has been filled in to get you started.

Barbary Pirates

- Why they were a threat: stole property and enslaved sailors
- Some nations responded by ______
- How Jefferson responded: ______

Challenges Faced by the United States

American Neutrality Challenged

- Causes: War between Britain and France leads to restrictions on U.S. trade
- Actions taken by Britain and France: ______
- U.S. response: Jefferson calls for an embargo on foreign trade; Congress passed the Embargo Act.
- Results of embargo:
  - ______
  - ______
  - ______
- Congress repealed Embargo Act in 1809.

Native American Unrest

- Cause of unrest: rapid westward settlement
- Effects on Native Americans
  - exposed to deadly diseases
  - ______
  - ______
  - ______
  - ______
- Tecumseh and Tenskwatawa urged Native Americans to:
  - resist
  - ______
- U.S. response to unrest: ______

Refer to this page to answer the Chapter 9 Focus Question on page 149.

Section 4
The War of 1812

Section 4 Focus Question

What were the causes and effects of the War of 1812? To begin answering this question,

- Find out why the United States moved toward war with Britain.
- Learn about the early days of the war.
- Read about the war in the West and South.
- Learn about the final battles of the war.

Section 4 Summary

The War of 1812 started badly for the United States. However, America's eventual victory increased **nationalism**, or the pride Americans felt about their country.

The Move Toward War

In 1809, when James Madison became President, Americans were angry with the British. The British supplied arms to Native Americans and impressed American sailors in the British navy. To most Americans, the honor of the country was being tested. Supporters of war with Britain were known as **war hawks.** Opposition to war was strongest in New England, where many believed war would hurt American trade.

Relations with Britain worsened in 1812 when the British told the United States they would continue impressing sailors. Meanwhile, Native Americans in the Northwest began new attacks on frontier settlements. In June, Congress declared war on Britain. ✓

Early Days of the War

Britain was still at war in Europe at the time. But it was not willing to meet American demands in order to avoid war. When the war began, Americans were confident they would win. However, because of military cuts under Jefferson, the United States military was not prepared for war.

At the beginning of the war, Britain set up a blockade of the American coast. A **blockade** is the action of shutting a port or road to prevent people or supplies from coming into an area or leaving it. By the end of the war, the British were able to close off all American ports. ✓

Key Events

1803	The United States purchases Louisiana from France.
1811	Americans defeat Native Americans at Battle of Tippecanoe.
1812	United States declares war on Britain.

✓ Checkpoint

Name the region in the United States where opposition to the war with Britain was strongest.

____

✓ Checkpoint

Name an action the British took at the beginning of the war.

____

✓ Checkpoint

List two commanders who led American forces to victory.

____

____

Vocabulary Builder

The word *negotiate* comes from the Latin word for "to carry on business." What do you think the word *negotiating* means in the underlined sentence?

____

____

Reading Strategy

The bracketed paragraph says that New England considered seceding from the United States. Reread the beginning of the summary. Underline the clue that explains why New England considered seceding from the United States.

Mark the Text

✓ Checkpoint

Name the battle that occurred after the peace treaty was signed.

____

The War in the West and South

In the West, the Americans and British fought for control of the Great Lakes and the Mississippi River. American troops under William Hull tried to invade Canada. They did not succeed. American forces under **Oliver Hazard Perry,** however, scored a victory against the British on Lake Erie. William Henry Harrison and his troops defeated the British at the Battle of the Thames. In the South, Creek warriors attacked several American settlements. **Andrew Jackson** led American troops to victory over the Creeks in the Battle of Horseshoe Bend. ✓

Final Battles

After the British defeated Napoleon in 1814, they sent more troops to fight against the United States. British troops attacked Washington, D.C. Then they moved on to Baltimore, where they tried to take Fort McHenry.

However, Britain soon tired of the war, so the two sides began negotiating a peace treaty. On Christmas Eve 1814, the United States and Britain signed the Treaty of Ghent, ending the war. It took weeks for the news to reach the United States. During this time, the two sides fought one last battle. American forces under General Andrew Jackson defeated the British at the Battle of New Orleans.

Around the same time, opponents of the war met in Hartford, Connecticut. Some wanted New England to **secede,** or withdraw, from the United States. However, the convention quickly ended when news of the treaty arrived.

To some Americans, the War of 1812 was the "Second War of Independence." Once and for all, the United States had secured its independence from Britain, and European nations would now have to treat the young republic with respect. American pride and confidence grew. ✓

Check Your Progress

1. What British actions led to the War of 1812?

____

____

2. Why was the United States unprepared for war?

____

____

Section 4 Notetaking Study Guide

Question to Think About As you read Section 4 in your textbook and take notes, keep this question in mind: **What were the causes and effects of the War of 1812?**

▶ Use these charts to record key information. Some information has been filled in to get you started.

The Move Toward War
The President during the War of 1812 was James Madison.
The two main reasons Americans wanted to go to war with Britain were ________ ________ and ________.
Supporters of the war were called ________.
New Englanders opposed the war because ________.

Early Days of the War
The war did not come at a good time for Britain because ________ ________.
Near the start of the war, the British Navy blockaded the U.S. coast.
The U.S. warship that won an early battle was the USS *Constitution*.

The War in the West and South
U.S. General William Hull invaded ________, and then he retreated. Then British General Isaac Brock ________.
The U.S. naval commander ________ won an important battle on Lake Erie. U.S. General William Henry Harrison won the Battle of ________ where ________ was killed.
________ defeated the Creeks in the Battle of ________.

Final Battles
In 1814, the British could send more troops to fight the war in the United States because ________.
During an attack on the nation's ________ in 1814, British troops burned ________.
During the British attack on Fort McHenry in Baltimore, Francis Scott Key wrote the words to ________.
The Treaty of ________ ended the War of 1812.
Before news of the war's end reached the U.S., ________ led the U.S. to victory in the Battle of ________.
Federalists met at the Hartford Convention where some suggested New England ________ from the U.S.

Refer to this page to answer the Chapter 9 Focus Question on page 149.

Chapter 9 Assessment

Directions: Circle the letter of the correct answer.

1. Which was a goal of President Thomas Jefferson?
   - **A** to declare war on Britain
   - **B** to add a Bill of Rights to the Constitution
   - **C** to reduce the size of the federal government

2. Who was the Treaty of Ghent between?
   - **A** the United States and Britain
   - **B** William Marbury and John Marshall
   - **C** the United States and France

3. What was an effect of the Embargo Act?
   - **A** increased unemployment in America
   - **B** higher prices for American crops
   - **C** war between Britain and France

Directions: Follow the steps to answer this question:

How might the United States be different today if the Louisiana Purchase had not occurred?

Step 1: Recall information: In the chart, list three benefits of the Louisiana Purchase for the United States.

Benefits of the Louisiana Purchase in 1803
•   •   •

Step 2: Now imagine what two ways the United States would be different today if it had been denied those benefits.

Differences in the United States Without Those Benefits
•   •

Step 3: Complete the topic sentence that follows. Then write two or three more sentences that support your topic sentence.

Without the Louisiana Purchase, the United States ____________________

____

____

____

____

Chapter 9 Notetaking Study Guide

Now you are ready to answer the Chapter 9 Focus Question: **How did Jefferson and Madison deal with unresolved problems?**

► Complete the following organizer to help you answer this question. Use the notes that you took for each section.

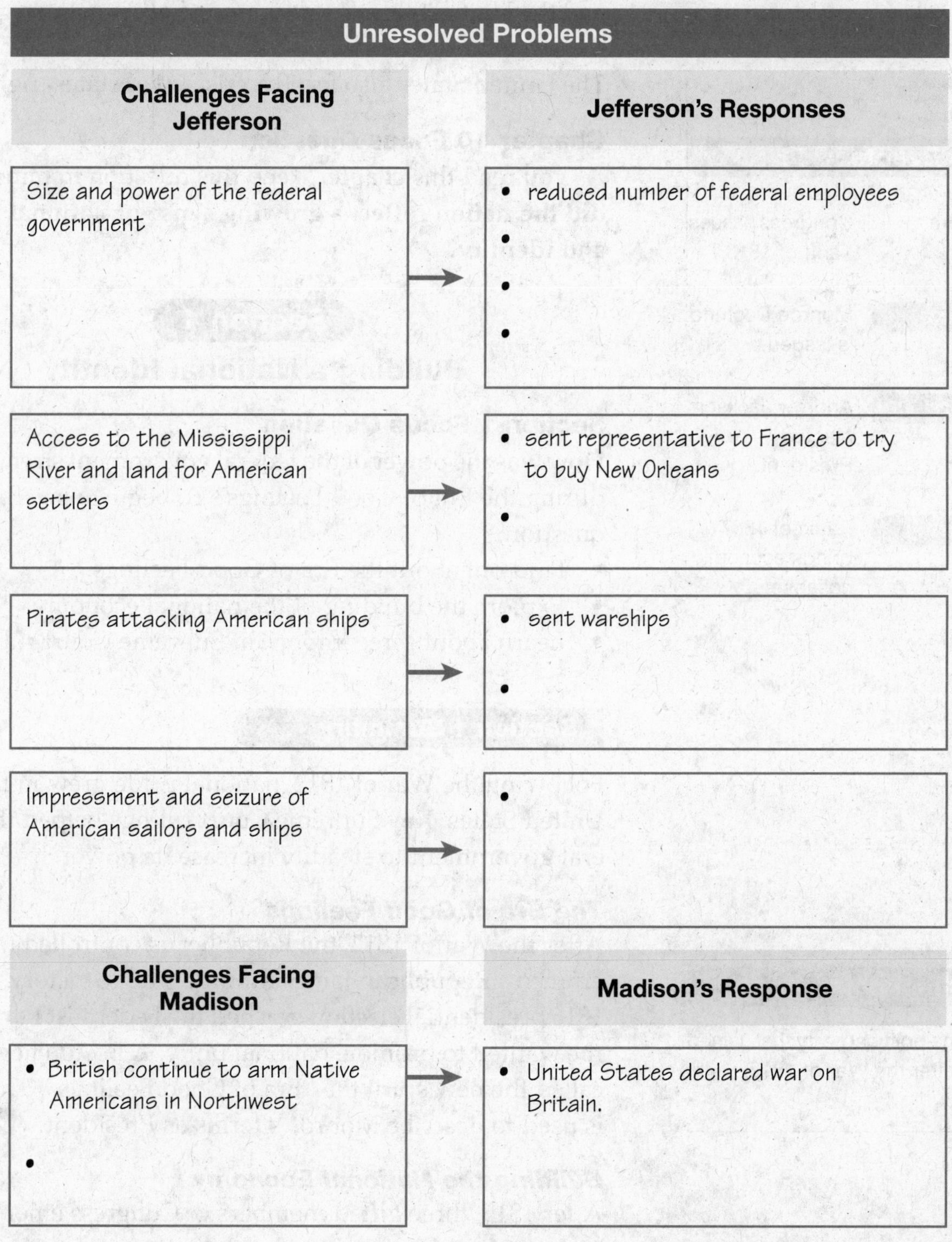

Unresolved Problems

Challenges Facing Jefferson		Jefferson's Responses
Size and power of the federal government	→	• reduced number of federal employees • • •
Access to the Mississippi River and land for American settlers	→	• sent representative to France to try to buy New Orleans •
Pirates attacking American ships	→	• sent warships •
Impressment and seizure of American sailors and ships	→	•

Challenges Facing Madison		Madison's Response
• British continue to arm Native Americans in Northwest •	→	• United States declared war on Britain.

Refer to this page to answer the Unit 3 Focus Question on page 167.

Chapter 10

A Changing Nation (1815–1840)

What You Will Learn

During the early to mid-1800s, federal authority increased, and the United States's status among other nations grew. At the same time, American politics became more democratic. The United States also faced a crisis over states' rights.

Chapter 10 Focus Question

As you read this chapter, keep this question in mind: **How did the nation reflect a growing sense of national pride and identity?**

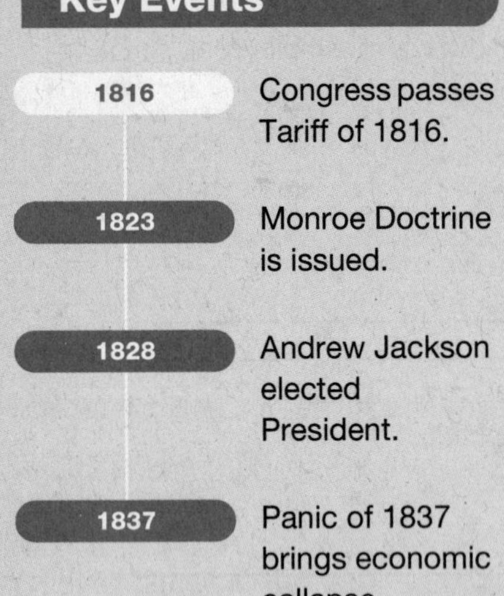

Key Events
1816
Congress passes Tariff of 1816.
1823
Monroe Doctrine is issued.
1828
Andrew Jackson elected President.
1837
Panic of 1837 brings economic collapse.

Section 1

Building a National Identity

Section 1 Focus Question

How was the power of the federal government strengthened during the Era of Good Feelings? To begin answering this question,

- Find out about the Era of Good Feelings.
- Explore the building of the national economy.
- Learn about three important Supreme Court rulings.

Section 1 Summary

Following the War of 1812, national pride grew in the United States. Key Supreme Court rulings helped the federal government to steadily increase its power.

The Era of Good Feelings

After the War of 1812, the Republicans controlled the government. Republican James Monroe's huge victory in the 1816 presidential election crushed the Federalist Party. Monroe wanted to promote national unity. A Boston newspaper called the new spirit the "Era of Good Feelings." This name is used to describe Monroe's terms as President. ✓

✓ Checkpoint

Name the political party that gained power after the War of 1812.

____

Building the National Economy

After 1815, three gifted members of Congress emerged. **Henry Clay** of Kentucky represented the West. **John C. Calhoun** of South Carolina spoke for southern interests.

Daniel Webster of Massachusetts was a leading politician for the Northeast.

The economy was one topic of debate. When the first Bank of the United States closed in 1811, the U.S. economy suffered. So in 1816, Congress established the second Bank of the United States. This helped business, but there were still problems. British companies began **dumping,** or selling manufactured goods in America below market price. This drove some New England companies out of business. So Congress passed the Tariff of 1816, which taxed some foreign goods. Such tariffs were popular in the North, where they protected local factories, but in the South, people resented paying higher prices.

Henry Clay defended tariffs in a plan called the American System. He said the money from tariffs could pay to build infrastructure. Clay argued that this would help all regions, but southerners rejected Clay's plan. ✓

Three Important Supreme Court Rulings

The Supreme Court issued three rulings that affected the economy and the power of the federal government. In *Dartmouth College* v. *Woodward* (1819), the Court protected private contracts. A **contract** is an agreement between two or more parties that can be enforced by law. This promoted **capitalism,** an economic system in which private businesses compete in a free market. In *McCulloch* v. *Maryland* (1819), the Court ruled that a state cannot pass a law that violates a federal law or interfere with federal institutions. This protected the second Bank of the United States from being taxed by the state of Maryland. In *Gibbons* v. *Ogden* (1824), the Court said that the state of New York could not give a steamboat company the sole right to run a ferry on the Hudson River. Because the trip was made between states, it was **interstate commerce,** or trade between states. Only Congress can regulate such trade. ✓

Check Your Progress

1. Why did Congress pass protective tariffs?

____

2. How did the Supreme Court's rulings increase the power of the federal government?

____

____

____

Reading Strategy

Using one of the blank pages at the back of the book, create a table that contrasts the views of the North and South on tariffs. Explain why northerners and southerners held those views.

✓ Checkpoint

Name three key members of Congress and the regions they represented.

Member: ____________________
Region: ____________________
Member: ____________________
Region: ____________________
Member: ____________________
Region: ____________________

✓ Checkpoint

Name the Supreme Court ruling that said states cannot pass laws that violate federal laws.

____

Section 1 Notetaking Study Guide

Question to Think About As you read Section 1 in your textbook and take notes, keep this section focus question in mind: **How was the power of the federal government strengthened during the Era of Good Feelings?**

▶ Use these charts to record key information from the section.

Important Political Figures During the Era of Good Feelings	
Henry Clay	Congressman from Kentucky who represented ________ interests; proposed the ________________
John C. Calhoun	Congressman from ____________ who represented ________ interests; emphasized states' rights
	Congressman from ____________ who represented northern interests; supported ________________

Important Economic Issues		
Topic	**Why It Was Needed**	**What It Did**
Second Bank of United States	____________ made too many loans and issued too much money.	Loaned money and controlled the ____________
Tariff of 1816	________ manufacturers were ____________, which hurt American businesses.	Raised taxes on foreign goods, pleasing __________ and upsetting __________

Key Supreme Court Cases	
Case	**Supreme Court Ruling**
________ v. ________ (______)	**Question:** Can Maryland tax a state branch of the ________________? **Decision:** States cannot ____________ federal institutions or violate ____________.
________ v. Woodward (1819)	**Question:** Can New Hampshire change the charter of ____________? **Decision:** The charter was a private contract protected by the ____________.
Gibbons v. Ogden (1824)	**Question:** Can ____________ grant a steamship company a ____________ on the Hudson River ferry? **Decision:** The ferry trip involved ________________, which only Congress can ________.

Refer to this page to answer the Chapter 10 Focus Question on page 166.

Section 2

Dealing With Other Nations

Section 2 Focus Question

How did U.S. foreign affairs reflect new national confidence? To begin answering this question,

- Learn about U.S. relations with Spain.
- Find out how Spanish colonies won independence.
- Learn about the Monroe Doctrine.
- Examine U.S. relations with Canada.

Section 2 Summary

After the War of 1812, the United States settled border disputes with Spain and Britain. Many Latin American colonies declared independence. The Monroe Doctrine tried to keep European powers from interfering with these nations or other U.S. interests in the Americas.

Relations With Spain

Spanish Florida was a source of conflict between the United States and Spain. Enslaved African Americans fled from Georgia and Alabama into Florida. Many joined the Seminole Nation. The Seminoles often crossed the border to raid American settlements. In 1817, the U.S. government sent Andrew Jackson to recapture escaped slaves. Jackson destroyed Seminole villages and then captured two Spanish towns. Spain realized that it could not defend Florida from the United States. So Spain **ceded,** or gave up, Florida to the United States in the Adams-Onís Treaty of 1819. ✓

Spanish Colonies Win Independence

Spain's control of its other American colonies was also fading. The people of Latin America were inspired by the American and French revolutions to seek independence. In 1810, **Father Miguel Hidalgo** (ee DAHL goh) led a local army against Spanish rule in Mexico. He failed. But another revolution broke out in 1820. Spain granted Mexico independence in 1821, and Mexico became a republic in 1823.

In South America, **Simón Bolívar** (see MOHN boh LEE vahr) led several struggles for independence. Known as the Liberator, Bolivar defeated the Spanish in 1819 and formed the Republic of Great Colombia. This included what are now Colombia, Ecuador, Panama, and Venezuela. The people of Central America soon followed by forming the

Key Events

1816	Congress passes Tariff of 1816.
1823	Monroe Doctrine is issued.
1828	Andrew Jackson elected President.
1837	Panic of 1837 brings economic collapse.

✓ Checkpoint

Name the reason Spain was willing to cede Florida to the United States.

____

____

Vocabulary Builder

To *liberate* means "to set free." Why do you think Simón Bolívar was called the Liberator?

____

____

____

✓ Checkpoint

Name two events that inspired Latin American independence movements.

____

____

Reading Strategy

Ask and answer a question about the Monroe Doctrine.

Question: ______________________

____

Answer: ______________________

____

____

✓ Checkpoint

Name the region covered by the Monroe Doctrine.

____

✓ Checkpoint

Name the act that reunited Canada in 1841.

____

United Provinces of Central America in 1823. By 1825, most of Latin America had thrown off European rule. ☑

The Monroe Doctrine

In 1822, the United States recognized the independence of Mexico and six other former colonies in Latin America. But European powers like France and Russia wanted to help Spain regain its colonies. In 1823, Britain suggested that the United States and Britain join together to protect the freedom of Latin America. President **James Monroe** approved. But Secretary of State **John Quincy Adams** argued that acting jointly would make the United States look like Britain's junior partner.

In December 1823, Monroe announced what is now called the Monroe Doctrine. The United States would not allow European powers to interfere with the free nations of Latin America. In truth, the United States could not have stopped European powers from acting. As U.S. power grew, however, the Monroe Doctrine boosted the influence of the United States in Latin America. ☑

Relations With Canada

Britain faced its own challenges in Canada. In 1791, this British colony was divided into Upper and Lower Canada. After each part rebelled in 1837, Britain rejoined the colony in 1841 under the Act of Union. This act gave Canadians greater **self-government**—the right of people to rule themselves independently.

Canadian relations with the United States were strained during the War of 1812 when U.S. forces tried to invade Canada. But relations improved as Britain and the United States settled several border disputes involving Canada from 1818 to 1846. Eventually, the United States and Canada established excellent relations. ☑

Check Your Progress

1. What are two reasons the United States was upset about relations with Spanish Florida?

____

____

____

2. Why did Adams not want the United States to work with Great Britain on the Monroe Doctrine?

____

____

Section 2 Notetaking Study Guide

Question to Think About As you read Section 2 in your textbook and take notes, keep this section focus question in mind: **How did U.S. foreign affairs reflect new national confidence?**

▶ Use these organizers to record key information from the section. Some information has been filled in to get you started.

Latin American Independence		
Region	**Country/countries to gain independence**	**When**
North America	Mexico: First a __________, then a __________	•
	People in this region declared their independence from Spain and formed the __________________.	• 1821 •
South America	____________________ made up of today's nations of Colombia, Ecuador, Panama, and Venezuela Brazil announced its independence from __________.	• •

U.S.-Foreign Relations

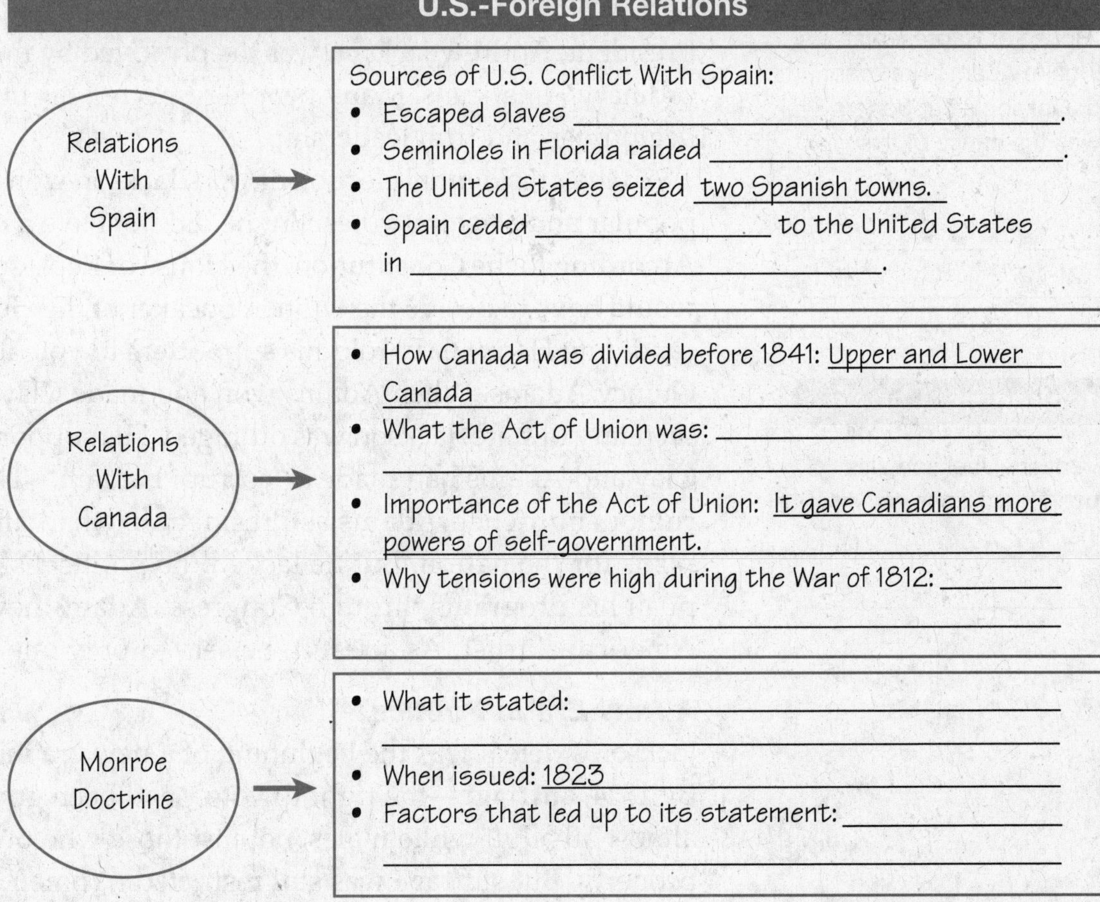

Relations With Spain →

Sources of U.S. Conflict With Spain:
- Escaped slaves ____________________.
- Seminoles in Florida raided ____________________.
- The United States seized two Spanish towns.
- Spain ceded __________ to the United States in ____________________.

Relations With Canada →

- How Canada was divided before 1841: Upper and Lower Canada
- What the Act of Union was: ____________________
- Importance of the Act of Union: It gave Canadians more powers of self-government.
- Why tensions were high during the War of 1812: ____________________

Monroe Doctrine →

- What it stated: ____________________
- When issued: 1823
- Factors that led up to its statement: ____________________

Refer to this page to answer the Chapter 10 Focus Question on page 166.

Section 3

The Age of Jackson

Key Events

1816	Congress passes Tariff of 1816.
1823	Monroe Doctrine is issued.
1828	Andrew Jackson elected President.
1837	Panic of 1837 brings economic collapse.

Reading Strategy

The result of the 1824 election was that the House of Representatives voted to make Adams President. What did Jackson's supporters believe was the cause of this event?

____

____

✓ Checkpoint

List two reasons Jackson was deeply loved by millions of Americans.

____

____

Section 3 Focus Question

How did the people gain more power during the Age of Jackson? To begin answering this question,

- Find out about the conflict between Adams and Jackson.
- Learn about a new era in politics.
- Discover how Jackson became President.

Section 3 Summary

The period from the mid-1820s to the end of the 1830s is called the Age of Jackson, after President Andrew Jackson. Under Jackson, everyday Americans were allowed to play a greater role in government.

Adams and Jackson in Conflict

Andrew Jackson began his life with very little. However, his toughness and determination helped him become wealthy. Jackson stood for the idea that ordinary people should take part in American political life. As a general and later as President, Andrew Jackson was deeply loved by millions of ordinary Americans. Many people respected his humble beginnings and firm leadership.

In the presidential election of 1824, Jackson won the most popular and electoral votes. But he did not have a majority. According to the Constitution, the House of Representatives would have to decide the winner. Speaker of the House and candidate Henry Clay told his supporters to vote for John Quincy Adams. When Adams won and made Clay his secretary of state, Jackson was outraged. His supporters said Clay and Adams had made a "corrupt bargain." These rumors burdened Adams as President. He had ambitious plans for the nation. But he lacked the political skill to push his programs through Congress. Adams never won Americans' trust. As a result, he served only one term. ✓

A New Era in Politics

Jackson's defeat was the beginning of a new era in politics. By 1824, **suffrage**—the right to vote—had been granted to almost all adult white males, not just those who owned property. But suffrage was still restricted. Women and enslaved African Americans could not vote. States also were changing how they chose presidential electors. Previously, state legislatures chose them. Now, that right went to voters. In 1824, voters in 18 out of 24 states chose their electors.

Greater voting rights were part of a growing belief in democratic ideas. Jackson and his supporters believed that ordinary people should vote and hold public office. Jackson did not trust the government and banks, which he felt favored the rich.

During the 1824 election, the Republican Party split. Jackson's supporters called themselves Democrats. Supporters of Adams called themselves National Republicans. In 1836, the new Whig Party replaced the Republicans. The two parties began to hold **nominating conventions,** or large meetings of party delegates who choose party candidates. Previously, a party's members of Congress held a **caucus**—a meeting of members of a political party. ✓

Jackson Becomes President

Three times as many people voted in 1828 as had voted in 1824. Most of these new voters supported Jackson, who easily defeated Adams. The election revealed growing sectional and class divisions among American voters. Jackson did best in the West and South. He also had strong support from farmers, small business people, and workers nationwide. Adams was most popular in New England.

Many people celebrated Jackson's victory as a win for the "common man." Some supporters called Jackson the "People's President." Once in office, Jackson quickly replaced some government officials with his own supporters. Although this was not a new practice, he claimed that bringing in new people furthered democracy. This practice of rewarding supporters with government jobs became known as the **spoils system.** ✓

Check Your Progress

1. What was different about the voting rights enjoyed by citizens in 1824 compared to earlier elections?

____

____

____

2. How did political parties change the way they chose candidates?

____

____

✓ Checkpoint

Name two political parties that formed during the Age of Jackson.

____

____

Vocabulary Builder

There is an old military saying, "to the victors belong the spoils." *Spoil* is another word for loot or prize. Why do you think the name *spoils system* was given to Jackson's practice of putting his supporters in office?

____

____

✓ Checkpoint

How many more people voted in the 1828 election than in the 1824 election?

____

Section 3 Notetaking Study Guide

Question to Think About As you read Section 3 in your textbook and take notes, keep this question in mind: **How did people gain more power during the Age of Jackson?**

► Use these charts to record key information from the section. Some information has been filled in to get you started.

Important Events During the Age of Jackson	
Year	**Event**
1824	**Presidential Election** • Who ran: ______ • Who won the electoral vote: Jackson • Problem with results: ______ • How election was decided: by a vote in the House of Representatives • Who was ultimately elected: ______
1824–1828	**John Quincy Adams's Presidency** • Burdened by charges of a ______ • Had ______ plans but accomplished little • Lacked the political skills to push his programs through ______
1828	**Presidential Election** • Who ran: ______ • Who won: ______ • Revealed growing ______ and class divisions
1832	**Presidential Election** • Who ran: ______ • Who won: ______

Key Political Changes During the Age of Jackson		
What Changed	**How It Changed**	**What It Replaced**
Suffrage	Almost all adult white males were allowed to vote and hold office.	Most states had required men to own property before they could vote.
Choosing the electoral college		
Choosing political candidates		
Ideas about who should participate in political life		Only those with money and power should vote and run for office.

Refer to this page to answer the Chapter 10 Focus Question on page 166.

Section 4

Indian Removal

Section 4 Focus Question

Why did Jackson use force to remove Indians from the Southeast? To begin answering this question,

- Learn about the Native Americans of the Southeast.
- Explore the conflict over land.
- Follow the Trail of Tears.

Section 4 Summary

As the population of white settlers in the Southeast grew, conflicts arose with Native Americans in the region. President Andrew Jackson decided to forcibly remove thousands of Native Americans and relocate them to the West.

Native Americans of the Southeast

In 1828, more than 100,000 Native Americans lived east of the Mississippi River. These groups included the Cherokee, Chickasaw, Choctaw, and Creek. They lived in parts of Alabama, Mississippi, Georgia, North Carolina, and Tennessee. The Seminoles, who lived in Florida, had an unusual origin. They were a combination of Creeks who had moved into Florida in the late 1700s, Florida Native Americans, and escaped African American slaves. Many of the southeastern Native Americans were farmers or lived in towns.

The Cherokees in particular adopted many white customs. Many became Christians. They also had businesses, schools, and even a newspaper. A leader named **Sequoyah** (sih KWOY uh) created the Cherokee alphabet. In 1827, the Cherokee set up a government with their own constitution and claimed status as a separate nation. ✓

Conflict Over Land

To many government leaders and white farmers, Native Americans blocked westward expansion. Native Americans lived on fertile land. White farmers wanted this land for growing cotton. Many Americans, including Thomas Jefferson, thought that the only way to prevent conflict and protect Native American culture was to send Native Americans west. After the War of 1812, the federal government signed treaties with several Native American groups in the Old Northwest. Groups agreed to give up their land and move west of the

Key Events

1816	Congress passes Tariff of 1816.
1823	Monroe Doctrine is issued.
1828	Andrew Jackson elected President.
1837	Panic of 1837 brings economic collapse.

✓ Checkpoint

List two white customs adopted by the Cherokees.

____

____

Vocabulary Builder

The "Old Northwest" is the name for land around the Great Lakes that was once the northwestern part of the United States. Why do you think we do not call the Southeast the "Old Southeast"?

____

____

Mississippi River. The pressure to move increased on the Native Americans who remained in the Southeast.

In 1828, Georgia tried to force the Cherokees to leave the state, but they refused to give up their lands. Instead, they sued the state of Georgia. The case *Cherokee Nation* v. *Georgia* reached the Supreme Court in 1831. The decision in this suit went against the Cherokees. But in *Worcester* v. *Georgia* (1832), the Court declared that Georgia's laws "can have no force" within Cherokee land. In his ruling, John Marshall pointed to treaties that the United States had signed with the Cherokees. These treaties guaranteed certain territory to Native Americans. Georgia could not take away Cherokee territory. President Andrew Jackson refused to support the Court's decision. Instead, he enforced the Indian Removal Act of 1830. This law gave him the power to offer Native Americans land west of the Mississippi in exchange for land in the East. ✓

✓ Checkpoint

Name the law that allowed President Jackson to move Native American groups to the West.

____

____

On the Trail of Tears

Believing they had no choice, most Native American leaders signed treaties agreeing to move to Indian Territory. Today, most of that area is in Oklahoma. The Choctaws moved between 1831 and 1833. The federal government did not give the Choctaws enough food and supplies for the long trip. As a result, many people died in the cold winter weather. President Martin Van Buren forced the Cherokees to move in the winter of 1838–1839. Once again, there were not enough supplies. Some 4,000 of the 15,000 Cherokees who began the journey died along the way. The route of this tragic trip is known as the Trail of Tears.

The Seminoles chose to fight rather than move. During the 1840s, most Seminoles were removed to Indian Territory. In their new homes, Native Americans struggled to rebuild their lives under very difficult conditions. ✓

Reading Strategy

Draw a time line on a blank page at the back of this book. On your time line, record the steps taken by the state of Georgia to remove the Cherokees from their land. Include dates for each action.

✓ Checkpoint

What was the Trail of Tears?

____

____

____

Check Your Progress

1. What did the Supreme Court rule in *Worcester* v. *Georgia*?

____

____

____

2. What happened to most of the Native American groups in the Southeast?

____

____

Section 4 Notetaking Study Guide

Question to Think About As you read Section 4 in your textbook and take notes, keep this section focus question in mind: **Why did Jackson use force to remove Indians from the Southeast?**

▶ Use these charts to record key information from the section. Some information has been filled in to get you started.

Time Line of Indian Removal

Date	Events
After 1812	Indian groups in the Old Northwest give up their land and move to Indian Territory.
1825, 1827	Georgia passes law that forces the Creeks to give up their land.
1827	The Cherokees form an independent government with a ______________________.
1828	The Cherokees refuse Georgia's order to leave, suing the state instead.
1832	The Supreme Court rules in *Worcester* v. *Georgia* that ______________________.
1831–1833	The U.S. government forces the Choctaws to leave the Southeast and settle in Indian Territory.
1838–1839	The U.S. government forces the Cherokees to leave the Southeast for Indian Territory. Thousands die on the journey known as ______________________.
1840s	Many of the __________ are forced to leave after fighting U.S. forces to resist removal to Indian Territory.

Cause and Effect: Indian Removal

Cause: Conflict Over Land

- Why government wanted Native American land: ______________________
- Why white settlers wanted Native American land: ______________________
- Native American groups living in the Southeast:
  1. Choctaw
  2.
  3.
  4.
  5.

→

Effect: Indian Removal

- Policies to move Native Americans from their land dated from the time of Thomas Jefferson.
- What the Indian Removal Act of 1830 did: ______________________
- Believing they had no choice, most Native Americans signed treaties agreeing to give up their land and move to Indian Territory.
- What happened on the Trail of Tears: ______________________

Refer to this page to answer the Chapter 10 Focus Question on page 166.

Section 5

States' Rights and the Economy

Key Events

1816	Congress passes Tariff of 1816.
1823	Monroe Doctrine is issued.
1828	Andrew Jackson elected President.
1837	Panic of 1837 brings economic collapse.

Section 5 Focus Question

How did old issues take a new shape in the conflict over a national bank and tariffs? To begin answering this question,

- Note the disagreement over the second Bank.
- Explore the viewpoints towards states' rights.
- Examine the nullification crisis.
- Find out about the end of the Jackson Era.

Section 5 Summary

Jackson faced two major political conflicts during his presidency. One involved the second Bank of the United States. The other dealt with the thorny issue of states' rights.

The Bank War

The second Bank of the United States earned the support of business people. The Bank was a safe place for the federal government to keep its money. It also loaned money to many businesses. The money it issued formed a stable currency. But Andrew Jackson and many other Americans believed that the Bank favored the rich and hurt everyday people. In the South and West, the Bank was blamed for the economic crisis of 1819, which cost many people their farms.

In 1832, Nicholas Biddle, the Bank's president, got Congress to renew the Bank's charter. Jackson vetoed the bill. Most voters stood behind Jackson, who won the 1832 election by a large margin. As a result, the Bank ceased to exist when its charter ran out in 1836. ✓

✓ Checkpoint

Name the two men who opposed each other over the Bank charter.

____

____

The Question of States' Rights

The Constitution gives the federal government many significant powers. At the same time, the Tenth Amendment says that powers not specifically given to the federal government are reserved to the States or to the people. Over the years, the issue of balancing federal and state power came up repeatedly. During Jackson's presidency, arguments over this issue caused a serious crisis. ✓

✓ Checkpoint

Name the Constitutional amendment that reserves certain powers to the states and people.

____

The Nullification Crisis

In 1828, Congress passed a new tariff on manufactured goods. This helped northern businesses but hurt southerners, who to pay more for goods. To many, the tariff issue was part of a larger problem. If the federal government could enforce laws southerners considered unjust, could it also use its power to ban slavery? John C. Calhoun argued that the states had the right of **nullification**—an action by a state that cancels a federal law to which the state objects.

Arguments For Nullification	Arguments Against Nullification
• The Union was formed by an agreement between the states. • States kept the right to nullify federal laws that the people of the state considered unfair.	• The Union had been formed by the American people, not the states. • The supreme power in the land lay with the American people, not the states.

When Congress passed another high tariff in 1832, South Carolina voted to nullify, or cancel, the tariffs. State leaders also threatened to secede, or leave the Union. Jackson asked Congress to allow the federal government to collect its tariff by force if necessary. But he also supported a compromise bill that lowered the tariffs. In 1832, Congress passed both laws. South Carolina accepted this agreement, ending the crisis peacefully. ✓

The End of the Jackson Era

Martin Van Buren, Jackson's Vice President, won the presidency in 1836. Soon after he took office, cotton prices fell. Cotton growers could not repay their bank loans, which caused hundreds of banks to fail. This led to the Panic of 1837. Van Buren's presidency was ruined. In 1840, the Whig candidate, **William Henry Harrison,** easily beat Van Buren. The Age of Jackson had ended. ✓

Check Your Progress

1. What did supporters and opponents of the second Bank believe?

____

____

____

2. What caused the nullification crisis?

____

____

____

Vocabulary Builder

To *nullify* means "to make of no value." To nullify a law means to take away its power. How was nullification supposed to protect states' rights?

____

____

____

✓ Checkpoint

Name the act of Congress that South Carolina was trying to nullify.

____

____

✓ Checkpoint

Name the crisis that ruined Van Buren's presidency.

____

____

Section 5 Notetaking Study Guide

Question to Think About As you read Section 5 in your textbook and take notes, keep this section focus question in mind: **How did old issues take a new shape in the conflict over a national bank and tariffs?**

▶ Use these charts to record key information from the section.

The Bank War
The second Bank of the United States held the __________ government's money and lent money to __________ banks. It also issued paper money, which helped create a __________ currency.
Many people blamed the Bank for the __________.
In 1832, Jackson __________ the bill to renew the Bank's charter. He won the 1832 election while __________ the Bank, which closed when its charter ran out in __________.

States' Rights and the Nullification Crisis
Americans had always debated about the balance between the powers of the __________ and state governments. The Constitution gave the federal government __________. The Tenth Amendment __________ federal power by stating that __________.
Congress passed a law in 1828 raising tariffs. It helped northern manufacturers, but __________ felt the law was unfair.
__________ argued that states had the right of nullification, which means they could __________. This theory was based on the idea that Union was formed from a voluntary agreement between __________.
The clearest argument against nullification came from Daniel Webster. He argued that the Union was formed by __________, not the states.
After Congress passed another tariff in 1832, __________ voted to nullify the tariffs. It threatened to secede if the federal government interfered. Federal threats to __________ as well as a lowering of the __________ led __________ to vote to __________.

The End of the Jackson Era
Jackson's choice to succeed him was __________, who won the presidential election of 1836. However, soon afterward, an economic collapse, called the __________, occurred. As a result of the hard times that followed, Van Buren did not __________.

Refer to this page to answer the Chapter 10 Focus Question on page 166.

Chapter 10 Assessment

Directions: Circle the letter of the correct answer.

1. Whose presidency became known as "The Era of Good Feelings"?

A James Monroe
B John Quincy Adams
C Andrew Jackson

2. What political change took place during the Age of Jackson?

A States began to require voters to own property.
B State legislatures began choosing electors.
C States allowed almost all adult white males to vote.

3. What is the name given to the journey to Indian Territory made by the Cherokees in the winter of 1838–39?

A The Great Migration
B The Trail of Tears
C The Long Walk

Directions: Follow the steps to answer this question:

What was the basis of the disagreement over nullification?

Step 1: Recall information: Briefly describe what those who supported nullification believed. Then briefly describe what those who opposed it believed.

Beliefs of Supporters of Nullification	Beliefs of Opponents of Nullification

Step 2: Compare: What justification did each side give for its position?

Arguments For Nullification	Arguments Against Nullification

Step 3: Draw conclusions: Complete the topic sentence that follows. Then write two or three more sentences that support your topic sentence.

Supporters and opponents of nullification disagreed about ____________________

____

____

____

____

Chapter 10 Notetaking Study Guide

Now you are ready to answer the Chapter 10 Focus Question: **How did the nation reflect a growing sense of national pride and identity?**

► Fill in the following chart to help you answer this question. Use the notes that you took for each section.

Building a National Identity
U.S.–Foreign Relations
• The Monroe Doctrine stated that ______________________ ____.   • How relations with Canada changed after the War of 1812: ______________
Federal Government Versus States' Rights
Key Supreme Court cases that strengthened the power of the federal government: 1. ______________________   2. ______________________   3. ______________________   • South Carolina said that states had the right to ______________________.
Indian Removal
• Why there was a conflict over land between white settlers and Native Americans: ______________________ ______________________   • Native Americans were forced ______________________.   • The Cherokees called their journey ______________________.
Democratic Reforms in the Age of Jackson
• States dropped property requirements for voting.   • Presidential electors were chosen by __________, not by ______________.   • Candidates for office were chosen by ______________ instead of caucuses.
A National Economy

• The second Bank of the United States
   • made loans to businesses.
   • was a safe place for the ______________ to keep its money.
   • issued ____________ that formed a stable ____________.
 • However, many Americans opposed the bank because ______________ ______________________.

Refer to this page to answer the Unit 3 Focus Question on page 167.

Unit 3 Pulling It Together Activity

What You Have Learned

Chapter 8 As the nation's first President, George Washington established the U.S. government's authority in domestic as well as foreign affairs. Political divisions and strife with France rocked John Adams's presidency.

Chapter 9 The Louisiana Purchase of 1803 doubled the size of the United States. At the same time, the United States struggled to remain neutral in its foreign policy. British support of Native Americans led to the War of 1812.

Chapter 10 During the early 1800s, the federal government increased its authority. At the same time, the Monroe Doctrine expanded U.S. influence in Latin America.

Think Like a Historian

Read the Unit 3 Focus Question: **What problems might a new nation face?**

▶ Use the organizers on this page and the next to collect information to answer this question.

What types of national problems did the new nation face? Some of them are listed in this organizer. Review your section and chapter notes. Then complete the organizer.

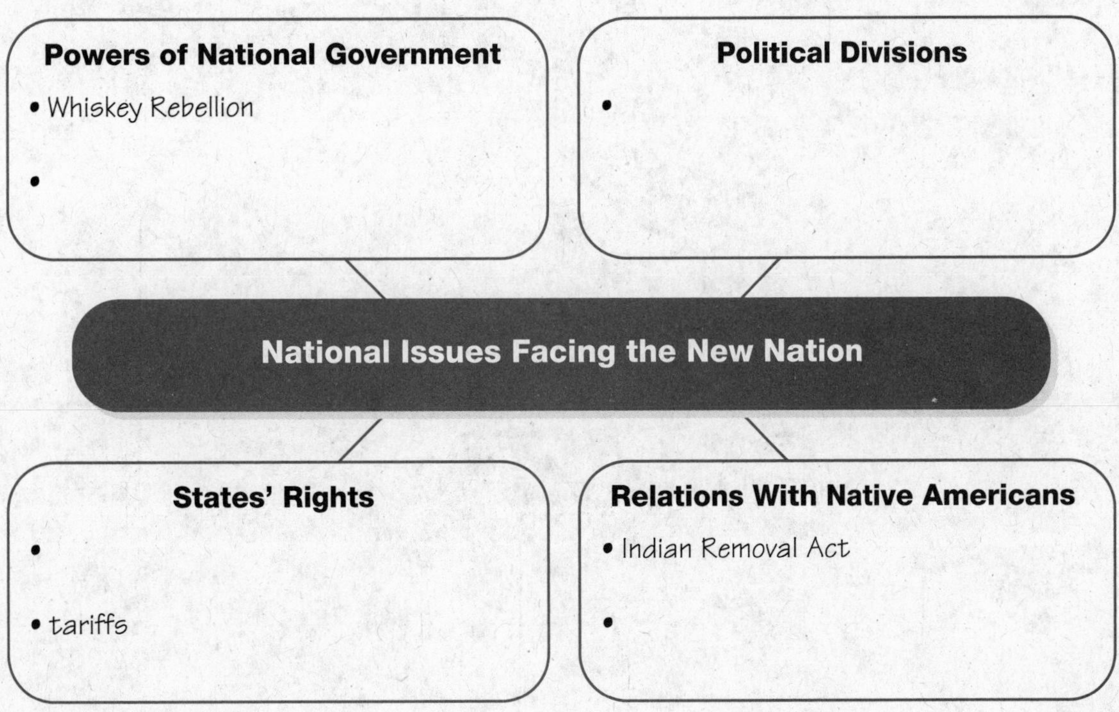

What types of international problems did the new nation face? The organizer below gives you a part of the answer. Review your section and chapter notes. Then fill in the rest of the organizer.

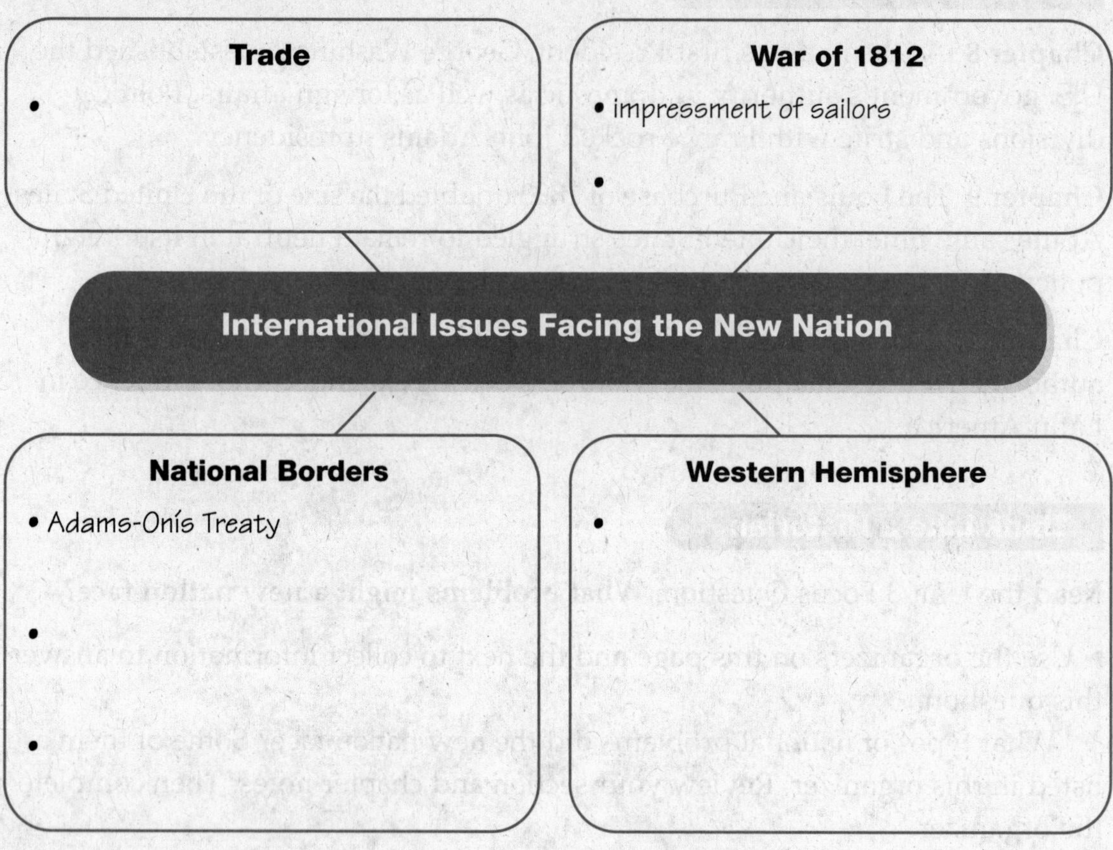

Unit 4

The Nation Expands and Changes

What You Will Learn

Chapter 11 The North industrialized and urbanized rapidly in the early to mid-1800s. The South became highly dependent on cotton and the slave labor needed to cultivate it. Tensions between North and South spread to the western territories.

Chapter 12 By the mid-1800s, Americans were seeking reform in education and abolition. Some sought equality for women. Artists and writers also began to develop a distinct style.

Chapter 13 In the mid-1800s, many Americans wanted the nation to expand westward to the Pacific Ocean. American settlers overcame hardships in making this happen.

Focus Your Learning As you study this unit and take notes, you will find the information to answer the questions below. Answering the Chapter Focus Questions will help build your answer to the Unit Focus Question.

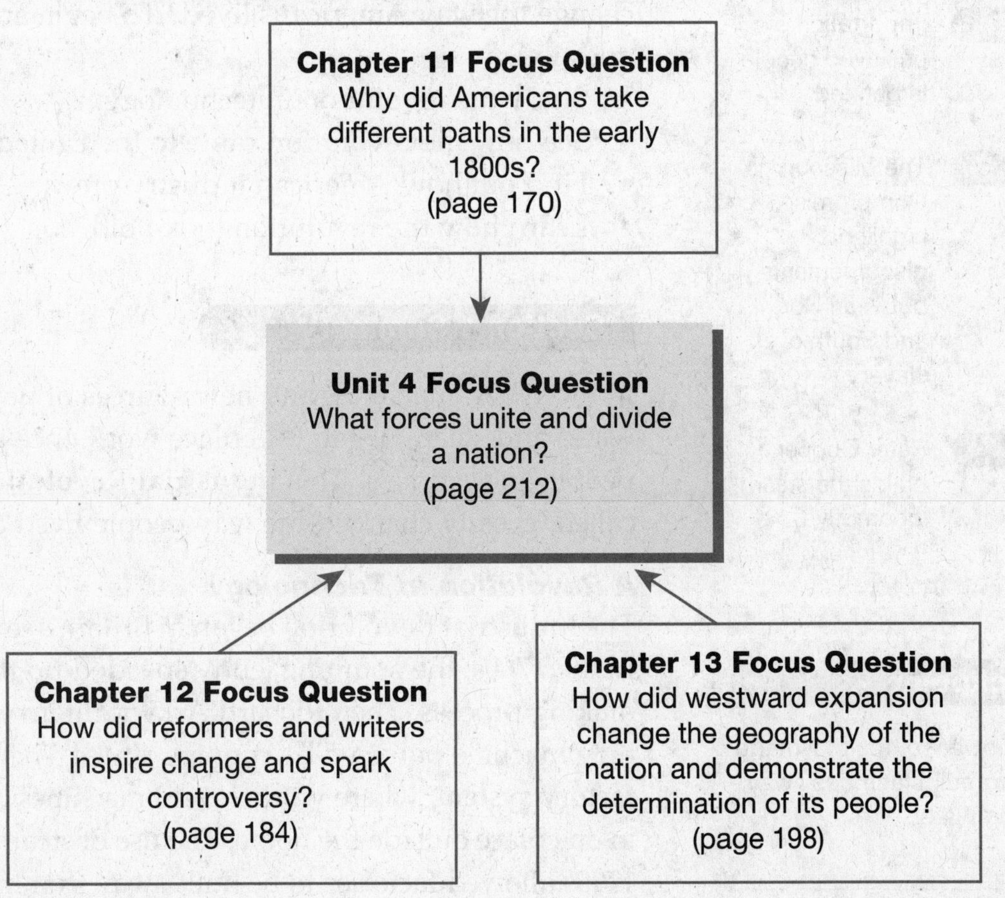

Chapter 11 Focus Question
Why did Americans take different paths in the early 1800s?
(page 170)
Unit 4 Focus Question
What forces unite and divide a nation?
(page 212)
Chapter 12 Focus Question
How did reformers and writers inspire change and spark controversy?
(page 184)
Chapter 13 Focus Question
How did westward expansion change the geography of the nation and demonstrate the determination of its people?
(page 198)

Chapter 11

North and South Take Different Paths

(1800–1845)

What You Will Learn

The North industrialized and urbanized rapidly in the early to mid-1800s. The South became highly dependent on cotton and the slave labor needed to cultivate it. Tensions between North and South spread to the western territories.

Chapter 11 Focus Question

As you read through this chapter, keep this question in mind: **Why did Americans take different paths in the early 1800s?**

Key Events
1794
Eli Whitney patents the cotton gin.
1808
Importation of enslaved people is banned.
1820
The Missouri Compromise highlights disagreements between North and South over slavery.
1830
Peter Cooper builds the steam locomotive.

Section 1

The Industrial Revolution

Section 1 Focus Question

How did the new technology of the Industrial Revolution change the way Americans lived? To begin answering this question,

- Study the revolution in technology.
- See how the revolution came to the United States.
- Find out how American industry grew.
- Learn how the revolution took hold.

Section 1 Summary

In the 1700s, machines and new sources of power such as water and steam began to replace work once performed by people and animals. This **Industrial Revolution,** as it was called, greatly changed the way people lived and worked.

A Revolution in Technology

The Industrial Revolution began in Britain's textile industry. In the 1760s, the spinning jenny speeded up the thread-making process. Then Richard Arkwright invented a spinning machine powered by running water. This led to the **factory system,** where workers and machines come together in one place outside the home. The use of steam power in the 1790s allowed factories to be built away from rivers. ✓

✓ Checkpoint

Name the power source that made it possible to build factories away from running water.

____

The American Industrial Revolution

Britain tried to guard its industrial secrets. In 1789, a young apprentice in a British factory, Samuel Slater, came to America. Working from his memory of the factories, Slater built new spinning machines for American merchant Moses Brown. Slater's mill became a great success. ☑

American Industry Grows

Industrialization started in the Northeast. During the War of 1812, Americans could not buy British products. They had to develop their own industries. **Francis Cabot Lowell** built a new kind of mill that combined spinning and weaving in a single factory. This led to the growth of a mill town called Lowell. The workforce was made up of young women known as "Lowell girls," who lived in boarding houses. ☑

The Revolution Takes Hold

Another key innovation in the growth of American industry was Eli Whitney's idea of interchangeable parts in the 1790s. **Interchangeable parts** are identical pieces that could be quickly put together by unskilled workers. Before, craftsmen had built machines by hand. No two parts were the same, making machinery slow to build and hard to repair. Whitney's idea led to **mass production**—the rapid manufacture of large numbers of identical objects. As a result, many goods became cheaper, and industry continued to grow.

Many factories, mills, and mines employed children as young as 7 or 8. These children had little chance for an education and worked in difficult conditions. Working conditions for adults were no better. Many spent 12- or 14- hour workdays in dimly lit factories with little fresh air. The machines were often dangerous, and injury was common. There were no payments for disabled workers. Conditions gradually improved, but the eight-hour workday was far in the future. ☑

Check Your Progress

1. How did the Industrial Revolution change working life?

____

____

2. How do interchangeable parts make mass production possible?

____

____

✓ Checkpoint

Name the person who brought new spinning technologies from Britain to the United States.

____

✓ Checkpoint

What were workers in the Lowell mills called?

____

Vocabulary Builder

How would replacing the word *exactly* with the word *mostly* change the meaning of the following sentence? "Interchangeable parts were exactly alike." Would this make interchangeable parts more or less useful?

____

____

✓ Checkpoint

Name a reason that factory work was unhealthy and dangerous.

____

____

Section 1 Notetaking Study Guide

Question to Think About As you read Section 1 in your textbook and take notes, keep this section focus question in mind: **How did the new technology of the Industrial Revolution change the way Americans lived?**

► Use these charts to record key information from the section. Some information has been filled in to get you started.

The Industrial Revolution
In the Industrial Revolution, ___machines___ took the place of many hand tools. Much of the power once provided by ______ and ______ began to be replaced, first by ______ and then by ______.
For centuries, workers had ___spun thread___ in their ______ on spinning wheels. In the 1760s, the ______ speeded up the thread-making process.
This system of working was replaced by the ______, which brought workers and ______ together in one place.
In 1764, ______ invented the ______, a spinning machine powered by ______ rather than human energy. Textile mills began to be built on ______.
In 1790, ______ built the first steam-powered ______. Factories no longer had to be built on ______.
______ built the first water-frame-style spinning machine in the United States.
In the 1790s, inventor ___Eli Whitney___ devised a system of ______ ______, identical pieces that could be assembled quickly by ______.
During the ___War of 1812___, the British navy blockaded U.S. ports. This caused ______ to grow significantly.
Francis Cabot Lowell and his partners built a mill that was organized a new way. It combined ______ and ______ in one building. Later, the town of Lowell, Massachusetts, was built. Factories there employed ______ from nearby farms.

Typical Factory Working Conditions
Length of workday: ___12–14 hours___ Factory conditions: ______ Safety conditions: ______ Treatment of disabled workers: ______

Refer to this page to answer the Chapter 11 Focus Question on page 183.

Section 2
The North Transformed

Section 2 Focus Question

How did urbanization, technology, and social change affect the North? To begin answering this question,

- Learn about northern cities.
- Explore the growth of northern industry.
- Find out about the transportation revolution.
- Learn about a new wave of immigrants.
- Examine the lives of African Americans in the North.

Section 2 Summary

New inventions and breakthroughs in transportation helped industry expand in the United States. Much of this industry was located in the North, where it encouraged the growth of cities.

Northern Cities

In the 1800s, the Industrial Revolution led to **urbanization**, or the growth of cities due to movement of people from rural areas to cities. Agricultural workers were attracted to the new types of work available in the cities. Cities in the East became crowded. So newly arrived immigrants headed west. Growing cities faced many problems. Poor sewers, a lack of clean drinking water, and filthy city streets encouraged the spread of disease. Citywide fires were another major concern since most city buildings were made of wood. ✓

The Growth of Northern Industry

American inventors helped industry grow. In 1844, **Samuel F.B. Morse** tested the telegraph. The **telegraph** was an invention that used electrical signals to send messages very quickly over long distances. The telegraph revolutionized communication. In the Midwest, Cyrus McCormick built a mechanical reaper that cut wheat much faster than could be done by hand. Such machines allowed more wheat to be grown and harvested using fewer workers. Other inventions revolutionized the way goods were made. The sewing machine was first introduced by Elias Howe in 1846 and improved by Isaac Singer. Sewing machines made clothes faster and cheaper than ever before. By 1860, ninety percent of business investment was concentrated in the North. ✓

Key Events

1794 Eli Whitney patents the cotton gin.

1808 Importation of enslaved people is banned.

1820 The Missouri Compromise highlights disagreements between North and South over slavery.

1830 Peter Cooper builds the steam locomotive.

✓ Checkpoint

List three factors that led to the spread of disease in cities.

____

____

____

✓ Checkpoint

Name two key American inventors and their inventions.

Inventor: ________________

Invention: ________________

Inventor: ________________

Invention: ________________

A Transportation Revolution

Improvements in transportation also spurred the growth of industry. Better transport allowed factories to make use of raw materials from farther away. Manufactured goods could be delivered to distant markets. American Robert Fulton built the first practical steamboat, the *Clermont*, in 1807. In 1850, a new type of American-built ship appeared, the clipper ship. Clipper ships were the fastest vessels on the ocean. They were eventually replaced by steamships.

Of all the forms of transportation, railroads did the most to tie together raw materials, manufacturers, and markets. In 1830, Peter Cooper built the first American-made steam locomotive. By 1840, the United States had 3,000 miles of railroad track. ✓

✓ Checkpoint

List three major breakthroughs in transportation.

____

____

____

A New Wave of Immigrants

In the 1840s, millions of immigrants came to the United States, mainly from western Europe. In 1845, disease wiped out the potato crop in Ireland. Ireland suffered from a **famine,** or widespread starvation. Huge numbers of Irish came to America. Many took jobs laying railroad track, or as household workers. Germans also came to the United States. Many were fleeing failed revolutions in Germany. Unlike the Irish, German immigrants came from many levels of society. Most moved to the Midwest.

Some Americans worried about the growing foreign population. These were **nativists,** or people who wanted to preserve the country for white, American-born Protestants. ✓

Reading Strategy

Reread the bracketed lines. Underline the cause and circle one effect of the Irish migration described in this paragraph.

Mark the Text

✓ Checkpoint

Name the countries from which most immigrants to the United States came in the 1840s.

____

____

African Americans in the North

African Americans in the North also faced discrimination. **Discrimination** is the denial of equal rights or equal treatment to certain groups of people. Though free, African Americans were often not allowed to vote or to work in factories and skilled trades. Public schools and churches were often segregated. So African Americans formed their own churches and publications. ✓

✓ Checkpoint

Define discrimination.

____

____

Check Your Progress

1. Name the invention that revolutionized communication.

____

2. How did better transportation help industry?

____

____

____

Section 2 Notetaking Study Guide

Question to Think About As you read Section 2 in your textbook and take notes, keep this section focus question in mind: **How did urbanization, technology, and social change affect the North?**

▶ Use these charts to record key information from the section. Some information has been filled in to get you started.

Key Inventions			
Invention	**Inventor(s)**	**When**	**What It Did**
Sewing machine	Elias Howe and Isaac Singer	1846	Made sewing clothes faster and cheaper
	Cyrus McCormick		Harvested more wheat with fewer workers
		1807	Made river travel faster and cheaper
	Peter Cooper		
Telegraph		1844	
Clipper ship	No single inventor		

Changes in Population			
	What Happened?	**Why Did It Happen?**	**Results**
Cities	Cities began growing rapidly, especially in the Northeast.	Factories moved to cities, followed by people moving from rural areas for factory jobs.	Cities faced the spread of disease and the threat of fire.
Immigration	Millions of immigrants from __________, particularly Ireland and Germany, came to the U.S. in the 1840s.	The Irish came to escape __________.	Nativists: __________
		The Germans came to escape __________.	Know-Nothings: __________
African Americans in the North	African Americans formed their own schools, churches, and publications.	__________	African Americans continued to face __________. They were often denied the right to __________. They were not allowed to work in factories or in __________.

Refer to this page to answer the Chapter 11 Focus Question on page 183.

Section 3

The Plantation South

Section 3 Focus Question

How did cotton affect the social and economic life of the South? To begin answering this question,

- Find out about the "Cotton Kingdom."
- Examine the life of African Americans in the South.

Section 3 Summary

Cotton production expanded in the South to supply the textile industry. Whether free or enslaved, African Americans in the South faced many hardships.

The Cotton Kingdom

As the textile industry in the North grew, the demand for cotton rose. Eli Whitney's invention of the **cotton gin** in 1793 allowed the South to meet this demand. The cotton gin used a spiked wooden cylinder to remove seeds from cotton fibers.

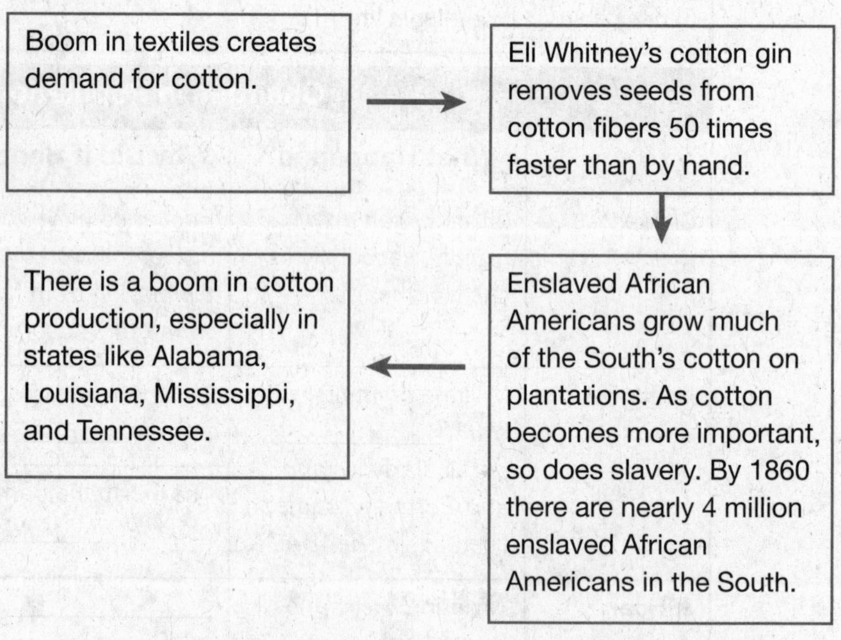

Boom in textiles creates demand for cotton.
Eli Whitney's cotton gin removes seeds from cotton fibers 50 times faster than by hand.
Enslaved African Americans grow much of the South's cotton on plantations. As cotton becomes more important, so does slavery. By 1860 there are nearly 4 million enslaved African Americans in the South.
There is a boom in cotton production, especially in states like Alabama, Louisiana, Mississippi, and Tennessee.

Cotton became the greatest source of wealth for the United States. The southern "Cotton Kingdom" society was dominated by slaveholding owners of large plantations. Supporters of slavery said that the system was more humane than the free labor system of the North. But critics pointed out that people held in slavery often suffered physical or other abuse from white owners. By the 1830s, some northerners were urging that slavery be banned. ✓

Key Events

1794 Eli Whitney patents the cotton gin.

1808 Importation of enslaved people is banned.

1820 The Missouri Compromise highlights disagreements between North and South over slavery.

1830 Peter Cooper builds the steam locomotive.

Vocabulary Builder

Gin is early English slang for "engine" or machine. What do you think the term *cotton gin* refers to?

____

✓ Checkpoint

Why did the invention of the cotton gin lead to a boom in cotton production?

____

____

____

African Americans in the South

About six percent of African Americans in the South were free. Many had purchased their freedom. But laws denied them even basic rights. By law they were excluded from most jobs. They could not vote, serve on juries, testify against whites in court, or attend public schools. Free African Americans were even discouraged from traveling. They also risked being kidnapped and sold into slavery.

However, enslaved African Americans faced even greater trials. They had no rights at all. Laws called **slave codes** controlled every aspect of their lives. A Kentucky court ruled in 1828 that "...a slave by our code is not treated as a person but as a ...thing...." Most enslaved African Americans did heavy farm labor. But many became skilled workers. Some worked in households. Wherever they worked, they faced the possibility of violent punishment.

Families of enslaved African Americans were often broken apart when slave owners sold one or more of their family members. After 1808, it was illegal to import enslaved Africans to the United States. Yet African Americans kept many African customs alive, including styles of music and dance. Many looked to the Bible for hope. They composed **spirituals**—religious folk songs that blended biblical themes with the realities of slavery.

African Americans found ways to resist slavery. Some worked slowly, broke equipment, and even fled to seek freedom in the North. Some led rebellions. **Nat Turner** led the most famous slave uprising in 1831. He and his companions killed some 60 whites. In reprisal, many innocent African Americans were executed. ✓

✓ Checkpoint

List three ways African Americans resisted slavery.

____
____
____

Check Your Progress

1. How were cotton and slavery connected?

____
____
____

2. In what ways did free African Americans in the South have their rights taken away?

____
____
____

Section 3 Notetaking Study Guide

Question to Think About As you read Section 3 in your textbook and take notes, keep this section focus question in mind: **How did cotton affect the social and economic life of the South?**

► Use these charts to record key information from the section. Some information has been filled in to get you started.

The Southern Economy	
Cotton gin	**What it was:** a machine invented by Eli Whitney in 1793 that speeded the processing of cotton **Impact on Economy:** • made cotton growing more ______ • increased the use and value of ______ • led to huge growth in ______ • made cotton the greatest ______ in the United States
Slave labor	**Argument for slave labor:**
	Arguments against slave labor: • •

African American Life in the South	
What	**Effect on African American Life**
Restrictions placed on free African Americans' rights	Could hold only menial jobs They were not allowed to: ______, ______, ______, ______ They were discouraged from ______.
Hardships faced on plantations	Enslaved African Americans • received ______ • had to perform ______ • families were often ______
Types of work enslaved African Americans performed	• • •
African American culture	Preserved African culture, ______, and ______ Composed ______
Ways of resisting slavery	• working slowly • • •

Refer to this page to answer the Chapter 11 Focus Question on page 183.

Section 4
The Challenges of Growth

Section 4 Focus Question

How did Americans move west and how did this intensify the debate over slavery? To begin answering this question,

- Follow along as Americans move west.
- Learn about roads and turnpikes.
- Find out about canals.
- Examine the extension of slavery.

Section 4 Summary

As the U.S. population grew, more people moved west to find new land. A transportation system of new roads and canals kept the country connected. Increasing differences between North and South became apparent when Missouri asked to join the Union as a slave state.

Moving West

By the 1750s, many immigrants began settling the backcountry between the Atlantic Coast and the Appalachian Mountains. In 1775, pioneer **Daniel Boone** helped create the Wilderness Road. This was a new route to the West. By the early 1800s, the flow of immigrants to the West had become a flood. Many areas applied to become states. Between 1792 and 1819, eight states joined the Union: Kentucky (1792), Tennessee (1796), Ohio (1803), Louisiana (1812), Indiana (1816), Mississippi (1817), Illinois (1818), and Alabama (1819). ✓

Roads and Turnpikes

Traveling west was not easy. Roads were unpaved, rough, and easily washed out by rain. The nation needed better roads. Farmers and merchants had to move their goods to market quickly and cheaply. Private companies began building **turnpikes,** or toll roads. In marshy areas, builders constructed **corduroy roads** out of sawed-off logs laid side by side. These roads were bumpy and dangerous. The first road built with federal money was the National Road. Begun in 1811 in Cumberland, Maryland, the road eventually reached Vandalia, Illinois, by 1850. ✓

Canals

Road construction was still slow and costly. The fastest, cheapest way to ship goods was by water. The solution was

Key Events

- **1794** Eli Whitney patents the cotton gin.
- **1808** Importation of enslaved people is banned.
- **1820** The Missouri Compromise highlights disagreements between North and South over slavery.
- **1830** Peter Cooper builds the steam locomotive.

✓ Checkpoint

Name two states admitted to the Union in the 1790s.

____

____

✓ Checkpoint

Name the first road built with federal money.

____

Reading Strategy

Reread the bracketed lines. Circle the word that tells you that the meaning of the word *canal* is being stated.

✓ Checkpoint

Name the two places connected by the Erie Canal.

___

✓ Checkpoint

Name the two states admitted to the Union under the Missouri Compromise.

___

___

[to build **canals,** or channels that are dug across land and filled with water. Canals allow boats to reach more places. The governor of New York suggested that a canal be built to connect the Hudson River and Lake Erie. Produce from the Midwest came across Lake Erie and passed through the Erie Canal. It was then carried down the Hudson River to New York City. New York City soon became the richest city in the nation. The success of the Erie Canal sparked a surge of canal building. ✓

The Extension of Slavery

In 1819, the nation consisted of 11 "slave states" and 11 "free states." Since 1817, Missouri had been seeking admission as a slave state. Adding another slave state would upset the balance in the Senate, where each state had two votes. Adding two more senators from a slave state would make the South more powerful than the North. Representative James Tallmadge of New York proposed that Missouri be admitted as a slave state. However, no more slaves could be brought into the state. The bill failed in the Senate. Then Maine applied to join the Union as a free state. The admission of both a free state and a slave state would maintain the balance in the Senate. In 1820, Senator **Henry Clay** persuaded Congress to adopt the Missouri Compromise. Maine would be admitted as a free state. Missouri would be admitted as a slave state. In addition, the Louisiana Territory north of the southern border of Missouri would be free of slavery. It also gave southern slave owners a right to pursue escaped fugitives into "free" regions and return them to slavery.

The Missouri Compromise revealed how sectional rivalries divided the states. The South was not happy that Congress discussed slavery. The North was not happy that another slave state had been admitted into the Union. Bitter feelings about slavery threatened national unity. ✓

Check Your Progress

1. Why were canals and better roads needed?

___

___

2. What was the Missouri Compromise?

___

___

___

___

Section 4 Notetaking Study Guide

Question to Think About As you read Section 4 in your textbook and take notes, keep this section focus question in mind: **How did Americans move west and how did this intensify the debate over slavery?**

▶ Use these organizers to record key information from the section. Some information has been filled in to get you started.

Roads and Canals		
Term	**What it was**	**Why it was important**
turnpike	A type of privately built toll road	Provided a much-needed way to move people and goods over land
	A road made of sawed-off logs	
		Allowed boats to reach more places
Project	**What it was and when it started**	**Why it was important**
	Road running from Cumberland, Maryland, to Vandalia, Illinois; 1811	
Erie Canal		• started a canal building boom • allowed goods to be shipped more ______ and cheaply between ______ and Midwest • helped make ______ the richest city in the nation

The Missouri Compromise

In 1820, Senator Henry Clay persuaded Congress to approve the Missouri Compromise. Its provisions:

1. ______ was admitted as a free state.
2. ______ was admitted as a slave state.
3. ______ north of Missouri's southern border was free of slavery.
4. Southern slave owners gained the right to pursue ______ into free regions.

Refer to this page to answer the Chapter 11 Focus Question on page 183.

Chapter 11 Assessment

Directions: Circle the letter of the correct answer.

1. Where did the Industrial Revolution begin?
   A the United States B Germany C Great Britain

2. What country experienced a famine that caused large numbers of people to emigrate to the United States in the 1840s?
   A France B Ireland C Spain

3. Which of the following did Eli Whitney invent?
   A the cotton gin B the telegraph C the clipper ship

4. The Missouri Compromise was a resolution to what issue?
   A the right of way for western railroads
   B the borders of the new Indian Territory
   C the expansion of slavery to western states

Directions: Follow the steps to complete this task: **Compare the economy of the North with the economy of the South.**

Step 1: Recall information: List one characteristic of the northern economy and one characteristic of the southern economy.

Section	Economy
North	industrial growth
South	

Step 2: Compare and contrast: Record how these characteristics are alike and how they are different.

	How They Are Alike	How They Are Different
Economies	cotton important to both regions	

Step 3: Complete the topic sentence that follows. Then write two or three more sentences that support your topic sentence.

The economies of the North and South ____________________

____

____

____

____

Chapter 11 Notetaking Study Guide

Now you are ready to answer the Chapter 11 Focus Question: **Why did Americans take different paths in the early 1800s?**

▶ Fill in the following charts to help you answer this question. Use the notes that you took for each section.

The North and South Take Different Paths	
The North	**The South**
Economy • Depended on industry • Some important inventions of the Industrial Revolution: 1. spinning jenny 2. 3. • The factory system is the ______________ ______________. • Labor conditions were poor. • ___Child___ labor was often used.	**Economy** • Depended on slavery • Eli Whitney's invention of the ______________ increased the South's dependency on slavery. • Cotton plantations were important because cotton became America's greatest ______________.
Society • Urbanization: the growth of cities due to movement from rural to urban areas. • Urban problems included __________ and poor ______________. • New advances in transportation included ____________, ____________, and ____________. These allowed goods to be shipped to distant markets. • Immigration provided ____________ for industry and caused a rapid growth in ____________.	**Society** • Society was dominated by ___slave-owning large landowners___. • Slave codes gave slaves no __________ and allowed every aspect of their lives to be ____________. • Free African Americans were not allowed to ____________ in elections or serve on ____________. Their children could not attend ______________, and they were discouraged from ______________.

Growing Sectional Differences
• In 1820, Senator Henry Clay proposed ___the Missouri Compromise___. • What this proposal involved: ______________________________ • How this revealed sectional tensions: 1. Southerners were not happy because ______________________________. 2. Northerners were not happy because ______________________________.

Refer to this page to answer the Unit 4 Focus Question on page 212.

Chapter 12

An Age of Reform (1820–1860)

What You Will Learn

By the mid-1800s, Americans were seeking reform in education and slavery. Some sought equality for women. Artists and writers also began to develop a distinct style.

Chapter 12 Focus Question

As you read through this chapter, keep this question in mind: **How did reformers and writers inspire change and spark controversy?**

Key Events

1831 William Lloyd Garrison starts antislavery newspaper.

1848 Women's rights convention is held in Seneca Falls, New York.

1850s American writers publish *The Scarlet Letter*, *Moby-Dick*, *Walden*, and *Leaves of Grass*.

Section 1

Improving Society

Section 1 Focus Question

How did key people bring about reform in education and society? To begin answering this question,

- Learn about the roots of the reforming spirit.
- Find out about temperance and prison reform.
- Explore education reform.

Section 1 Summary

The expansion of democracy during the presidency of Andrew Jackson and the Second Great Awakening led many to organize efforts to reform American society.

The Reforming Spirit

In the 1830s, many Americans became interested in **social reform,** or organized attempts to improve conditions of life. Social reform had its roots in both politics and religion. The political system was becoming fairer in the spirit of Jacksonian democracy. People began to support other causes, such as rights for women and the end of slavery.

Religious ideas also encouraged reform. In the early 1800s, some ministers questioned whether God alone decided a person's fate. This movement was known as the Second Great Awakening. Its leaders argued that people's own actions determined their salvation. In 1826, the minister **Charles Finney** held the first of many **revivals,** or huge outdoor religious meetings to convert people. The Second Great Awakening encouraged people to try to improve themselves and society.

Some reformers experimented with building utopian, or ideal, communities. In 1825, Robert Owen founded a utopian community called New Harmony in Indiana. Residents were supposed to produce enough food and goods to make the community self-sufficient. But New Harmony, like most utopian communities, did not last very long. ✓

✓ Checkpoint

Name the person who held the first revival meetings.

___

Social Reformers at Work

Meanwhile, other reformers tried to change the existing society. The **temperance movement** was an organized effort to end alcohol abuse and the problems created by it. Many women were drawn to this movement. Most citizens favored temperance, or moderation in drinking. But others supported **prohibition,** or a total ban on the sale and consumption of alcohol.

Reading Strategy

Meanwhile tells you that two things were going on at the same time. Circle the sentence starting with *Meanwhile*. Then draw an arrow up to the other event or process that was going on at the same time.

Dorothea Dix, a schoolteacher, wanted to improve the prison system. She supported the building of new, cleaner, and more humane prisons. She also urged the government to create separate institutions, called asylums, for people with mental illnesses. ✓

✓ Checkpoint

Name the schoolteacher who took up the cause of prison reform.

___

Education Reform

Many reformers thought that a better education system was needed. They called for **public schools,** or free schools supported by taxes. These schools would create better-informed voters, and could help immigrants become part of American culture.

The leader of education reform was Horace Mann of Massachusetts. With his encouragement, colleges were created to train teachers, the salaries of teachers were raised, and the school year was lengthened. These improvements did little for African Americans. But in 1855, Massachusetts became the first state to admit African Americans to public schools. ✓

✓ Checkpoint

Name the main leader of the movement for education reform.

___

Check Your Progress

1. What religious movement contributed to reform?

___

2. What is the difference between temperance and prohibition?

___

___

Section 1 Notetaking Study Guide

Question to Think About As you read Section 1 in your textbook and take notes, keep this section focus question in mind: **How did key people bring about reform in education and society?**

► Complete this chart to record key information from the section.

Improving Society
The Reforming Spirit of Jacksonian Democracy
Some people worked to make the political system fairer. They supported causes such as legal rights for ___women___ and the end of ___slavery___.
How the Second Great Awakening encouraged reform: • Doctrine of free will: __________ • Charles Finney: __________ • If people had the power to improve themselves, they could __________.
Utopian Communities • Definition: communities that tried to create perfect societies • Robert Owen: __________ • Results: __________
Social Reformers at Work
Temperance Movement • Definition: an organized effort to ___end alcohol abuse and the problems it creates___ • Many women supported this movement because __________. • Some reformers supported prohibition, which is __________.
Movement to Reform Prisons • Dorothea Dix worked to support the building of __________. • Dix urged the government to create ___asylums___ for ___the mentally ill___.
Education Reform • Public schools were supported as a way to create more informed __________ and help new __________. • Horace Mann: reformer from Massachusetts who __________ • Reformers of African American education __________. • First state to admit African Americans to public schools: __________ • Ashmun Institute: __________

Refer to this page to answer the Chapter 12 Focus Question on page 197.

Section 2
The Fight Against Slavery

Section 2 Focus Question

How did abolitionists try to end slavery? To begin answering this question,

- Learn about the roots of the antislavery movement.
- Discover why there was growing opposition to slavery.
- Find out about the Underground Railroad.
- Explore why some opposed the abolition of slavery.

Section 2 Summary

The reform movement of the 1800s led to growing calls to end slavery. However, other Americans continued to defend slavery.

Roots of the Antislavery Movement

Many leaders of the early republic, such as Alexander Hamilton and Benjamin Franklin, opposed slavery. They thought that slavery went against the principle that "all men are created equal." In 1780, Pennsylvania became the first state to pass a law gradually ending slavery. By 1804, every northern state had ended or pledged to end slavery.

In 1817, the American Colonization Society began an effort to gradually free and then send slaves back to Liberia, a colony in Africa. This movement did not work because most enslaved people had been born in America and did not want to return to Africa. By 1830, only about 1,400 African Americans had migrated to Liberia. ✓

Growing Opposition to Slavery

Antislavery feeling increased during the Second Great Awakening when preachers like Charles Finney began to condemn slavery. By the mid-1800s, more Americans had become **abolitionists**, reformers who wanted to abolish slavery. Instead of gradual change, they supported a complete and immediate end to slavery. **William Lloyd Garrison** was an abolitionist leader who founded an abolitionist newspaper, the *Liberator*, in 1831. He supported giving all African Americans full political rights. Garrison also cofounded the New England Anti-Slavery Society.

African Americans in the North also joined the abolitionist movement. In 1829, David Walker wrote his *Appeal: to the*

Key Events

1831	William Lloyd Garrison starts antislavery newspaper.
1848	Women's rights convention is held in Seneca Falls, New York.
1850s	American writers publish *The Scarlet Letter, Moby-Dick, Walden*, and *Leaves of Grass*.

✓ Checkpoint

Name the first state to pass a law gradually ending slavery.

____

Vocabulary Builder

What word in the underlined sentence could be replaced by the word *oppose*?

____

Reading Strategy

Reread the bracketed paragraph. Circle its main idea. Then underline two details in the paragraph that support the main idea.

✓ Checkpoint

Name the organization William Lloyd Garrison cofounded.

____

✓ Checkpoint

Name the escaped slave who led over 300 slaves to freedom on the Underground Railroad.

____

✓ Checkpoint

Why did some northern factory owners oppose abolitionism?

____

____

Coloured Citizens of the World, It called on slaves to rebel to gain their freedom. Perhaps the most powerful speaker for abolitionism was **Frederick Douglass.** Born into slavery, he had escaped to freedom. He gave speeches before large crowds. He also published an antislavery newspaper, the *North Star*.

Abolitionists won the support of a few powerful people. Former President John Quincy Adams, now a member of Congress, supported abolition. He read antislavery petitions in the House of Representatives. He also introduced a constitutional amendment to ban slavery in new states. ✓

The Underground Railroad

Some abolitionists helped people escape from slavery using a system known as the Underground Railroad. People called "conductors" helped runaway slaves move between "stations." These were usually abolitionists' homes, churches, or caves. One Quaker, Levi Coffin, helped 3,000 slaves escape. Escaped slave **Harriet Tubman** escorted over 300 slaves to freedom. In total, as many as 50,000 may have used the Underground Railroad to reach freedom. ✓

Opposing Abolition

Abolitionists faced opponents in the North and the South. Northern textile mill owners and merchants needed the cotton produced by slave labor. Northern workers feared that freed slaves might take their jobs. Some northerners reacted violently towards abolitionists. In 1835, a mob dragged William Lloyd Garrison through the streets of Boston with a rope around his neck.

Southerners had long defended slavery as a positive force. As support for abolition grew, they went on the offensive. Southerners won passage of a "gag rule" in Congress that blocked discussion of antislavery petitions. ✓

Check Your Progress

1. Describe Frederick Douglass' roles in abolitionism.

____

____

2. What was the Underground Railroad?

____

____

Section 2 Notetaking Study Guide

Question to Think About As you read Section 2 in your textbook and take notes, keep this section focus question in mind: **How did abolitionists try to end slavery?**

▶ Complete this chart to record key information from the section.

The Fight Against Slavery
Roots of the Antislavery Movement
• 1780: Pennsylvania became the first state to pass a law gradually ending slavery. • Ohio was the first state to ________. • By 1804, ________ had ended or pledged to end slavery. • The American Colonization Society ________, but it was ________.
Growing Opposition to Slavery
Abolitionists • definition: ________
William Lloyd Garrison • important abolitionist leader who founded the newspaper *the Liberator* in 1831 • supported giving all African Americans ________ • cofounded the ________
David Walker • wrote ________ in 1829, a pamphlet that called on enslaved people to ________
Frederick Douglass • an escaped ________ and powerful ________ • published the *North Star*, an ________
John Quincy Adams • As a member of Congress, he read ________. • spoke to the Supreme Court for ________
The Underground Railroad
• definition: ________ • "conductors": people who helped runaway slaves move between "stations" • "stations": usually ________ • Harriet Tubman: nicknamed ________, escorted ________
Opposition to Abolition
In the North: • Northern textile mill owners and merchants relied on cotton produced by enslaved people. • Northern workers feared that ________.
In the South: • defended slavery as a ________ • Southerners in Congress won passage of a "gag rule," which blocked discussion of ________.

Refer to this page to answer the Chapter 12 Focus Question on page 197.

Key Events

1831	William Lloyd Garrison starts antislavery newspaper.
1848	Women's rights convention is held in Seneca Falls, New York.
1850s	American writers publish *The Scarlet Letter*, *Moby-Dick*, *Walden*, and *Leaves of Grass*.

✓ Checkpoint

List three things women could not do in 1820.

____

____

____

Vocabulary Builder

Exclude, in the underlined sentence, means to "keep out" or "reject." What would be an antonym of *exclude*?

____

Section 3

A Call for Women's Rights

Section 3 Focus Question

How did the women's suffrage movement begin? To begin answering this question,

- Learn about the start of the women's rights movement.
- Read about the Seneca Falls Convention.
- Find out about new opportunities for women.

Section 3 Summary

Women reformers organized the women's rights movement, which led to new civil and legal rights and new educational and career opportunities for women.

The Struggle Begins

In 1820, women had limited civil and legal rights. They could not vote or serve on juries, attend college, or enter professions like medicine or law. They also had limited educational opportunities. Married women could not even own property or keep the money they earned. Women were expected to stay in the private world of the home.

Women who were active in abolition and other reform movements began to demand rights as equal citizens. Among these women was **Sojourner Truth,** a former slave who spoke on behalf of both African Americans and women. **Lucretia Mott,** a Quaker, was also an abolitionist. Mott had organization skills and public speaking experience that most women of her day did not. ✓

Seneca Falls Convention

In 1840, Mott traveled to London to attend an antislavery convention. There, she met another abolitionist, **Elizabeth Cady Stanton.** <u>They were angry to learn that women were excluded from taking an active role in the meeting.</u> So, they organized a convention for women's rights. It was held in Seneca Falls, New York, in 1848. Over 300 men and women attended the convention.

Stanton wrote a Declaration of Sentiments based on the Declaration of Independence. It declared that all men and women are created equal. It also listed injustices against women. The declaration demanded full equality for women in all areas of life. Stanton's argument was the beginning of the battle for **women's suffrage,** or the right of women to vote. Some delegates, including Lucretia Mott, feared that demanding suffrage might harm other causes because it was so controversial. Still, the convention approved the demand for women's suffrage. ✓

New Opportunities for Women

The Seneca Falls Convention launched the women's rights movement. The **women's rights movement** was the organized effort to improve the political, legal, and economic status of women in American society. Stanton and Susan B. Anthony, a former schoolteacher, abolitionist, and temperance supporter, founded the National Woman Suffrage Association in 1869. They also convinced New York to pass a law protecting women's property rights. Many other states followed.

The women's rights movement focused much attention on education. Before this time, girls seldom studied subjects like math and science. In 1821, Emma Willard founded the Troy Female Seminary in New York. It served as a model for girls' schools everywhere. Then in 1837, Mary Lyon founded the first college for women, Mount Holyoke Female Seminary.

American society came to accept that girls could be educated, and women could be teachers. Some women tried to enter other professions as well. Margaret Fuller, a journalist, scholar, and literary critic, wrote about the need for women's rights in the book *Women in the Nineteenth Century*. Other women entered science. Elizabeth Blackwell was the first woman to graduate from a medical school. Astronomer Maria Mitchell was the first professor hired at Vassar College. She was also the first woman elected to the American Academy of Arts and Sciences. ✓

Check Your Progress

1. Why did many reformers, including Lucretia Mott, oppose the demand for women's suffrage?

____

____

2. What other movement were both Sojourner Truth and Lucretia Mott involved in before they began to demand rights for women?

____

✓ Checkpoint

Name the document that demanded full equality for women in all areas of life.

____

Reading Strategy

Circle the three words or phrases in the underlined sentence that describe Susan B. Anthony.

✓ Checkpoint

Name the first college for women in the United States.

____

Section 3 Notetaking Study Guide

Question to Think About As you read Section 3 in your textbook and take notes, keep this section focus question in mind: **How did the women's suffrage movement begin?**

▶ Complete this chart to record key information from the section.

Women's Rights Movement
Roots of the Movement
Important leaders • Sojourner Truth: former slave who spoke on behalf of African Americans and women • Lucretia Mott: __________ • Elizabeth Cady Stanton: __________
Seneca Falls Convention
How it came about: Lucretia Mott and Elizabeth Cady Stanton were not allowed to take an active role in an antislavery convention. In response, they organized a __________ in Seneca Falls, New York, in 1848.
Declaration of Sentiments • the beginning of the battle for __________ • It demanded __________.
Suffrage • definition: full equality for women in all areas of life
New Opportunities for Women
The Seneca Falls Convention launched the women's rights movement. • Stanton and Susan B. Anthony founded __________ in 1869. • In 1860, Stanton and Anthony convinced New York to pass a law __________.
Education • Emma Willard: founded __________, which served as __________ • Mary Lyon: founded __________, the first __________
Careers • Margaret Fuller: wrote __________, which was about the need for women's rights • Elizabeth Blackwell: the first __________ • Maria Mitchell: the first __________ and the first __________

Refer to this page to answer the Chapter 12 Focus Question on page 197.

Section 4
American Literature and Arts

Section 4 Focus Question

How did American literature and arts have an impact on American life? To begin answering this question,

- Discover how a distinctly American culture developed.
- Find out about the flowering of American literature.
- Learn about new American styles of art and music.

Section 4 Summary

In the 1800s, America developed its own unique culture. This included many new ideas and changes in literature, art, and music.

An American Culture Develops

Before 1800, American writers and artists modeled their work on European styles. But by the mid-1800s, Americans had begun to develop their own styles. <u>These new styles reflected the optimism of the reform era.</u>

Writer Washington Irving based many of his stories, such as "The Legend of Sleepy Hollow," on the Dutch history of early New York. James Fenimore Cooper wrote about a character named Natty Bumppo, a frontiersman who kept moving westward.

By the early 1800s, a new artistic movement called Romanticism took shape in Europe. It was a style of writing and painting that placed value on nature, strong feelings, and the imagination. Americans developed their own form of Romanticism, called **transcendentalism.** Its goal was to explore the relationship between man and nature through emotions rather than through reason.

Transcendentalists tried to live simply, and sought an understanding of beauty, goodness, and truth. The writings and lectures of transcendentalist **Ralph Waldo Emerson** stressed **individualism,** or the unique importance of the individual. He influenced **Henry David Thoreau,** another important writer and thinker. In his 1854 book *Walden*, Thoreau urged people to live simply. He also encouraged **civil disobedience,** the idea that people should disobey unjust laws if their consciences demand it. ✓

Key Events

1831 William Lloyd Garrison starts antislavery newspaper.

1848 Women's rights convention is held in Seneca Falls, New York.

1850s American writers publish *The Scarlet Letter*, *Moby-Dick*, *Walden*, and *Leaves of Grass*.

Vocabulary Builder

If the word *optimum* means "best" and the suffix *-ism* means "belief," what do you think *optimism* in the underlined sentence means?

____

____

Reading Strategy

Based on clues in the text, which artistic movement was the first to develop: Romanticism or Transcendentalism?

____

✓ Checkpoint

List two important United States transcendentalists.

____

____

Flowering of American Literature

Herman Melville and **Nathaniel Hawthorne** changed the optimistic tone of American literature. They introduced psychological themes and extreme emotions. Melville's novel, *Moby-Dick* (1851), was the story of a ship captain who destroyed himself, his ship, and his crew chasing a whale. Hawthorne's stories used historical themes to explore the dark side of the mind. **Louisa May Alcott** wrote about a heroine as a believable, imperfect person.

Poets helped create a new national voice. Henry Wadsworth Longfellow based poems on American history. He wrote "Paul Revere's Ride." His long poem *The Song of Hiawatha*, was one of the first works to honor Native Americans.

Walt Whitman published *Leaves of Grass* in 1855. Whitman is seen as the poet who best expresses the democratic American spirit. His poetry celebrated the common man. Other poets used their poetry for social protest and social reform. John Greenleaf Whittier and Frances Watkins Harper wrote poems that described and condemned the evils of slavery. ✓

✓ Checkpoint

Name the first writer to create realistic heroines.

____

Art and Music

After 1820, artists focused on the landscapes around them or the daily lives of Americans. The Hudson River school of artists was inspired by Romanticism. These artists stirred emotion by painting about the beauty and power of nature. Other painters, such as George Caleb Bingham, painted scenes of everyday life. George Catlin captured the ways and dignity of Native Americans in his art.

American music also began to develop its own identity. A wide variety of new songs emerged, including work songs and spirituals. The era's most popular songwriter was Stephen Foster. Many of his tunes, such as "Camptown Races," are still familiar today. ✓

✓ Checkpoint

Name the school of painting inspired by Romanticism.

____

Check Your Progress

1. What aspect of the reform era was reflected in American literature and art?

____

2. How did Herman Melville and Nathaniel Hawthorne change the tone of American literature?

____

____

Section 4 Notetaking Study Guide

Question to Think About As you read Section 4 in your textbook and take notes, keep this section focus question in mind: **How did American literature and arts have an impact on American life?**

▶ Complete this chart to record key information from the section.

American Literature and Arts
Development of an American Culture
• Before 1800, American writers and artists modeled their work on European styles. By the mid-1800s, American writers and artists developed styles that reflected American ______ and ______.
Early Writers • Washington Irving based many of his stories on the ______; he wrote "The Legend of Sleepy Hollow" and "Rip Van Winkle." • James Fenimore Cooper wrote about ______.

• Romanticism: a European ______ that placed value on ______
• Transcendentalism: goal was to explore ______
  • Ralph Waldo Emerson stressed ______.
  • Henry David Thoreau urged people to ______ and encouraged civil disobedience.

Flowering of American Literature
Herman Melville and Nathaniel Hawthorne changed the tone of American literature by introducing psychological themes and extreme emotions.
Louisa May Alcott: first to write about a heroine as a ______
Poetry • Henry Wadsworth Longfellow based his poems on ______. • Walt Whitman rejected ______ and expressed the ______. • John Greenleaf Whittier and Frances Watkins Harper wrote poems that described and condemned ______.
Art
Hudson River school: The school's artists sought to reproduce ______. George Caleb Bingham's paintings showed ______. George Catlin's paintings showed ______.
Music
A new American style of song emerged, including ______ chanted by sailors and laborers, and ______ developed among African Americans.

Refer to this page to answer the Chapter 12 Focus Question on page 197.

Chapter 12 Assessment

Directions: Circle the letter of the correct answer.

1. Who was an important leader of education reform?
   A Lucretia Mott **B** Harriet Tubman **C** Horace Mann

2. What document declared that all men and women are created equal and listed injustices against women?
   A the U.S. Constitution
   B the Declaration of Sentiments
   C *Moby-Dick*

3. Whose writings changed the tone of American literature by introducing psychological themes and extreme emotions?
   A Charles Finney
   B Henry David Thoreau
   C Herman Melville

Directions: Follow the steps to answer this question:

How did religious ideas encourage an era of social reform?

Step 1: Recall information: Define *social reform* and identify its roots.

Social Reform		
Concept	**Definition**	**Rooted In**
Social Reform		

Step 2: Explain the new religious movement and how it was spread.

Second Great Awakening	How It Was Spread

Step 3: Complete the topic sentence that follows. Then write two or three more sentences that support your topic sentence.

Religious ideas helped spark an era of social reform by ______________________

____

____

____

____

Chapter 12 Notetaking Study Guide

Now you are ready to answer the Chapter 12 Focus Question: **How did reformers and writers inspire change and spark controversy?**

▶ Complete the following chart to help you answer this question.

American Reforms and Ideas

Society and Education

Social reform: organized attempts to improve conditions of life

- Two factors encouraging reform:
  1. the expansion of democracy
  2. ______________________
- The temperance movement was ______________________.

Prison reform

- Dorothea Dix convinced state legislatures to build ______________ and create ______________.

Education reform

- ______________ called for colleges to train teachers and higher teacher salaries.
- ______________ was the first state to admit African Americans to public schools.

Slavery

Abolitionists: reformers who wanted to abolish slavery

- William Lloyd Garrison cofounded the *Liberator*, an ______________________.
- Frederick Douglass: an escaped slave and powerful speaker

The Underground Railroad

- "Conductors" helped slaves move between "stations."
- ______________, an escaped slave, escorted over 300 slaves to freedom.

Opposing Abolition

- Northerners relied on cotton produced by slaves.
- The "gag rule" blocked ______________________.

Women's Rights

Women's rights movement

- Women began to demand equal rights as citizens.
- Elizabeth Cady Stanton wrote ______________________.

The Seneca Falls Convention

- birthplace of ______________
- 1869: Stanton and Susan B. Anthony founded the ______________.

New Opportunities

- Women started schools for girls and women.
- career "firsts" in medicine, ______________, ______________

Culture

Ideas

- Transcendentalism was a form of ______________, a European artistic movement.
- The writings of ______________ and ______________ reflected transcendentalism.
- Louisa May Alcott was the first to depict a woman as ______________________.
- American artists began to focus on landscapes around them or ______________________.

Refer to this page to answer the Unit 4 Focus Question on page 212.

Chapter 13

Westward Expansion (1820–1860)

What You Will Learn

In the mid-1800s, many Americans wanted the nation to expand westward to the Pacific Ocean. American settlers overcame hardships in making this happen.

Chapter 13 Focus Question

As you read this chapter, keep this question in mind: **How did westward expansion change the geography of the nation and demonstrate the determination of its people?**

Section 1

The West

Section 1 Focus Question

What cultures and ideas influenced the development of the West? To begin answering this question,

- Explore what "the West" was.
- Learn about the Mexican settlements.
- Understand the concept of Manifest Destiny.

Section 1 Summary

The lands that made up the West were constantly changing. Americans believed they were destined to take possession of the West.

What Was "The West"?

As the nation grew, the lands that made up "the West" changed. At first, the West was the land between the Appalachian Mountains and the Mississippi River. Then the West became the lands beyond the Mississippi.

The Great Plains lay between the Mississippi and the Rockies, but it was overlooked by settlers. They did not think it was good for farming because it was covered by thickly rooted grasses that would be hard to clear. Instead, they looked to the Northwest and Southwest.

The Northwest had fertile lands stretching from the Rocky Mountains to the Pacific Ocean. The United States, Great Britain, Russia, and Spain all claimed this area.

Key Events

1821	William Beck-nell opens the Santa Fe Trail.
1836	Texas declares independence from Mexico.
1849	California gold rush begins.

Reading Strategy

Reread the bracketed paragraph. It describes a cause and an effect. Underline the cause and circle the effect.

The Southwest included present-day California, Utah, Nevada, Arizona, New Mexico, Texas, and half of Colorado. It was a vast area that was ruled first by Spain, then by Mexico. Its culture was very different from that of the United States. ✓

Mexican Settlements

Spain followed a policy of mercantilism in its colonies. Settlers in New Spain could not trade with other nations.

Spanish missionaries tried to convert the local Native Americans to Catholicism. Many Native Americans were forced to live and work at missions. Here, thousands of Native Americans died from overwork or disease.

Over the years, Spanish settlers mixed with Native Americans to create a blended culture. The new culture included the Spanish language, law, and religion. It also included Native American foods and building materials.

In 1821, Mexico won its independence from Spain. The Mexican government opened up the region to trade with foreign countries, including the United States. It also removed the missions from church control. It gave their lands in large **land grants,** or government gifts of land, to Mexican settlers. Many of these grants were made to **rancheros,** or owners of ranches. Much of this land belonged to Native Americans. They responded by raiding ranches. However, they were soon crushed. Soon, their population in the Southwest was drastically reduced. ✓

Manifest Destiny

Many Americans were interested in westward **expansion,** or extending the nation beyond its existing borders. The Louisiana Purchase had doubled the size of the nation. But just forty years later, Americans were looking even farther west. A newspaper editor coined the phrase "manifest destiny" in 1845. The phrase described the belief that the United States was destined, or meant, to stretch from coast to coast. ✓

Check Your Progress

1. Why weren't the Great Plains settled quickly?

____

____

2. What phrase described American feelings about westward expansion?

____

✓ Checkpoint

List three areas that made up the West after the 1820s.

____

____

____

Vocabulary Builder

Reread the bracketed paragraph. Based on context clues in the paragraph, what do you think the word *missions* means?

____

____

____

✓ Checkpoint

Name two changes that Mexico made when it took control of the Southwest.

____

____

____

✓ Checkpoint

Name the term that described the idea that the United States should stretch from coast to coast.

____

Section 1 Notetaking Study Guide

Question to Think About As you read Section 1 in your textbook and take notes, keep this section focus question in mind: **What cultures and ideas influenced the development of the West?**

▶ Use this chart to record key information from the section. Some information has been filled in to get you started.

Westward Expansion

The Great Plains

Where: between the Mississippi River and the Rocky Mountains

Problem with land: ______

For many settlers, the Great Plains was: ______

The Northwest

Where: ______

Included present-day states of Washington and Oregon

Claimed by: ______

Settlers attracted to ______

Manifest Destiny

From the beginning, Americans were interested in westward expansion. The Louisiana Purchase, which doubled the territory of the nation, helped with this goal. Forty years later, the idea of Manifest Destiny became popular. It meant ______.

Mexican Settlement

The Southwest included the present-day states of: California, Utah ______.

Spanish Missions

- Purpose: ______
- Effect of missions on Indians: ______

Blended culture

- Spanish influence: ______
- Native American influence: ______
- Creoles were children born in Southwest to Spanish settlers
- Mestizos were ______.

Trade under Spanish rule: ______

Trade under Mexican rule: ______

Under Spanish rule, land grants were given mostly to ______.
Under Mexican rule, missions were removed from ______ control. Their lands were given as land grants to ______.
Much of this land belonged to ______, who responded by ______.
But soon ______ and their population ______.

Refer to this page to answer the Chapter 13 Focus Question on page 211.

Section 2
Trails to the West

Section 2 Focus Question

Why did people go west, and what challenges did they face? To begin answering this question,

- Find out how traders led the way into the West.
- Explore the Oregon Trail.
- Learn about life in the West.

Section 2 Summary

Whether they went to find gold, become a trader, work as a missionary, or farm, people who went west suffered many hardships.

Traders Lead the Way

Trade drove the first western crossings. Traders were looking for new markets in which to sell goods. In the process, they blazed important trails for those who followed.

After Mexico won independence, it allowed trade with the United States. In 1821, Captain **William Becknell** led a wagon train filled with merchandise from Independence, Missouri, to Santa Fe, New Mexico. It was a difficult journey, but the group succeeded. The Santa Fe Trail soon became a busy international trade route.

John Jacob Astor, a German fur merchant, sent the first American fur-trading expedition to Oregon. On the way, one group in the expedition found the South Pass through the Rocky Mountains. This important trade route helped open up the Northwest.

Mountain men, or fur trappers, supplied Astor with furs. For most of the year, they lived isolated lives, but once a year they gathered for a **rendezvous** (RAHN day voo), or a meeting where they would trade furs for supplies.

Beaver fur was in great demand in the East. However, by the 1830s, the supply of beavers was nearly exhausted. Most of the trappers moved back east to become farmers, merchants, or even bankers. Others stayed as guides for the thousands of settlers who came west. ✓

The Oregon Trail

The first white easterners to build permanent homes in Oregon were missionaries, who began to travel west in the

Key Events

1821	William Becknell opens the Santa Fe Trail.
1836	Texas declares independence from Mexico.
1849	California gold rush begins.

Vocabulary Builder

The word *isolated* comes from the Latin word *insula*, which means "island." Think about the position of an island relative to the mainland. What do you think the word *isolated* means as it is used in the text?

____

____

✓ Checkpoint

List three people or groups who developed trade in the West.

____

____

____

1830s to bring their religion to the Indians. The missionaries' glowing reports of Oregon led more easterners to make the journey west. Farmers sought the free and fertile land, the mild climate, and the plentiful rainfall in river valleys.

Most settlers followed the Oregon Trail, a route that stretched over 2,000 miles from Missouri to Oregon. Travelers left in the spring and had five months to make their journey. If they were caught in the Rocky Mountains during the winter, their chances of survival were slim.

Pioneers on the Oregon Trail banded together in wagon trains for mutual protection. The wagons carried their goods, while most people walked the thousands of miles of trail. The trip was dangerous. Disease and accidents killed one out of every ten travelers. Clean, safe water was hard to find. Still, over 50,000 people reached Oregon between 1840 and 1860. ✓

✓ Checkpoint

List two groups of people who went to Oregon.

____

____

Life in the West

Settlers in the West had few possessions and little money. They worked hard to clear land, plant crops, and build shelters. Disease, accidents, and natural disasters were a constant threat.

Because western families relied on women's labor to survive, women had a higher status in the West. In 1869, Wyoming Territory became the first area of the United States to grant women the vote.

Native Americans in Oregon lived in an uneasy peace with the white settlers. Native Americans in southern Oregon usually got along with whites. However, in the north, Native Americans were angered by the presence of strangers on their land. When gold was discovered in northern Oregon in the 1850s, a large number of white and Chinese miners arrived in the area. In 1855, war broke out briefly between the Native Americans and miners. After the U.S. government intervened, the tribes were forced to accept peace treaties. ✓

✓ Checkpoint

List three dangers that settlers in Oregon faced.

____

____

____

Check Your Progress

1. What first drove people to find safe trails to the West?

____

____

2. Why did western women have a higher status?

____

____

Section 2 Notetaking Study Guide

Question to Think About As you read Section 2 in your textbook, keep this question in mind: **Why did people go west, and what challenges did they face?**

▶ Use this chart to record key information from the section.

Traders Lead the Way

The Santa Fe Trail

- In 1821, ______________________ led a wagon train from Independence, Missouri to ______________________.
- Hardships experienced along the way: ______________________
- Importance: established a route for ____________ trade with ____________ that stretched about ______ miles

The Oregon Fur Trade

- John Jacob Astor sent the first American fur-trading expedition to Oregon and established the ____________ Fur Company in 1808.
- Trappers who supplied furs were called mountain men.
- What happened to the fur trade in the 1830s ______________________

The Oregon Trail

Missionaries Travel West to Oregon in the 1830s

- Purpose: to bring their religious beliefs to the Indians
- Famous missionary couple: ______________________
- How missionaries spurred settlement of the West: ______________________

On the Trail

- Trail stretched more than ______ miles from ____________ to ____________
- Travelers left in spring and had to reach Oregon in 5 months. If they did not make it in time, they risked ______________________.
- Between 1840 and 1860, more than ____________ people reached Oregon.

Life in the West

Pioneer Life

- Settlers had only ____________ to clear the land, ____________, and build shelters.
- Threats included ____________, ____________, and ____________.

Women in the West

- Reason women's status was raised in the West: ______________________
- In 1869, Wyoming was the first area to grant women the right to ____________.

Native Americans and Settlers

- Relationship between the two groups: uneasy peace
- In the 1850s, ______________________ brought large numbers of ____________ to ____________ Oregon. In 1855, ____________ broke out there briefly.

Refer to this page to answer the Chapter 13 Focus Question on page 211.

Section 3

Conflict With Mexico

Key Events

1821	William Becknell opens the Santa Fe Trail.
1836	Texas declares independence from Mexico.
1849	California gold rush begins.

Section 3 Focus Question

What were the causes and effects of the Texas War for Independence and the Mexican-American War? To begin answering this question,

- Find out how Texas won independence.
- Learn how Texas and Oregon were annexed.
- Discover the causes of the Mexican-American War.
- Explore how the United States achieved Manifest Destiny.

Section 3 Summary

The United States acquired Oregon from Britain, but U.S. expansion in the Southwest resulted from war with Mexico.

Texas Wins Independence

In 1820, the Spanish gave Moses Austin a land grant to establish a small colony in Texas. After Moses Austin died, his son, **Stephen Austin,** led a group of some 300 settlers there. Then Mexico won its independence from Spain. Texans did not like the Mexican government. They wanted a democratic government that would ensure fair representation.

In 1833, General Antonio López de Santa Anna became president of Mexico. He started a **dictatorship,** or one-person rule, that clamped down on Texas. Stephen Austin led Texans to declare independence from Mexico. The Republic of Texas was created in 1836.

Sam Houston, commander of Texan forces, finally defeated Santa Anna. Houston became president of the Republic of Texas. Texans hoped the U.S. would **annex,** or add on, their republic to the Union. ✓

✓ Checkpoint

Name the three men who played major roles in the war over Texas.

____

____

____

Annexing Texas and Oregon

[Adding Texas became a political issue because Texas would come in as a slave state. How could the balance of slave and free states be maintained? President **James K. Polk** solved this problem by persuading Britain to give up Oregon. In 1845, Texas was admitted as a slave state. Oregon came in as a free territory.]

But Mexico had never recognized Texas independence. Now Mexico claimed that the southern border of Texas was the Nueces River, not the Rio Grande. Polk pressured Mexico to accept the Rio Grande border.

Reading Strategy

Reread the bracketed paragraph. What is the problem that it discusses? What was the solution used to solve the problem?

Problem: ______________________

____

Solution: ______________________

____

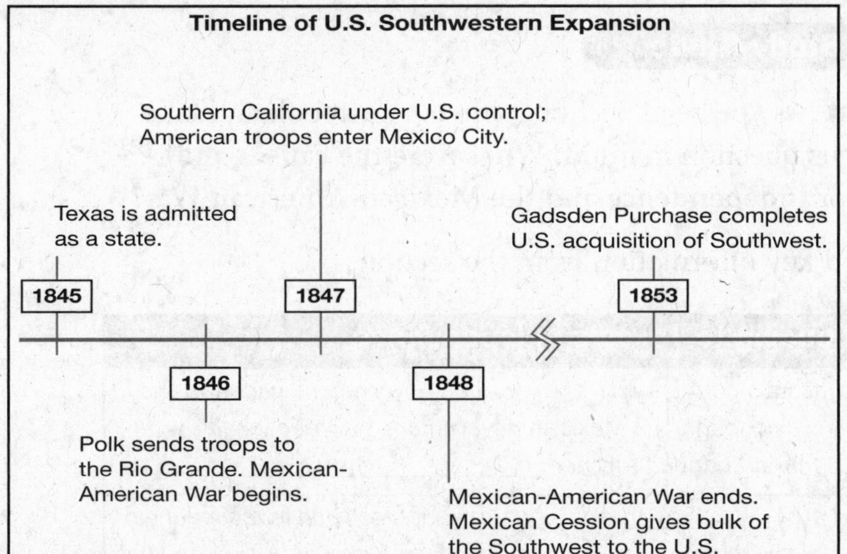
Timeline of U.S. Southwestern Expansion
Southern California under U.S. control; American troops enter Mexico City.
Texas is admitted as a state.
Gadsden Purchase completes U.S. acquisition of Southwest.
1845
1847
1853
1846
1848
Polk sends troops to the Rio Grande. Mexican-American War begins.
Mexican-American War ends. Mexican Cession gives bulk of the Southwest to the U.S.

✓ Checkpoint

List the two rivers that were claimed as Texas's southern border.

___

___

The Mexican-American War

Mexico would not accept the Rio Grande border. It also refused to **cede**, or give up, California and New Mexico. So Polk sent General Zachary Taylor to the Rio Grande. Mexico saw this as an act of war and attacked. Polk then urged Congress to declare war. He sent Stephen Kearny to capture Santa Fe. **John C. Frémont**, an explorer, led a rebellion against Mexican rule in California.

General Taylor invaded Mexico and defeated Santa Anna at the Battle of Buena Vista. General Winfield Scott marched to Mexico City. Santa Anna fled, and Mexico was under U.S. occupation. ✓

✓ Checkpoint

Name four Americans who led the United States in the Mexican-American War.

___

___

___

___

Achieving Manifest Destiny

The United States and Mexico signed the Treaty of Guadalupe-Hidalgo in 1848. Mexico recognized Texas as a U.S. state. The Mexican Cession gave the Southwest to the U.S. for $18 million. This included California, Nevada, Utah, parts of Wyoming, Colorado, Arizona, and New Mexico.

In the 1853 Gadsden Purchase, the United States bought a narrow strip of present-day Arizona and New Mexico from Mexico for $10 million. The United States had fulfilled what it saw as its destiny to occupy the West. ✓

✓ Checkpoint

List the two things that gave the United States the entire Southwest.

___

___

Check Your Progress

1. What did Texans want from the Mexican government?

___

2. What action started the Mexican-American War?

___

___

Section 3 Notetaking Study Guide

Question to Think About As you read Section 3 in your textbook and take notes, keep this section focus question in mind: **What were the causes and effects of the Texas War for Independence and the Mexican-American War?**

▶ Use these charts to record key information from the section.

Events Leading to Texas's Independence
American settlers in Texas came into conflict with the Mexican government because they were slaveholders even though the Mexican government had abolished ______. In 1830, Mexico banned further ______.
After Santa Anna established a(n) ______, Texans declared independence. Mexican troops laid siege to the Alamo, a mission in San Antonio. Although the Texans were defeated, this event inspired ______. Later, the Texans defeated Santa Anna's army at ______.
______ became president of the new Republic of Texas. He hoped that the United States would annex Texas. However, public opinion in the United States was divided because ______.

Annexing Texas and Oregon
James K. Polk negotiated a treaty with Britain to divide Oregon, which became the states of ______, ______, and ______.
Tensions with Mexico increased because Mexico had never ______. Also, the United States claimed that the southern Texas border was the Rio Grande, while Mexico claimed it was the ______.

The Mexican-American War
When war broke out between Mexico and the United States, it was most popular among ______ and westerners who wanted ______. Many ______, however, opposed the war because they thought it was an attempt to ______.
Stephen Kearny led troops that captured ______ and later California.
______ won a victory at the Battle of Buena Vista. An American army under ______ captured Veracruz and then marched on to Mexico City.
The Treaty of ______ formally ended the war. Under the treaty, Mexico recognized ______ and ceded a vast territory known as ______ to the United States. This territory included present-day California, Nevada ______.
In the ______ of 1853, the United States paid Mexico $10 million for a narrow strip of present-day ______.

Refer to this page to answer the Chapter 13 Focus Question on page 211.

Section 4
A Rush to the West

Section 4 Focus Question

How did Mormon settlement and the gold rush lead to changes in the West? To begin answering this question,

- Learn about Mormon settlement in Utah.
- Find out about the California gold rush.
- Explore California's changing population.

Section 4 Summary

Mormons migrated to Utah in search of religious freedom. Fortune seekers flocked to California in search of gold.

Mormons Settle Utah

In 1830, **Joseph Smith,** a New York farmer, founded a new church: the Mormon Church. Although the church grew quickly, its teachings angered others. For example, Smith favored **polygamy,** or the practice of having more than one wife at a time.

Hostile communities forced the Mormons to move from New York. In Illinois, Joseph Smith was murdered. In 1847, **Brigham Young,** the new Mormon leader, led the group to the valley of the Great Salt Lake in Utah.

Utah became a territory of the United States in 1848. The Mormons immediately came into conflict with the U.S. government over three issues. The first was over the election process. It was controlled by the church, which gave non-Mormons no say. Another was that the church supported Mormon-owned businesses. So, non-Mormons had difficulty doing business in the territory. Third, polygamy was illegal in the rest of the country. In time, Congress passed a law that took control of elections away from the Mormon Church. Church leaders agreed to ban polygamy and to stop favoring Mormon-owned businesses. ✓

The California Gold Rush

At the time of the Mexican Cession, there were about 10,000 Californios, or Mexican Californians, living in California. Some easterners began migrating to the territory. Then a flood of settlers came when gold was discovered in 1848 near Sacramento. The prospect of finding gold attracted about 80,000 fortune seekers. These people who came to

Key Events

1821	William Becknell opens the Santa Fe Trail.
1836	Texas declares independence from Mexico.
1849	California gold rush begins.

✓ Checkpoint

List three issues that were a source of conflict between the Mormons and the U.S. government.

____

____

____

Vocabulary Builder

Reread the underlined sentence. Which of the following words could replace *prospect*, as it is used in the sentence?

a. hope
b. guarantee
c. mining claim

California in search of gold were known as the **"forty-niners."** In two years, the population of settlers in California zoomed from 14,000 to 100,000.

Since much of California was desert, disputes over water rights were common. **Water rights** are the legal rights to use the water in a river, stream, or other body. Often such disputes erupted in violence.

Mining towns sprang up overnight. Since California was not yet a state, federal law did not apply within mining towns. Often **vigilantes,** or self-appointed law enforcers, punished people for crimes. But they had no legal right to do so.

Other migrations in U.S. history included men and women, young and old. The forty-niners, however, were mainly young men.

Few forty-niners struck it rich. After the gold rush, many people continued to search for gold throughout the West. Others settled in the West for good. ✓

✓ Checkpoint

Name one way the gold rush was different from other migrations in U.S. history.

___

___

___

California's Changing Population

The gold rush brought enormous ethnic diversity to California. People came from Europe, Asia, Australia, and South America. After news of the gold rush reached China, about 45,000 Chinese men went to California.

Although some southerners brought slaves with them, slavery did not take root in California. Other miners objected to anyone profiting from mining who did not participate in the hard labor of finding gold.

The gold rush brought tragedy for Native Americans in California. Miners swarmed onto Indian lands, and vigilante gangs killed many Indians. About 100,000 Indians died during the gold rush. This was nearly two thirds of the Native American population in California.

By 1850, only 15 percent of Californians were Mexican. Many Mexicans lost their land to the new settlers. ✓

Reading Strategy

Reread the bracketed paragraph. Circle the main idea, and underline two supporting details.

✓ Checkpoint

Describe one reason why slavery did not take root in California.

___

___

___

Check Your Progress

1. Why did the Mormons migrate to Utah?

___

___

2. How did California's population change after gold was discovered in the state?

___

___

Section 4 Notetaking Study Guide

Question to Think About As you read Section 4, keep this question in mind: **How did Mormon settlement and the gold rush lead to changes in the West?**

▶ Use these charts to record key information from the section.

Mormons Move West

Seeking Refuge

The Mormon Church was founded by Joseph Smith in 1830. Hostility forced the Mormons to move from ________ to Ohio, and then to ________. After ________ was murdered, ________ led the Mormons to the valley of Utah's ________.

Conflict With the Government

Utah became part of the United States in ______. The Mormons almost immediately came into conflict with the U.S. government over three issues:

1. *Problem*: ________
   Solution: Congress took away control of elections from the Mormon Church.
2. *Problem*: ________
   Solution: Church leaders agreed to stop favoring Mormon-owned businesses.
3. *Problem*: Polygamy, which is ________, was illegal in the United States.
   Solution: ________

Finally, in ______, Utah became a state.

The California Gold Rush

Gold Is Discovered

In January _____, gold was discovered at Sutter's Mill near Sacramento. Fortune seekers, called ________, came to California in search of gold. In just two years, the population of settlers in California zoomed from ________ to ________.

Miners and Mining Towns

Mining towns supplied miners with ________, ________, and ________. Since California was not yet a state, federal law did not apply within mining towns, so ________, or ________, punished people for crimes.

California's Changing Population

During the gold rush, people from ________, Asia, ________, and ________ came to California. Chinese workers faced ________ and were usually hired only for ________. Some southerners brought their slaves to California, but slavery did not take root because ________ ________. California's Native American population declined by about ______ thirds during the gold rush. Its people were killed by ________ gangs who wanted their land. By 1850, only ______ percent of Californians were ________.

Refer to this page to answer the Chapter 13 Focus Question on page 211.

Chapter 13 Assessment

Directions: Circle the letter of the correct answer.

1. The largest region of the West was
- **A** the Southwest.
- **B** the Northwest.
- **C** the Great Plains.

2. Most early travelers to the West were
A missionaries. **B** farmers. **C** traders.

3. Which of the following was a result of the Mexican-American War?
- **A** the Mexican Cession
- **B** the annexation of Texas
- **C** the Gadsden Purchase

4. Which of the following was a result of the gold rush in California?
- **A** Many people became rich from mining.
- **B** Slavery became widespread in the territory.
- **C** California's population became more diverse.

Directions: Follow the steps to answer this question:

How did the Mexican-American War help achieve Manifest Destiny?

Step 1: Define Manifest Destiny.

____

____

____

Step 2: Recall information: Describe the results of the Mexican-American War.

Results of the Mexican-American War
•
•

Step 3: Complete the topic sentence that follows. Then write two or three more sentences that support your topic sentence.

The effect of the Mexican-American War helped achieve Manifest Destiny by

____

____

____

____

____

Chapter 13 Notetaking Study Guide

Now you are ready to answer the Chapter 13 Focus Question: **How did westward expansion change the geography of the nation and demonstrate the determination of its people?**

▶ Complete the following chart to help you answer this question. Use the notes that you took for each section.

Westward Expansion Changes the Nation's Geography

The West

- **What was the West?** By the 1820s, lands west of the Mississippi
  - **Northwest:** Land that stretched from ___the Rockies___ to the ______________ ______________; in the early 1800s was claimed by ______________ ______________
  - **Southwest:** Lands in the southwest that included present-day California, Utah, Nevada, Arizona, New Mexico, Texas, and half of Colorado; ruled first by Spain, then by Mexico
- **What was Manifest Destiny?** ______________

Trails to the West

- **The Santa Fe Trail:** overland trade route that carried merchandise from Independence, Missouri to Santa Fe, New Mexico
- **The Oregon Trail:** ______________
- **Life in the West**
  - **For women:** ___improved status because their work was necessary for survival___
  - **For Native Americans and settlers:** ______________ ______________

Texas and the Mexican-American War

- **Texans rebel against Mexico because** of religious differences, conflicts over slavery, and a lack of democracy.
- **Annexation of Texas was controversial in the United States because** ______________.
- **The solution that led to the annexation of Texas was that** ______________ ______________.
- **Causes of the Mexican War:** ______________ ______________
- **Results of the Mexican War:** The nation's geography greatly changed after the United States acquired a vast territory under the Mexican Cession.

A Rush to the West

- **Who were the Mormons?** a religious group founded by Joseph Smith in 1830
- **Why did they migrate to Utah?** to escape conflict with ______________
- **Discovery in 1848 that brought a flood of settlers to California:** ___gold___

Refer to this page to answer the Unit 4 Focus Question on page 212.

Unit 4 Pulling It Together Activity

What You Have Learned

Chapter 11 The North industrialized and urbanized rapidly in the early to mid-1800s. The South became highly dependent on cotton and the slave labor needed to cultivate it. Tensions between North and South spread to the western territories.

Chapter 12 By the mid-1800s, Americans were seeking reform in education and abolition. Some sought equality for women. Artists and writers also began to develop a distinct style.

Chapter 13 In the mid-1800s, many Americans wanted the nation to expand westward to the Pacific Ocean. American settlers overcame hardships in making this happen.

Think Like a Historian

Read the Unit 4 Focus Question: **What forces unite and divide a nation?**

▶ Use the organizers on this page and the next to collect information to answer this question.

What forces united the nation? Some of them are listed in this chart. Review your section and chapter notes. Then complete the chart.

Factors That United the North and the South, 1800–1860	
Area	**Uniting Factors**
Economy	• *transformed by the Industrial Revolution*
Technology	• *new methods of transportation: steamboat, railroad* • •
Labor	•
Arts	•
Issues	• •

Look at the second part of the Unit Focus Question. It asks about the forces that divide a nation. The chart below gives you a part of the answer. Review your section and chapter notes. Then fill in the rest of the chart.

Factors That Divided the North and the South, 1800–1860		
Area	**In North**	**In South**
Economy	• industrial • based on manufacturing and trade	• agricultural • dependent on cotton
Key technology	• •	•
Where people lived and worked	• •	• rural; many plantations and small farms
Source of labor	• unskilled factory workers including immigrants	•
Reform movements	• •	•
Slavery	• •	• •

Unit 5

Civil War and Reunion

What You Will Learn

Chapter 14 With the addition of new western lands, tension over the slavery issue erupted into violence. The election of Abraham Lincoln led to seven states leaving the Union and marked the coming of the Civil War.

Chapter 15 People in the North and the South hoped for an early victory, but the Civil War went on for years. Hundreds of thousands of Americans were killed before the war ended.

Chapter 16 At the end of the Civil War, Americans faced the problem of how to reunite the nation. Disagreements over Reconstruction led to conflicts in government and in the South. With the end of Reconstruction, African Americans in the South lost many of the rights they had gained.

Focus Your Learning As you study this unit and take notes, you will find the information to answer the questions below. Answering the Chapter Focus Questions will help build your answer to the Unit Focus Question.

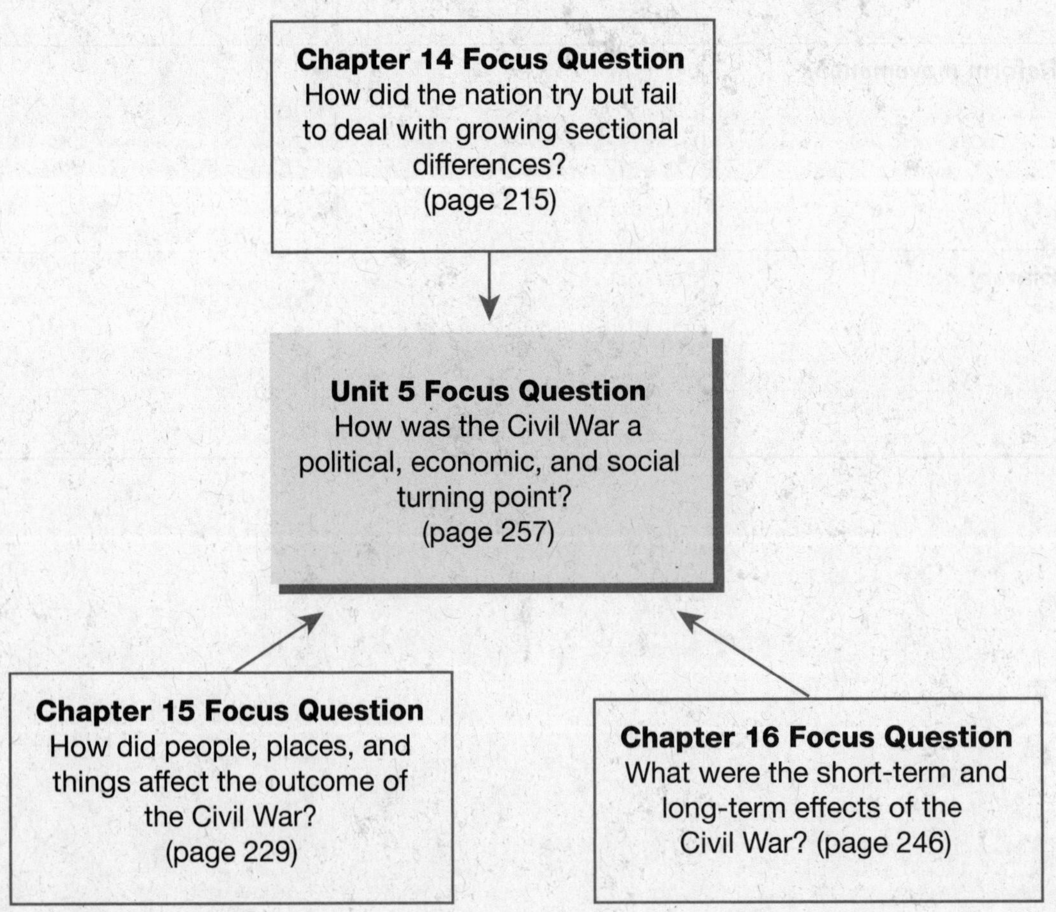

Chapter 14 Focus Question
How did the nation try but fail to deal with growing sectional differences?
(page 215)
Unit 5 Focus Question
How was the Civil War a political, economic, and social turning point?
(page 257)
Chapter 15 Focus Question
How did people, places, and things affect the outcome of the Civil War?
(page 229)
Chapter 16 Focus Question
What were the short-term and long-term effects of the Civil War? (page 246)

Chapter 14

The Nation Divided (1846–1861)

What You Will Learn

With the addition of new western lands, tension over the slavery issue erupted into violence. The election of Abraham Lincoln led to seven states leaving the Union and marked the coming of the Civil War.

Chapter 14 Focus Question

As you read through this chapter, keep this question in mind: **How did the nation try but fail to deal with growing sectional differences?**

Key Events

1852	Harriet Beecher Stowe publishes *Uncle Tom's Cabin*.
1857	Supreme Court ruling in Dred Scott case declares Missouri Compromise unconstitutional.
1861	The Civil War begins with Confederate bombardment of Fort Sumter.

Section 1

Growing Tensions Over Slavery

Section 1 Focus Question

How did the question of admission of new states to the Union fuel the debate over slavery and states' rights? To begin answering this question,

- Learn about slavery and the Mexican-American War.
- Explore the bitter debate over slavery.

Section 1 Summary

The vast new lands the United States won in the Mexican-American War restarted the national debate on slavery.

Slavery and the Mexican-American War

Between 1820 and 1848, there was a balance of free and slave states. The Missouri Compromise did not apply to the huge territory gained from Mexico in 1848, however. Would this territory be organized as states that allowed slavery?

The issue was important to northerners who wanted to stop slavery from spreading. Representative David Wilmot of Pennsylvania feared that the South would gain too much power. In 1846, he proposed that Congress ban slavery in all territory that might become states as a result of the Mexican-American War. This proposal was called the Wilmot Proviso. Slaveholding states saw the proviso as an attack on slavery by the North.

Vocabulary Builder

Sovereign comes from a Latin word meaning "above." If the states were sovereign, and made their own laws, what law would they be above?

____

✓ Checkpoint

List the three parties and their candidates in the 1848 election.

____

____

____

Reading Strategy

Reread the bracketed paragraph. Underline a cause and circle the two possible effects that cause might have.

✓ Checkpoint

List two issues that caused debate in the Congress.

____

____

____

____

Neither the Democrats nor the Whigs took a strong stand on slavery. Each party needed support in both the North and the South to win the presidential election of 1848.

In 1848, the Democratic candidate for president was Senator Lewis Cass of Michigan. He backed the idea of **popular sovereignty.** This meant people in each territory would vote directly on the issue of slavery, rather than having their elected representatives decide for them.

Many antislavery Whigs and Democrats created the Free-Soil Party. They wanted to ban slavery in all territory gained in the Mexican-American War. This would make it "free soil." Their candidate, Martin Van Buren, took enough votes from Cass to keep him from winning. General Zachary Taylor of the Whig Party became President. ✓

A Bitter Debate

Southerners feared that California's admission to the Union would give free states a majority in the Senate. Then the South could no longer block antislavery laws. Southern leaders threatened to **secede,** or withdraw, from the Union if California came in as a free state.

There were other issues that divided the North and South. Northerners wanted the slave trade abolished in Washington, D.C. Southerners wanted laws forcing northerners to return **fugitive,** or runaway, slaves.

[In 1850, Senator **Henry Clay** of Kentucky made proposals to save the Union. A great debate arose in the Senate. South Carolina Senator **John C. Calhoun** was against these proposals. He said if California came in as a free state, there were only two ways to preserve the South's way of life. One was a constitutional amendment protecting states' rights, and the other was secession.]

Senator **Daniel Webster** of Massachusetts supported Clay. He said both sides must compromise to save the Union. Both sides seemed deadlocked. ✓

Check Your Progress

1. What was the Wilmot Proviso?

____

____

2. Why did southerners fear California entering the Union as a free state?

____

____

Section 1 Notetaking Study Guide

Question to Think About As you read Section 1 in your textbook and take notes, keep this question in mind: **How did the question of admission of new states to the Union fuel the debate over slavery and states' rights?**

► Use this chart to record key information from the section. Some information has been filled in to get you started.

The Debate Over Slavery and States' Rights		
If	**Then**	**Who Benefits?**
The Wilmot Proviso passes,	1. slavery will be banned in all territory from the Mexican-American War that becomes part of the United States; slave states will be outnumbered and weakened.	North
Lewis Cass (Democrat) becomes President,	2. ______	Both
Martin Van Buren (Free-Soil) becomes President,	3. ______	
Zachary Taylor (Whig) becomes President,	4. ______	
California enters the Union as a free state,	5. ______	
Fugitive slave laws are enforced,	6. slavery is enforced in the North and the South.	South
Henry Clay's proposals are accepted,	7. according to Calhoun, the South ______	
Slavery remains an unresolved issue,	8. Bitter debates will continue to divide the nation.	

Refer to this page to answer the Chapter 14 Focus Question on page 228.

Section 2

Compromises Fail

Key Events

1852	Harriet Beecher Stowe publishes *Uncle Tom's Cabin*.
1857	Supreme Court ruling in Dred Scott case declares Missouri Compromise unconstitutional.
1861	The Civil War begins with Confederate bombardment of Fort Sumter.

Section 2 Focus Question

What was the Compromise of 1850, and why did it fail? To begin answering this question,

- Learn about the Compromise of 1850.
- Find out about *Uncle Tom's Cabin*.
- Learn about the Kansas-Nebraska Act.
- Read about the violence in Bleeding Kansas.

Section 2 Summary

Efforts to calm the slavery debate, such as the Compromise of 1850, ultimately failed, and the debate only grew fiercer.

The Compromise of 1850

In 1850, Congress passed five bills based on Henry Clay's proposals. The President signed them into law. These bills were known as the Compromise of 1850. To please the North, California was admitted as a free state. Also, the slave trade was banned in the nation's capital. To please the South, popular sovereignty would be used to decide the slavery issue in the rest of the Mexican Cession. Southerners also got a tough fugitive slave law.

The Fugitive Slave Act allowed government officials to arrest anyone accused of being a runaway slave. A person could be declared a runaway slave if just one white person said it was true. Northerners were supposed to help capture runaway slaves.

The Fugitive Slave Act became the most controversial part of the Compromise of 1850. Northerners hated the new law. They were outraged to see many African Americans suddenly arrested and shipped South. Thousands of African Americans fled to Canada for safety. ✓

✓ Checkpoint

Name two parts of the Fugitive Slave Act.

____

____

____

____

Uncle Tom's Cabin

Harriet Beecher Stowe was a northerner against slavery. In 1852, she published *Uncle Tom's Cabin*. It was about a kind slave abused by a cruel master. Many white southerners attacked the book as **propaganda**, or false or misleading information that is spread to further a cause. The book was a bestseller in the North. It shocked thousands of people who were previously unconcerned about slavery. Stowe's book showed that slavery was not just a political conflict, but a real human problem. ☑

The Kansas-Nebraska Act

In 1854, Illinois Senator **Stephen A. Douglas** pushed the Kansas-Nebraska Act through Congress. It formed two new territories—the Kansas Territory and the Nebraska Territory. At first, southerners objected because both territories lay in an area closed to slavery by the Missouri Compromise. This meant that the states created from these territories would enter the Union as free states.

Douglas tried to win southern support. He proposed that slavery in the new territories be decided by popular sovereignty. This in effect undid the Missouri Compromise. Northerners were angered that the slavery issue was to be reopened in the territories. Southern support enabled the Kansas-Nebraska Act to pass in both houses of Congress. ☑

Bleeding Kansas

In March 1855, Kansas held a vote on whether to enter the Union as a free or slave state. Thousands of proslavery people from Missouri voted illegally. Kansas had only 3,000 voters, but 8,000 votes were cast. A proslavery government was elected. Antislavery Kansans refused to accept these results and put a second government in place.

Violence soon broke out. Pro- and antislavery groups terrorized the countryside, attacking and killing settlers. It grew so bad that the territory was called Bleeding Kansas. Violence even spilled onto the floor of the U.S. Senate. ☑

Check Your Progress

1. What did each side get in the Compromise of 1850?

___

___

___

2. What was the effect of the Kansas-Nebraska Act?

___

___

___

✓ Checkpoint

What was the reaction of many northerners to *Uncle Tom's Cabin*?

___

___

Vocabulary Builder

Circle the definition of *propose* that most closely matches the meaning used in the underlined sentence.

A. to put forward for consideration
B. to nominate for an office
C. to make an offer of marriage

✓ Checkpoint

Name the method used to determine the status of slavery in the Kansas and Nebraska territories.

___

✓ Checkpoint

Kansas election of 1855:

Number of voters: ___
Number of votes cast: ___

Section 2 Notetaking Study Guide

Question to Think About As you read Section 2 in your textbook and take notes, keep this section focus question in mind: **What was the Compromise of 1850 and why did it fail?**

▶ Use this chart to record key information from the section. Some information has been filled in to get you started.

Compromises Fail		
Compromise of 1850 Proposed by Henry Clay	**Terms:** • California admitted as a free state • Slave trade banned in ______ • ______ would decide slavery in the rest of the Mexican Cession. • Southerners got a tough new ______	**Goal of Compromise:** To end slavery crisis by giving supporters and opponents of slavery some of what they wanted.
Fugitive Slave Act of 1850	**Terms:** • Government officials may arrest any person accused of being a ______ ______ by any white person. • Suspects had no right to a ______. • ______ were required to help authorities capture accused runaway slaves if asked.	**Results:** • Most ______ part of the Compromise of 1850 • Thousands of northern African Americans fled to ______.
Kansas-Nebraska Act of 1854 Proposed by ______	**Terms:** • Slavery in the new Kansas and Nebraska territories was to be decided by ______	**Results:** • Undid the Missouri Compromise • Reopened the issue of ______ in territories • ______ outraged
Kansas Election of 1855	**Events:** • Both proslavery and antislavery settlers flooded Kansas and wanted to hold the ______ in the territory. • Thousands of Missourians entered Kansas illegally to select a territorial legislature. • Antislavery settlers held a second ______.	**Results:** • Kansas now had two ______. • Violence broke out and earned Kansas the name ______ ______.

Refer to this page to answer the Chapter 14 Focus Question on page 228.

Section 3
The Crisis Deepens

Section 3 Focus Question

Why did the Lincoln-Douglas debates and John Brown's raid increase tensions between the North and South? To begin answering this question,

- Learn how a new antislavery party came to be.
- Explore the impact of the Dred Scott decision.
- Find out about the Lincoln-Douglas debates.
- Learn about John Brown's raid.

Section 3 Summary

The Lincoln-Douglas debates and John Brown's raid caused more controversy and anger over slavery.

A New Antislavery Party

The Whig Party split apart in 1854. Whigs who took a strong antislavery stand joined the new Republican Party. Its main platform was to stop slavery from spreading to the western territories. Northern Democrats and Free-Soilers also joined the Republican Party. It quickly became powerful. In the 1856 presidential election, the first Republican candidate, John C. Frémont, won 11 of the 16 free states. Still, the Democratic candidate, James Buchanan, won the presidential election. ✓

The Dred Scott Decision

In 1857, the Supreme Court decided the case of *Dred Scott* v. *Sandford*. **Dred Scott** was an enslaved person who sued for his freedom because he had lived with his master in states where slavery was illegal.

Supreme Court Chief Justice **Roger B. Taney** ruled that Scott had no right to sue in federal court because African Americans were not citizens. Taney also declared that living in a free state did not make enslaved people free. They were property, and the property rights of their owners were protected in all states.

This meant that Congress did not have the power to prohibit slavery in any territory, and that the Missouri Compromise was unconstitutional. Slavery was legal again in all territories. Supporters of slavery rejoiced at this ruling. Northerners, however, were stunned. ✓

Key Events

1852	Harriet Beecher Stowe publishes *Uncle Tom's Cabin*.
1857	Supreme Court ruling in Dred Scott case declares Missouri Compromise unconstitutional.
1861	The Civil War begins with Confederate bombardment of Fort Sumter.

✓ Checkpoint

List three groups that joined the Republican Party.

____

____

____

✓ Checkpoint

Name the kind of right that protected slavery in all states, according to the Dred Scott decision.

____

Reading Strategy

Complete the following cause-and-effect pair:

Cause: ________________________

____

Effect: Lincoln ran for the Illinois Senate seat.

Vocabulary Builder

Entitle, in the underlined sentence, means "to give a right to something." What does this tell you about the way Lincoln felt about the rights of African Americans?

____

____

✓ Checkpoint

List two points Lincoln made in the debates about slavery and African Americans.

____

____

____

____

✓ Checkpoint

Name the part of the country in which John Brown was considered a hero.

____

The Lincoln-Douglas Debates

Abraham Lincoln, an Illinois attorney, was elected to the House as a Whig. He voted for the Wilmot Proviso. After one term, he returned to his Springfield law practice.

Lincoln's opposition to the Kansas-Nebraska Act brought him back into politics. In 1858, Lincoln ran for the Illinois Senate seat against Stephen Douglas, the author of the Kansas-Nebraska Act. Lincoln accepted the Republican nomination in 1858. Many southerners believed that Lincoln was an abolitionist. Lincoln then challenged Douglas to a series of public debates.

Douglas strongly defended popular sovereignty. He said people in each state could decide the slavery issue for themselves. He accused Lincoln of being an abolitionist who wanted equality for African Americans.

Lincoln took a stand against slavery. He stated that slavery was wrong and would die on its own. In the meantime, slavery had to be kept out of the West. While Lincoln did not promote equal rights for African Americans, he stated that there was no reason they should not be "entitled to all the rights" in the Declaration of Independence.

Douglas won the Senate election, but the debates made Lincoln nationally known. Two years later, the men would be rivals again for the presidency. ✓

John Brown's Raid

John Brown was an abolitionist. He had been driven out of Kansas after the Pottawatomie Massacre. He returned to New England and hatched a plot to raise an army to free people in the South who were enslaved. In 1859, Brown attacked Harpers Ferry, Virginia. He hoped to take control of the guns stored there by the U.S. Army. He would give the arms to enslaved African Americans and lead them in a revolt.

Brown and his men were captured. Brown was executed, but his cause was celebrated in the North. Many people there considered him a hero. More than ever, southerners thought that the North wanted to destroy their way of life. ✓

Check Your Progress

1. Why was the Republican Party formed?

____

____

2. Why did John Brown attack Harpers Ferry?

____

____

Section 3 Notetaking Study Guide

Question to Think About As you read Section 3 in your textbook and take notes, keep this section focus question in mind: **Why did the Lincoln-Douglas debates and John Brown's raid increase tensions between the North and South?**

▶ Use these charts to record key information from the section.

The Dred Scott Decision

- Dred Scott was an enslaved person who sued for his freedom.
- Supreme Court Chief Justice ___Roger B. Taney___ ruled that Scott had no right to sue in federal court because African Americans were not ____________.
  - Slaves were property, and the ____________ of their owners were protected in all states.
- This meant Congress did not have the power to prohibit slavery in any territory, and the ____________ was unconstitutional.
- Supporters of slavery ____________ at this ruling but northerners were ____________.

Abraham Lincoln-Stephen Douglas Debates

- Occurred during Illinois Senate race in the year ________.
- Lincoln's opposition to the ___Kansas-Nebraska Act___ led him to run as a Republican against Senator Stephen Douglas, the author of the ____________.
- The goal of the new Republican Party was to ____________
  ____________.

Douglas's stand on popular sovereignty:	Lincoln's stand on African Americans:	Lincoln's stand on slavery:	Lincoln's position on the Union:
Each state has the right to choose slavery if it pleases.	a. ____ b. ____	a. ____ b. ____ c. ____	____

John Brown's Raid

Who was John Brown?	His plan in 1859:	Southerners were worried because:
____	____	____

Refer to this page to answer the Chapter 14 Focus Question on page 228.

Key Events

1852 Harriet Beecher Stowe publishes *Uncle Tom's Cabin*.

1857 Supreme Court ruling in Dred Scott case declares Missouri Compromise unconstitutional.

1861 The Civil War begins with Confederate bombardment of Fort Sumter.

Section 4

The Coming of the Civil War

Section 4 Focus Question

Why did the election of Abraham Lincoln spark the secession of southern states? To begin answering this question,

- Learn how the nation divided.
- Find out how the Civil War began.

Section 4 Summary

By the time Lincoln became President, the division over slavery was too deep to heal. The Civil War began.

The Nation Divides

As the election of 1860 drew near, Americans everywhere felt a sense of crisis. The long debate over slavery had left the nation divided. Southern Democrats wanted the party to support slavery in the territories. But northerners refused to do so, and the party split in two.

Northern Democrats nominated Stephen Douglas, but southern Democrats picked Vice President John Breckinridge from Kentucky. Some southerners still hoped to heal the split between North and South. They formed the Constitutional Union Party and nominated John Bell of Tennessee. He promised to protect slavery *and* keep the nation together. The Republicans chose Abraham Lincoln as their candidate. His criticisms of slavery during his debates with Douglas made him popular in the North.

The election showed just how fragmented the nation had become. Lincoln won every free state. Breckinridge won every slaveholding state except four. Bell won Kentucky, Tennessee, and Virginia. Douglas won only Missouri. Lincoln carried only 40 percent of the popular vote. But he received enough electoral votes to win the presidency.

To many southerners, Lincoln's election meant that the South no longer had a voice in the national government. They believed that the President and Congress were set against their interests. South Carolina was the first southern state to secede from the Union. Six more states followed.

Not all southerners favored secession, but they were overwhelmed by those who did. When leaders from the seven seceding states met in Montgomery, Alabama, they formed a new nation they called the Confederate States of

Vocabulary Builder

Confederate comes from a Latin word meaning "to unite." The Confederate States of America, then, means what?

____

____

America. By the time Lincoln took office in March, the Confederate leaders had written a constitution. They named former Mississippi Senator Jefferson Davis as their president. ✓

The Civil War Begins

In Lincoln's inaugural address, he assured the seceding states that he meant them no harm. He stated that he had no plan to abolish slavery where it already existed. Lincoln's assurance of friendship was rejected. The seceding states took over post offices, forts, and other federal property within their borders.

One of those forts was Fort Sumter, on an island in the harbor of Charleston, South Carolina. The fort's commander would not surrender. South Carolina authorities decided to starve the fort's troops into surrender. They had been cut off from supplies since late December. They could not hold out much longer.

Lincoln did not want to give up the fort. But he feared that sending troops might cause other states to secede. He decided to send food to the fort. But he sent it on supply ships carrying no troops or guns. Confederate leaders decided to capture the fort. On April 12, they opened fire. The troops inside finally surrendered.

This attack marked the beginning of the American Civil War. A **civil war** is a war between opposing groups of citizens of the same country. Americans continue to debate whether it could have been avoided. But by 1861, the North and South were so bitterly opposed that most Americans saw war as inevitable. At stake was the nation's future. ✓

Check Your Progress

1. How did Lincoln win the presidential election without receiving a majority of the popular vote?

____

____

2. What is a civil war?

____

____

✓ Checkpoint

List the four presidential candidates in 1860.

____

____

____

____

Reading Strategy

Reread the underlined sentence. Circle the cause, and draw an arrow to the possible effect.

✓ Checkpoint

Name the event that marked the beginning of the American Civil War.

____

Section 4 Notetaking Study Guide

Question to Think About As you read Section 4 in your textbook and take notes, keep this question in mind: **Why did the election of Abraham Lincoln spark the secession of southern states?**

▶ Use this chart to record key information from the section. Some information has been filled in to get you started.

Chain of Events Leading to Civil War	
The Election of 1860	• There were four candidates in the election because proslavery and antislavery factions of the Democratic Party chose different candidates; some Southerners formed the Constitutional Union Party. • Northern Democratic candidate: ______ • Southern Democratic candidate: ______ • Constitutional Union candidate: ______ • Republican candidate: ______ • Although he did not receive a majority of the popular vote, Lincoln received enough ______ to win the election. • The election showed how ______ the nation was.
Secession	• After South Carolina learned that Lincoln had won the election, it responded by seceding from the Union. • Southern leaders who opposed secession: 1. ______ 2. ______ • First state to secede from the Union: ______ • Name of the new southern nation: ______ • President of the southern nation: ______ • Lincoln's message to seceding states: ______ • Response of seceding states to Lincoln's message: 1. ______ 2. ______
Fort Sumter	• Lincoln's plan to deal with the siege of Fort Sumter: ______ • South Carolina's response to Lincoln's plan: ______

Refer to this page to answer the Chapter 14 Focus Question on page 228.

Chapter 14 Assessment

Directions: Circle the letter of the correct answer.

1. The main question raised by the Southwest territory was
   - **A** should slavery be abolished?
   - **B** should the Missouri Compromise be used?
   - **C** would slavery be allowed in the West?

2. What was an effect of the Kansas-Nebraska Act?
   - **A** *Uncle Tom's Cabin* gained popularity.
   - **B** It undid the Missouri Compromise.
   - **C** The Free-Soil Party was formed.

3. The Republicans' first presidential candidate was
   - **A** Abraham Lincoln. **B** John C. Frémont. **C** Stephen Douglas.

4. Most southerners believed Lincoln
   - **A** would abolish slavery.
   - **B** would defend Fort Sumter.
   - **C** would accept secession.

Directions: Follow the steps to answer this question:

How did the issue of slavery bitterly divide the nation?

Step 1: Recall information: Describe each of the following pieces of legislation.

Legislation	What It Said
Wilmot Proviso	
Fugitive Slave Act of 1850	

Step 2: How did these acts affect the nation?

____

____

Step 3: Complete the topic sentence that follows. Then write two or three more sentences that support your topic sentence.

Legislation like the Wilmot Proviso and the Fugitive Slave Act of 1850 ________

____

____

____

____

Chapter 14 Notetaking Study Guide

Now you are ready to answer the Chapter 14 Focus Question: **How did the nation try but fail to deal with growing sectional differences?**

▶ Complete the following chart to help you answer this question. Use the notes that you took for each section.

<table>
<tr><th colspan="2">The Nation Divided</th></tr>
<tr><th colspan="2">Growing Tensions Over Slavery</th></tr>
<tr><td>The Wilmot Proviso
• Description: ______________
____
Its fate: Blocked in __________, slaveholding states saw it as an ___attack___ on slavery.</td><td>California
• Both sides realized its admission to the Union would upset the balance of free and slave states.
• The South threatens: __________</td></tr>
<tr><th colspan="2">Compromises Fail</th></tr>
<tr><td>To please the North, Compromise of 1850
• admitted California as a free state.
•</td><td>To please the South, Compromise of 1850
•
•</td></tr>
<tr><td colspan="2">The Kansas-Nebraska Act essentially undid ______________.</td></tr>
<tr><td colspan="2">Harriet Beecher Stowe published ___propaganda___ in 1852. A bestseller in the North, it was written off as ______________ in the South.</td></tr>
<tr><th colspan="2">The Crisis Deepens</th></tr>
<tr><td colspan="2">In the Dred Scott case, the Supreme Court declared ______________ unconstitutional and opened all territories ___to slavery___.</td></tr>
<tr><td colspan="2">• Abraham Lincoln ran against ______________ for the Illinois Senate in 1858.
• In their debates, Lincoln took a stand against slavery, saying African Americans should be entitled to the rights stated in ______________.
• After he was executed for raiding Harpers Ferry and trying to lead a slave revolt, ______________ was considered a hero by many northerners.</td></tr>
<tr><th colspan="2">The Coming of the Civil War</th></tr>
<tr><td>To many southerners, the election of Lincoln meant that the South no longer had a voice in ______________.</td><td>Lincoln's assurance of friendship in his inaugural address was ______________ by the seceding states.</td></tr>
<tr><td colspan="2">The Confederate attack on ______________ marked the beginning of the Civil War.</td></tr>
</table>

Refer to this page to answer the Unit 5 Focus Question on page 257.

Chapter 15

The Civil War (1861–1865)

What You Will Learn

People in the North and the South hoped for an early victory, but the Civil War went on for years. Hundreds of thousands of Americans were killed before the war ended.

Chapter 15 Focus Question

As you read this chapter, keep this question in mind: **How did people, places, and things affect the outcome of the Civil War?**

Section 1

The Call to Arms

Section 1 Focus Question

Why did each side in the Civil War think the war would be won easily? To begin answering this question,

- Discover how sides were taken in the war.
- Explore the strengths of the North and the South.
- Learn the two sides' strategies.
- Find out about the First Battle of Bull Run.
- Explore the details of a soldier's life.

Section 1 Summary

Both North and South prepared for a short war. They soon realized, however, they were in for a long struggle.

Taking Sides in the War

After Fort Sumter was captured, President Lincoln asked for troops to subdue the Confederacy. He also had to deal with the four **border states**—slave states that did not secede. These were Delaware, Kentucky, Missouri, and Maryland. If Maryland seceded, the U.S. capital would be in Confederate territory, so eastern Maryland was put under **martial law.** This is a type of rule in which the military is in charge and citizens' rights are suspended. ✓

North Against South

When the war began, people on both sides were confident of victory. To win the war, the North would have to invade the

Key Events

1861	Eleven states secede from the Union, creating the Confederacy.
1863	Lincoln delivers the Emancipation Proclamation.
1864	Grant invades South and lays siege to Petersburg.
1865	Lee's surrender at Appomattox brings Union victory.

✓ Checkpoint

List the four border states.

____

____

____

____

✓ Checkpoint

List three advantages the North had in the war.

______

______

______

✓ Checkpoint

Name the main goal of the Union blockade.

______

______

✓ Checkpoint

Name the Union army's goal in marching into Virginia.

______

✓ Checkpoint

List two dangers faced by soldiers in prison camps.

______

______

South. Southerners would be fighting on their own territory. They would also be led by some of the nation's best officers. The North also had some advantages. It had a larger population, more farmland, and more factories.

Two thirds of eligible northern and three fourths of eligible southern men served in the military. But the North had 3.5 million men in this age group, while the South had only 1 million. The North thus had a much larger army. ✓

The Two Sides Plan Strategies

To isolate the South, the North set up a naval **blockade**, a military action to prevent traffic to and from an area. The North also wanted to control the Mississippi River and capture Richmond, the Confederate capital. Southerners had a simple strategy: defend their land until northerners gave up. They would pay for the war with continued trade with Britain. They also hoped Britain would support the South. ✓

First Battle of Bull Run

Popular demand led Union General Irvin McDowell to march into Virginia before his troops were ready. The armies met in the First Battle of Bull Run on July 21, 1861. The South held firm while the Union troops panicked and ran. ✓

A Soldier's Life

Soldiers spent most of their time in camp, not fighting. They spent much of the time training. Camp conditions were often miserable. Soldiers often did not have clean water, which led to outbreaks of disease.

Conditions in prison camps were even worse. In over-crowded camps, prisoners died each day from starvation and exposure. ✓

Check Your Progress

1. What were the Union and Confederate war strategies?

______

______

______

2. What was the result of the First Battle of Bull Run?

______

______

Section 1 Notetaking Study Guide

Question to Think About As you read Section 1 in your textbook and take notes, keep this section focus question in mind: **Why did each side in the Civil War think the war would be won easily?**

▶ Use this chart to record key information from the section. Some information has been filled in to get you started.

The Call to Arms

The North

1. How did two border states bolster northern confidence? Kentucky and Delaware supported the Union.
2. What Virginia event helped the North?
3. What four things did the North have much more of than the South had?
4. What were three parts of the northern strategy?
5. Who was the Union general in the First Battle of Bull Run?

The South

1. How did two border states bolster southern confidence? Maryland and Missouri supported the South, and northern troops had to be used to subdue them.
2. Which generals left the U.S. Army to join the Confederate Army?
3. What were two advantages the South had?
4. What was the South's strategy? to defend its land until the North got tired of fighting, and seek aid from European nations
5. Why was the South hopeful that Britain would support it? because Britain was a major trading partner that needed southern cotton

Hardships of Both Sides

1. What effect did the war have on American families?
2. What were the camp conditions for soldiers? often miserable and diseased, lack of clean water
3. What were the conditions for prisoners of war in the North and the South?

Refer to this page to answer the Chapter 15 Focus Question on page 245.

Section 2

Early Years of the War

Key Events

1861	Eleven states secede from the Union, creating the Confederacy.
1863	Lincoln delivers the Emancipation Proclamation.
1864	Grant invades South and lays siege to Petersburg.
1865	Lee's surrender at Appomattox brings Union victory.

Section 2 Focus Question

How did each side in the war try to gain an advantage over the other? To begin answering this question,

- Learn about new technology of the war.
- Read about the war in the East.
- Find out about the war in the West.

Section 2 Summary

Unable to win a quick victory, Union forces met Confederate troops in a series of battles made more bloody by new technology.

New Technology in the War

New weapons made the Civil War more deadly than any previous war. Older muskets and cannons were not very accurate and took a long time to reload. Generals usually sent their troops charging at the enemy forces to overwhelm them. During the Civil War, improvements in gun technology made charging the enemy more dangerous. Rifles were more accurate and had a greater range than the old muskets. They could also be reloaded very quickly. Unfortunately, Civil War generals were slow to recognize the problem and change tactics. Thousands of soldiers died charging across open fields into rifle fire during the Civil War.

Ironclads, or warships covered with protective iron plates, were another new invention. Cannons could not sink these ships. The Confederacy used ironclads against the Union's naval blockade, and the Union used them to control the Mississippi River. ✓

✓ Checkpoint

List three way rifles were better than older guns.

____

____

____

The War in the East

After its defeat at Bull Run, the Union army got a new commander, General **George McClellan.** He was a very cautious leader who spent seven months training his army. In March 1862, he finally moved 100,000 soldiers southeast of Richmond. His forces could easily have defeated the 15,000 Confederate soldiers facing them, but McClellan stopped to ask for more troops. Almost a month passed before he started up again.

Reading Strategy

The underlined phrase describes General McClellan. Circle examples that support the idea that he was a very cautious general.

This gave the Confederates time to reinforce their army. They stopped McClellan outside Richmond on May 31, 1862, and forced him to retreat in late June. General Lee decided to invade the North, hoping a victory on Union soil would win European support for the South. He moved his army into western Maryland.

McClellan learned that Lee had divided his army and attacked the larger half at Antietam Creek on September 17, 1862. The Union suffered 12,000 **casualties,** a military term for persons killed, wounded, or missing in action. The South lost nearly 14,000 soldiers. Lee had to retreat to Virginia. McClellan could have followed Lee and attacked him again, but he did not. ✓

The War in the West

In the West, Union generals were not so cautious. General **Ulysses S. Grant** was the most successful of these generals. In February 1862, Grant captured Fort Henry, just south of the Kentucky-Tennessee border, and then Fort Donelson. These victories opened up the South to invasion from two different water routes. Grant continued on to Corinth, Mississippi, an important railroad center.

Before Grant reached Corinth, Confederate General Albert Sidney Johnston attacked. On April 6, 1862, he surprised Grant's forces at Shiloh, a costly battle for both sides. The Union army forced the Confederate army to withdraw. In this way, it won control of Corinth. The Union now controlled western Tennessee and part of the Mississippi River.

Two weeks after the Battle of Shiloh, Union commander David Farragut entered the Mississippi River from the Gulf of Mexico, capturing New Orleans. By the summer of 1862, the Union controlled almost all of the Mississippi River. ✓

Check Your Progress

1. What effect did rifles have at the beginning of the Civil War?

____

____

2. What two events show the differences between Grant's and McClellan's approaches after victory?

____

____

____

Vocabulary Builder

Fill in the first blank below with a synonym for *reinforce*. Fill in the second blank with an antonym for *reinforce*.

Union delays allowed Confederates to __________ their army near Richmond. McClellan thought that not having enough troops would __________ his army.

✓ Checkpoint

Name the error McClellan made before facing Lee's troops near Richmond.

____

____

✓ Checkpoint

List three key places Grant and his troops captured.

____

____

____

Section 2 Notetaking Study Guide

Question to Think About As you read Section 2 in your textbook and take notes, keep this section focus question in mind: **How did each side in the war try to gain an advantage over the other?**

▶ Use this chart to record key information from the section. Some information has been filled in to get you started.

Early Years of the War		
New Technology		
New ______ and ______ were more accurate and had greater range than previous weapons. Ironclads were a great improvement over older wooden warships.		
Event	**Military Leader**	**Outcome**
Forts Henry and Donelson, February 1862	Union: Grant	• The Union takes control of two water routes into the western Confederacy.
Use of ironclads		• ______ • ______
Battle of Shiloh, April 1862	Union: Grant Confederacy: A. S. Johnston	• ______
New Orleans, April 1862	Union:	• The North controls almost all of the Mississippi River.
Outside Richmond, Virginia, May and June 1862	Union:	• ______
Battle of Antietam, September 1862	Union: McClellan Confederacy:	• ______

Refer to this page to answer the Chapter 15 Focus Question on page 245.

Section 3

The Emancipation Proclamation

Section 3 Focus Question

What were the causes and effects of the Emancipation Proclamation? To begin answering this question,

- Find out about emancipating the enslaved.
- Learn how African Americans helped the Union.

Section 3 Summary

After the Emancipation Proclamation was issued, the Civil War became a struggle to end slavery as well as a battle to save the Union.

Emancipating the Enslaved

Northern abolitionists assumed that Lincoln's main war goal was to end slavery, because that was what they wanted most. But Lincoln's main goal was to preserve the Union. If that could be done without outlawing slavery, Lincoln would not outlaw slavery. He did not want to free the slaves at the outset of the war. This action might lead the border states to secede. Furthermore, he knew that most northerners did not care enough about slavery to fight a war to end it. Lincoln had no plan to **emancipate,** or free, enslaved people when the war began.

But by mid-1862, Lincoln realized slavery was important to the southern war effort. Slaves kept farms and factories producing when their owners were away fighting the war. Lincoln decided slavery had to end.

On January 1, 1863, Lincoln issued the Emancipation Proclamation. He had been ready to do this in the summer of 1862, but nervous Cabinet members had feared the people would not like it. They had urged him to wait until the Union army had more victories under its belt. Then northerners would still be willing to fight, even if they did not care about ending slavery.

The proclamation was not the sweeping rejection of slavery abolitionists wanted and expected. It freed slaves only in areas that were fighting the Union. Slaves in border states and the West were not affected, and southern states under Union control were not affected. In addition, the states that had seceded did not have to obey the law because

Key Events

1861	Eleven states secede from the Union, creating the Confederacy.
1863	Lincoln delivers the Emancipation Proclamation.
1864	Grant invades South and lays siege to Petersburg.
1865	Lee's surrender at Appomattox brings Union victory.

Reading Strategy

Reread the bracketed paragraph. Underline the sentences that explain why Lincoln did not focus on freeing the slaves at the start of the war.

Vocabulary Builder

Proclamation comes from a Latin word that means "to cry out." Use context clues from this section to write your own short definition of *proclamation*.

____

____

____

they did not recognize the U.S. government. In short, very few slaves were actually freed in 1863.

Some abolitionists protested that the proclamation did not go far enough; others accepted it as a start. Northern African Americans rejoiced. Southerners, on the other hand, claimed Lincoln was trying to start a slave rebellion. For the most part, Union soldiers supported the law because they knew it weakened the South's ability to fight. Whether people supported the proclamation or not, it changed the nature of the Civil War. It now became a war to end slavery.

Also, the proclamation ended southern hopes of British support. Britain would not back a government identified as fighting for slavery. ✓

✓ Checkpoint

Name Lincoln's main goal in fighting the Civil War.

____

____

African Americans Help the Union

African Americans in the North were not allowed to fight in the Union army at first. After the Emancipation Proclamation, it was easier for African Americans to enlist. By the end of the war, 189,000 had served in the army or navy. Over half were former slaves.

All African Americans fighting in the Civil War faced grave danger—slavery or death—if taken prisoner by southerners. They served in all-black regiments in the army and alongside whites in the navy. They were paid less than white soldiers. Still, they fought bravely, often deep in southern territory. African Americans also served as cooks, wagon drivers, and hospital aides.

Enslaved people in the South did what they could to hurt the Confederate war effort. Many slaves whose owners went away to war refused to work. ✓

✓ Checkpoint

List four ways that African Americans served in the Union army and navy.

____

____

____

____

Check Your Progress

1. How did the Emancipation Proclamation change the Civil War?

____

____

2. What were some of the extra risks African Americans took by serving in the Union army?

____

____

Section 3 Notetaking Study Guide

Question to Think About As you read Section 3 in your textbook and take notes, keep this section focus question in mind: **What were the causes and effects of the Emancipation Proclamation?**

▶ Use this chart to record key information from the section. Some information has been filled in to get you started.

The Emancipation Proclamation

Emancipating the Enslaved

Lincoln's main war goal was to ______preserve the Union______. He did not free slaves at the beginning of the war in order to avoid ______________________________.

Lincoln issued the ______________________ on January 1, 1863. However, it only freed slaves in ______________________, so very few enslaved people were immediately freed. Most Union soldiers supported the proclamation because it ______________________.

The ______Emancipation Proclamation______ caused the Civil War to become a ______________________. It also kept Britain from ______________________.

African Americans Help the Union

More than half of African American volunteers serving in the Union army were ______________________.

Confederates did not treat captured African American soldiers as ______________________; they faced ______________________.

Noncombat positions held by free African Americans in the Union army:

-
- wagon drivers
-

Ways enslaved African Americans hurt the Confederate war effort:

-
- refused to work

Refer to this page to answer the Chapter 15 Focus Question on page 245.

Section 4

The Civil War and American Life

Key Events

1861 Eleven states secede from the Union, creating the Confederacy.

1863 Lincoln delivers the Emancipation Proclamation.

1864 Grant invades South and lays siege to Petersburg.

1865 Lee's surrender at Appomattox brings Union victory.

Vocabulary Builder

The term *habeas corpus* comes from a Latin phrase meaning "to have the body." Why would the term *habeas corpus* be used to describe imprisonment?

____

____

____

✓ Checkpoint

Name three ways people disrupted the war effort.

____

____

____

Section 4 Focus Question

How did the war affect people and politics in the North and the South? To begin answering this question,

- Explore divisions over the war.
- Find out about the draft laws.
- Learn about the economic strains caused by the war.
- Explore the role of women in the Civil War.

Section 4 Summary

Neither the North nor the South presented a united front in the war. Divisions existed between states and social classes.

Divisions Over the War

The North may have faced the South in the war, but in reality, neither side was united in its opinions on the war and slavery. Not all northerners supported a war to end slavery. Many opposed the Emancipation Proclamation. Nor did they all want to restore the Union. Some northerners blamed Lincoln and the Republicans for forcing the South into a war. Northern Democrats who opposed the war were called Copperheads, after the poisonous snake. Copperheads criticized the war and called for peace with the Confederacy.

Not all southerners supported slavery or secession. Poor backcountry regions with few enslaved people were less supportive of the war. Strong support for states' rights created other divisions. For example, the governors of Georgia and North Carolina did not want the Confederate government to force men from their states to do military service.

People on both sides tried to disrupt the war effort. Some helped prisoners of war escape, encouraged soldiers to desert, or held peace protests. Both Abraham Lincoln and Jefferson Davis tried to keep order by suspending the right of **habeas corpus.** This is the constitutional protection against unlawful imprisonment. ✓

The Draft Laws

Because so many soldiers on both sides deserted, both sides established a **draft,** a system of required military service.

The southern draft began in 1862, and the northern draft in 1863. All eligible men were required to serve.

But there were ways around the draft. The wealthy could hire substitutes to serve for them. In the South, a man who held at least 20 enslaved people did not have to serve. In the North, anyone who paid $300 to the government was allowed to stay home. Only the well-off could afford this.

People on both sides objected that poor people were fighting the war. Draft riots broke out in many northern cities in 1863 as poor people destroyed draft offices and other property. ✓

✓ Checkpoint

List three ways someone could avoid the draft.

____

____

____

The War and Economic Strains

While northern industries thrived on war production, the government could not cover the costs of the war. Congress introduced the first **income tax** in August 1861. This is a tax on the money people receive. Congress also printed $400 million in paper money. Putting this additional money into circulation led to **inflation**, or a general rise in prices. In the North, prices went up 80 percent on average.

In the South, money was also scarce. This caused much worse inflation than in the North. On top of this, food production fell as Union armies invaded farmland. Shortages led to riots in the South. ✓

✓ Checkpoint

Name the effect the printing of paper money had in the North.

____

Women in the Civil War

Women in both the North and the South contributed to the war effort. Some disguised themselves as men and enlisted in the army. Some were spies. But most women took up the roles of absent male family members. Women ran businesses and farms, worked in factories, taught school, and served on the battlefield, in army camps, and in hospitals. Elizabeth Blackwell, the first American woman to earn a medical degree, trained nurses for the Union army. Clara Barton cared for Union soldiers on the battlefield and later founded the American Red Cross. ✓

✓ Checkpoint

Name two women who helped heal soldiers during the war.

____

____

Check Your Progress

1. Why would suspending habeas corpus keep the peace?

____

____

2. How did most women support the war effort?

____

____

Section 4 Notetaking Study Guide

Question to Think About As you read Section 4, keep this question in mind: **How did the war affect people and politics in the North and the South?**

► Use this chart to record key information from the section.

The Civil War's Effect on American Life	
Divisions	
In the North, some people: • • believed the South had the right to secede • Northern Democrats opposed to the war were called ______________.	Areas of South less supportive of war: • Opposition to the war was strongest in ___Georgia___ and ______. Divisions were also created by strong support for ______________.
Disruptions	
Ways people disrupted the war effort: • encouraged soldiers to desert • • • Both sides dealt with disruptions in some areas by ______________.	
Draft Laws	
• ______________ was a problem for both sides. Many soldiers left their units to ______________. • Each side established a ________, a system of required ______________. Anger at exceptions to this requirement caused ___riots___ in many places.	
Economic Strains	
Congress levied the first ___income tax___ to pay for the war. The Union printed large amounts of ______________, causing the cost of goods to ___increase___. Union blockades of the South caused ________ that made goods ________.	
Women in the Civil War	
Women's contributions to the war effort on both sides: • disguised themselves as men to join the army • • • Barriers for women fell, especially in the field of ___nursing___.	

Refer to this page to answer the Chapter 15 Focus Question on page 245.

Section 5
Decisive Battles

Section 5 Focus Question

How did Lincoln and his generals turn the tide of the war? To begin answering this question,

- Learn about the turning points of the war.
- Find out how the Union closed in on the Confederacy.
- Discover how peace came at last.

Key Events

1861	Eleven states secede from the Union, creating the Confederacy.
1863	Lincoln delivers the Emancipation Proclamation.
1864	Grant invades South and lays siege to Petersburg.
1865	Lee's surrender at Appomattox brings Union victory.

Section 5 Summary

Under Grant, the Union finally won the war. Both sides suffered terrible losses in the final two years of the war.

The Tide Turns

The Union army had a new commander in 1862, General Ambrose Burnside, who was determined to act more boldly than General McClellan had. Burnside marched toward Richmond in December 1862, to attack Confederate General Lee's army. But Burnside ordered traditional charges, sending thousands of men running into Confederate gunfire. The Union lost 13,000 men in the Battle of Fredericksburg. The South lost only 5,000.

Burnside was replaced by General Joseph Hooker, who also marched toward Richmond. In May 1863, his army was defeated at the Battle of Chancellorsville.

After these victories, Lee decided to invade the North once more. On July 1, 1863, Lee's army attacked a Union army led by General George Meade outside the town of Gettysburg, Pennsylvania. The battle lasted three days. The Union won the Battle of Gettysburg, but it lost 23,000 men. The South lost 28,000.

The day after the Battle of Gettysburg ended, the city of Vicksburg, Mississippi—one of the last cities on the river still in southern hands—fell to Union General Grant. Grant had laid **siege** to the city for two months. A siege is an attempt to capture a place by surrounding it with troops and cutting it off until its people surrender. Grant's victory and Lee's defeat were the turning points of the war, giving the Union the advantage. ✓

✓ Checkpoint

Name three Union commanders.

____

____

____

Closing In on the Confederacy

President Lincoln put Grant in charge of the Union army. Grant marched toward Richmond. He fought a series of battles in Virginia in the spring of 1864, losing about 55,000 men. The South lost 35,000. Grant knew his men could be replaced, however, while the South was running out of soldiers. Grant settled into a siege south of Richmond.

Meanwhile, in a push across the South, Union General **William Tecumseh Sherman** practiced **total war.** This is an all-out attack aimed at destroying not only an enemy's army, but also its resources and its people's will to fight. His troops burned buildings, seized crops and livestock, and pulled up railroad tracks. Sherman captured Atlanta in September 1864. He then marched toward the Atlantic Ocean. This "March to the Sea" devastated an area 60 miles wide.

Reading Strategy

Circle the term "total war," and reread its definition. Underline phrases that describe the effects of the total war that Sherman carried out.

Mark the Text

✓ Checkpoint

Name the general who practiced total war and led the Union "March to the Sea."

____

Steps to a Union Victory

1. Meade defeats Lee at Gettysburg.
2. Vicksburg falls to Grant.
3. Grant is made commander of the Union army.
4. Grant fights a series of battles that cost Lee soldiers who can't be replaced.
5. Sherman's "March to the Sea" devastates land, resources, and people.
6. Grant reinforces his army and captures Richmond.

✓

Peace at Last

By March 1865, Lee knew the war was lost. Lincoln knew it too and asked the North to welcome the South back to the Union. He said, "with malice toward none, [and] charity for all; . . . let us strive together . . . to bind up the nation's wounds." On April 2, Grant captured Richmond. After a brief retreat, Lee surrendered. On April 9, Grant and Lee signed a surrender agreement. The Union allowed Confederates to return home without punishment.

The war left its mark on the nation. Around 260,000 southerners and over 360,000 northerners had died, including 37,000 African Americans. ✓

Vocabulary Builder

Using everyday language, write your own version of Lincoln's statement "with malice toward none, and charity for all; ... let us strive together ... to bind up the nation's wounds."

____

____

____

✓ Checkpoint

How many soldiers died in the Civil War?

Northerners: ______________

Southerners: ______________

Check Your Progress

1. Why did Burnside suffer such high casualties?

____

____

2. What happened to Confederate soldiers under the terms of the surrender agreement?

____

____

Section 5 Notetaking Study Guide

Question to Think About As you read Section 5 in your textbook and take notes, keep this section focus question in mind: **How did Lincoln and his generals turn the tide of the war?**

▶ Use these charts to record key information from the section.

Turning the Tide of War

General	Battle(s)	Result
1. Ambrose Burnside	__________	__________
2. Joseph Hooker	__________	__________
3. George Meade	Gettysburg	Union victory that forced Lee out of the North and cost Lee nearly a third of his soldiers, who could not be replaced.
4. Ulysses Grant	Vicksburg	__________
5. Ulysses Grant	Petersburg	__________
6. __________	Atlanta	__________
7. William Sherman	"March to the Sea"	__________
8. __________	Richmond	Confederate national capital is taken and Lee is forced to surrender his army.

The End of the War

Lincoln looked ahead to victory in a speech in 1863 called __________.
The capture of Atlanta gave Lincoln a victory in the presidential election.
Number of Union soldiers killed in the Civil War: __________
Number of Confederate soldiers killed in the Civil War: __________
Key results of the Civil War:

-
- It put an end to slavery.

Refer to this page to answer the Chapter 15 Focus Question on page 245.

Chapter 15 Assessment

Directions: Circle the letter of the correct answer.

1. Which does ***not*** describe public reaction to the start of the Civil War?
- **A** Most believed the war would be short.
- **B** The border states all sided with the Confederacy.
- **C** Not everyone supported the war.

2. Where were slaves actually freed by the Emancipation Proclamation?
- **A** areas still fighting the Union
- **B** parts of the South already under Union control
- **C** the border states

3. What year was the turning point in the war, when the Union took the upper hand?
A 1862 **B** 1863 **C** 1864

Directions: Follow the steps to answer this question:

How did the North finally gain the upper hand in the Civil War?

Step 1: Recall information: In the chart, fill in the result of each Union victory.

Event	Result
Gettysburg	1.
Vicksburg	2.
Battles in northern Virginia	3.
Sherman's "March to the Sea"	4.

Step 2: How did these events affect the North and the South?

Events' Effects on North and South	
North	
South	

Step 3: Complete the topic sentence that follows. Then write two or three more sentences that support your topic sentence.

By 1864, the tide had turned in the North's favor because ________________

____

____

____

____

Chapter 15 Notetaking Study Guide

Now you are ready to answer the Chapter 15 Focus Question: **How did people, places, and things affect the outcome of the Civil War?**

▶ Complete the following chart to help you answer this question. Use the notes that you took for each section.

People, Places, and Things That Affected the Outcome of the Civil War

People	Places	Things
Lincoln: • His main goal was to restore the Union. • Effects of the Emancipation Proclamation: 1. 2.	Border states: The Union's control over these states helped the Union war effort.	Railroads: The North had many more miles of railroad tracks than the South.
	First Battle of Bull Run:	Manufacturing:
Ulysses S. Grant: • Attacks in the West led to Union control of the Mississippi. • He became the Union army's top commander.	Shiloh: helped the Union control western Tennessee	New rifles and cannons were deadlier than earlier weapons: • more accurate • had a longer range • Ironclads: • protected from cannon fire • used against Union naval blockade •
	Antietam:	
African Americans served in the army and navy as: • • • •	Gettysburg: important Union victory stopped the Confederate advance into northern territory	
	Vicksburg: led to	Economic challenges: In the North: • Congress levied the first income tax to pay war costs. • Increased currency supply led to inflation and higher prices. In the South: • •
How women participated: • • • •	Battles in northern Virginia/Petersburg: • • Lee's soldiers and supplies ran low.	

Refer to this page to answer the Unit 5 Focus Question on page 257.

Chapter 16

Reconstruction and the New South

(1863–1896)

What You Will Learn

As the Civil War ended, disagreements over Reconstruction led to conflict, and African Americans lost many of the rights they had gained.

Chapter 16 Focus Question

As you read through this chapter, keep this question in mind: **What were the short-term and long-term effects of the Civil War?**

Key Events

1863	President Lincoln proposes a mild Reconstruction plan.
1867	Radical Reconstruction begins.
1870	The 15th Amendment is ratified by the states.
1896	Supreme Court rules to permit separate facilities for blacks and whites.

Section 1

Rebuilding the Nation

Section 1 Focus Question

How did the government try to solve key problems facing the nation after the Civil War? To begin answering this question,

- Explore the challenges of preparing for reunion.
- Learn about the services of the Freedmen's Bureau.
- Find out about Abraham Lincoln's assassination and its aftermath.

Summary

As the Civil War ended, the country faced the challenge of reuniting the nation. With President Lincoln's assassination, hopes of a lenient Reconstruction policy faded away.

Preparing for Reunion

As the Civil War came to a close, much of the South lay in ruins, the homeless needed food and shelter, and many in the North and the South had hard feelings toward each other. The process of bringing the North and the South back together again, known as Reconstruction, would occupy the nation for years to come.

Abraham Lincoln and some fellow Republicans thought a lenient Reconstruction policy would strengthen the Republican Party in the South. The Radical Republicans

Reading Strategy

Reread the bracketed paragraph. There are several challenges stated. Underline the challenges and circle the nation's reaction.

Mark the Text

disagreed and claimed only a "hard," or strict, Reconstruction policy would keep the South from rising again.

Reconstruction	
Lenient	**Strict**
Lincoln: Ten Percent Plan - loyalty oath from 10% of state's voters needed to create new state government - abolition of slavery by state government - former Confederates who swear loyalty pardoned	**Radical Republicans: Wade-Davis Bill** - loyalty oath from 50% of state's voters needed before reentering Union - abolition of slavery by state government - Confederate volunteers barred from voting and holding office

✓

The Freedmen's Bureau

Congress created the Freedmen's Bureau to help **freedmen**, or enslaved people who had been freed by the war, as well as other war refugees. The bureau's first duty was to provide emergency relief to people displaced by war. It also set up schools for African Americans, helped freedmen find jobs, and settled disputes between blacks and whites. ✓

Lincoln Is Murdered

As the war drew to a close, President Lincoln hoped for a peaceful Reconstruction. But Lincoln had no chance to put his plans into practice. He was shot on April 14, 1865, by **John Wilkes Booth**, a Confederate sympathizer. Lincoln died hours later.

Lincoln's successor was Andrew Johnson from Tennessee. A southern Democrat who had remained loyal to the Union, Johnson had expressed bitterness toward the Confederates, and many expected him to take a hard line on Reconstruction. ✓

Check Your Progress

1. What was one major difference between the Ten Percent Plan and the Wade-Davis Bill?

____

____

2. How did the Freedmen's Bureau help former states?

____

____

Vocabulary Builder

If *strict* is the opposite of *lenient*, what do you think *lenient* means?

____

____

____

✓ Checkpoint

List two problems that faced the nation during Reconstruction.

____

____

✓ Checkpoint

What was the main purpose of the Freedmen's Bureau?

____

____

____

✓ Checkpoint

Name the person who succeeded Abraham Lincoln as President.

____

Section 1 Notetaking Study Guide

Question to Think About As you read Section 1 in your textbook and take notes, keep this section focus question in mind: **How did the government try to solve key problems facing the nation after the Civil War?**

▶ Use this chart to record key information from the section. Some of the information has been filled in to get you started.

Rebuilding a Nation	
Challenges that the Nation Faced	**Proposed Solutions**
1. How would Confederate states and sympathizers be treated?	a. Lincoln's Ten Percent Plan • loyalty oath: 10% of each state's voters must take oath • slavery: each state's government must abolish slavery • former Confederates: pardoned if signed loyalty oath
	b. The Wade-Davis Bill • loyalty oath: ________ • former Confederates: ________
2. What provisions would be made for those freed from slavery?	The Freedmen's Bureau a. main purpose: ________ b. examples: • ________ • ________ • ________

Murder of Abraham Lincoln		Vice President Becomes President	
When	April 14, 1865	Who	Andrew Johnson
How		From where	
By whom		Political party	
National reaction		Expected impact on Reconstruction	People thought he would take a strict approach.

Refer to this page to answer the Chapter 16 Focus Question on page 256.

Section 2

The Battle Over Reconstruction

Section 2 Focus Question

How did disagreements over Reconstruction lead to conflict in government and in the South? To begin to answer this question,

- Learn how conflict grew between the President and Congress during Reconstruction.
- Discover the significance of the Fourteenth Amendment.
- Understand the policies of Radical Reconstruction.

Key Events

1863	President Lincoln proposes a mild Reconstruction plan.
1867	Radical Reconstruction begins.
1870	The 15th Amendment is ratified by the states.
1896	Supreme Court rules to permit separate facilities for blacks and whites.

Summary

During the Johnson presidency, there were many clashes over Reconstruction. The Radical Republicans took hold of Congress, and African Americans made strides into politics for the first time.

A Growing Conflict

Like President Lincoln, **Andrew Johnson** wanted to restore the Union quickly and easily, so he proposed a lenient plan for Reconstruction. Johnson's plan required southern states to ratify the Thirteenth Amendment, which banned slavery and forced labor. His plan also offered amnesty to most Confederates and allowed southern states to form new governments and to elect representatives to Congress.

Congress rejected Johnson's plan and appointed a committee to form a new plan for the South. The committee learned that some southern states passed **black codes**, or laws to control African Americans. In response, Congress adopted a harder line against the South. The Radical Republicans took the hardest stance. They wanted to prevent former Confederates from regaining control of southern politics and to make sure freedmen had the right to vote. ✓

✓ Checkpoint

List two goals of the Radical Republicans.

____

____

____

____

The Fourteenth Amendment

The struggle for Reconstruction continued in 1866. Congress passed the Civil Rights Act of 1866. President Johnson vetoed it and another bill extending the Freedmen's Bureau. Congress then voted to overturn the vetoes.

Congress also drew up the Fourteenth Amendment. It declared all people born or naturalized in the United States to be citizens. It also barred the states from passing laws to take away a citizen's rights. The Fourteenth Amendment

✓ Checkpoint

Name two elements of the Fourteenth Amendment.

______

______

______

______

Reading Strategy

In the bracketed paragraph, underline the topic sentence. Circle the result of Congress's actions.

Mark the Text

Vocabulary Builder

Servitude comes from the Latin word *servus*, which means "slave." What do you think *servitude* means?

______

______

✓ Checkpoint

List two effects of the Reconstruction Act of 1867.

______

______

______

______

also stopped states from taking away property or liberty "without due process of law." Despite opposition from President Johnson, the amendment was ratified in 1868. ✓

Radical Reconstruction

Violence directed at African Americans pushed Congress to adopt a stricter form of Reconstruction called Radical Reconstruction. The Reconstruction Act of 1867 threw out the governments of all states that refused to adopt the Fourteenth Amendment, and it imposed military rule on these states. By June of 1868, all of these states had ratified the Fourteenth Amendment and written new constitutions.

For the first time, African Americans in the South played an important role in politics. Some other accomplishments of Radical Reconstruction included public schools in southern states, even taxation, and property rights for women.

Meanwhile, the Radical Republicans tried to remove President Johnson from office by **impeachment.** Impeachment means formally bringing charges against a public official. Johnson escaped removal by one vote in the Senate.

Ulysses S. Grant won the presidential election for the Republicans in 1868. Grant was a war hero and a moderate with support from many northern business owners. Radicals then began to lose their grip on the Republican Party.

Over Democratic opposition, Congress approved the Fifteenth Amendment in 1869. It barred all states from denying the right to vote "on account of race, color, or previous condition of servitude."

Angry at being shut out of power, some whites resorted to violence against African Americans and their white allies. The most feared secret society was the Ku Klux Klan. In the face of terrorism from the Klan and other groups, voting by African Americans declined. The stage was set for the end of Reconstruction. ✓

Check Your Progress

1. What were the main features of Andrew Johnson's plan for Reconstruction?

______

______

2. List three accomplishments of Reconstruction.

______

______

Section 2 Notetaking Study Guide

Question to Think About As you read Section 2 in your textbook and take notes, keep this section focus question in mind: **How did disagreements over Reconstruction lead to conflict in government and in the South?**

▶ Use these organizers to record key facts from the section. Some information has been filled in to get you started.

Reconstruction

Johnson's Plan

- issued broad amnesty to Confederates
- allowed southern states to organize new governments and ______

↓

Congress

- refused to seat southern representatives
- appointed committee to form a plan for the South
- passed ______ of 1866, which granted citizenship to African Americans and guaranteed their civil rights

↓

Johnson

- ______ the Civil Rights Act of 1866
- vetoed a bill that extended the life of ______

↓

Congress

- ______ Johnson's vetoes
- passed ______
  - All people born or naturalized in the United States are citizens.
  - All citizens are guaranteed rights.
  - Citizens are promised due process of law.
  - Denying the vote to any male citizen will reduce a state's representation in Congress.

Radical Reconstruction

Actions of the Radicals

- imposed military rule on states that rejected ______
- to join the Union, states had to:
  1. ______
  2. ______
- allowed ______ to register to vote
- opened public schools in the South
- built a strong following with three key groups:
  1. scalawags
  2. ______
  3. ______
- spread out taxes more evenly
- gave ______ to women
- impeached ______
- passed ______
  - states could not deny the right to vote based on ______, ______, or previous condition of servitude

Responses to Radicals

- General ______ elected President in 1868
- ______ terrorized African Americans and their white allies

Refer to this page to answer the Chapter 16 Focus Question on page 256.

Section 3

The End of Reconstruction

Key Events

1863	President Lincoln proposes a mild Reconstruction plan.
1867	Radical Reconstruction begins.
1870	The 15th Amendment is ratified by the states.
1896	Supreme Court rules to permit separate facilities for blacks and whites.

Section 3 Focus Question

What were the effects of Reconstruction? To begin to answer this question,

- Understand Reconstruction's conclusion.
- Learn how African Americans lost many rights with the end of Reconstruction.
- Discover how many freedmen and whites became locked in a cycle of poverty.
- Understand how the end of Reconstruction marked a time of industrial growth in the South.

Summary

Support for Radical Republicans declined. Reconstruction came to a halt with the election of 1876. Southern African Americans gradually lost their rights and fell into a cycle of poverty. Meanwhile, the South's economy flourished.

Reconstruction's Conclusion

Support for Radical Republicans declined as many northerners lost faith in the Republicans and their policies. The Grant presidency suffered from controversy and corruption. Meanwhile, many northerners and southerners alike were calling for the withdrawal of federal troops and amnesty for former Confederates. Beginning in 1869, Democrats regained power in the South state by state.

The end of Reconstruction was finalized with the election of Rutherford B. Hayes in 1876. Although he was a Republican, Hayes vowed to end Reconstruction. He removed all federal troops from the South. ✓

✓ Checkpoint

List two reasons that Reconstruction came to an end.

____

____

____

____

African Americans Lose Rights

With the end of Reconstruction, African Americans began losing their remaining political and civil rights in the South. Southern whites passed a number of laws to prevent blacks from voting without technically violating the Fifteenth Amendment. A **poll tax,** or a tax to be paid before voting, kept many blacks and poor whites from voting. Another law required voters to pass a **literacy test,** or a test to see if a person could read or write, before voting. Most southern blacks had not been educated and could not pass the test.

Reading Strategy

Reread the bracketed paragraph. Underline the main idea. Circle two measures taken by southerners that support the main idea.

Mark the Text

Southern states created laws, known as Jim Crow laws, requiring **segregation**, or enforced separation of races. In the *Plessy* v. *Ferguson* case, the Supreme Court ruled that law could require "separate" facilities as long as they were "equal." The "separate but equal" rule was in effect until the 1950s. However, the facilities for African Americans were rarely equal. ✓

A Cycle of Poverty

At emancipation, most freedmen were very poor. Most in rural areas became sharecroppers. A **sharecropper** is a farmer who rents land and pays a share of each year's crop as rent. Sharecroppers hoped to save money and eventually buy land of their own. But weather conditions and the ups and downs of crop prices often caused sharecroppers to lose money and become locked in a cycle of debt. They would then become poorer and poorer each year. Opportunities also dwindled for African Americans in southern cities and towns. Most urban African Americans had to take whatever menial jobs they could find. ✓

Industrial Growth

During Reconstruction, the South's economy slowly began to recover. By the 1880s, new industries appeared. Agriculture was the first industry to recover, with cotton production setting new records by 1875.

Industries that turn raw materials into finished products, such as the textile industry, came to play an important role in the South's economy. New mills and factories also grew to use the South's natural resources such as iron, timber, and oil. By 1900, the South was no longer dependent on "King Cotton." A "New South" based on manufacturing was emerging. ✓

Check Your Progress

1. How did the rights of African Americans change after the end of Radical Reconstruction?

____

____

____

2. What led to southern industrial growth in the 1880s?

____

____

✓ Checkpoint

Name two ways that southern African Americans were prevented from voting.

____

____

Vocabulary Builder

Use the context clues in the bracketed paragraph to write a definition of the word *menial*.

____

____

✓ Checkpoint

List two reasons that sharecropping was not profitable.

____

____

✓ Checkpoint

Name three industries that contributed to the South's economic recovery.

____

____

____

Section 3 Notetaking Study Guide

Question to Think About As you read Section 3 in your textbook and take notes, keep this section focus question in mind: **What were the effects of Reconstruction?**

▶ Use this organizer to record key information from the section. Some information has been filled in to get you started.

The End of Reconstruction

African Americans' Rights

- Southern states passed laws to prevent African Americans from voting. These included
  - literacy tests
  - ______________
  - grandfather clauses
- Southern states passed ________ laws, which enforced ______________.

Freedmen in Poverty

- Most rural freedmen became ______________.
  - rented land and paid with share of the crops
  - dependent on ______________ and crop prices
- Opportunities declined for urban African Americans.
  - skilled labor jobs closed to African Americans

Reconstruction's Conclusion

- Support for Radical Republicans declined.
- Many people called for:
  - withdrawal of troops from the South
  - ______________
- Disputed Election of 1876
  - ______________ vowed to end Reconstruction
  - all troops removed

Industrial Growth in the South

- Investors started or expanded industries to turn ______________ into ______________.
- The __________ industry came to play an important role in the southern economy.
- New mills and factories grew up to use the South's iron, ________, and ________.

Refer to this page to answer the Chapter 16 Focus Question on page 256.

Chapter 16 Assessment

Directions: Circle the letter of the correct answer.

1. The case of *Plessy* v. *Ferguson* provided the legal basis for
   A poll taxes. **B** sharecropping. **C** segregation.

2. Which of the following was a result of violence by the Ku Klux Klan?
   A Andrew Johnson was impeached.
   B Fewer African Americans voted.
   C The South became more industrialized.

3. Slavery and forced labor were banned by the
   A Emancipation Proclamation.
   B Freedmen's Bureau Bill.
   C Thirteenth Amendment.

4. The process of bringing the nation together after the Civil War became known as
   A Reconstruction. **B** Emancipation. **C** Radicalization.

Directions: Follow the steps to answer this question:

What do the differences between Johnson's plan and Radical Reconstruction say about their supporters' attitudes about the South?

Step 1: Recall information: List two policies of Johnson's plan. Then list two policies of Radical Reconstruction.

Johnson's Plan	Radical Reconstruction
• •	• •

Step 2: Compare these policies in the chart.

How Plans Differ	What Differences Suggest

Step 3: Complete the topic sentence that follows. Then write two or three more sentences that support your topic sentence.

The details of Johnson's plan and Radical Reconstruction reveal that

____

____

____

Chapter 16 Notetaking Study Guide

Now you are ready to answer the Chapter 16 Focus Question: **What were the short-term and long-term effects of the Civil War?**

► Complete the following chart to help you answer this question. Use the notes that you took for each section.

Rebuilding a Nation

As the Civil War ended, the nation faced enormous challenges:

- much of the South lay in ruins
-
-

Lincoln's Plan	Radical Republican Plan
Ten Percent Plan • • • 10% state voter loyalty oath	Wade-Davis Bill • • •

The first duty of the Freedmen's Bureau was to ______________________________.

Battle Over Reconstruction

Johnson's Plan	Radical Republican Goals
• Southern states ratify Thirteenth Amendment • •	• •

Radical Reconstruction

- ____________________ imposed military rule on all southern governments that did not ratify the Fourteenth Amendment.
- During Radical Reconstruction, ____________________ played an important role in politics, and women were given ____________________.
- Southern states opened ____________________ for the first time.
- Legislators spread ____taxes____ more evenly and made fairer ______________.

End of Reconstruction

As Radical Republican support died, many called for local self-government and ______________________________.

The end of Reconstruction was finalized with ____the election of Rutherford B. Hayes____.

Southern whites prevented African Americans from voting with techniques such as ______________ and ______________.	The South's economy began to ______________ due to industries based on ______________.

Refer to this page to answer the Unit 5 Focus Question on page 257.

Unit 5 Pulling It Together Activity

What You Have Learned

Chapter 14 With the addition of new western lands, tension over the slavery issue erupted into violence. The election of Abraham Lincoln led to seven states leaving the Union and marked the coming of the Civil War.

Chapter 15 People in the North and the South hoped for an early victory, but the Civil War went on for years. Hundreds of thousands of Americans were killed before the war ended.

Chapter 16 At the end of the Civil War, Americans faced the problem of how to reunite the nation. Disagreements over Reconstruction led to conflicts in government and in the South.

Think Like a Historian

Read the Unit 5 Focus Question: **How was the Civil War a political, economic, and social turning point?**

▶ Use the organizers on this page and the next to collect information to answer this question.

What political, economic, and social factors existed before the Civil War? Some of them are listed in this organizer. Review your section and chapter notes. Then complete the organizer.

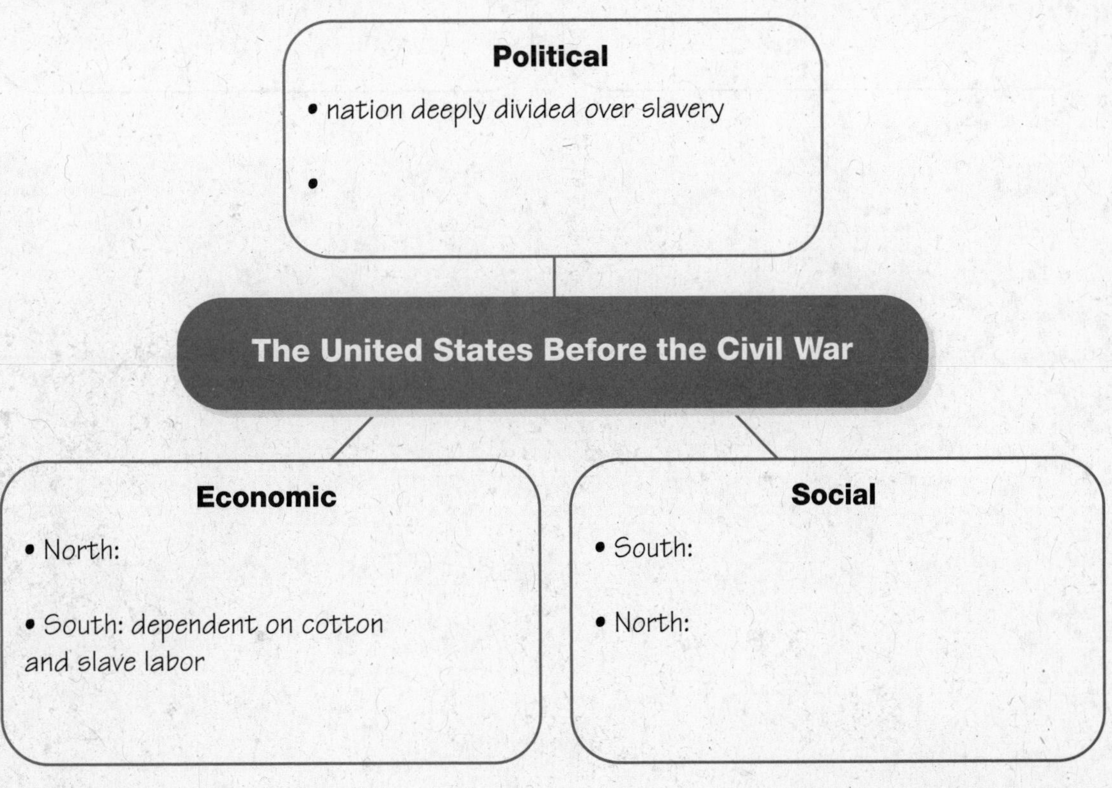

What political, economic, and social factors changed because of the Civil War? The organizer below gives you a part of the answer. Review your section and chapter notes. Then fill in the rest of the organizer.

The United States After the Civil War

Economic

- inflation
- The South was physically destroyed and economically ruined.
-
-

Political

- 13th Amendment abolished slavery.
-
-
- African Americans hold political office.
-

Social

- Many people killed or injured.
-
-
- Freedmen needed education and jobs.
-

Unit 6

An Age of Industry

What You Will Learn

Chapter 17 Miners and railroad builders led to settlement of the West. Native Americans struggled to maintain their way of life. Western farmers faced many challenges.

Chapter 18 In the late 1800s, industrialization caused urban growth, altered the way business was run, and prompted reforms in education. A new wave of immigration to America occurred during this period.

Chapter 19 During the late 1800s and early 1900s, Americans organized to press for reforms in many areas of government and society.

Focus Your Learning As you study this unit and take notes, you will find the information to answer the questions below. Answering the Chapter Focus Questions will help build your answer to the Unit Focus Question.

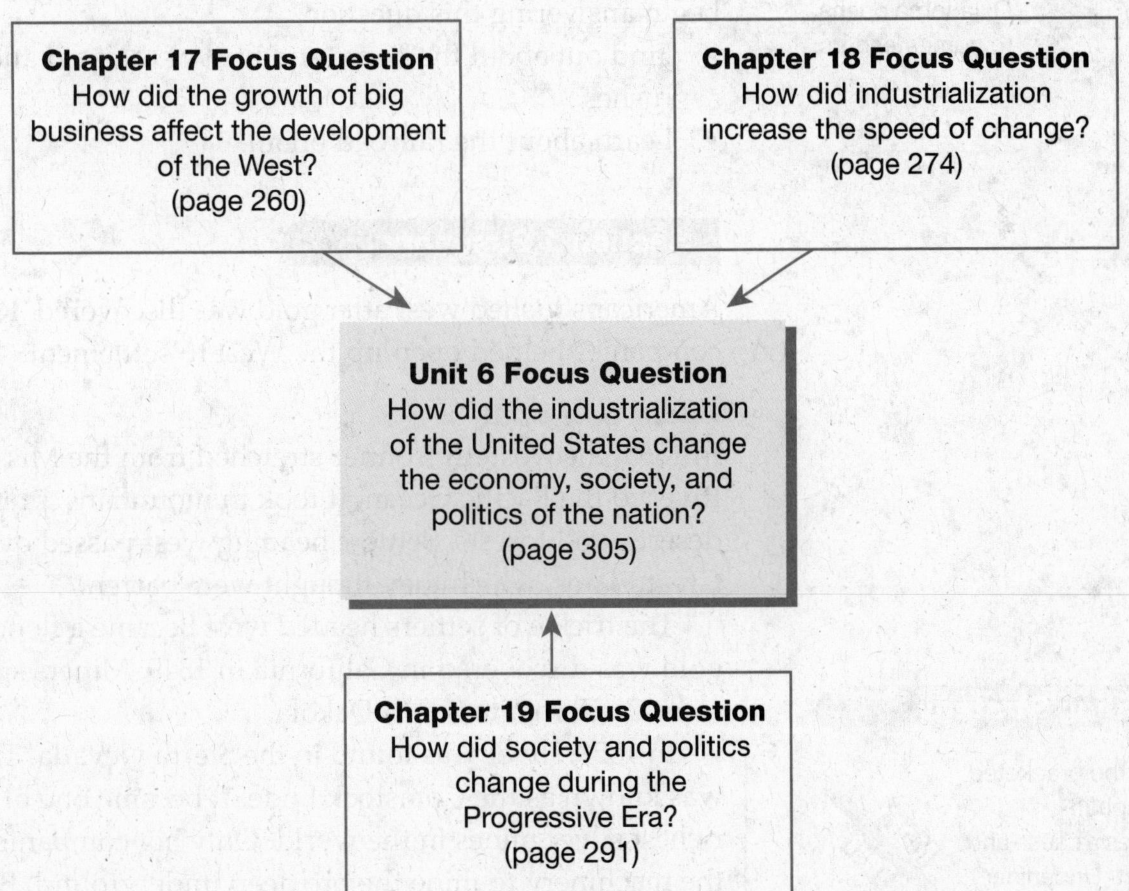

Chapter 17 Focus Question
How did the growth of big business affect the development of the West?
(page 260)
Chapter 18 Focus Question
How did industrialization increase the speed of change?
(page 274)
Unit 6 Focus Question
How did the industrialization of the United States change the economy, society, and politics of the nation?
(page 305)
Chapter 19 Focus Question
How did society and politics change during the Progressive Era?
(page 291)

Chapter 17

The West Transformed (1860–1896)

What You Will Learn

Miners and railroad builders led to settlement of the West. Native Americans struggled to maintain their way of life. Western farmers faced many challenges.

Key Events

- **1867** First cattle drive on Chisholm Trail.
- **1887** Dawes Act breaks up Native American tribal lands.
- **1889** Oklahoma opens to homesteaders.

Chapter 17 Focus Question

As you read this chapter, keep this question in mind: **How did the growth of big business affect the development of the West?**

Section 1

Mining and Railroads

Section 1 Focus Question

How did mining and railroads draw people to the West? To begin answering this question,

- Find out about the boom and bust of the gold and silver rushes.
- Learn about the railroad boom.

Section 1 Summary

Americans rushed west after gold was discovered. Railroad companies helped open up the West to settlement.

Boom and Bust

In 1865, the western frontier stretched from the Mississippi River to the Pacific Ocean. It took in mountains, prairies, deserts, and forests. Settlers heading west passed over the Great Plains, which they thought were barren.

The trickle of settlers headed west became a flood when gold was discovered in California in 1849. Miners spread from California to South Dakota.

[In 1859, silver was found in the Sierra Nevada. The find was known as the Comstock Lode. It became one of the richest silver mines in the world. Only big companies had the machinery to mine the ore deep underground. By the 1880s, western mining had become big business.]

Reading Strategy

Reread the bracketed paragraph. It describes a cause and an effect. Underline the cause and circle the effect.

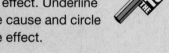

Miners lived in boomtowns that sprang up overnight. These towns supplied food, board, and tools to the miners at very high prices. Women could make a good living running boarding houses, restaurants, and laundries.

Almost half of miners were foreign-born. They often faced hostility and discrimination. For example, laws restricted Chinese miners to claims abandoned by others.

Mining towns sprouted so fast that law and order were hard to find. People formed groups of **vigilantes,** or self-appointed law keepers. Vigilantes hunted down people they considered criminals and punished people as they saw fit. As towns grew, residents created more lasting forms of government. But in some towns, when all the ore was taken, miners and merchants left. Boomtowns became ghost towns. ✓

The Railroad Boom

Before 1860, the railroads stopped at the Mississippi River. The federal government offered the railroad companies **subsidies,** or grants of land and money, to build out their lines. For every mile of track they laid, railroads got ten square miles of land next to the track. Very quickly, the railroads owned over 180 million acres.

In 1862, Leland Stanford and his partners won the right to build a railroad eastward from Sacramento. Their company was called the Central Pacific Railroad. It would build the western leg of the **transcontinental railroad,** a railroad line spanning the continent. At the same time, the Union Pacific Railroad was building west from Omaha. On May 10, 1869, the two lines met in Promontory, Utah.

With the transcontinental railroad in place, the west became a fixed part of the U.S. economy. Goods flowed between the East and the West. Railroad stops turned into towns that grew rapidly. Eight western territories became states in the period from 1864 to 1890. ✓

Check Your Progress

1. What was the Comstock Lode?

____

____

2. How did railroads come to own millions of acres of land?

____

____

Vocabulary Builder

Based on context clues in your reading, write your own definition of a boom.

____

✓ Checkpoint

List three kinds of businesses women ran in boomtowns.

____

____

____

✓ Checkpoint

Name the two companies that built the transcontinental railroad.

____

____

Section 1 Notetaking Study Guide

Question to Think About As you read Section 1 in your textbook and take notes, keep this section focus question in mind: **How did mining and railroads draw people to the West?**

▶ Use these charts to record key information from the section. Some information has been filled in to get you started.

The Discovery of Gold and Silver in the West

The Comstock Lode

- Discovered in Nevada in 1859
- Importance: one of the richest ______________
- Effect: made Nevada a center for ______________

The Boom Spreads

- Few prospectors became rich because ______________________________
- By the 1880s, western mining had become a big business.

Life in Mining Towns

- Tent cities arose around mining camps and quickly became boomtowns.
- Nearly half of all miners were ______________.
- Because mining towns grew so quickly, it was hard to find __________ and order. So, miners formed groups of ______________, who ______________ and ______________.
- As towns grew, local residents looked for more lasting forms of ______________.
- In some towns, all the ore was soon extracted, and mines ______________, miners ______________, businesses failed, and merchants ______________.

The Railroad Boom

Aid to Railroads

- To encourage the growth of railroads, the federal government offered railroads ______________, which are ______________________________.
- Railroads also received ______________.

The Transcontinental Railroad

- A transcontinental railroad is a railroad line that ______________.
- In 1862, the ______________ Railroad won the right to build a line eastward from ______________. The ______________ Railroad would build west from ______________.
- The railroads hired thousands of workers, including 10,000 ______________.
- On May 10, ______, the two lines met in ______________, ______.

Effects of the Railroads

- On population: ______________________________
- Political changes: Became states: Nevada, Colorado, ______________________________

Refer to this page to answer the Chapter 17 Focus Question on page 273.

Section 2

Native Americans Struggle to Survive

Section 2 Focus Question

What were the consequences of the conflict between the Native Americans and white settlers? To begin answering this question,

- Discover who the people of the Plains were.
- Find out about broken treaties.
- Learn about the last stand for Custer and the Sioux.
- Read about Native American efforts at resistance.
- Understand the failure of reform.

Section 2 Summary

The gold rush and the railroads meant disaster for Native Americans of the West.

People of the Plains

When Europeans arrived, they introduced horses and guns to Native Americans. This allowed Native Americans to kill more game and travel faster and farther. Many Plains nations followed the buffalo herds. As a result, buffalo hunting played a key role in people's survival.

In many Plains nations, women managed village life. Men were hunters and warriors. Often, they also led religious life. ✓

Broken Treaties

U.S. treaties promised to safeguard Native American lands. As miners and settlers pushed west, they broke the treaties. In 1851, Plains nations signed the Fort Laramie Treaty. This treaty said their lands would be protected by the United States if they stopped following the buffalo. However, the United States soon broke the treaty.

Native Americans protested. In response, Colonel John Chivington and 700 volunteers attacked a band of Cheyenne under army protection at Sand Creek in eastern Colorado in 1864. Chivington attacked anyway. The Sand Creek Massacre helped to ignite an era of war. ✓

Last Stand for Custer and the Sioux

Native Americans were moved to **reservations,** or land set aside for Native Americans to live on. But they were unable to thrive on them. The land they were given was so poor no

Key Events

1867	First cattle drive on Chisholm Trail.
1887	Dawes Act breaks up Native American tribal lands.
1889	Oklahoma opens to homesteaders.

✓ Checkpoint

Describe the roles of women and men in the Plains nations.

Women: ______________________

____

Men: ______________________

____

✓ Checkpoint

Name the event that helped start an era of war.

____

Reading Strategy

Why are the events described in this section called a "Last Stand"?

____

____

____

✓ Checkpoint

Name two Native American leaders who resisted the reservation system.

____

____

✓ Checkpoint

Name the event that marked the end of the Indian Wars.

____

✓ Checkpoint

List two things the Dawes Act did.

____

____

settlers would take it. If gold was discovered on reservation land, the land was taken away.

In June 1876, Colonel George Custer attacked the Sioux and Cheyennes. He was ordered to force them onto a reservation. Chiefs **Sitting Bull** and Crazy Horse won the Battle of Little Bighorn, but the Sioux and Cheyennes were rounded up a winter or two later by a larger force. ✓

Other Efforts at Resistance

Under pressure, many Nez Percés agreed to go to a reservation. When Chief Joseph and a large band of Nez Percés tried to flee to Canada, they were captured near the border.

The Navajos of the Southwest resisted removal to reservations until 1864. They were then sent to the Pecos River in Arizona. The Apaches, led by Geronimo, fought until 1886, when they, too, were sent to a reservation.

In the 1880s, soldiers worried about the Ghost Dance. Native Americans said the dance gave them visions of returning to their old ways. In 1890, Sitting Bull was killed by Native American police sent to stop the dance. Then soldiers surrounded a group of Sioux fleeing to avoid more violence. While the Sioux were giving up their guns, a shot was fired. The army opened fire. They killed nearly 200 Sioux men, women, and children. This Battle of Wounded Knee ended the Indian Wars. ✓

The Failure of Reform

Reformers criticized the government for its harsh treatment of Native American nations. Hoping to improve Native American life, Congress passed the Dawes Act in 1887. The act tried to end Native Americans' wandering and turn them into farmers. It set up schools and gave Native American men 160 acres to farm. But few Native Americans took to farming, and with the buffalo hunt gone, they remained poor. Many grew dependent on the government. ✓

Check Your Progress

1. How did the Plains nations' lives change after the arrival of Europeans?

____

____

2. Why did the Dawes Act fail?

____

____

Section 2 Notetaking Study Guide

Question to Think About As you read Section 2 in your textbook and take notes, keep this section focus question in mind: **What were the consequences of the conflict between the Native Americans and white settlers?**

▶ Use this chart to record key information from the section. Some information has been filled in to get you started.

Native Americans in the West

People of the Plains

- For centuries, the Plains people lived by gathering wild foods, hunting, and fishing.
- The Europeans introduced ________ and guns.
- Many Plains nations began ________________.

Broken Treaties

- As Americans moved west, U.S. officials tried to convince the Plains nations to stop ________________ and settle down permanently.
- In 1851, Native American leaders signed the ________________ Treaty. The U.S. government promised to ________________. However, after the treaty was signed, ________________.
- In 1864, ________________ attacked a band of ________ at ________. The ________ helped ignite an era of war.

Native American Resistance

- Southern Plains nations were moved to reservations in Oklahoma. Life there was a disaster because ________________.
- Many Sioux and Cheyennes gathered on land set aside for them in the ________ of South Dakota. When a ________________ in 1874 brought ________ to the area, ________ and ________ led attacks to keep whites out.
- In 1876, ________________ tried to force Native Americans onto a reservation. He and all his men died in the Battle of ________________.
- Chief Joseph led the ________________ to ________________. The U.S. Army ________________, and Chief Joseph ________________.
- After years of war, the ________________ were defeated in 1864 in Arizona, and they were forced to move to a spot near the Pecos River.
- In the late 1880s, Native Americans began performing the ________________, which they believed would make their ________________ and the ________________ return and would cause ________________ to leave the Plains. Soldiers saw this as the beginning of an ________________. In a struggle, ________________ was killed. Later, troops killed nearly ______ Sioux men, women, and children at the Battle of ________________.

Efforts at Reform

- Congress passed the ________ Act in 1887, which gave Native American men ________________ and set up ________________. The measure failed because few Native Americans ________________.

Refer to this page to answer the Chapter 17 Focus Question on page 273.

Section 3

The Cattle Kingdom

Key Events

1867	First cattle drive on Chisholm Trail.
1887	Dawes Act breaks up Native American tribal lands.
1889	Oklahoma opens to homesteaders.

Section 3 Focus Question

What factors led to boom and bust in the cattle industry? To begin answering this question,

- Find out about the rise of the cattle industry.
- Explore life on the trail.
- Learn about the Wild West.
- Learn why the cattle boom went bust.

Section 3 Summary

Cattle towns and the life of the cowhand on the trail helped create the Wild West. But the boom was short-lived.

The Rise of the Cattle Industry

Wild longhorn cattle had roamed the **open range,** or unfenced land, of Texas for years. When the railroads crossed the Plains in the 1860s, Texas ranchers saw a way to get these cattle to market. They could drive the cattle to the railroad towns. Then the cattle could be shipped by rail to slaughterhouses and then sold in the East. These **cattle drives** meant herding cattle over very long distances. Texan cattle were driven as far as 1,000 miles to rail lines. ✓

✓ Checkpoint

Name the type of cattle that roamed the open range of Texas.

____

Life on the Trail

Cowhands who drove the cattle had to have nerves of steel. They had to control thousands of cows and keep the herds together through rivers, fires, and droughts. Yet, for all their efforts, their pay was low.

The first cowhands were the Spanish and Mexican **vaqueros** (vah KAYR os). This Spanish word for cowhand or cowboy comes from *vaca*, the Spanish word for "cow." Americans learned how to ride, rope, and brand from vaqueros. They also adopted the vaqueros' spurs, chaps, and cowboy hats. About one third of all cowhands on the trails were Mexican. Many others were African American or white Civil War veterans. ✓

✓ Checkpoint

Name three types of clothes American cowhands borrowed from the vaqueros.

____

____

____

The Wild West

Railroad towns were the destination of the cattle drives. Abilene, Kansas, was the first big **cow town,** or settlement at the end of a cattle trail. It was founded in 1867 by Joseph

McCoy, where the Chisholm Trail met the Kansas Pacific Railroad.

Cow towns were filled with unruly men. Their saloons, gambling, dance halls, and gun fighting helped spread the myth of the Wild West.

William "Buffalo Bill" Cody promoted the Wild West with his traveling show. Starting in 1883, it had gun-slinging cowboys, Native Americans on horseback, and reenactments of battles from the Indian Wars. But the West was being transformed. Native Americans were on reservations, and big companies ran mining and ranching. Most cow towns were quieting down. ✓

Boom and Bust in the Cattle Kingdom

The cattle boom lasted from the 1860s to the 1880s. At its height, ranchers could buy a calf for $5 and sell a grown steer for $60. The region dominated by the cattle industry and its ranches, trails, and cow towns became known as the **cattle kingdom**.

By the 1880s, the open range had more cattle than the land could support. Two years of hard weather in 1886 and 1887 killed millions of cattle. A depression in eastern cities lowered demand for beef. Farmers fenced in the open range. As the railroads expanded, their lines moved closer to the ranches. The cattle drives ended, as did the cattle boom itself. ✓

Check Your Progress

1. Why did ranchers have to drive their cattle so far?

___

___

2. How was Buffalo Bill's Wild West show out of date?

___

___

___

___

Vocabulary Builder

Reread the bracketed paragraph. Based on context clues in the paragraph, write a definition of the word *transform*.

___

___

✓ Checkpoint

List three ways the West was changing in the 1880s.

___

___

___

___

___

✓ Checkpoint

List three factors that hurt the cattle industry.

___

___

___

Section 3 Notetaking Study Guide

Question to Think About As you read Section 3 in your textbook and take notes, keep this section focus question in mind: **What factors led to boom and bust in the cattle industry?**

► Use this chart to record key information from the section. Some information has been filled in to get you started.

The Cattle Kingdom: Causes and Effects	
Causes	**Effects**
1. Railroads swept across the Plains.	1. Texas ranchers began driving cattle to the rail lines to get cattle to distant markets. Cowhands followed trails such as the ________ Trail and the ____________ Trail.
2. Cowhands who drove cattle needed to unwind at the end of the trail, where they faced dangers such as panicked animals, stampedes, fires, and thieves.	2. __________ sprang up along rail lines. Here, ________, ________, hotels, and ________ served the cowhands.
3. Cowhands borrowed much from early ________ and Mexican ________.	3. Cowhands learned how to ride, rope, and brand. They wore spurs and chaps and broad-brimmed hats.
4. ______________ created a traveling Wild West show.	4. The myth of the Wild West as a place of violence, adventure, and endless opportunity was spread.
5. ________ rose. New breeds of cattle had fewer ________ and more meat than longhorns.	5. The cattle industry booms. Backers from the East and Europe invested ______ in ____________.
6. In the 1880s, there was bad weather, economic depression, lower demand for beef, and competition with sheep. Farmers fenced in the open range.	6. The cattle industry __________.
7. Railroads expanded and their lines moved closer to the ranches.	7. Large roundups and long __________ vanished. The cattle boom ____________.

Refer to this page to answer the Chapter 17 Focus Question on page 273.

Section 4
Farming in the West

Section 4 Focus Question

How did farmers on the Plains struggle to make a living? To begin answering this question,

- Find out about the impact of homesteading.
- Discover the hardships of life on the Plains.
- Learn about the last rush for land.
- Read about how farmers organized politically.

Section 4 Summary

Homesteading boomed in the West after the Civil War, but times were not easy for farmers.

Homesteading

The Homestead Act of 1862 offered 160 acres on the Great Plains to those who agreed to live on and farm the land for five years. This created thousands of **homesteaders,** settlers who acquired free land offered by the government.

But only one third of homesteaders on the Great Plains lasted the required five years. On the dry Plains, 160 acres was not enough land to support a family.

The railroads also promoted farming. They gave away some of the 180 million acres that they got from the government. More farms meant more shipping for the railroads. ✓

A Hard Life on the Plains

Life on the Great Plains was not easy. Water was scarce, and crops were hard to grow. The soil of the Plains was fertile, but the tough **sod,** a thick layer of roots of grasses tangled with soil, had to be removed. This was backbreaking work.

New farming methods helped Plains farmers. They used steel plows, which were stronger and lighter than other plows. New drills allowed them to bury seeds deep down where there was moisture. They used reapers to harvest crops and threshers to beat off the hard coverings of the grains. Farmers used windmills to pump water from deep underground. They used barbed wire, a new type of twisted wire, to keep cattle from trampling their crops.

By the 1880s, 70,000 African Americans had settled in Kansas. They were known as Exodusters because they felt like the Jews who fled slavery in Egypt, a biblical story told in the book of Exodus. ✓

Key Events

1867	First cattle drive on Chisholm Trail.
1887	Dawes Act breaks up Native American tribal lands.
1889	Oklahoma opens to homesteaders.

Vocabulary Builder

Based on context clues, define *homestead*.

____

____

✓ Checkpoint

Name two conditions that homesteaders had to live up to.

____

____

✓ Checkpoint

List two things that made farming the Plains so difficult.

____

____

✓ Checkpoint

How much land was up for grabs in the Oklahoma Land Rush?

____

Reading Strategy

Reread the bracketed paragraphs. Then, using one of the blank pages at the back of this book, create a timeline of the events described in the paragraphs.

✓ Checkpoint

Name two things that Populists wanted.

____

____

____

____

A Last Rush for Land

By the 1880s, few areas on the Plains remained free to settlers. In 1889, nearly 100,000 people gathered at a line in Oklahoma. They were ready to enter what was once Indian Territory to claim some of the two million acres being offered by the government. A few people, known as **sooners,** had already sneaked onto the land. They came out of hiding to claim the best land. By 1890, the free land had run out. ✓

Farmers Organize

As in mining and ranching, farming had a few big organizations that did well. But small farmers scraped by. Overproduction drove down prices. Small farmers borrowed money to expand or to buy new equipment. When prices for their crops fell, the farmers could not pay off the loans, and they lost their land.

Many farmers formed **granges,** groups that met for lectures, sewing bees, and other events. In 1867, local granges joined to form the National Grange. In the 1870s and 1880s, Grangers demanded the low rates from railroads and grain warehouses that big farmers got. In time, **farm cooperatives** were formed. These were groups of farmers who pooled their money to make large purchases of tools, seed, and other supplies at a discount.

In 1892, farmers joined labor unions to form the Populist Party. They pushed for social reforms like public ownership of railroads and warehouses to control rates. They called for both an income tax to replace property taxes and an eight-hour workday. Populists also wanted the government to back the dollar with silver as well as gold. They hoped this would bring on **inflation,** or a general rise in prices. This would raise crop prices. But after the presidential election of 1896, which Populist candidate **William Jennings Bryan** lost, Populism faded away. ✓

Check Your Progress

1. Why did railroads support farming on the Plains?

____

____

2. What did the National Grange demand?

____

____

Section 4 Notetaking Study Guide

Question to Think About As you read Section 4 in your textbook and take notes, keep this question in mind: **How did farmers on the Plains struggle to make a living?**

► Use these charts to record key information from the section.

Farming in the West	
Homestead Act of 1862	• Offered 160 acres to anyone who resided on the land for five years • Thousands became homesteaders, which were ________________.
Railroads	• To the railroads, more farms meant more ________. • So railroads gave away ________________.
New Farming Methods	• Steel plows that could break through sod • ________ to bury seed • ________ to harvest crops • ________ to beat off the hard coverings of grain
Farm Families	• Role of men: ________________ • Role of children: tended animals and did chores • Role of women: ________________
Exodusters	• Thousands of ________ came to the Plains. • They were known as Exodusters because ________________.
Spanish-speaking Farmers	• Many had been there since before ________. • Mexican immigrants arrived with the coming of the railroads. • Large landowners were known as ________.
Sooners	• The federal government opened up what was once ________ in Oklahoma to homesteaders in April 1889. • A few people known as sooners ________________.
Farmers Organize	• Granges were groups of farmers who met for lectures, sewing bees, and other events. In 1867, local granges ________________. • Grangers demanded ________________. • Farm cooperatives were groups of farmers who pooled their money to ________________. • Unhappy farmers joined with ________ to form the Populist Party, which pushed for ________.

Refer to this page to answer the Chapter 17 Focus Question on page 273.

Chapter 17 Assessment

Directions: Circle the letter of the correct answer.

1. Which of the following was true of miners in the late 1800s?
   - **A** Most worked for big mining companies.
   - **B** Most received government subsidies.
   - **C** Almost half were foreign-born.

2. What was the goal of the Dawes Act?
   - **A** to protect Native Americans' way of life
   - **B** to turn Native Americans into farmers
   - **C** to prohibit settlers from trespassing on Native American lands

3. Why did Populist farmers want inflation?
   - **A** to raise crop prices
   - **B** to lower equipment prices
   - **C** to hurt big farmers

Directions: Follow the steps to answer this question:

What was the main issue that led to the outbreak of the Indian Wars?

Step 1: Recall information: In the chart, recall the issues behind the events leading up to the Indian Wars.

Fort Laramie Treaty	Sand Creek Massacre
• Provision for Native Americans: ______	• Events leading up to massacre: ______
• In return, the U.S. wanted: ______	• What happened: ______
• What happened: ______	• Result: ______

Step 2: Decide: What was the basic conflict between the U.S. government and Native Americans?______

Step 3: Complete the topic sentence that follows. Then write two or three more sentences that support your topic sentence.

The Indian Wars were caused by a conflict over ______

______

______

______

______

Chapter 17 Notetaking Study Guide

Now you are ready to answer the Chapter 17 Focus Question: **How did the growth of big business affect the development of the West?**

▶ Complete the following organizers to help you answer this question. Use the notes that you took for each section.

Mining and Railroads	Effects on Native Americans
Gold and silver rushes • People raced to the West to mine. • By the 1880s, big businesses had taken over mining.	**Gold discoveries** • Led miners onto traditional Native American lands • Conflict erupted
Railroads laid tracks to mines and boomtowns. Effects: • • Western population grew rapidly.	**Railroad expansion and the buffalo** Railroads had buffalo killed to • feed their crews • Effect:
	Westward settlement • Native Americans were forced onto ______________, or areas set aside for them to live.

The Influence of Big Business on the West

Cattle Kingdoms	Farming in the West
Effect of railroads: •	**Railroads promoted farming by** •
Reasons the cattle industry boomed: • • new breeds had fewer diseases and more meat	**Big farmers versus small farmers:** • Big farms tended to do well, while many small farms struggled.
Reasons the cattle boom ended: • • decline in demand •	**Farm groups pushed for silver standard** • Why farmers wanted this: • Why banks and businesses opposed: They argued that inflation would ruin the economy • Result:
Reason cattle drives ended: •	

Refer to this page to answer the Unit 6 Focus Question on page 305.

Chapter 18

Industry and Urban Growth (1865–1915)

What You Will Learn

In the late 1800s, industrialization caused urban growth, altered the way business was run, and prompted reforms in education. A new wave of immigration into America occurred during this period.

Chapter 18 Focus Question

As you read through this chapter, keep this question in mind: **How did industrialization increase the speed of change?**

Key Events

1869 Knights of Labor, a major labor union, is formed.

1889 Jane Addams founds Hull House to help city poor.

1892 Ellis Island opens as major entry station for European immigrants.

1913 Henry Ford sets up assembly line to mass produce automobiles.

Section 1

A New Industrial Revolution

Section 1 Focus Question

What conditions spurred the growth of industry? To begin answering this question,

- Find out why industry boomed.
- Learn about inventors and inventions.
- Explore a transportation revolution of the late 1800s.

Section 1 Summary

After the Civil War, the United States experienced rapid industrial growth. Westward expansion, government policy, and new technology helped the nation become a leading industrial power.

Why Industry Boomed

As the nation expanded westward, industry grew. Government policy also helped to spur growth. It gave land grants to railroads and businesses and placed high tariffs on imports. Tariffs helped American industry by raising the price of foreign goods.

New technology also spurred industrial growth. Inventors developed the Bessemer process, a method to make stronger steel at a low cost. Steel replaced iron as the basic building material of cities and industry. The oil industry

Reading Strategy

The pronoun "It" in the underlined sentence is a substitute for a word in the previous sentence. Circle that word.

developed refining methods to turn crude oil into lubricants for machines and to power engines and cars. "Black gold," as oil was called, later became gasoline for automobiles.

Railroads fueled the new Industrial Revolution. Trains transported goods and people to the West and raw materials to the East. Big rail lines sought ways to limit competition and keep prices high. Many small farmers became angry over high rail rates to transport their goods. Many joined the Granger and Populist movements. ✓

✓ Checkpoint

List three factors that influenced industrial growth.

____

____

____

Inventors and Inventions

In the late 1800s, Americans created many new inventions. **Thomas Edison**'s "invention factory" produced the light bulb and motion picture camera. In 1882, Edison opened the nation's first electrical power plant. The plants provided power to homes, streetcars, and factories.

Inventions that improved communication prompted growth in business. Telegraphs transmitted messages from Europe more quickly. **Alexander Graham Bell**'s invention of the telephone in 1876 helped speed up the pace of business. The typewriter made office work faster and cheaper. African Americans such as Jan Matzeliger also contributed to the flood of inventions. ✓

✓ Checkpoint

Name three inventions that helped businesses to grow.

____

____

____

A Transportation Revolution

Technology revolutionized transportation. The invention of the automobile ushered in an era of faster and faster transportation. **Henry Ford** made the automobile affordable for millions. Ford perfected a system to mass produce cars. Ford introduced the **assembly line,** a manufacturing method in which a product is put together as it moves along a belt.

In 1903, **Wilbur and Orville Wright**'s gas-powered airplane took flight. Airplanes began to alter the world by making travel quicker and easier. ✓

Vocabulary Builder

Reread the underlined sentence.

Think about how airplanes affected travel. Based on this information, what do you think the word *alter* means?

____

✓ Checkpoint

List two inventions that made transportation faster.

____

____

Check Your Progress

1. How did government policy influence industrial growth?

____

____

____

2. How did Henry Ford make the automobile affordable to millions of people?

____

____

Section 1 Notetaking Study Guide

Question to Think About As you read Section 1 in your textbook, keep this question in mind: **What conditions spurred the growth of industry?**

▶ Use these charts to record key information from the section.

Factors Leading to the Industrial Boom

Factor	Effect
Westward expansion	• provided access to vast deposits of coal, iron, lead, and copper • Pacific Northwest furnished ______ for ______
Government policies	• Congress gave ______ and other ______ to ______ and other ______. • kept ______ high, which made ______ expensive
Railroads	• Trains carried ______ and ______ west.

Inventions That Spurred Industry, Business, and Transportation

Invention	Impact
Bessemer process	• allowed people to make stronger steel at a lower cost • Steel replaced iron as the basic building material of industry.
Oil refining methods	Crude oil refined into ______ and ______
Electrical power plant	• ______ opened first one in ______ in ______ • allowed people to use inventions such as the ______, the phonograph, and the ______
Telegraph	• improved communication for ______
Underwater telegraph	• sped up communications with ______
Telephone	• invented by ______ in ______ • device that carried ______
Typewriter	• made office work ______ and ______
Automobile	• ushered in an era of ______ and ______ transportation
Assembly line	• introduced by ______ in ______ to mass produce ______
Gas-powered airplane	• first tested by ______ in ______ • later used by the ______ during ______

Refer to this page to answer the Chapter 18 Focus Question on page 290.

Section 2

Big Business and Organized Labor

Section 2 Focus Question

How did big business change the workplace and give rise to labor unions? To begin answering this question,

- Learn about new ways of doing business.
- Find out about growth in "big business."
- Explore changes in the workplace.
- Learn how workers organized.

Section 2 Summary

Without government regulation, big business grew. A few owners accumulated vast wealth, while factory workers tried to form unions to improve poor working conditions.

New Ways of Doing Business

Entrepreneurs (ahn treh preh NYOORZ) led business expansion. An **entrepreneur** is someone who sets up a business to make a profit. These entrepreneurs needed capital, or money, to expand. Many businesses became **corporations**, or businesses owned by many investors. Corporations raise large amounts of capital by selling stock, or shares in a business. Stockholders receive a share of profits and pick directors to run the company.

Banks lent money to corporations and industries to spur faster growth. One banker, J. P. Morgan, became the most powerful force in the American economy by gaining control of key industries such as railroads and steel mills. ✓

Growth of Big Business

Congress seldom made laws to regulate business practices. This encouraged the growth of what came to be known as "big business." Entrepreneurs formed giant corporations and monopolies. A **monopoly** is a company that controls all or nearly all business in a particular industry.

Andrew Carnegie's companies controlled every step of making steel. **John D. Rockefeller** ended competition in the oil industry by creating the Standard Oil Trust. A **trust** is a group of corporations run by a single board of directors. Trusts dominated many of the nation's industries.

Some Americans criticized big business practices as threats to free enterprise. **Free enterprise** is the system in

Key Events

1869	Knights of Labor, a major labor union, is formed.
1889	Jane Addams founds Hull House to help city poor.
1892	Ellis Island opens as major entry station for European immigrants.
1913	Henry Ford sets up assembly line to mass produce automobiles.

✓ Checkpoint

Name two industries that J. P. Morgan controlled.

____

____

Vocabulary Builder

Mono comes from the Greek word meaning "one." *Poly* comes from the Greek word meaning "many." What do you think the word *monopoly* means?

____

____

____

✓ Checkpoint

Name the people who held monopolies in the steel and oil industries.

____

____

✓ Checkpoint

List three reasons used to justify the poor conditions of factories.

____

____

____

Reading Strategy

Compare the Knights of Labor and the American Federation of Labor. What was one major difference between the two unions?

____

____

____

____

✓ Checkpoint

Name three issues that workers organized to change.

____

____

____

which privately owned businesses compete freely. Others praised big business for expanding the economy, creating jobs, and lowering prices. Some used a philosophy called Social Darwinism to support their views. Social Darwinists applied the idea of "survival of the fittest" to entrepreneurs who beat out competition. ✓

Changes in the Workplace

Industry attracted millions of workers who toiled in dangerous conditions for low wages. Even young children worked in hazardous jobs. But factory owners tried to justify the harsh conditions. They said that the conditions were necessary to cut costs, to increase production, and to ensure survival of the business. ✓

Workers Organize

Workers attempted to organize against unsafe working conditions, low wages, and long hours. In 1869, workers formed a union called the Knights of Labor. The union was for skilled and unskilled workers.

However, violent labor disputes undercut the union's successes. The American Federation of Labor became the country's leading union. It admitted only skilled workers, who were difficult to replace. This union relied on collective bargaining to achieve its goals. In **collective bargaining,** unions negotiate with management for workers as a group.

In 1893, the nation plunged into an economic depression. Many business owners fired workers and cut wages. A wave of violent strikes swept the country. Federal troops were used to end some strikes, which often resulted in more violence. Most Americans sided with owners because they saw unions as radical and violent. ✓

Check Your Progress

1. What were the two differing views of big business?

____

____

____

____

2. Why did most Americans not favor unions?

____

____

Section 2 Notetaking Study Guide

Question to Think About As you read Section 2 in your textbook and take notes, keep this question in mind: **How did big business change the workplace and give rise to labor unions?**

► Use these organizers to record key information from the section.

Big Business	
Corporation	• businesses owned by investors • raised capital by ______ • run by a board of directors • limited risk for ______ • shareholders received ______
Trust	• consisted of a group of corporations run by a ______ • by 1900, dominated ______ • used ______ to justify efforts to limit competition
Monopoly	a company that controls ______
Banks	• huge loans helped industry ______ • J. Pierpont Morgan: most powerful force in ______
Andrew Carnegie	• controlled steel industry • according to Carnegie's Gospel of Wealth philosophy, ______ ______
John D. Rockefeller	• used profits from investing in an oil refinery to buy other oil companies • formed ______, which ______ ______
Debate over big business	Arguments for: • lowered the price of goods • ______ • ______ Arguments against: • ______ • ______

Workplace Conditions and Labor Unions	
Workplace	**Labor Unions**
Hours: long Pay: ______ Conditions: ______ Employers not required to ______ ______ for workplace injuries	Goals: safer working conditions, ______, ______ Early unions: • ______ • ______

Refer to this page to answer the Chapter 18 Focus Question on page 290.

Section 3

Cities Grow and Change

Key Events

1869 Knights of Labor, a major labor union, is formed.

1889 Jane Addams founds Hull House to help city poor.

1892 Ellis Island opens as major entry station for European immigrants.

1913 Henry Ford sets up assembly line to mass produce automobiles.

Section 3 Focus Question

What were the causes and effects of the rapid growth of cities? To begin answering this question,

- Learn about the rapid growth of cities.
- Find out about problems of urban life.
- Explore the excitement of city life.

Section 3 Summary

The Industrial Revolution reshaped American cities. Millions of people moved to cities in search of jobs. Cities and reformers battled the problems caused by such rapid growth. City life also offered excitement.

Rapid Growth of Cities

The rate of urbanization during the late 1800s was astonishing. **Urbanization** is the rapid growth of city populations. Cities attracted industry, and industry attracted people.

Cities near waterways drew industry because they provided easy transport for goods. Technology such as electricity and steel also helped cities grow. Growing urban populations and public transportation gave rise to suburbs. **Suburbs** are living areas on the outskirts of a city. Cities began to expand upward as well as outward. By 1900, skyscrapers towered over city streets.

Living patterns in cities also changed. The poor crowded into the old downtown sections of cities. The middle class lived in outlying row houses or apartments. The wealthy built fine homes on the cities' outskirts. ✓

Problems of Urban Life

Rapid urbanization created many problems. Fire was a constant threat to tightly packed neighborhoods. In downtown slums, poor people lived in crowded tenements. **Tenements** are buildings divided into many tiny apartments. As many as 10 people might live in a single room. Sanitation was perhaps the worst problem. Streets in slums were strewn with garbage, and outbreaks of cholera and other diseases were common. Babies ran the greatest risk. In one Chicago slum, half of all babies died before the age of one.

✓ Checkpoint

List three effects of urbanization.

____

____

____

Reading Strategy

Reread the bracketed paragraphs on this page and on page 281. Underline two problems of city life. Draw arrows to their corresponding solutions.

Mark the Text

To improve urban life, cities set up police, fire, and sanitation departments. They paved streets and installed street lights. Public health officials waged war on disease. Religious groups served the poor. Some set up hospitals and clinics, or places where people could receive medical treatment for little or no money, for people who could not afford a doctor. Others provided food and shelter to the homeless. Reformers like **Jane Addams** worked hard for city dwellers. She opened Hull House, one of America's first settlement houses. **Settlement houses** were centers offering help to the urban poor. Volunteers taught immigrants English and provided entertainment for young people and nurseries for children of working mothers. ✓

✓ Checkpoint

Name three problems created by urbanization.

____

____

____

The Excitement of City Life

Despite hardships, cities offered attractions and excitement not available in the country. Downtown shops attracted crowds of people. In time, the department store appeared on the scene. In such stores, many types of goods were sold in separate sections.

Long hours on the job made people value their free time. The division between work and play led to a new interest in leisure. To meet this need, cities provided forms of entertainment. Attractions included museums, orchestras, theatres, and circuses. City parks, zoos, and gardens let city dwellers take a break from crowded city streets.

After the Civil War, professional sports teams began to spring up in cities. The most popular professional sport was baseball. Football gained popularity in American colleges. In 1891, James Naismith came up with a winter sport called basketball. ✓

Vocabulary Builder

The text states that people found leisure in a city's entertainment. Based on the context clues, write a definition of the word *leisure*.

____

____

✓ Checkpoint

List three attractions found in cities.

____

____

____

Check Your Progress

1. How did living patterns change in cities during the Industrial Revolution?

____

____

____

2. What services did settlement houses provide?

____

____

____

Section 3 Notetaking Study Guide

Question to Think About As you read Section 3 in your textbook and take notes, keep this section focus question in mind: **What were the causes and effects of the rapid growth of cities?**

▶ Use these charts to record key information from the section.

Growth of Cities		
Urbanization	**Expanding Cities**	**Living Patterns**
Urbanization: the rapid growth of ________ Why people were attracted to cities: ________ ________ To meet the needs of shoppers, merchants developed the department store, which ________ ________ Kinds of leisure activities cities offered: ________ ________ ________ ________	Public transportation: subways, streetcars, elevated trains Public transportation gave rise to new living areas called ________. ________ helped speed up the growth of suburbs. New types of buildings: ________ ________	Lived in oldest sections at cities' centers: ________ Lived away from city centers in row houses and apartments: middle class Lived in fine homes on outskirts of cities: ________

Urban Problems and Solutions	
Problems of Urban Life	**Solutions to Problems**
Fires endangered ________ ________. Tenement life was bleak. Slum streets were ________ with ________. Disease was caused by ________.	Provided by cities: • ________ • ________ • ________ Provided by religious groups: • ________ • food, clothing, and shelter Provided by reformers: • ________ • ________

Refer to this page to answer the Chapter 18 Focus Question on page 290.

Section 4

The New Immigrants

Section 4 Focus Question

How was the experience of immigrants both positive and negative? To begin answering this question,

- Learn why immigrants sought a fresh start in America.
- Explore how immigrants started a new life.
- Find out how immigrants became American.
- Learn about a new wave of nativism.

Section 4 Summary

Starting in the late 1800s, millions of immigrants came to America seeking freedom and economic opportunities. Immigrants worked hard and gradually became part of American culture.

A Fresh Start

Some 25 million immigrants entered the United States between 1865 and 1915. Some people emigrated in search of employment. Others wanted to escape political and religious persecution in their home countries.

The wave of "new immigrants" in the late 1800s came from southern and eastern Europe, as well as from Asia and the Pacific. ✓

Starting a New Life

Most immigrants came to the United States crammed into the steerage of ships. **Steerage** consisted of large compartments that usually held cattle. After 1892, most people from Europe went through the receiving center on Ellis Island in New York City. Asian immigrants entered through Angel Island in San Francisco Bay. About two thirds of immigrants settled in cities. Many settled near other people from the same country in ethnic neighborhoods. ✓

Becoming American

Many newcomers to America clung to their traditional ways while trying to assimilate. **Assimilation** is the process of becoming part of another culture. Surrounded by English-speakers at school, children of immigrants learned the language more quickly and were more easily assimilated.

Immigrant labor was essential to the new economy. Immigrants worked in steel mills, meat-packing plants, and

Key Events

1869	Knights of Labor, a major labor union, is formed.
1889	Jane Addams founds Hull House to help city poor.
1892	Ellis Island opens as major entry station for European immigrants.
1913	Henry Ford sets up assembly line to mass produce automobiles.

✓ Checkpoint

List three regions from where the "new immigrants" came.

____

____

____

✓ Checkpoint

About what fraction of immigrants settled in cities?

____

Vocabulary Strategy

Assimilate means "to make similar." If you assimilate, you become similar to something. How does the immigrant experience reflect this meaning?

____

____

____

garment factories. They helped build skyscrapers, railroads, subways, and bridges. With hard work and saving, they slowly advanced economically.

Some Notable Immigrants		
Immigrant	**Place of Origin**	**Important Contribution**
Alexander Graham Bell	Scotland	invented the telephone
Andrew Carnegie	Scotland	steel magnate; donated money to charities
Samuel Goldwyn & Louis Mayer	Eastern Europe	helped establish the motion picture industry in California
Arturo Toscanini	Italy	orchestra conductor
Leo Baekeland	Belgium	invented plastic

✓

✓ Checkpoint

Which immigrant invented the telephone?

____

A New Wave of Nativism

As immigration increased, a new wave of nativists sought to preserve the country for native-born Americans. Nativists charged that foreigners would never assimilate and also that they took jobs from Americans.

In the West, nativist feelings against Chinese drove many Chinese immigrants from mining camps and cities. The Chinese Exclusion Act of 1882 excluded, or kept out, Chinese laborers from the United States. In 1917, Congress passed a law that barred immigrants who could not read their own language from entering the country. ✓

✓ Checkpoint

List two restrictions placed on immigration.

____

____

____

____

Check Your Progress

1. Why was it easier for children of immigrants to assimilate?

____

____

2. Why did nativists oppose immigration?

____

____

Section 4 Notetaking Study Guide

Question to Think About As you read Section 4 in your textbook and take notes, keep this section focus question in mind: **How was the experience of immigrants both positive and negative?**

► Fill in these charts to record key information from the section.

Reasons for Migration

- Employment opportunities
- ________ persecution: Russian Jews were the victims of ________.
- Political unrest: Many Mexicans were driven out of their homes because of ________.
- Most "new immigrants" came from southern Europe and ________. Smaller numbers came from ________ and the Pacific.

Starting New Lives

- Most immigrants were received at ________ and ________.
- About two thirds of immigrants settled in cities.
- Living in ethnic neighborhoods, immigrants could speak ________ and celebrate ________.

Becoming American

- Assimilation is the process of ________.
- Children of immigrants assimilated more quickly because ________.
- Immigrants worked in ________, ________, ________, and ________. They helped build skyscrapers, ________, ________, and ________.
- Many immigrants advanced economically by ________.
- Immigrants who made major contributions: ________, ________, ________, ________, ________, ________

A New Wave of Nativism

- Nativists sought to ________.
- Nativists charged that immigrants took away jobs from ________.
- Many Americans associated immigrants with ________, crime, and ________.
- The Chinese Exclusion Act of 1882 ________.
- In 1917, Congress passed a law that denied entry to immigrants who could not ________.

Refer to this page to answer the Chapter 18 Focus Question on page 290.

Section 5

Education and Culture

Key Events

1869	Knights of Labor, a major labor union, is formed.
1889	Jane Addams founds Hull House to help city poor.
1892	Ellis Island opens as major entry station for European immigrants.
1913	Henry Ford sets up assembly line to mass produce automobiles.

Vocabulary Strategy

Reread the underlined sentence. What meaning would be lost if the word *compulsory* were replaced with the word *voluntary*?

____

____

____

✓ Checkpoint

Which states were reluctant to pass compulsory education laws?

____

Section 5 Focus Question

What were the causes and effects of an expanded educational system? To begin answering this question,

- Learn about American education.
- Find out about new American writers.
- Explore the newspaper boom.

Section 5 Summary

Public education expanded during the economic boom. Compulsory education eventually became commonplace in all states. With better education, Americans took more interest in reading. Newspapers vied for readers' attention with sensational headlines and colorful features.

Educating Americans

The nation's growing industry needed a more educated workforce. States improved public schools. In 1852, Massachusetts passed the first compulsory education law. **Compulsory education** is the requirement that children attend school up to a certain age. Southern states were more reluctant to pass compulsory education laws than northern or western states. <u>But by 1918, compulsory education became the norm in all states.</u>

By 1900, there were 6,000 high schools in the country. Higher education also expanded. Private colleges for men and women opened, and states built universities that offered free or low-cost education.

Education for adults also improved. Wealthy people funded the building of public libraries in towns and cities. Adults could also study at the Chautauqua (shuh TAWK wuh) Society in New York. It began as a summer school for Bible teachers. After one year, the school was opened to the public. ✓

New American Writers

As education became available to more people, reading habits changed. Americans began to read more books and magazines. In the 1880s, a new crop of American writers appeared. Many were **realists**, writers who try to show life as it is. Stephen Crane wrote about the hardships of city slums. Californian Jack London wrote about miners and sailors on the West Coast who put their lives at risk. Kate Chopin shocked readers by writing about an unhappily married woman. Paul Laurence Dunbar was the first African American to make a living as a writer.

Mark Twain, the pen name of Samuel Clemens, was the most popular writer of the time. Twain made his stories realistic by capturing the speech patterns of southerners living and working along the Mississippi River. ✓

A Newspaper Boom

The number of newspapers increased dramatically in the late 1800s. By 1900, half of the newspapers in the world were printed in the United States.

The spread of education was one cause of growth in the newspaper industry. Urbanization was another reason for the newspaper boom. In small towns, news spread by word of mouth. But people in cities depended on newspapers to stay informed.

Immigrant **Joseph Pulitzer** created the first modern, mass-circulation newspaper. In 1883, he purchased the *New York World*. Pulitzer cut the price of the newspaper to make it more affordable.

Pulitzer added crowd-pleasing features to his newspaper, including color comics. The *New York World* also became known for its sensational headlines. As a result, readership of the *New York World* skyrocketed. Soon other newspapers tried to follow suit.

The Yellow Kid, a tough but sweet slum boy, became the first popular American comic strip character. Because of the Yellow Kid, critics of the *New York World* coined the term **yellow journalism** to describe the sensational reporting style of the *World* and other papers. ✓

Check Your Progress

1. Why did education become such an important issue in the late 1880s?

____

____

2. What caused the newspaper boom?

____

____

____

✓ Checkpoint

List three well-known writers of the time.

____

____

____

Reading Strategy

Why is the title of this section of text "A Newspaper Boom"? Did newspapers really "boom"?

____

____

✓ Checkpoint

Name three ways in which Joseph Pulitzer changed the newspaper industry.

____

____

____

Section 5 Notetaking Study Guide

Question to Think About As you read Section 5 in your textbook and take notes, keep this section focus question in mind: **What were the causes and effects of an expanded educational system?**

▶ Use these organizers to record key information from the section.

Education and Culture

Better-Educated Americans

- States improved public schools because ________________.
- States in the ________________ were more reluctant to pass compulsory education laws than states in the ________________ and West. Still, by ________________ every state required children to attend school.
- Elementary school students learned reading, ________________, and West.
- ________________ offered free or low-cost higher education.
- Wealthy individuals funded the building of ________________ in cities and towns.
- The Chautauqua Society offered ________________ and later began ________________.

Americans Read More Books and Magazines

What or Who People Read	Description or Accomplishment
Many bestsellers	low-priced paperbacks that told tales of the "Wild West" or "rags-to-riches" stories
Realists	
Stephen Crane	
Jack London	wrote about the lives of miners and sailors
Kate Chopin	
Paul Dunbar	
Mark Twain	

A Newspaper Boom

By 1900, half the newspapers in the world were printed in the United States.

Causes:

- spread of education
- ________________

New York World

- first modern ________________ newspaper
- created by ________________, who cut prices so people could ________________ the paper
- known for ________________ and ________________
- term used to describe its reporting style: ________________

Refer to this page to answer the Chapter 18 Focus Question on page 290.

Chapter 18 Assessment

Directions: Circle the letter of the correct answer.

1. Which of the following created a trust in the oil industry?
   - A J. P. Morgan
   - B John D. Rockefeller
   - C Andrew Carnegie

2. Westward expansion was important to industrial growth because
   - A it provided new land on which to build factories.
   - B it created the need for more automobiles.
   - C it made raw materials readily available.

3. The sensational reporting style of the *New York World* and other newspapers became known as
   - A yellow journalism.
   - B trustbusting.
   - C realism.

4. Which of the following was ***not*** a result of urbanization?
   - A rise of the newspaper industry
   - B building of skyscrapers
   - C rise in the price of oil

Directions: Follow the steps to complete this task:

Decide whether the changes to cities were positive or negative.

Step 1: Recall information: In the chart, list ways rapid urbanization changed cities and the way people lived in them.

Changes to Cities	Effect on City Dwellers

Step 2: Analyze effects: which were positive? Which were negative?

____

____

Step 3: Explore consequences: Complete the topic sentence that follows. Then write two or three more sentences that support your topic sentence.

The rapid growth of cities led to ______________________________

____

____

____

Chapter 18 Notetaking Study Guide

Now you are ready to answer the Chapter 18 Focus Question: **How did industrialization increase the speed of change?**

► Fill in the following organizer to help you answer this question.

Industrial Growth

Caused by:

- Westward expansion: Industries gained access to natural resources, including coal, ______, ______, ______, and ______.
- Government policies: Congress gave land grants and other subsidies to ______ and other businesses. The government also kept high ______ on imports, making foreign goods ______.
- Technology: The Bessemer process made stronger ______ at a lower cost. ______ was increasingly used to fuel machines and became a valuable resource.
- Improvements in transportation: ______ carried people and goods to the West and raw materials to eastern ______.

Furthered by Inventions:

- light bulb
- electric power plant
- ______
- ______
- ______
- ______

Supported by Labor from Immigration:

- The "new immigrants" came from ______.
- Many immigrants came to America in search of ______. Others wanted to escape religious persecution or ______ in their home countries.
- Many immigrants tried to maintain familiar traditions while trying to ______ to American culture.
- Immigrants worked in steel mills, ______, ______, and ______. They built ______, ______, ______ and ______.

The Growth of Cities

Problems of cities

- poor sanitation
- ______
- ______

Attractions and leisure activities:

- department stores
- ______
- sporting events
- ______

The Rise of Big Business

- Role of corporations and trusts: ______
- Conditions of factory work: ______
- Labor unions were formed to: ______

Improved Educational System

- Why education was needed: ______
- Better educated Americans took more interest in reading. This spurred a boom in newspapers.

Refer to this page to answer the Unit 6 Focus Question on page 305.

Chapter 19

Political Reform and the Progressive Era (1870–1920)

What You Will Learn

During the late 1800s and early 1900s, Americans organized in support of several different kinds of reform.

Chapter 19 Focus Question

As you read through this chapter, keep this question in mind: **How did society and politics change during the Progressive Era?**

Section 1

The Gilded Age and Progressive Reform

Section 1 Focus Question

How did reformers try to end government corruption and limit the influence of big business? To begin answering this question,

- Learn about reform during the Gilded Age.
- Find out about the Progressives' political reforms.
- Learn about the muckrakers.

Section 1 Summary

The Progressives supported efforts to end government corruption and limit the influence of big business.

Reform in the Gilded Age

The period after the Civil War was called the Gilded Age. It was a time of economic growth. But there were problems in society. One problem was the spoils system, which is the rewarding of political supporters with government jobs. Many believed the spoils system encouraged corruption. The Pendleton Act (1883) created the Civil Service Commission. The **civil service** is a system that includes government jobs, except elected positions, judges, and soldiers. Jobseekers were to be hired on skills instead of political connections.

Several laws put limits on big business. The Interstate Commerce Act (1887) prohibited rebates. It also set up the Interstate Commerce Commission to regulate railroads. The

Key Events

1890	Sherman Antitrust Act bars businesses from limiting competition.
1909	Reformers found the NAACP to promote rights of African Americans.
1920	Nineteenth Amendment guarantees women the right to vote.

Vocabulary Builder

Gilded means "coated with a thin layer of gold paint." How was this appropriate for describing America after the Civil War?

____

____

✓ Checkpoint

List two laws that regulated big business.

____

____

✓ Checkpoint

List three reforms of state government.

____

____

____

✓ Checkpoint

Name the type of journalist who exposed corruption.

____

Sherman Antitrust Act (1890) was supposed to stop businesses from using trusts to destroy competition. However, this was hard to enforce. Instead, the law was mainly used to limit the power of labor unions.

Corruption was a serious problem in city governments. Politicians called bosses controlled work done in many cities. They demanded bribes from businesses that wanted work from the city. ✓

Progressives and Political Reform

The Progressive movement aimed to end corruption and promote the public interest, or the good of all the people. The Wisconsin Idea was a set of state government reforms that got rid of political bosses and used commissions to solve problems. One important reform was the **primary,** or election in which voters, rather than party leaders, choose their party's candidate for an election.

Some states carried out reforms to give more power to voters. One was the **recall,** a process by which people may vote to remove an elected official from office. Another reform was the **initiative,** a process that allows voters to put a bill before a state legislature. A third political reform was the **referendum,** a way for people to vote directly on a proposed law. Many reformers supported two new amendments. The Sixteenth Amendment (1913) gave Congress the power to pass a federal income tax. The Seventeenth Amendment (1913) provided for the direct election of U.S. senators by the people instead of state legislatures. ✓

The Muckrakers

The press played an important role in exposing corruption and other problems. Ida Tarbell wrote about unfair business practices. Upton Sinclair exposed grisly practices of the meatpacking industry. Using photographs, Jacob Riis revealed the shocking conditions of slum life. **Muckraker** became a term for a crusading journalist. ✓

Check Your Progress

1. What was the practice of rewarding political supporters with government jobs?

____

2. What were the two constitutional amendments supported by Progressive reformers, and what did each do?

____

____

Section 1 Notetaking Study Guide

Question to Think About As you read Section 1 in your textbook and take notes, keep this section focus question in mind: **How did reformers try to end government corruption and limit the influence of big business?**

▶ Use this chart to record key information from the section. Some information has been filled in to get you started.

The Gilded Age and Progressive Reform

Reform in the Gilded Age

Two Political Concerns of the Gilded Age

- The wealthy were making themselves rich at the public's expense.
- There was widespread ______________ in government.

Reforming the Spoils System

- The spoils system rewarded political supporters with ______________.
- In 1883, the ______________ created the ______________, which filled jobs on the basis of merit.

Controlling Big Business

- In 1887, the Interstate Commerce Act forbade ______________ and set up the ______________ to oversee railroads.
- Although difficult to enforce, the Sherman Antitrust Act of 1890 was designed to ______________.

Corruption: A Serious Problem in City Government

- Politicians called ______________ controlled work locally and demanded ______________ from businesses.

Progressives and Political Reform

The Progressive Movement

- The ______________ Idea was a set of Progressive reforms proposed by Governor Robert La Follette. These reforms included the creation of ______________, made up of experts, to solve problems.
- Some states instituted reforms to put more power in the hands of ______________. These included the recall, the ______________, and the ______________.

Constitutional Amendments

- The Sixteenth Amendment gave Congress the power to ______________.
- The ______________ (1913) required the direct election of U.S. senators.

Muckrakers

- Muckraker became a term for a ______________.
- Muckrakers played an important role in exposing ______________ and other problems.
- Three well known muckrakers were Ida Tarbell, ______________, and ______________.

Refer to this page to answer the Chapter 19 Focus Question on page 304.

Section 2

The Progressive Presidents

Key Events

1890	Sherman Antitrust Act bars businesses from limiting competition.
1909	Reformers found the NAACP to promote rights of African Americans.
1920	Nineteenth Amendment guarantees women the right to vote.

Section 2 Focus Question

How did the Progressive Presidents extend reforms? To begin answering this question,

- Learn about Theodore Roosevelt, the first Progressive President.
- Find out about Roosevelt's Square Deal.
- Explore Taft and Wilson's accomplishments.

Section 2 Summary

The Progressive Presidents were Theodore Roosevelt, William Howard Taft, and Woodrow Wilson. New areas of reform included conservation of natural resources, consumer protection laws, and banking reform.

The First Progressive President

Theodore Roosevelt was the first Progressive President. A former war hero and governor, Vice President Roosevelt took office after President McKinley was killed.

Roosevelt was a **trustbuster,** a person who worked to destroy monopolies and trusts. He distinguished between "good trusts," which did not do any harm, and "bad trusts," which cheated workers and the public. Roosevelt believed the government must control or break up bad trusts. In a case involving Northern Securities, the Supreme Court ruled that the company had violated the Sherman Antitrust Act. It was the first time the act had been used to break up trusts, not unions. Roosevelt also forced mine owners to negotiate with striking coal miners. ✓

✓ Checkpoint

Why was the Northern Securities court case important?

____

____

____

The Square Deal

The Square Deal was Roosevelt's platform during the presidential election of 1904. It promised that everyone, not just big businesses, would have the same opportunity to succeed. It helped him win an overwhelming victory.

Roosevelt was a strong supporter of **conservation,** or the protection of natural resources. He created the U.S. Forest Service to manage the nation's woodlands. He also created **national parks,** or natural areas protected and managed by the federal government.

Vocabulary Builder

Platform in this context means a set of policies that a politician or political party proposes.

Roosevelt also supported reforms to protect consumers from unsafe food and drugs. He and others were influenced by writers of the day. Muckrakers exposed the unhealthy practices and false claims made by food and drug companies. The Pure Food and Drug Act required food and drug makers to list all ingredients on packages. ✓

Taft and Wilson

In 1908, Roosevelt supported **William Howard Taft** for President. Taft won easily. Taft's approach differed from Roosevelt's. He was quiet and more cautious. Taft broke up more trusts than Roosevelt. He also favored a graduated income tax, approved new mine safety rules, and started to regulate child labor. However, Taft lost Progressive support when he raised tariffs and changed some of Roosevelt's conservation policies.

In 1912, Roosevelt ran against Taft for the Republican presidential nomination. Republican leaders sided with Taft and made him the nominee. Roosevelt then formed the Progressive, or Bull Moose, Party so he could run. Democrats nominated **Woodrow Wilson.** He was a cautious reformer often criticized for being unwilling to compromise. Wilson won the election of 1912 because Taft and Roosevelt split the Republican votes between them.

President Wilson had a program called the New Freedom. It aimed to restore free competition. The Federal Trade Commission (1914) helped restore competition by investigating and then stopping companies that used unfair trade practices. The Clayton Antitrust Act (1914) banned other business practices that limited competition. The Federal Reserve Act (1913) set up a system of federal banks. It also gave the government the power to change interest rates and control the money supply. ✓

Check Your Progress

1. What actions did President Roosevelt take to promote conservation?

____

____

2. Why did Woodrow Wilson win the election of 1912?

____

____

✓ Checkpoint

List two causes Roosevelt supported.

____

____

Reading Strategy

Taft lost the support of Progressives because of certain policies. However, on the whole he is considered a Progressive. Circle four of Taft's Progressive achievements.

✓ Checkpoint

List three parts of Wilson's New Freedom program.

____

____

____

Section 2 Notetaking Study Guide

Question to Think About As you read Section 2 and take notes, keep this section focus question in mind: **How did the Progressive Presidents extend reforms?**

▶ Use this chart to record key information from the section. Some information has been filled in to get you started.

The Progressive Presidents
Theodore Roosevelt
• war hero, former governor, Vice President • became President in 1901 after ________________ • believed the government had to control or __________ bad trusts • launched lawsuits against __________ • Northern Securities: first time that the Sherman Antitrust Act was used to break up a trust • 1902 Pennsylvania coal miners strike: first time that ________________ • During the 1904 presidential campaign, Roosevelt promised Americans a Square Deal. By this, he meant ________________. • Conservation is ____________. • In 1905, Roosevelt created __________ to conserve the nation's woodlands. He had thousands of acres of land set aside for __________. • Roosevelt supported consumer protection reforms. The __________ required food and drug makers to list all ingredients on packages.
William Howard Taft
• Roosevelt's secretary of war, won presidency in 1908 with Roosevelt's support • Unlike Roosevelt, Taft was ____________. • supported Progressive reforms: graduated __________, new rules for mines, government workers, child labor • lost Progressive support because he __________ and modified conservation policies • Roosevelt broke with Taft and started the ____________. • In the presidential election of 1912, Roosevelt and Taft ____________, so Woodrow Wilson won.
Woodrow Wilson
• had served as a university president and a __________ • was known as a brilliant scholar and a cautious reformer • His program to restore free competition was called __________. It included the creation of the Federal Trade Commission (1914), the __________, and the __________.

Refer to this page to answer the Chapter 19 Focus Question on page 304.

Section 3

The Rights of Women

Section 3 Focus Question

How did women gain new rights? To begin answering this question,

- Learn about the women's suffrage movement.
- Find out about new opportunities for women.
- Learn about the temperance movement.

Section 3 Summary

After decades of effort, the movement for women's rights won the right to vote. New educational and career opportunities also opened for women.

Women Win the Vote

The Seneca Falls Convention of 1848 marked the start of an organized women's rights movement in the United States. After the Civil War, Elizabeth Cady Stanton and Susan B. Anthony formed the National Woman Suffrage Association to push for a constitutional amendment to give women the right to vote.

The suffrage movement had its first successes in the late 1800s in the western states. By giving women the right to vote, the states recognized the contributions of pioneer women to the settlement of the West.

In the early 1900s, support for women's suffrage grew. One reason was that more women were beginning to work outside the home. Women wage earners believed that they deserved a say in the laws that affected them.

A new generation of leaders took over after the deaths of Stanton and Anthony. **Carrie Chapman Catt** created a strategy for winning suffrage state by state. The plan coordinated the work of **suffragists,** or people who worked for women's right to vote, across the nation.

More states began giving women the right to vote, but women still could not vote in federal elections. Suffragists pushed for a constitutional amendment. **Alice Paul** and other suffragists met with President Wilson on the matter. Wilson pledged his support for a constitutional amendment. The Nineteenth Amendment finally gave women the right to vote in federal elections. ✓

Key Events

1890	Sherman Antitrust Act bars businesses from limiting competition.
1909	Reformers found the NAACP to promote rights of African Americans.
1920	Nineteenth Amendment guarantees women the right to vote.

Vocabulary Builder

A synonym is a word that is similar in meaning to another word. Which of the following words is a synonym for *coordinated*: organized, ruined, or finished?

____

✓ Checkpoint

Name the change that increased support for women's suffrage in the early 1900s.

____

____

____

New Opportunities for Women

Women also struggled for better jobs and educational opportunities. Starting with the first granting of a Ph.D. to a woman in the late 1870s, more and more women earned advanced degrees at graduate schools. By 1900, there were thousands of women doctors and lawyers.

During the late 1800s, many women joined clubs. The earliest clubs sought to help women improve their minds. For instance, women met to discuss books. Over time women's clubs became more concerned with improving society. They raised money for libraries, schools, and parks, and pushed for laws to protect women and children, to ensure pure foods and drugs, and to win the right to vote.

African American women also formed clubs. The National Association of Colored Women sought to end segregation and violence against African Americans. Its members also supported the women's suffrage movement.

Many women became reformers during the Progressive Era. Florence Kelley fought for safe working conditions and organized a boycott of manufacturers who used child labor. Some women entered the field of social work, helping poor city-dwellers. ✓

Reading Strategy

The underlined sentence makes a general statement about the activities of women during the Progressive Era. Circle specific examples given in the bracketed paragraphs.

Mark the Text

✓ Checkpoint

List three fields women entered.

____

____

____

The Crusade Against Alcohol

Women were leaders of the temperance movement, which tried to ban alcohol. The Woman's Christian Temperance Union was founded in 1874. Its president **Frances Willard** encouraged women to also support women's suffrage. Carry Nation was a more radical crusader for temperance. She gained publicity for the movement by attacking saloons, or places that sold liquor, with a hatchet. The temperance crusade reached its goal in 1919 with the ratification of the Eighteenth Amendment. It enforced **prohibition**, or a ban on the sale and consumption of alcohol. ✓

✓ Checkpoint

Name two leaders of the temperance movement.

____

____

Check Your Progress

1. Where did women first gain the right to vote? Why?

____

____

2. How did the concerns of women's clubs change over time?

____

____

Section 3 Notetaking Study Guide

Question to Think About As you read Section 3 in your textbook and take notes, keep this section focus question in mind: **How did women gain new rights?**

▶ Use these charts to record key information from the section. Some information has been filled in to get you started.

Women's Suffrage	
Seneca Falls Convention (1848)	Importance: Marked the start of an organized women's rights movement in the United States
National Woman Suffrage Association	Goal: Passage of ______________ . Founders: ______________ , ______________
Western states	By the late 1800s, women won voting rights in Wyoming , ______________ , ______________ , and ______________ .
Reasons for increased support for women's suffrage	• More women ______________ and demanded ______________ . • New leaders: ______________ , ______________ • A detailed strategy to ______________
Nineteenth Amendment	Ratified: 1920 What it did: ______________

New Opportunities
Higher Education
• Women began to earn advanced degrees .
Clubs and Reform
• At first women's clubs focused on advancing ______________ .
• The focus of many switched to social reforms:
1. raised money for libraries , ______________ , and ______________ .
2. pressed for laws to ______________ , to ______________ , and to ______________ .
• Racial barriers forced ______________ to form their own clubs.

Temperance	
Temperance	Campaign against ______________
Woman's Christian Temperance Union	Goal: ______________ Led by: Francis Willard , ______________
Eighteenth Amendment	Ratified: ______________ What it did: ______________

Refer to this page to answer the Chapter 19 Focus Question on page 304.

Section 4

Struggles for Justice

Section 4 Focus Question

What challenges faced minority groups? To begin answering this question,

- Read about how African Americans responded to discrimination.
- Explore how Mexican Americans lived.
- Find out about challenges faced by Asian Americans.
- Learn about prejudice faced by religious minorities.

Key Events

1890	Sherman Antitrust Act bars businesses from limiting competition.
1909	Reformers found the NAACP to promote rights of African Americans.
1920	Nineteenth Amendment guarantees women the right to vote.

Section 4 Summary

African Americans and other groups faced discrimination with little support from Progressives.

African Americans

African Americans faced discrimination in the North and South. **Booker T. Washington** urged African Americans to learn trades and move up gradually in society. In time, they would have the money and power to demand equality. Washington set up an institute to train African Americans in industrial and agricultural skills.

The scholar **W.E.B. Du Bois** had a different approach. He urged blacks to fight discrimination rather than yield to it. Du Bois helped found the National Association for the Advancement of Colored People.

Ida B. Wells tried to stop the **lynching**, or the murder by mobs, of African Americans. She encouraged African Americans to protest lynching and to boycott white-owned stores and segregated streetcars.

In spite of many obstacles, some African Americans succeeded. The scientist George Washington Carver discovered hundreds of new uses for peanuts and other crops. Sarah Walker started a line of hair care products for African American women. Many black-owned businesses also served the African American community. Churches helped train new leaders. ✓

Vocabulary Builder

Reread the underlined sentence. One meaning of *discriminate* is "to treat differently." In the context of this sentence, does *discrimination* mean African Americans were treated better or worse than white Americans?

____

✓ Checkpoint

Name Ida B. Wells' main goal.

____

____

Mexican Americans

By 1900, about half a million Mexican Americans lived in the United States. They also faced legal segregation. Around 1910, famine and the Mexican Revolution led many more

Mexicans to settle in the United States. Mexican Americans were confined to unskilled jobs and were paid less than Anglo workers.

Many Mexican Americans lived in barrios, or ethnic Mexican American neighborhoods, which helped preserve their language and culture. The largest barrio was in Los Angeles. In the barrio, mutualistas, or mutual aid groups, were formed. They helped provide insurance and legal advice and collected money to care for the sick and needy. ✓

Asian Americans

The Chinese Exclusion Act of 1882 stopped Chinese immigration to the United States. Employers on the West Coast hired workers from other parts of Asia, mainly the Philippines and Japan.

Many Japanese settled in California where they became successful farmers. When San Francisco forced all Asians into segregated schools, Japan protested. Unions and other groups wanted President Roosevelt to limit Japanese immigration. A "Gentlemen's Agreement" was made. Japan agreed to stop workers from moving to the United States. In exchange, Japanese women whose husbands had already migrated to the United States were allowed to join them. ✓

Religious Minorities

Religious minorities also faced prejudice. Nativist groups tried to restrict immigration of Roman Catholics and Jews. Both native-born and immigrant Catholics and Jews faced discrimination in housing and jobs.

To avoid prejudice in schools, Catholics set up church-sponsored schools. Jewish Americans founded the Anti-Defamation League to promote understanding and fight prejudice against Jews. (Defamation means the spreading of false, hateful information.) ✓

Check Your Progress

1. How did Washington's and Du Bois's views on ending discrimination differ?

____

____

____

2. What was one way that Mexican Americans preserved their language and culture?

____

✓ Checkpoint

Name three ways mutualistas helped residents of barrios.

____

____

____

Reading Strategy

In the bracketed paragraph, circle the factors that led to the Gentlemen's Agreement.

✓ Checkpoint

List the terms of the "Gentlemen's Agreement" between Japan and the United States.

____

____

____

____

✓ Checkpoint

List two religious minorities that faced discrimination.

____

____

Section 4 Notetaking Study Guide

Question to Think About As you read Section 4 in your textbook and take notes, keep this section focus question in mind: **What challenges faced minority groups?**

▶ Use this chart to record key information from the section.

Struggles for Justice
African Americans
• Booker T. Washington founded the ________________. He advised African Americans to learn trades and move up gradually in society.
• W.E.B. Du Bois helped found the ________________. He urged African Americans to ________________.
• ________________ fought against lynching, or ________________.
Mexican Americans
• Before 1900, about half a million Mexican Americans lived in the United States. Like ________________, they faced legal ________________. • In 1910, ________________ and ________________ swept Mexico. As a result, thousands of Mexicans fled into the United States. • Mexican Americans created barrios, or ________________. • Mexican immigrants and Mexican Americans formed ________________, or mutual aid groups. Members pooled money to pay for ________________ and ________________. They also collected money for the sick and needy.
Asian Americans
• More than ________________ Japanese entered the United States in the early 1900s. • Most first went to Hawaii to work on ________________. • In 1906, the city of ________________ forced Asian students to attend separate ________________. • This led to a compromise called the ________________ between the United States and Japan. Japan would stop any more ________________ from going to the United States. The United States, in exchange, allowed ________________ ________________.
Religious Minorities
• ________________ groups worked to restrict immigration. Even ________________ and ________________ who were not immigrants faced discrimination in jobs and ________________. • American Catholics set up ________________ schools. • American Jews set up the ________________, which worked to fight ________________, or prejudice against Jews.

Refer to this page to answer the Chapter 19 Focus Question on page 304.

Chapter 19 Assessment

Directions: Circle the letter of the correct answer.

1. Which did President Theodore Roosevelt strongly support?
   - **A** women's rights
   - **B** conservation
   - **C** African American rights

2. Women first won voting rights in several states in the
   - **A** Northeast.
   - **B** West.
   - **C** South.

3. Which reformer urged African Americans to fight discrimination?
   - **A** Booker T. Washington
   - **B** Carry Nation
   - **C** W.E.B. Du Bois

Directions: Follow the steps to answer this question:

How did the reforms of the Wisconsin Idea help to achieve its goals?

Step 1: Recall information: What was the Wisconsin Idea and its goals?

The Wisconsin Idea	
Description	
Goals	• •

Step 2: Describe these reforms associated with the Wisconsin Idea.

The Wisconsin Idea Reforms	
Reform	**Description**
Primary	
Initiative	
Recall	
Referendum	

Step 3: Complete the topic sentence that follows. Then write two or three more sentences that support your topic sentence.

The Wisconsin Idea reforms ______________________________

____

____

____

____

Chapter 19 Notetaking Study Guide

Now you are ready to answer the Chapter 19 Focus Question: **How did society and politics change during the Progressive Era?**

▶ Complete the following chart to help you answer this question. Use the notes that you took for each section.

Change in the Progressive Era	
The Gilded Age and Progressive Reform	
• ______________, or dishonesty in government, was widespread. • Critics said a key part of the problem was the ______________.	
Efforts to Control Big Business • ______________ • Interstate Commerce Commission • ______________	**Political Reforms** • Wisconsin Idea • ______________ • ______________
Progressive Presidents	
Theodore Roosevelt • In 1904, he campaigned on the promise of a ______________ for all Americans. • He also pressed for ______________, or the protection of natural resources. He had thousands of acres set aside to become ______________.	
William H. Taft • reputation: ______________ • Despite strong Progressive policy record, he lost Progressive support.	**Woodrow Wilson** • reputation: ______________ • Goal of New Freedom program: ______________
Rights of Women	
Two significant suffragist leaders: ______________ and ______________.	The Nineteenth Amendment guaranteed women the right to vote.
Struggles for Justice	
Booker T. Washington • founded: ______________ • believed: Blacks should learn trades and earn money, then demand equality	**W.E.B. Du Bois** • helped found: ______________ • believed: ______________
Mexican Americans • Barrio: ______________	**Asian Americans** • Gentlemen's Agreement: ______________
Two religious minorities who faced discrimination: ______________ and ______________	

Refer to this page to answer the Unit 6 Focus Question on page 305.

Unit 6 Pulling It Together Activity

What You Have Learned

Chapter 17 Miners and railroad builders led to settlement of the West. Native Americans struggled to maintain their way of life. Western farmers faced many challenges.

Chapter 18 In the late 1800s, industrialization caused urban growth, altered the way business was run, and prompted reforms in education. A new wave of immigration to America occurred during this period.

Chapter 19 During the late 1800s and early 1900s, Americans organized to press for reforms in many areas of government and society.

Think Like a Historian

Read the Unit 6 Focus Question: **How did the industrialization of the United States change the economy, society, and politics of the nation?**

▶ Use the organizers on this page and the next to collect information to answer this question.

What were some developments made during the industrialization of the United States? Some of them are listed in this chart. Review your section and chapter notes. Then complete the chart.

Growth of U.S. Industry		
Inventions	**Transportation**	**Other Industries**
• phonograph • camera • electric power plants • • •	• railroads • •	• cattle • • •

What aspects of the industrialization of the United States caused changes in territorial expansion, growth of cities, and the Progressive movement and labor unions? The organizer below gives you a part of the answer. Review your section and chapter notes. Then fill in the rest of the organizer.

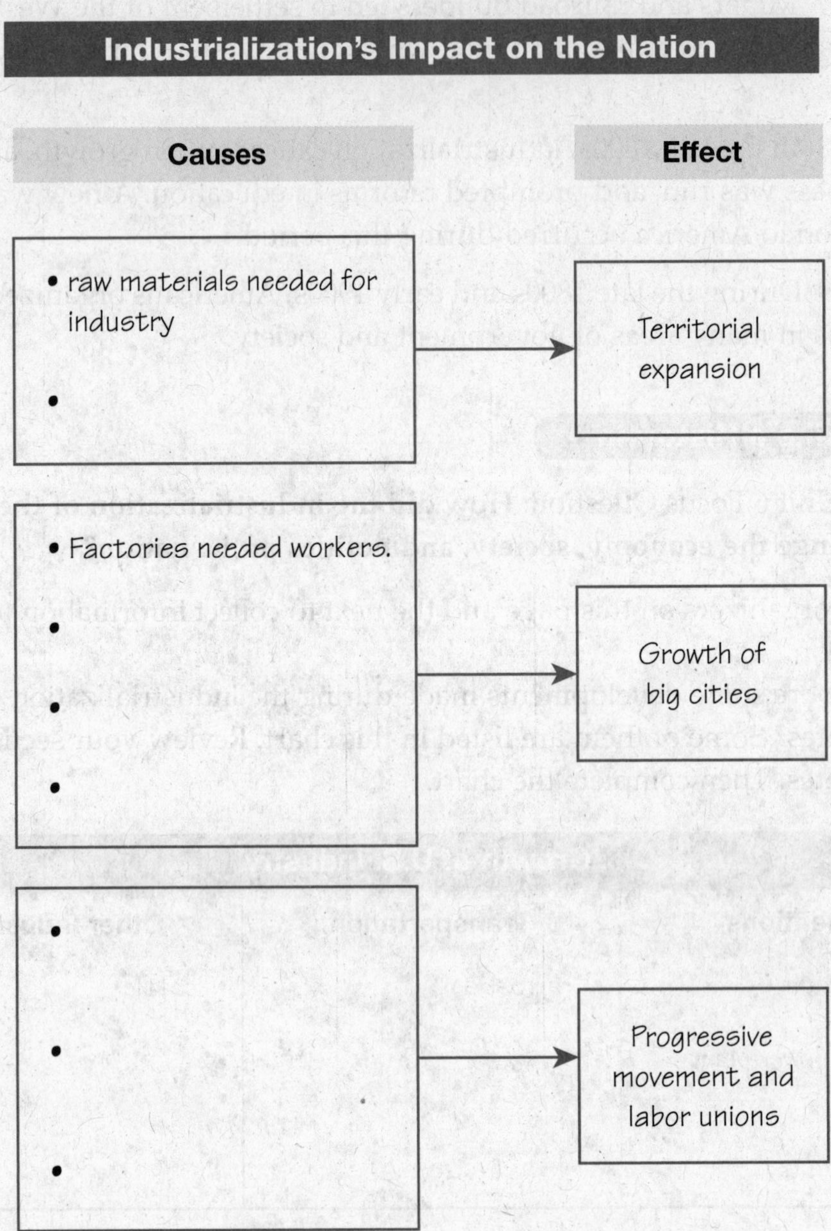

Unit 7

A New Role in the World

What You Will Learn

Chapter 20 By the late 1800s, the United States acquired new territories in the Pacific and strengthened its trade ties with Asia. The Spanish-American War led to increased involvement in Latin America.

Chapter 21 In 1914, a war broke out in Europe. Although the United States at first remained neutral, it eventually joined the war. The conflict, which we now call World War I, had important effects around the world.

Chapter 22 The decade following World War I marked great changes for the U.S. Republicans returned the country to pre-war isolationism and supported big business. Cultural changes affecting the lives and values of Americans sparked conflicts and tensions.

Focus Your Learning As you study this unit and take notes, you will find the information to answer the questions below. Answering the Chapter Focus Questions will help build your answer to the Unit Focus Question.

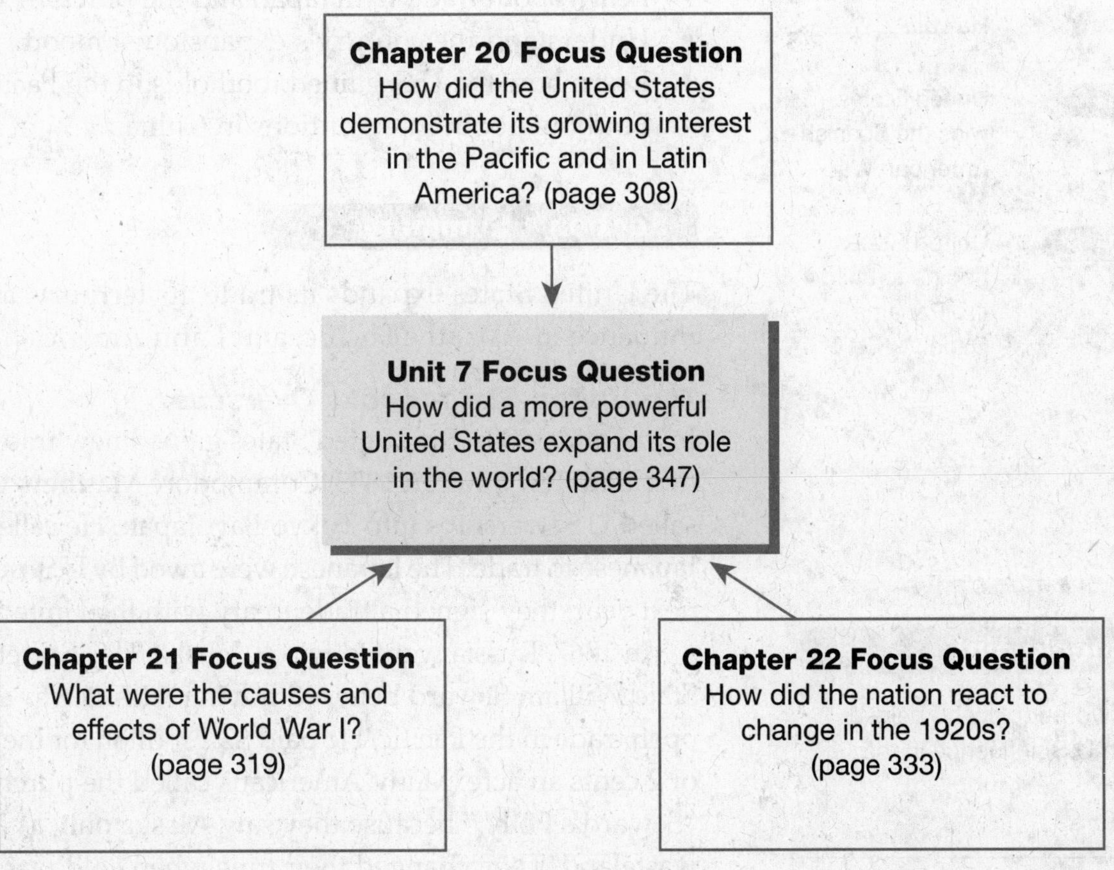

Chapter 20 Focus Question
How did the United States demonstrate its growing interest in the Pacific and in Latin America? (page 308)
Unit 7 Focus Question
How did a more powerful United States expand its role in the world? (page 347)
Chapter 21 Focus Question
What were the causes and effects of World War I? (page 319)
Chapter 22 Focus Question
How did the nation react to change in the 1920s? (page 333)

Chapter 20

The United States Looks Overseas

(1853–1915)

What You Will Learn

By the late 1800s, the United States had new territories in the Pacific and strengthened its trade ties with Asia. The Spanish-American War led to more involvement in Latin America.

Chapter 20 Focus Question

As you read this chapter, keep this question in mind: **How did the United States demonstrate its growing interest in the Pacific and in Latin America?**

Section 1

Eyes on the Pacific

Section 1 Focus Question

How did the U.S. acquire new territory and expand trade in the Asia-Pacific region? To answer this question,

- Learn about trade with Japan and the purchase of Alaska.
- Understand the country's expansionist mood.
- Learn how the U.S. gained footholds in the Pacific region.
- Find out about interventions in China.

Section 1 Summary

The United States expands its trade, its territory, and its influence in Asia, the Pacific, and Latin America.

The United States Looks Overseas

In the mid-1800s, the United States gained new trading partners and new land. In 1853, Commodore **Matthew C. Perry** sailed U.S. warships into Tokyo Bay, Japan. He called on the Japanese to trade. The Japanese were awed by U.S. power. The next year, they signed a trade treaty with the United States.

In 1867, Russia wanted to sell Alaska. U.S. Secretary of State William Seward believed buying Alaska was a way to open trade in the Pacific. He paid $7.2 million for the territory, or 2 cents an acre. Many Americans called the purchase "Seward's Folly," because they saw Alaska only as a frozen wasteland. They changed their tune when gold was discovered there. ✓

Key Events

1893	American planters stage a revolt in Hawaii.
1898	United States wins the Spanish-American War.
1904	United States begins to build the Panama Canal.

✓ Checkpoint

Name two people who helped develop U.S. influence in the Pacific.

____

____

The Expansionist Mood

Until the late 1800s, the United States believed in **isolationism.** It avoided involvement in the affairs of other countries. Several European nations, however, began to build empires. Many U.S. leaders believed that **imperialism,** or building empires by establishing political and economic control over peoples around the world, could provide a new frontier. The United States could find new natural resources and markets for its products, as well as spread "American values." ✓

✓ Checkpoint

Give two reasons why imperialism appealed to some U.S. leaders.

____

____

Gaining Footholds in the Pacific

American expansionists became interested in two groups of islands in the Pacific—Samoa and Hawaii. Britain and Germany were also interested in Samoa as a place to refuel their ships. War nearly broke out over the islands, but in 1899, Germany and the United States agreed to divide Samoa.

By 1887, American planters in Hawaii had already gained great power over the government. Queen **Liliuokalani** tried to prevent Hawaii from losing its independence. The planters tried to overthrow the queen with help from U.S. Marines, but President Grover Cleveland did not support the revolt. President William McKinley did, however. In 1898, Congress voted to make Hawaii a U.S. territory. ✓

✓ Checkpoint

Name the two Pacific island groups that became U.S. possessions.

____

____

Carving Up China

In the late 1800s, Japan and Europe divided China into **spheres of influence,** or areas where another nation has economic and political control. U.S. leaders feared America would be left out, so Secretary of State John Hay issued the Open Door Policy. It called for all nations to be able to trade in China on an equal basis. The Chinese hated foreign influence. A Chinese group known as the Boxers attacked westerners in 1900. The United States and other countries sent troops to crush the Boxer Rebellion. Hay then issued a second Open Door message. It stated that China should remain one country. ✓

✓ Checkpoint

Explain what caused the Boxer Rebellion.

____

____

Check Your Progress

1. What three new lands did the United States acquire?

____

____

2. What nations became new trading partners with the United States?

____

____

Section 1 Notetaking Study Guide

Question to Think About As you read Section 1 in your textbook and take notes, keep this section focus question in mind: **How did the United States acquire new territory and expand trade in the Asia-Pacific region?**

▶ Use this chart to record key information from the section. Some information has been filled in to get you started.

<table>
<tr><th colspan="2">The United States Looks Overseas</th></tr>
<tr><td>Japan
• The United States could not trade with Japan because Japan <u>blocked outside trade</u> and ______.
• <u>Commodore Perry</u> sailed warships into ______. The Japanese were awed by his ______ and ______.
• As a result, the Japanese ______.</td><td>Alaska
• Secretary of State ______ bought Alaska from <u>Russia</u> for ______ in 1867.
• Many people called Alaska ______ because they thought it was a ______.
• They changed their tune when ______ led to the ______ of 1897–1898.</td></tr>
<tr><td colspan="2">The Expansionist Mood
• In late 1800s, the idea of <u>expansionism</u> replaced ______.
• Historian ______ concluded that the American ______ was gone.
• American leaders thought if the United States did not act soon, it might be shut out of ______ and denied .
• Alfred T. Mahan said that future U.S. prosperity depended on building up ______, and the key was a ______.
• Many Americans believed they had a divine duty to spread ______ and ______ around the world.</td></tr>
<tr><td colspan="2">Gaining Footholds in the Pacific
• Expansionists wanted more U.S. influence and trade in the ______.</td></tr>
<tr><td>Samoa
• Besides the United States, ______ and ______ wanted possession of Samoa.
• After a ______ prevented a war, ______ and ______ divided Samoa.</td><td>Hawaii
• In 1887, ______ forced the Hawaiian king to accept a new constitution.
• Queen ______ refused to recognize the constitution.
• On July 7, 1898, the U.S. Congress voted to ______.</td></tr>
<tr><td colspan="2">The Boxer Rebellion
A secret Chinese society, called the Boxers, tried to ______. Outside powers <u>crushed the rebellion</u>. To prevent other powers from seizing more Chinese territory, ______.</td></tr>
</table>

Refer to this page to answer the Chapter 20 Focus Question on page 318.

Section 2

The Spanish-American War

Section 2 Focus Question

What were the causes and effects of the Spanish-American War? To begin answering this question,

- Understand American interest in the Cuban rebellion.
- Learn what caused the U.S. to declare war on Spain.
- Find out how the United States governed its newly won territories.

Section 2 Summary

War broke out between Spain and Cuba, where the United States had business interests. The United States entered the war and gained territories in the Caribbean and the Pacific.

War Clouds Loom

Spain had ruled Cuba since Columbus landed in 1492. In 1868, Cubans revolted but were defeated. In 1895, a new revolt broke out. Spain responded with a policy of **reconcentration,** or the forced movement of large numbers of people into detention camps for military or political reasons. After about 200,000 Cubans died in the camps, Cuban exile **José Martí** appealed to the United States for help. Many Americans were sympathetic toward the Cuban cause. Others, who had money invested in Cuba, wanted the United States to intervene to protect their interests.

Neither President Cleveland nor President McKinley would intervene. Newspaper publishers **William Randolph Hearst** and Joseph Pulitzer, however, pushed Americans to call for war. Through yellow journalism, they ran headlines and stories that played up the horror in Cuba. When fighting broke out in Cuba's capital of Havana, President McKinley agreed to send the battleship *Maine* to protect American lives and property. On February 15, 1898, the ship exploded and sank, killing 260 men. Americans blamed Spain. "Remember the *Maine*" became the battle cry of revenge. ✓

The United States Goes to War

President McKinley wanted to make peace with Spain. He finally gave in and asked Congress to declare war on April 11, 1898. The first battle was fought not in Cuba, but in

Key Events

1893	American planters stage a revolt in Hawaii.
1898	United States wins the Spanish-American War.
1904	United States begins to build the Panama Canal.

Vocabulary Builder

Intervene comes from the Latin words *inter* ("between") and *venere* ("to come"). Using these meanings and the context clues in the text, explain what some Americans wanted the United States to do in Cuba.

____

____

✓ Checkpoint

Name the two publishers who fanned the flames of war in their newspapers.

____

____

the Philippines, another Spanish colony. Assistant Secretary of the Navy Theodore Roosevelt ordered Commodore George Dewey to move American ships to the Philippines. On May 1, Dewey's small fleet entered Manila Bay and sank all of the Spanish ships there without losing one U.S. ship or life. Dewey then received help from a Philippine rebel leader, **Emilio Aguinaldo.** He was fighting to overthrow Spanish rule. Americans were soon in control of the islands.

When the war shifted to Cuba, the main fighting took place near the city of Santiago and at sea. Roosevelt, who had given up his navy post, led the Rough Riders unit in a successful charge up San Juan Hill, which became a highlight of the war. The U.S. Navy then destroyed the Spanish fleet trapped in Santiago Harbor. Within two weeks, the Spanish surrendered Cuba. Soon, the United States invaded and controlled the Spanish island of Puerto Rico. ✓

✓ Checkpoint

List the three Spanish possessions where fighting occurred in the Spanish-American War.

____

____

____

An American Empire

In December 1898, the United States and Spain signed a peace treaty. Cuba gained its independence. The United States paid Spain $20 million and took control of Puerto Rico, the Philippines, and the Pacific islands of Guam and Wake. Many Americans were unhappy about acquiring colonies. The expansionists, however, were eager to open new businesses and to spread the idea of democratic government.

Reading Strategy

Reread the bracketed paragraph. Circle the sentence that summarizes the main idea. Draw arrows to details that support the main idea.

Mark the Text

The United States replaced Spain as a colonial power in the Caribbean. Congress forced the Cuban government to adopt the Platt Amendment in its constitution. This amendment limited Cuba's power and made it a U.S. **protectorate,** an independent country whose policies are controlled by an outside power. The Foraker Act of 1900 gave Puerto Rico limited self-rule. Puerto Ricans became U.S. citizens, but many wanted their freedom. In the Philippines, Emilio Aguinaldo led a revolt against U.S. rule. In 1901, he was captured and the fighting ended. ✓

✓ Checkpoint

Name the rebel leader who led Filipinos against American rule.

____

Check Your Progress

1. Why were expansionists eager to acquire colonies?

____

____

2. What new territories did the United States acquire?

____

____

Section 2 Notetaking Study Guide

Question to Think About As you read Section 2 in your textbook and take notes, keep this section focus question in mind: **What were the causes and effects of the Spanish-American War?**

▶ Use this chart to record key information from the section. Some information has been filled in to get you started.

The Spanish-American War	
Cause	**Effect**
Cubans rose up against Spanish rule in 1895.	Spain began a policy of reconcentration.
Many Americans were sympathetic toward Cuba. Others wanted to safeguard American investments in Cuba.	____________
• Yellow journalists ____________. • Americans blamed Spain for ____________.	Americans called for the United States to declare war on Spain.
• Dewey's warships sank the Spanish squadron at ____________. • With help from ____________, Dewey seized Manila.	The United States gained control of the Philippine Islands.
In a battle along the Cuban coast, U.S. ships destroyed the Spanish fleet.	____________
Spain and the United States signed a peace treaty.	• Spain accepted Cuban independence. • Spain granted ____________ to the United States. • The United States paid ____________.
The United States forced Cuba to add the Platt Amendment to its constitution.	• Limited Cuba's ____________ • Gave the United States ____________ • Allowed the United States to ____________
The Foraker Act of 1900 was passed, setting up a government in Puerto Rico.	• Gave Puerto Ricans ____________
Filipino rebels renewed their fight for independence.	• After 3 years of fighting, ____________ was captured and fighting came to an end.

Refer to this page to answer the Chapter 20 Focus Question on page 318.

Key Events

1893	American planters stage a revolt in Hawaii.
1898	United States wins the Spanish-American War.
1904	United States begins to build the Panama Canal.

✓ Checkpoint

Explain why the United States backed the Panamanian rebels.

____

____

____

Reading Strategy

Ask and answer a question about the Panama Canal.

Question: _______________

____

Answer: _______________

____

Section 3

The United States and Latin America

Section 3 Focus Question

How did the United States use the Monroe Doctrine to justify intervention in Latin America? To begin answering this question,

- Learn why the United States built the Panama Canal.
- Read how President Roosevelt dealt with European interference in Latin America.
- Learn about President Taft's "dollar diplomacy."
- Read about President Wilson's troubles with Mexico.

Section 3 Summary

The United States intervened in Latin American conflicts. Building the Panama Canal was central to its goals in world trade and managing distant possessions.

Linking the Oceans

Before the 1900s, the shortest sea route from San Francisco to Cuba was around the tip of South America. The 14,000-mile journey took over two months. The United States needed a canal to connect the Atlantic and the Pacific oceans. A canal would improve shipping and help the United States police its new empire.

In 1902, the **Isthmus** of Panama, a narrow strip of land between the Caribbean Sea and the Pacific Ocean, was a province of Colombia. The United States offered Colombia $10 million and a yearly rent of $250,000 to use the isthmus. Colombia wanted more money. So President Theodore Roosevelt urged Panamanians to revolt against Colombian rule. The revolt, supported by the U.S. military, took place on November 3, 1903. Three days later, the United States took control of the 10-mile-wide zone across the Isthmus of Panama. ✓

The Panama Canal

Work on the Panama Canal began in 1904. The first big problem was disease. Malaria and yellow fever sickened many workers and halted work. Mosquitoes carried the diseases. **William C. Gorgas** was an American expert on tropical diseases. He had workers drain swamps to wipe out mosquitoes' breeding grounds. By 1906, the diseases had been greatly reduced. Canal construction moved forward with difficulty. Six thousand workers died as they cut through the earth, constructed dams, and built giant locks. Many more thousands of men changed miles of mud into the great canal. The canal opened on August 15, 1914. ✓

Wielding a "Big Stick" in Latin America

Roosevelt was fond of an old West African proverb, "Speak softly and carry a big stick; you will go far." In other words, if diplomacy failed, the United States would use military force. In 1904, Roosevelt applied his "big stick" policy in Latin America. He announced that the United States would use police power against foreign nations that got involved in disputes with Latin America. The policy came to be known as the Roosevelt Corollary to the Monroe Doctrine. A **corollary** is a logical extension of a doctrine or proposition.

President Taft, Roosevelt's successor, had a different approach. He believed in **dollar diplomacy.** This policy stated that economic ties were the best way to expand American influence. He urged businesses to invest heavily in Asia and Latin America. Taft's dollar diplomacy led to many military interventions in Latin American. ✓

Relations With Mexico

Woodrow Wilson became President in 1913. His foreign policy goal was to support and nurture democracy throughout the world. Wilson's ideas were first tested in Mexico, which was involved in a violent revolution after a dictator was overthrown. Wilson adopted a "watchful waiting" policy, hoping that Mexico would become a democratic nation. But when two U.S. sailors were briefly arrested in Mexico, Wilson sent in the navy and almost caused a war. Two years later, the rebel general **Francisco** "Pancho" **Villa** killed 18 Americans. General John J. Pershing led U.S. troops into Mexico looking for Villa, but failed to capture him. ✓

Check Your Progress

1. Why did Roosevelt want to build the Panama Canal?

____

____

____

2. What was meant by Roosevelt's "big stick" policy?

____

____

✓ Checkpoint

Name the first obstacle that interfered with building the Panama Canal.

____

Vocabulary Builder

A *succession* is the following of one thing after another. What, then, is the meaning of a *successor*?

____

____

____

✓ Checkpoint

Name the earlier policy that the Roosevelt Corollary extended.

____

✓ Checkpoint

Explain Wilson's foreign policy goal.

____

____

Section 3 Notetaking Study Guide

Question to Think About As you read Section 3 in your textbook and take notes, keep this section focus question in mind: **How did the United States use the Monroe Doctrine to justify intervention in Latin America?**

▶ Use this chart to record key information from the section. Some information has been filled in to get you started.

The United States and Latin America
The United States and Panama
• In 1902, the United States wanted to build a canal across Panama linking the ____________ and ____________ oceans. • After helping Panama win its independence from Colombia, the United States and Panama signed a treaty that gave the United States ____________. • In return, the United States paid Panama ____________. • Construction of the ____________ began in 1904 and was completed in ______.
Roosevelt's Foreign Policy
• Roosevelt wanted the world to know that the United States ____________ ____________. • In 1904, European nations considered ____________ in the Dominican Republic. Roosevelt wanted to prevent this. He announced a new policy that became known as the ____________ to the ____________. • This policy stated that the United States had the right to ____________ ____________.
Taft's Dollar Diplomacy
• Dollar diplomacy was based on the idea that economic ties were the best way to expand American influence. • As a result, American bankers and business leaders ____________ ____________. • Dollar diplomacy led to U.S. military intervention in ____________, ____________, and ____________.
Woodrow Wilson's Foreign Policy
• Wilson believed that U.S. foreign policy should ____________. • After Porfírio Díaz was overthrown, Wilson's policy toward Mexico was one of ____________. • In 1914, Wilson intervened in Mexico after American sailors were arrested in Tampico. • In 1916, the United States was drawn into Mexican affairs again when ____________ ____________. The United States responded by ____________.

Refer to this page to answer the Chapter 20 Focus Question on page 318.

Chapter 20 Assessment

Directions: Circle the letter of the correct answer.

1. In the late 1800s and early 1900s, the United States changed
- **A** from trade to "gunboat diplomacy."
- **B** from expansionism to isolationism.
- **C** from isolationism to expansionism.

2. With which countries did the United States engage in battle?
- **A** Japan and China **B** China and Spain **C** Japan and Spain

3. Woodrow Wilson supported
- **A** isolationism.
- **B** spreading democracy.
- **C** dollar diplomacy.

Directions: Follow the steps to answer this question:

How were U.S. policies between 1853 and 1915 toward countries in the Pacific and in Latin America similar and different?

Step 1: Recall information: In the chart, list U.S. actions in each area.

Japan	
Alaska	
Hawaii	
China	
Cuba	
Panama	
Mexico	

Step 2: Write each country under the type of U.S. action that occurred there.

Peaceful Intervention	Military Intervention

Step 3: Complete the topic sentence that follows. Then write two or three sentences summarizing how U.S. actions were similar and different.

Between 1853 and 1915, U.S. actions were ______________________________

____

____

Chapter 20 Notetaking Study Guide

Now you are ready to answer the Chapter 20 Focus Question: **How did the United States demonstrate its growing interest in the Pacific and in Latin America?**

▶ Complete the following chart to help you answer this question. Use the notes that you took for each section.

The United States Looks Overseas	
Commodore Perry's mission to Japan	• Opened up ____________ with Japan • Effect on Japan: set out to transform its feudal society into an industrial nation
The purchase of Alaska and the annexation of Hawaii	• Secretary of State ____________ saw Alaska as a stepping stone for trade with ____________ and the ____________. • Why expansionists were interested in Hawaii: ____________ • How Hawaii became a U.S. territory: ____________
Open Door Policy in China	• The first Open Door Policy: ____________ • The second Open Door Policy: repeated the principle of free trade and said China should not be broken up
Spanish-American War	• The United States intervened in the conflict in Cuba to protect ____________. • Terms of the treaty ending the war: ____________
Panama Canal	• The United States gained access to the Isthmus of Panama after helping Panama gain its independence from ____________. • The canal linked the ____________ and ____________.
Foreign relations under Theodore Roosevelt	• Roosevelt's Big Stick Policy: ____________ • The Roosevelt Corollary: ____________
Foreign relations under Taft	• Taft's policy was called ____________. • What it was: a policy based on the idea that economic ties were the best way to expand American influence
Foreign relations under Wilson	• Wilson's foreign policy: ____________ • Led to two incidents in ____________

Refer to this page to answer the Unit 7 Focus Question on page 347.

Chapter 21

World War I (1914–1919)

What You Will Learn

In 1914, a war broke out in Europe. Although the United States at first remained neutral, it eventually joined the war. World War I had important effects throughout the world.

Chapter 21 Focus Question

As you read this chapter, keep this question in mind: **What were the causes and effects of World War I?**

Key Events

1914	World War I begins in Europe.
1917	United States declares war on Germany.
1918	Armistice ends World War I.
1919	U.S. Senate rejects the Treaty of Versailles.

Section 1

The Road to War

Section 1 Focus Question

What were the causes of World War I? To begin answering this question,

- Understand the factors that led to the outbreak of war.
- Learn why World War I was so deadly.
- Find out how American neutrality was tested.
- Understand the events that led the U.S. into the war.

Section 1 Summary

As competition for colonies increased, European nations began to take sides in case war broke out. War finally erupted. The U.S. tried to remain neutral but later joined the Allies.

Origins of World War I

European **militarism**, or the glorification of the military, grew in the early 1900s. **Nationalism**, or pride in one's national or ethnic group, also rose. The Balkan countries became tense as Balkan nationalists sought independence from Austria-Hungry. Two alliance systems formed among European nations. On June 28, 1914, a Serbian nationalist killed the heir to the Austro-Hungarian throne, Archduke Franz Ferdinand. In July, Austria-Hungary invaded Serbia. The alliance system soon drew more than twenty nations into the war. Britain, France, and Russia led the Allies. They fought against the Central powers of Germany, Austria-Hungary, and the Ottoman Empire. ✓

✓ Checkpoint

Name the two sides in World War I.

____

____

✓ Checkpoint

List three factors that made World War I much deadlier than previous wars.

____

____

____

The Deadliest War

Everyone hoped for a quick victory. Both sides used new weapons that made the battles more deadly, however, which lengthened the war. Airplanes, tanks, rapid-fire guns, and heavy artillery took a heavy toll. **Trench warfare,** in which soldiers fired on one another from opposite lines of dugouts, was brutal. The most feared weapon was poison gas. ☑

✓ Checkpoint

Name two ethnic American groups that supported the Central powers.

____

____

American Neutrality

Officially, the United States remained neutral, yet many German and Irish Americans supported the Central powers. Americans of British, Italian, and Slavic heritage generally supported the Allies. To strengthen American support, Britain used **propaganda,** or spreading stories about enemy brutality that were often exaggerated or made up.

American banks made loans to the Allies. U.S. businesses traded mostly with the Allies. And in any case, Britain's naval blockade of Germany prevented U.S. merchant ships from entering German ports. Germany announced it would use U-boats, or submarines, to blockade Britain and France. On May 7, 1915, a U-boat sank the British passenger ship *Lusitania,* with 128 Americans aboard. Afraid that the United States would enter the war, Germany promised not to target neutral merchant ships or passenger liners. ☑

✓ Checkpoint

State the event that prevented the United States from allying with a tyrant.

____

Entering the War

Wilson was reelected in 1916 on the slogan "He kept us out of war." But in February 1917, the British intercepted the Zimmermann Telegram. In it, Germany asked Mexico to join the Central powers in exchange for help in regaining New Mexico, Texas, and Arizona. Americans were furious. Then U-boats sank three U.S. ships. In March, a revolution overthrew the Russian tsar. Wilson could now enter the war without fighting on the same side as a tyrant. On April 2, 1917, Congress declared war on the Central powers. ☑

Check Your Progress

1. What event sparked World War I on June 28, 1914?

____

____

2. What three events led the United States into the war?

____

____

Section 1 Notetaking Study Guide

Question to Think About As you read Section 1 in your textbook and take notes, keep this section focus question in mind: **What were the causes of World War I?**

▶ Use this chart to record key information from the section. Some information has been filled in to get you started.

Events Leading to U.S. Entry into World War I	
Prior to June 1914	European imperialism led to a rise in militarism and nationalism. European nations formed alliances: • ________: Germany allied with ________ and ________ • ________: France allied with Britain and Russia
June 28, 1914	A Serbian nationalist assassinated ________, heir to the ________.
July 29, 1914	Austria-Hungary invaded ________.
July 31, 1914	Russia ________.
August 1, 1914	Germany declared war on ________.
August 3, 1914	Germany declared war on ________.
August 4, 1914	Germany invaded ________. ________ declared war on Germany.
May 1915	A German U-boat sank the passenger ship ________, then told the United States that ________.
November 1916	________ is reelected on the slogan "________."
February 1917	Britain intercepted the ________ in which Germany proposed that Mexico join the war on Germany's side in return for help in reconquering New Mexico, Texas, and Arizona. Other events followed: • The Germans ________. • In Russia, ________.
April 1917	Wilson asks ________ to make the world "________."

Refer to this page to answer the Chapter 21 Focus Question on page 332.

Key Events

1914	World War I begins in Europe.
1917	United States declares war on Germany.
1918	Armistice ends World War I.
1919	U.S. Senate rejects the Treaty of Versailles.

✓ Checkpoint

Name three groups of people who were not subject to the draft yet chose to volunteer for military service.

____

____

____

Section 2

Supporting the War Effort

Section 2 Focus Question

What steps did the U.S. government take to prepare the nation for war? To begin answering this question,

- Find out how the United States quickly mobilized.
- Learn about the agencies that helped to manage the war.
- Read how antiwar opinions were suppressed.

Section 2 Summary

After declaring war on the Central powers, the United States had to raise, train, and equip an army. It also had to coordinate industrial production and boost public support.

Building the Military

Although the United States had a large navy, its army was small. The nation had to quickly **mobilize,** or prepare for war. Many men volunteered to fight, but there were too few to build an army. Therefore, Congress passed the Selective Service Act, which required men between the ages of 21 and 30 to register for the draft. By the end of the war, almost four million Americans had entered the armed services.

More than 30,000 women volunteered, most of them as nurses for the army and navy. Others did clerical work as members of the navy and marines. Some leading women were against the war. **Jeannette Rankin,** the first woman elected to Congress, refused to send men to fight because she, as a woman, was unable to do so. Suffragists, however, urged women to support the war effort. They hoped their contributions would help them gain the right to vote.

Many Native Americans, not yet U.S. citizens, volunteered. Some 380,000 African Americans also served, but only 10 percent saw combat. They were placed in segregated units. Several members of the Harlem Hell Fighters received France's highest medal for bravery.

For many soldiers from poor rural areas, the military was a great educator. The military taught these soldiers how to fight and read. The soldiers also learned about nutrition, personal hygiene, and patriotism. ✓

Managing the War Effort

President Wilson chose **Herbert Hoover** to head a new Food Administration. It made sure that there was enough food for troops and civilians. Many people planted "victory gardens" to grow their own food. Wilson also created the War Industries Board. The Board told industries what and how much to make, and how much to charge.

As immigration dropped and more men served in the military, industries experienced a severe labor shortage. Women and African Americans, who migrated to factories in the Midwest and Northeast, filled many of the jobs. ✓

Shaping Public Opinion

Another government agency, the Committee on Public Information, kept public support high for the war. It recruited "Four-Minute Men" to give patriotic speeches at movie theaters and ballparks. It hired artists to produce pro-war cartoons and posters, and movie stars to sell war bonds.

In contrast, criticism of the war was harshly suppressed. The Espionage Act of 1917 and the Sedition Act of 1918 closed newspapers and jailed people for expressing antiwar opinions. **Eugene V. Debs,** a labor leader and Socialist Party candidate for president, was among those jailed. Debs, who urged people not to support the war, made this ironic comment: "It is extremely dangerous to exercise the constitutional right of free speech in a country fighting to make democracy safe in the world."

Private organizations encouraged people to spy on their neighbors and report anyone who did not comply with pro-war behavior. The American Protective League hired 200,000 people to open mail, tap phones, and pry into medical records. German Americans, who were shunned and even attacked, probably suffered worst of all. ✓

Check Your Progress

1. What was the purpose of the Selective Service Act?

____

____

2. What steps did the Committee on Public Information take to promote pro-war support?

____

____

✓ Checkpoint

List two government agencies that helped manage resources during the war.

____

____

Reading Strategy

Review the bracketed paragraphs.

Underline the phrase that signals you are reading about contrasting ideas.

Vocabulary Builder

When you *comply* with something, you go along with it. With what did the American people need to comply?

____

____

✓ Checkpoint

Name two acts that punished the expression of antiwar views.

____

____

Section 2 Notetaking Study Guide

Question to Think About As you read Section 2 in your textbook and take notes, keep this section focus question in mind: **What steps did the U.S. government take to prepare the nation for war?**

▶ Use this chart to record key information from the section. Some information has been filled in to get you started.

Building the Military

- Many men volunteered to fight but there were too few to form an army, so Congress passed the Selective Service Act. Men between the ages of 21 and 30 had to ____________________.
- Women were not drafted, but more than 30,000 __________. Suffragists hoped women's wartime service would help them __________ after the war.
- Other volunteers included __________ and __________.
- For poor, rural recruits, the war was a great educator because ____________________.

Managing the War Effort

- Herbert Hoover was appointed to head the __________ in order to ____________________.
- People grew __________ in order to __________.
- Wilson also created the __________ to oversee the shift to __________.
- A drop in immigration and __________ led to a __________. Women and __________ filled many of the vacancies.

Shaping Public Opinion

- The Committee on Public Information recruited "__________" to deliver __________. It also hired artists to produce __________ and movie stars to __________.
- Two Acts were passed to suppress criticism of the war: the __________ and the __________, which ____________________.
- At times, war fever collided with personal freedoms. Private organizations, such as the __________, enlisted people to snoop on their neighbors.

Refer to this page to answer the Chapter 21 Focus Question on page 332.

Section 3
Americans at War

Section 3 Focus Question

How did the arrival of American troops in Europe affect the course of the war? To begin answering this question,

- Learn how the first U.S. troops in Europe were received.
- Find out how the American troops aided the Allies.
- Read about President Wilson's plan for the armistice.

Section 3 Summary

German military might became stronger after making a treaty with Russia. Then the Americans joined the Allies, and together their combined efforts overcame the Central powers.

Joining the Fight

From February through April 1917, German submarines sank 844 Allied ships. To get supplies from the United States, the Allies developed a **convoy** system. Allied destroyers accompanied large groups of merchant ships sailing together. This system greatly decreased Allied losses.

Meanwhile, American forces prepared to enter the war. The American Expeditionary Force, as it was called in Europe, was under the leadership of **John J. Pershing.** On President Wilson's orders, Pershing insisted that American troops not integrate with Allied units. Wilson wanted the United States to make its own victorious showing. He believed this would allow the United States to influence the peace settlement. The first troops to arrive in Paris in June were not ready for combat. They did lift French morale, however, showing America's commitment to the war. ✓

Setbacks and Advances

While the Allies waited for more American troops, their situation grew worse. Fighting bogged down on the Western Front. The Central powers won a major victory in Italy.

Then Russia's new government, under Bolshevik leader **Vladimir Lenin,** pulled out of the war and signed a peace treaty with Germany. Lenin wanted to concentrate on taking his country toward **communism.** This is an economic and political system based on the idea that social classes and

Key Events

1914	World War I begins in Europe.
1917	United States declares war on Germany.
1918	Armistice ends World War I.
1919	U.S. Senate rejects the Treaty of Versailles.

✓ Checkpoint

Describe two ways the United States assisted the Allies.

____

____

____

Reading Strategy

Read the bracketed text. Think about the treaty it describes. Underline the two sentences that tell the effects of the treaty.

Mark the Text

✓ Checkpoint

Name the treaty that allowed Germany to concentrate solely on the Western Front.

____

____

Vocabulary Builder

To *abdicate* means "to give up a high position in government." What position did Wilhelm II abdicate?

____

____

✓ Checkpoint

Name the two nations that dictated the terms of the armistice.

____

____

private property should be eliminated. Russia and Germany signed the Treaty of Brest-Litovsk in March 1918. The treaty gave Germany about 30 percent of Russia's territory. Peace with Russia allowed Germany to move a huge number of troops to the Western Front. Germany hoped to defeat the Allies before the American troops arrived.

On March 21, 1918, the Germans launched a series of daring attacks. They moved through Belgium and into France. The situation became so grave that General Pershing turned over all U.S. resources to the French. He even allowed the French to command American troops. It was a good decision. Twice during that summer, American and Allied troops pushed the Germans back from the Marne River, keeping them away from Paris. By September, the Allies—including one million American soldiers—advanced against German positions in northeastern France. By November, the German defenses had crumbled. ✓

The Armistice

Germany's leaders decided to seek an **armistice,** a halt in fighting, to discuss the conditions of a peace treaty. The remaining Central powers also agreed to an armistice. Germany had hoped the settlement would be based on Wilson's peace plan, founded on principles of international cooperation. In the end, however, Wilson's plan had little effect. Instead, Britain and France dictated the terms of the agreement. Germany had to pull its troops from the Western Front, cancel the Treaty of Brest-Litovsk, and surrender all of its U-boats. At Wilson's urging, Kaiser Wilhelm II had to abdicate his throne so that Germany could develop a republic.

The armistice went into effect on November 11, 1918, at 11 A.M. The bloodiest and most brutal war the world had yet seen was over. About 10 million soldiers had died. Millions of other soldiers were maimed for life. Some historians think civilian deaths equaled the number of military deaths. ✓

Check Your Progress

1. Why did Russia pull out of the war?

____

____

2. What were the terms of the armistice?

____

____

Section 3 Notetaking Study Guide

Question to Think About As you read Section 3 in your textbook and take notes, keep this section focus question in mind: **How did the arrival of American troops in Europe affect the course of the war?**

▶ Use this chart to record key information from the section. Some information has been filled in to get you started.

Americans at War	
Cause	**Effect**
1. German U-boats destroy many Allied ships.	• U.S. supplies cannot get to the Allies •
2. President Wilson wants the United States to make its own victorious showing.	•
3. First Division of the American Expeditionary Force arrives in Paris.	•
4. Russia signs a peace agreement with Germany.	•
5. Daring German attacks create a grave situation for the Allies.	•
6. Allied forces push forward along a line that stretches from the North Sea to Verdun.	• German defenses crumble •
Terms of the armistice: • • • • Kaiser Wilhelm II forced to abdicate throne	
War dead: Total military personnel France Britain Germany Russia American Civilian no one knows; some historians believe civilian deaths equaled military deaths	

Refer to this page to answer the Chapter 21 Focus Question on page 332.

Section 4

Shaping the Peace

Key Events

1914	World War I begins in Europe.
1917	United States declares war on Germany.
1918	Armistice ends World War I.
1919	U.S. Senate rejects the Treaty of Versailles.

✓ Checkpoint

List the three main ideas that the Fourteen Points addressed.

____

____

____

Section 4 Focus Question

How did the Treaty of Versailles and the League of Nations disappoint President Wilson? To answer this question,

- Learn about President Wilson's Fourteen Points.
- Find out how the Treaty of Versailles punished Germany.
- Learn why Congress rejected the League of Nations.

Section 4 Summary

President Wilson insisted that the Treaty of Versailles set up a peacekeeping body. The treaty did set up the League of Nations. Congress, however, rejected U.S. membership in the League.

The Fourteen Points

President Wilson presented his peace plan, the Fourteen Points, to Congress before the war even ended. The first five points dealt with some of the causes of the war. Wilson called for an end to secret agreements. He sought freedom of the seas and free trade among nations. He asked for smaller armies, and a settlement of colonial claims. The next eight points dealt with territorial issues created by the war, especially **self-determination** for minority groups in Austria-Hungary and the Ottoman Empire. Under Wilson's plan, they would be able to decide for themselves what kind of government they would have. The fourteenth point was a call for an international peacekeeping body. ✓

Peace Conference in Paris

Cheering crowds greeted President Wilson in Paris in January 1919. The war-weary population approved of Wilson's Fourteen Points. Not in agreement were the other three members of the "Big Four"—prime ministers Georges Clemenceau of France, David Lloyd George of Britain, and Vittorio Orlando of Italy. They had already signed secret treaties dividing up the colonies of the Central powers.

The final peace agreement, known as the Treaty of Versailles (ver SĪ) forced Germany to accept full responsibility for the war and to pay huge **reparations,** or payments to cover war damages. Wilson disagreed with the harsh treaty, but he went along with the Allies in order to win his international peacekeeping organization. The Versailles Treaty included an organization like the one in Wilson's plan. It was called the League of Nations. On June 28, 1919, Germany signed the treaty.

Other treaties led to Austria, Hungary, and Czechoslovakia becoming separate states. The Balkan peoples formed Yugoslavia. Poland became independent. Britain and France divided Germany's African colonies and the Middle Eastern lands of the Ottoman Empire. The Ottoman Empire became the new republic of Turkey. ✓

Battle Over the League

The U.S. Senate strongly opposed the Treaty of Versailles. Senator **Henry Cabot Lodge** led the opposition. He felt that the League of Nations would limit America's ability to act independently in its own interests. He asked for changes that would reduce United States ties to the League. Wilson would not give in. Instead, he tried to rally public support for the League. He gave speeches around the country. Despite Wilson's efforts to save the League, he failed. The Senate voted against the Treaty of Versailles. This decision crippled the League of Nations' peacekeeping power. ✓

Postwar Troubles

The postwar years were troubled times. A worldwide epidemic of influenza (flu) killed more people than the war had. Soldiers returning home could not find jobs. Union workers demanding higher wages went on strike. Many Americans thought the Communists, or "Reds," were behind the labor troubles. Attorney General Palmer ordered thousands of immigrants suspected of radical views to return to their home countries. Eventually the public turned against Palmer's tactics, and the panic ended. ✓

Check Your Progress

1. Why did Wilson's Fourteen Points have little influence?

____

____

____

2. Why did Wilson agree to the Treaty of Versailles?

____

____

✓ Checkpoint

Name the "Big Four" and the nations they represented.

____

____

____

____

✓ Checkpoint

Name the U.S. senator who led the opposition to the Treaty of Versailles.

____

____

Vocabulary Builder

A person with *radical* views usually promotes extreme political, economic, or social changes. What radical view did the Americans fear during the postwar years?

____

✓ Checkpoint

List three major problems the United States faced after World War I.

____

____

____

Section 4 Notetaking Study Guide

Question to Think About As you read Section 4 in your textbook and take notes, keep this section focus question in mind: **How did the Treaty of Versailles and the League of Nations disappoint President Wilson?**

► Use this chart to record key information from the section. Some information has been filled in to get you started.

Shaping the Peace

The "Big Four" met in Paris in 1919.
U.S. President: ______________________
Prime Minister of France: ______________________
Prime Minister of Britain: ______________________
Prime Minister of Italy: Vittorio Orlando

Wilson's Goals	What Eventually Resulted
End to secret international agreements →	Britain, France, and Italy signed secret agreements dividing up territories and colonies of the Central powers.
Deal fairly with Germany →	______________________
Self-determination for minority peoples →	• Austria, __________, and __________ became separate states. • Balkan people __________ • Poland __________ • __________ replaced the Ottoman Empire • Britain and France divided __________
International peacekeeping body →	______________________
Ratification of the Treaty of Versailles →	______________________

U.S. *Opposition to The Treaty of Versailles*
The United States opposed the Treaty of Versailles. Senator __________ objected to the Treaty's peacekeeping body, the __________, because __________. Wilson campaigned to __________, but his efforts failed.

Refer to this page to answer the Chapter 21 Focus Question on page 332.

Chapter 21 Assessment

Directions: Circle the letter of the correct answer.

1. Who made up the Central powers?
   - **A** Germany, Italy, Japan
   - **B** Germany, Austria-Hungary, Italy
   - **C** Germany, Austria-Hungary, Ottoman Empire

2. Which of the following was ***not*** a result of World War I?
   - **A** the League of Nations
   - **B** Communist ideology
   - **C** the breakup of the Ottoman Empire

3. Woodrow Wilson supported
   A dividing Germany. **B** secret treaties. **C** League of Nations.

Directions: Follow the steps to answer this question:

Which minority peoples of Central Europe gained the right to determine their own government as a result of the Treaty of Versailles?

Step 1: Recall information: In the chart, list the colonial status before and after the war.

Nation	Pre-War Colonies	Post-War Changes
Germany	Controlled colonies in ________	Lost ________
Austria-Hungary	Controlled ________	Lost ________ Became ________
Ottoman Empire	Controlled ________	Lost ________ Became ________
Britain	had colonial empire throughout world	Gained half of ________
France	had colonies in West Africa and West Indies	Gained half of ________

Step 2: List the minority peoples who gained self-determination after the war.

Gained Self-determination	Did Not Gain Self-determination

Step 3: Complete the topic sentence that follows. Then write two or three sentences summarizing the degree to which Wilson's point calling for self-determined governments was fulfilled.

The Treaty of Versailles allowed ________________________________

____

____

Chapter 21 Notetaking Study Guide

Now you are ready to answer the Chapter 21 Focus Question: **What were the causes and effects of World War I?**

▶ Complete the charts to help you answer this question. Use the notes that you took for each section.

Causes of World War I

Imperialism	Nationalism	Alliance Systems
• Germany had colonies in ______________. • Austria-Hungary ruled ______________. • Ottoman Empire ruled other nationalities in the Middle East and Africa.	Ethnic groups in the Balkan region wanted to free themselves of ______________.	• ______, ______, and ______ formed the Central powers. • The nations of ______, ______, and ______ formed the Allies.

World War I Begins

On June 28, 1914, a Serbian nationalist assassinated ______________ of Austria-Hungary. As a result, Austria-Hungary declared war on ______________. Britain, France, and ______________ came to its aid. Germany, and later the Ottoman Empire, ______________.

Events that Brought America into the War

At first, America ______________, allowing it to trade with both sides, although most American trade and banking helped the ______________. President Wilson cut off diplomatic relations with Germany when Germany ______________. America finally entered the war after Germany tried to get Mexico to join forces with the Central Powers and ______________.

Results of the Allied Victory

The Treaty of Versailles punished ______________ and changed the map of Europe. Germany had to pay ______________ and lost ______________. Austria-Hungary and the Ottoman Empire were ______________. The Treaty established a peacekeeping organization called the ______________. The U.S. rejected ______________ because ______________.

Refer to this page to answer the Unit 7 Focus Question on page 347.

Chapter 22

The Roaring Twenties

(1919–1929)

What You Will Learn

After World War I, U.S. presidents shifted the country's focus to domestic issues. Mass culture was transformed. The decade was prosperous but had serious economic problems.

Chapter 22 Focus Question

As you read this chapter, keep this question in mind: **How did the nation react to change in the 1920s?**

Section 1

Adjusting to Peacetime

Section 1 Focus Question

What problems at home and abroad challenged the nation after World War I? To begin answering this question,

- Learn about the administrations of Hoover and Coolidge.
- Understand what postwar isolationism meant.
- Read about the Red Scare.

Section 1 Summary

Due to a poor economy and threats of violence, people voted largely Republican in the election of 1920. This began an era of big business, isolationism, and immigration restrictions.

Return to Normalcy

President Wilson had expected to return home from the Paris Peace Conference a hero. Instead, the failure of the United States to sign the Treaty of Versailles, plus an economic recession, cost his Democratic Party the election of 1920. Labor strikes, racial violence, and threats of communism also disturbed Americans. Voters hoped new leadership would lead the decade into peace and prosperity.

President **Warren Harding** of Ohio promised a return to "normalcy." He supported business interests and appointed friends to government jobs. These men often used their jobs to make personal fortunes, leading to many scandals. Upon

Key Events

1919	18th Amendment prohibits the consumption and sale of alcoholic beverages.
1924	Teapot Dome and other government scandals become public.
1927	Lindbergh flies alone across the Atlantic.

Vocabulary Builder

Decade comes from *decem*, the Latin word for "ten." How many years are in a decade?

____

✓ Checkpoint

List three reasons the Democrats lost favor in 1920.

____

____

____

✓ Checkpoint

List two ways the United States participated in international affairs during the Coolidge administration.

____

____

Reading Strategy

Read the underlined sentence. Find and circle the stated cause. Draw an arrow to the effect.

Mark the Text

✓ Checkpoint

Name the two men who symbolized the Red Scare.

____

____

Harding's death in 1923, Vice President **Calvin Coolidge** became President. People saw him as an honest man. He went on to win the 1924 election by a large margin. The economy revived and the 1920s began to "roar." ✓

Foreign Policy

World War I had made the United States an international power. Yet most Americans favored isolationism. The United States did not cut itself off completely from world affairs, however. It participated in international conferences to promote **disarmament,** or the reduction of weapons. With France, the United States sponsored the Kellogg-Briand Pact, which condemned military aggression and outlawed war. In addition, Coolidge felt the United States could get involved in foreign conflicts when America's business interests were threatened. This happened several times in Latin America. ✓

The Red Scare

President Wilson had refused to recognize the Soviet Union's new Communist government. **Communism** is an anti-democratic political system in which the single-party government controls all means of production. The fear of Communists, or Red Scare, reached a peak in 1919. In addition, **anarchists,** or people who oppose organized government, set off a series of bombings. Many anarchists were foreign born. Thousands of anarchists and "Reds" were deported.

The 1920 trial of Nicola Sacco and Bartolomeo Vanzetti symbolized the public hysteria of the time. Both were charged with murder. There was little evidence of their guilt. <u>They were convicted and executed mostly because they were foreign anarchists.</u>

Fear of radical immigrants, along with fear of losing jobs to newcomers, led Congress to pass an emergency immigration law in 1921. The law limited European immigration and stopped all Asian immigration. ✓

Check Your Progress

1. What did Harding promise that won him the presidency?

____

____

2. What two actions did the U.S. government take to stop anarchists and Communists?

____

____

Section 1 Notetaking Study Guide

Question to Think About As you read Section 1 in your textbook and take notes, keep this section focus question in mind: **What problems at home and abroad challenged the nation after World War I?**

► Use this chart to record key information from the section. Some information has been filled in to get you started.

Adjusting to Peacetime

Return to Normalcy

President Wilson expected to return home a hero, but several factors put Democrats out of power:

- Mishandling of the peace treaty at Versailles, an economic ______, labor disputes that led to ______, and fear that ______ would overthrow the government

Harding Administration

- Harding promised a ______.
- Appointed businessmen, including ______ as secretary of the treasury
- Slashed the ______
- Scandals marred Harding's presidency, including the Teapot Dome scandal, after which ______ became the first Cabinet member sent to prison.
- After Harding died, Vice President ______ took office.

Foreign Policy

Most Americans favored ______ after World War I.
The United States, however, continued to participate in world affairs:

- Encouraged ______, or limiting weapons
- Joined the ______, limiting powerful navies
- Sponsored the ______, which outlawed war
- Coolidge sent troops to ______ to protect American business interests.

The Red Scare

Alarm about ______ affected American foreign policy and events at home.
Postwar strikes led Americans to believe that a revolution was beginning.

- A series of bombings by ______ led to many Communists being hunted down, arrested, and ______.
- Two Italian immigrants, ______ and ______, were arrested and executed based on the fact that both were ______ and ______.
- Immigration was limited because of fears about ______, and American workers feared for their jobs.
- Immigration law limited people from ______ and prohibited immigration from ______.

Refer to this page to answer the Chapter 22 Focus Question on page 346.

Key Events

1919 18th Amendment prohibits the consumption and sale of alcoholic beverages.

1924 Teapot Dome and other government scandals become public.

1927 Lindbergh flies alone across the Atlantic.

✓ Checkpoint

Name the amendments that established and repealed Prohibition.

____

____

Reading Strategy

Reread the bracketed paragraph. Underline a signal word that shows two things are being compared. Circle a phrase signaling that two things are being contrasted.

Mark the Text

Section 2
Changes in American Society

Section 2 Focus Question

How did social change and social conflict mark the 1920s? To begin answering this question,

- Find out how Prohibition affected the nation.
- Learn about the changing social position of women.
- Read about inventions that created a new mass culture.
- Understand the conflicts created by rapid change.

Section 2 Summary

American society saw many social and political changes in the 1920s. Prohibition laws led to more crime. Women gained the right to vote, and social conflicts split the nation.

Prohibition

During World War I, the temperance movement gained public support. In 1919, the states ratified the Eighteenth Amendment, which prohibited the making, selling, and transporting of alcohol. The new law ushered in the age of Prohibition. Saloons closed, but illegal ones called **speakeasies** took their place. A smuggling industry known as bootlegging arose. **Bootleggers** transported alcohol from Canada and the Caribbean into the country. Organized crime made huge amounts of money from bootlegging. As a result, gang warfare and lawlessness increased. It soon became clear that Prohibition could not be enforced. The Twenty-first Amendment repealed Prohibition in 1933. ✓

Changing Lives of Women

[The Nineteenth Amendment was ratified before the 1920 election, giving women the right to vote for president. Before long, they were joining political parties. Some were elected to office. Both Wyoming and Texas elected women governors. In spite of these new freedoms, women's lives remained restricted in other ways. Many universities and professional schools, such as medical schools, still did not admit them. In some states, they could not serve on juries. Some married women could not keep the money they earned. More women were holding jobs, however.

Meanwhile, a younger generation of women was showing another kind of independence. They wore short dresses and "bobbed" their hair. These young women, called "flappers," shocked many people but became the symbol for women of the 1920s. ✓

> **✓ Checkpoint**
>
> Identify the purpose of the Nineteenth Amendment.
>
> ______________________________
>
> ______________________________

A New Mass Culture

Another symbol of the 1920s was the automobile. Henry Ford introduced the assembly line, which made the Model T Ford faster to produce and cheaper to buy. New roads with gas stations and restaurants increased travel and tourism.

The first commercial radio station began broadcasting in 1920. By 1926, more than 700 stations and a national radio network were bringing the same radio shows into millions of homes. Motion pictures also became popular. ✓

> **✓ Checkpoint**
>
> List two forms of media that contributed to a mass culture in the 1920s.
>
> ______________________________
>
> ______________________________

Social Conflict

Rapid change created conflict between old and new social values. One such conflict was the 1925 Scopes trial. John Scopes was a high school biology teacher in Dayton, Tennessee. He went against religious leaders and state law by teaching Charles Darwin's theory of evolution to his students. Clarence Darrow, a famous Chicago lawyer, defended Scopes. Darrow lost the case, and Scopes lost his job. The trial, however, ridiculed the old way of thinking.

Racial conflict became another problem. Many African Americans moved from the South to find jobs in northern cities. This so-called Great Migration led to racial tensions and violent riots. In response, Marcus Garvey, an immigrant from Jamaica, created the Universal Negro Improvement Association (UNIA). It promoted black pride and black unity. At the same time, the Ku Klux Klan—an organization opposed to blacks, immigrants, Catholics, and Jews—gained power. It spread from the South to the Midwest and the West before its decline. ✓

> **✓ Checkpoint**
>
> Name the organization founded by Marcus Garvey.
>
> ______________________________
>
> ______________________________

Check Your Progress

1. What were three main social conflicts during the 1920s?

____

____

2. What effect did the Model T Ford have on American culture?

____

____

Section 2 Notetaking Study Guide

Question to Think About As you read Section 2 in your textbook and take notes, keep this section focus question in mind: **How did social change and social conflict mark the 1920s?**

▶ Use this chart to record key information from the section. Some information has been filled in to get you started.

Changes in American Society
Prohibition
During World War I, prohibition was supported as a way to conserve ____________. • In 1919, the states ratified the ____________, which prohibited the making, selling, or transporting of alcohol. • Saloons closed, but the law proved impossible to ____________. • ____________ made huge profits importing illegal alcohol. • Every large town had a ____________. • Prohibition led to the growth of ____________. • In February 1933, Prohibition was repealed by the ____________.
Changing Lives of Women
• ____________ gave women the right to vote in the 1920 presidential election. • Two women governors: ____________ and ____________ • In some states, women could not serve on ____________ or keep their ____________. • Younger women known as ____________ became the symbol of women in the 1920s.
A New Mass Culture
• Henry Ford introduced the ____________, which made the price for a Model T ____________. • The automobile became the symbol of ____________. • New businesses created by the automobile: ____________ • Cars made it easier for families to move to ____________, and people in rural areas were less ____________. Cars also encouraged tourism. • The first commercial radio station: ____________ • Families listened to ____________ and political conventions. • The first major "talking" movie: ____________
Social Conflict
• The Scopes trial pitted religion against scientific theory. • Many African Americans moved north in the ____________. • Race riots broke out, with the worst occurring in ____________ in 1919. • Jamaican immigrant ____________ created the ____________ ____________. It promoted ____________ and encouraged African Americans to ____________. • Social tensions led to the growth of ____________.

Refer to this page to answer the Chapter 22 Focus Question on page 346.

Section 3
The Jazz Age

Section 3 Focus Question

What arts and culture symbolized the Jazz Age? To begin answering this question,

- Read about the new pastimes of the 1920s.
- Learn about a unique American musical sound.
- Find out about writers who chronicled the social values of the 1920s.
- Understand the Harlem Renaissance.

Section 3 Summary

During the 1920s, American culture saw new fads and heroes. America's popular dance, music, and literature expressed hopes and conflicts of a new generation.

Fads and Heroes

The 1920s was a decade of prosperity that saw many new enthusiasms. Lively dances, such as the Charleston and the Lindy Hop, were the rage. Fads such as flagpole sitting and dance marathons swept the country. The Chinese game of mah-jongg became popular.

The sports hero became a new kind of celebrity during the 1920s. Athletes such as baseball's Babe Ruth, swimmer Johnny Weissmuller, and champion golfer Bobby Jones became famous. The most popular celebrity of all was **Charles Lindbergh**, who made the first solo nonstop flight across the Atlantic. His nickname was Lucky Lindy. He came to symbolize the optimism of the decade. ✓

An American Sound

Jazz is a style of music that combined rhythms from West Africa and the Caribbean, work chants and spirituals from the rural South, and harmonies from Europe. African American musicians developed jazz in the nightclubs and dance halls of New Orleans. From there, jazz moved north during the Great Migration. Famous jazz stars were Louis Armstrong, Bessie Smith, and Duke Ellington.

Radio helped spread jazz, too. White composers and bandleaders, such as George Gershwin and Paul Whiteman, took on the style and gave it their own stamp. Jazz became one of the most important American contributions to world

Key Events

1919	18th Amendment prohibits the consumption and sale of alcoholic beverages.
1924	Teapot Dome and other government scandals become public.
1927	Lindbergh flies alone across the Atlantic.

✓ Checkpoint

List three fads that were popular in the 1920s.

____

____

____

Reading Strategy

Reread the bracketed paragraph. Use your own words to express the main idea of this paragraph.

____

____

____

✓ Checkpoint

List two ways in which jazz spread from New Orleans to other parts of the country.

______

______

Vocabulary Builder

The word *renaissance* means "rebirth." Why do you think the Harlem Renaissance was given this name?

______

______

______

✓ Checkpoint

List three major novelists of the 1920s.

______

______

______

culture. It was so popular that the 1920s are known as the Jazz Age. Yet like many other cultural movements, it widened the gap between older and younger generations. ✓

Literature of the 1920s

American literature in the 1920s showed both the decade's energy and its excesses. The novels of F. Scott Fitzgerald, Ernest Hemingway, and **Sinclair Lewis** were social criticisms as well as fictional stories. Fitzgerald's *The Great Gatsby* expressed disillusionment with the emptiness of rich people's lives. Hemingway's *The Sun Also Rises* and *A Farewell to Arms* captured the growing antiwar feelings. Lewis's *Babbitt* criticized the loose values and hypocrisy of middle-class culture. Fitzgerald and Hemingway, among others, actually left the United States to live abroad for extended periods.

During the 1920s, a vibrant African American culture known as the Harlem Renaissance emerged. Harlem was a large African American neighborhood of New York City. It attracted thousands of African Americans from the South. A different kind of social criticism arose among the black writers, musicians, and poets who settled in Harlem. Their moving works were a reaction to racial prejudice as well as an expression of hope. **Langston Hughes** expressed black pride in poetry that tried to capture the beat of jazz. James Weldon Johnson combined poetry and politics. He wrote editorials for the *New York Age*, an important black-owned newspaper. He also worked for the NAACP, an organization dedicated to the advancement of African Americans. Novelist and anthropologist Zora Neale Hurston recorded and explained many African American folk songs and folk tales. ✓

Check Your Progress

1. Who was the favorite celebrity of the 1920s and why?

______

______

2. Who were some of the major figures of the Harlem Renaissance?

______

______

Section 3 Notetaking Study Guide

Question to Think About As you read Section 3 in your textbook and take notes, keep this section focus question in mind: **What arts and culture symbolized the Jazz Age?**

► Use this chart to record key information from the section. Some information has been filled in to get you started.

Arts and Popular Culture of the Jazz Age

Fads

Dance fads that expressed the energy and optimism of the 1920s included the ___Charleston___, ______________, ______________, and ______________. Other fads included ______________, ______________, and ______________.

Heroes of the 1920s

- Baseball player ___Babe Ruth___
- Swimmer ______________
- Football player ______________
- Golf champion ______________
- Tennis stars ______________
- Boxer ______________

The most loved hero of the decade was ______________, whose Atlantic flight symbolized ______________.

Jazz Greats

Jazz was born in the nightclubs and dance halls of ______________.
It combined ___rhythms from West Africa and the Caribbean___, ______________, and ______________.

Famous jazz artists included ______________, ______________, and ______________.

Jazz emphasizes ______________ and ______________.

Notable Writers

Some novels reflected ___exuberance___ of the era as well as criticized its ______________, such as F. Scott Fitzgerald's ______________ and Sinclair Lewis's ______________.

Ernest Hemingway's novel ______________ captured ______________.

In a New York City neighborhood, a vibrant African American culture known as the ______________ occurred.

African American writers reacted to ______________.

The works of writers such as ______________, ______________, and ______________ expressed ______________.

Refer to this page to answer the Chapter 22 Focus Question on page 346.

Section 4

The Economy of the 1920s

Key Events

1919	18th Amendment prohibits the consumption and sale of alcoholic beverages.
1924	Teapot Dome and other government scandals become public.
1927	Lindbergh flies alone across the Atlantic.

✓ Checkpoint

List three reasons for increased consumer spending in the 1920s.

____

____

____

Section 4 Focus Question

What economic problems threatened the economic boom of the 1920s? To begin answering this question,

- Learn about the decade's industrial growth.
- Find out about margin buying on the stock market.
- Understand Americans' failure to see the signs of economic trouble.
- Read about the election of Herbert Hoover.

Section 4 Summary

Many people regarded the 1920s as prosperous. New purchases and a booming stock market, however, existed alongside rural poverty and unemployment.

Industrial Growth

A huge increase in industrial production pulled the nation out of the postwar economic recession. As more goods came to market, prices dropped. Advertisements, chain stores, and mail-order catalogs presented labor-saving devices for the home, such as washing machines, vacuum cleaners, and toasters. These enticed consumers to spend their money. **Installment buying,** or buying on credit, meant that people could enjoy expensive purchases such as cars, refrigerators, and radios long before they had paid for them in full.

Government policies kept the economy going. High taxes on imported goods resulted in Americans buying from U.S. businesses. Tax cuts for the wealthy encouraged spending. These measures made the economy boom. At the same time, however, they encouraged reckless spending. ✓

A Booming Stock Market

In a strong economy, more people are able to afford to buy stocks, or shares of companies. During the 1920s, the stock market became a **bull market.** This meant that stock values were rising. Investors began **buying on margin.** They paid a percentage of the stock's cost when they bought it, and paid the rest when they sold it. As long as the market value continued to rise, this was not a risk. If the market fell, however, investors could be left owing money for stock that wasn't worth much. Some economists began to worry about margin buying. But most people listened to positive economists such as Irwin Fisher who felt prosperity would last forever. In reality, only 5 percent of Americans were rich. Many of the rest worked hard yet barely survived. ✓

Signs of Trouble

Among those who did not share in the decade's prosperity were farmers. Before World War I, they had sold their surplus crops to foreign markets. During the pre-war years, farmers took out loans to buy land and equipment. However, many postwar nations were too poor to buy crops. With less income, farmers were unable to pay their debts.

Some factory workers fared well, but others did not. Some companies offered their employees benefits such as vacations and pensions. With the rise of the assembly line, however, unskilled workers were taking the jobs of skilled workers for less pay. Unemployment was high even during the more prosperous years. ✓

The Election of 1928

The Republicans, who held the presidency throughout the 1920s, took credit for the prosperity. Republican Secretary of Commerce Herbert Hoover ran for President in 1928. His Democratic opponent, Alfred E. Smith, was the first Catholic to run for President. Religion and the economy became the major issues in the election. Hoover won with the slogan "a chicken in every pot and a car in every garage." Hoover lost the largest cities, but he carried 41 states. This was a significant victory for Republicans. It showed that many poor, rural voters still placed their hopes in the Republican Party. Hoover believed he could satisfy those hopes. ✓

Check Your Progress

1. What were two factors in the economy that indicated a period of prosperity?

____

____

2. What two groups in American society did not share in the prosperity of the 1920s?

____

____

✓ Checkpoint

Explain why buying stocks on margin could be a risky practice.

____

____

Reading Strategy

Reread the bracketed paragraph.

Underline the statement that best summarizes the farmers' ultimate problem.

✓ Checkpoint

Explain why farmers were unable to repay their loans.

____

____

Vocabulary Builder

Something that is *significant* has a major or important effect. Why was Hoover's victory significant?

____

____

✓ Checkpoint

Name the two major issues in the election of 1928.

____

____

Section 4 Notetaking Study Guide

Question to Think About As you read Section 4 in your textbook and take notes, keep this section focus question in mind: **What economic problems threatened the economic boom of the 1920s?**

▶ Use this chart to record key information from the section. Some information has been filled in to get you started.

The Economy of the 1920s	
Industrial Growth • From 1922 to 1928, ________ ________ climbed 70 percent. • As more goods came to market, ________. • Rising incomes gave consumers more to spend. • To encourage spending, businesses offered ________. • Chain stores and ________ made it easier for people to buy goods. • A new ________ culture arose. • High tariffs on ________ stopped competition with domestic products. • Taxes on the wealthy were ________ to encourage spending. • Americans developed a ________ about spending.	**A Booming Stock Market** • Many people could now afford to ________, or shares of companies. • A bull market occurred, and stocks were so profitable that people began ________. • Some economists began to worry, and a few experts warned that ________. • Most investors ________ the warnings. • Most people at the time were not prosperous. • The wealthiest Americans made up ________ of the population.
Signs of Trouble	
Farmers Many farmers lived in poverty. Reasons for an agricultural depression: • Farmers grew more than the American public could consume. • After World War I, other nations were too poor to buy farmers' ________ crops. • Many farmers were unable to pay off their ________.	**Workers** • Workers' ________ were rising. • Some companies offered ________, such as pensions and ________. • Unemployment was ________. • Unskilled workers who worked on an ________ were squeezing out skilled labor for less wages.
Election of 1928 • The ________ Party held the presidency throughout the 1920s. • The Republican candidate for the 1928 presidential election: ________ • The Democratic candidate for the 1928 presidential election: ________ • Two issues highlighted in the election: ________ • Winner: ________; Slogan: ________	

Refer to this page to answer the Chapter 22 Focus Question on page 346.

Chapter 22 Assessment

Directions: Circle the letter of the correct answer.

1. Who were the Republican Presidents of the 1920s?
   A Wilson, Coolidge, Hoover
   B Wilson, Harding, Coolidge
   C Harding, Coolidge, Hoover

2. Which amendment to the Constitution gave women the right to vote?
   A Eighteenth **B** Nineteenth **C** Twentieth

3. Who of the following was ***not*** a writer of the 1920s?
   A Louis Armstrong
   B Langston Hughes
   C Sinclair Lewis

Directions: Follow the steps to answer this question:

How might American culture be different if three major events had not occurred in the 1920s?

Step 1: Recall information: List one effect each event below had on American culture.

Three Major Events of the 1920s	Effect
• Increase of installment buying • Nineteenth Amendment passed into law • Birth of Jazz	• • •

Step 2: Hypothesize: Now imagine three ways the American culture would be different today if these events had never occurred.

Differences in American Culture Without Those Events
• • •

Step 3: Complete the topic sentence that follows. Then write two or three sentences that support the topic sentence.

American culture today would be much different if ______________________

____

____

____

Chapter 22 Notetaking Study Guide

Now you are ready to answer the Chapter 22 Focus Question: **How did the nation react to change in the 1920s?**

▶ Fill in the following chart to help you answer this question. Use the notes that you took for each section.

Change in the 1920s	
Areas of Change	**Results of Change**
The Red Scare and Immigration	• Thousands of radical anarchists, Communists, and other foreigners are deported from the country. • • •
Ratification of Amendments • Eighteenth Amendment • Nineteenth Amendment	• •
Mass Culture • Automobile • Entertainment	• •
The Great Migration	• • Racial tensions increase, resulting in riots •
Arts and Culture • Literature • Music	• • •
The Economy • Consumer market • Stock market • Job market	• • • Farmers in debt, skilled workers losing jobs to assembly lines and unskilled workers, high unemployment

Refer to this page to answer the Unit 7 Focus Question on page 347.

Unit 7 Pulling It Together Activity

What You Have Learned

Chapter 20 By the late 1800s, the United States had gained new territories in the Pacific and strengthened its trade ties with Asia. The Spanish-American War led to increased involvement in Latin America.

Chapter 21 In 1914, a war broke out in Europe. The United States remained neutral at first, but it eventually joined the war. The conflict, which we now call World War I, had important effects throughout the world.

Chapter 22 The decade following World War I marked dramatic changes for the United States. Republicans returned the country to pre-war isolationism and supported big business. Cultural changes sparked conflicts and tensions.

Think Like a Historian

Read the Unit 7 Focus Question: **How did a more powerful United States expand its role in the world?**

▶ Use the organizers on this page and the next to answer this question.
How did the United States expand its territorial, economic, and political roles? Review your section and chapter notes. Then complete the charts.

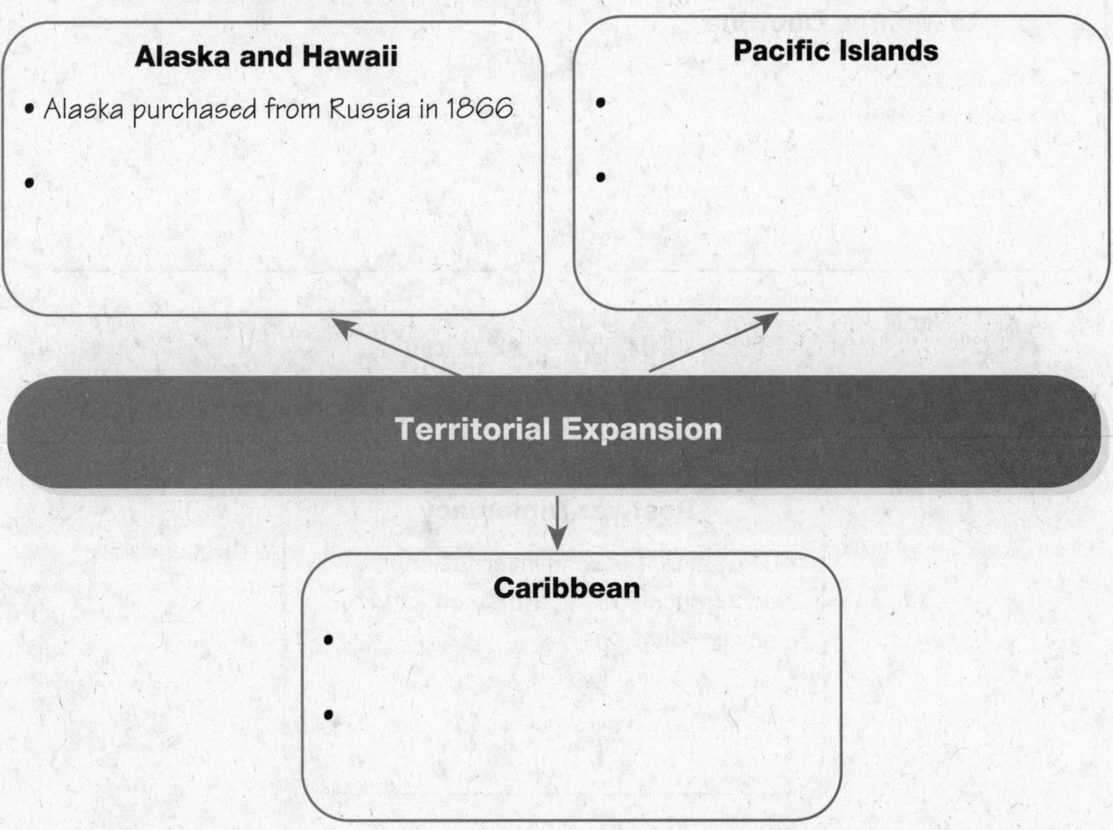

Japan and China

- Commodore Perry opens trade with Japan in 1854
-

Alaska and Hawaii

-
-

Economic Expansion

Dollar Diplomacy

-

Panama

-

Roosevelt Corollary to Monroe Doctrine

-

Treaty of Versailles

-

Political Expansion

Postwar Diplomacy

- U.S. participates in international conferences for disarmament and naval reductions
-

Unit 8

Depression and War

What You Will Learn

Chapter 23 The Great Depression was the worst economic crisis in American history. Millions of people lost their jobs, homes, and savings. President Franklin Roosevelt responded with measures called the New Deal.

Chapter 24 World War II was the bloodiest conflict in history, with fighting in Europe and the Pacific. Both U.S. soldiers and civilians made major contributions to winning the war.

Chapter 25 After World War II, conflict with the Soviet Union developed into a Cold War. U.S. policy aimed to contain the spread of communism. At home, important social and economic changes took place.

Focus Your Learning As you study this unit and take notes, you will find the information to answer the questions below. Answering the Chapter Focus Questions will help build your answer to the Unit Focus Question.

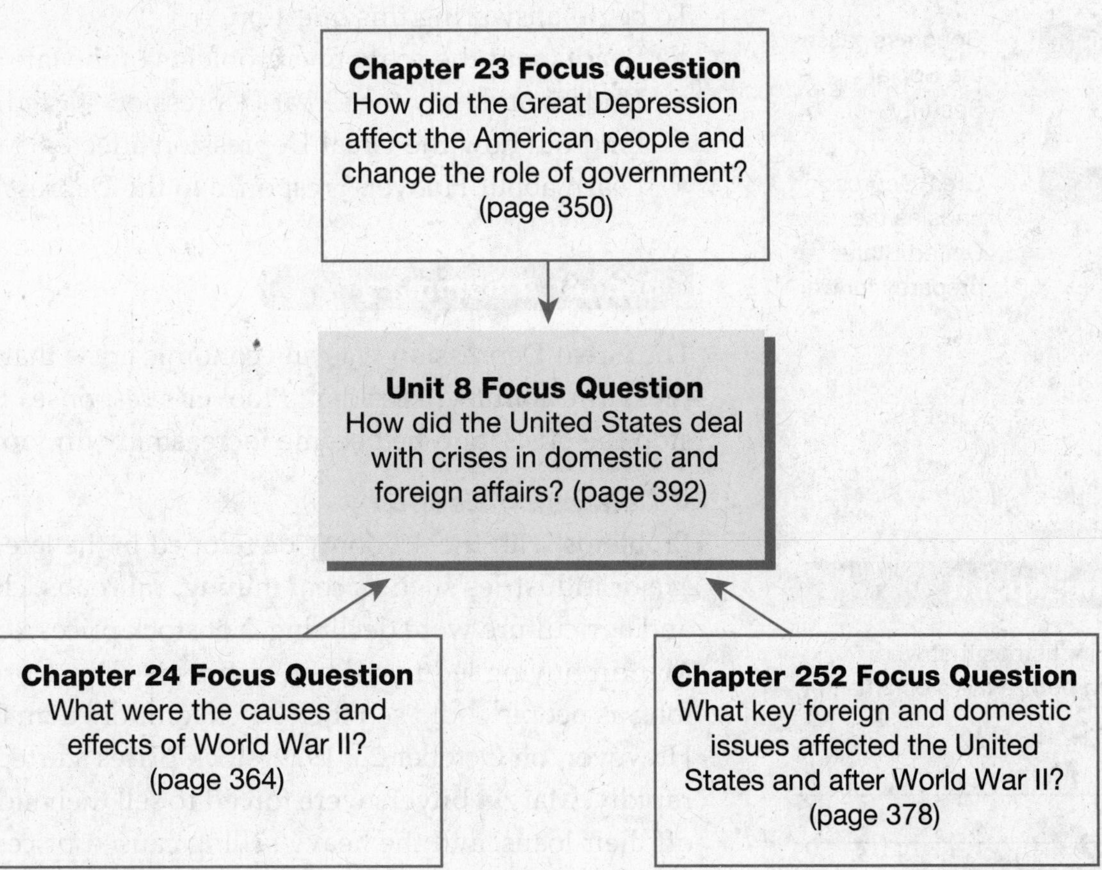

Chapter 23 Focus Question
How did the Great Depression affect the American people and change the role of government? (page 350)
Unit 8 Focus Question
How did the United States deal with crises in domestic and foreign affairs? (page 392)
Chapter 24 Focus Question
What were the causes and effects of World War II? (page 364)
Chapter 252 Focus Question
What key foreign and domestic issues affected the United States and after World War II? (page 378)

Chapter 23

The Great Depression and the New Deal

(1929–1941)

What You Will Learn

The Great Depression was the worst economic crisis in American history. Millions of people lost their jobs, homes, and savings. President Roosevelt responded with the New Deal.

Chapter 23 Focus Question

As you read this chapter, keep this question in mind: **How did the Great Depression affect the American people and change the role of government?**

Key Events

1929	Stock market crash marks the beginning of the Great Depression.
1933	President Roosevelt launches the New Deal.
1935	Congress passes the Social Security Act.
1941	Great Depression ends as the United States prepares for war.

Section 1

Hoover and the Crash

Section 1 Focus Question

Why did the economy collapse after the stock market crash? To begin answering this question,

- Read about the economic problems of the late 1920s.
- Understand how the Great Depression started.
- Find out how the Great Depression affected Americans.
- Learn about Hoover's response to the Depression.

Section 1 Summary

The Great Depression was an economic crisis that affected the entire country. President Hoover's responses failed to stop the crisis, and he became increasingly unpopular.

A Collapsing Economy

Problems with the economy developed in the late 1920s. Major industries such as coal mining, railroads, clothing, and agriculture were declining. Yet stock prices kept rising. Margin buying led to risky investments. This worked as long as people could sell their stock for more than they paid. However, on October 23, 1929, stock prices started falling rapidly. Margin buyers were forced to sell their stock to pay off their loans, and the heavy selling caused prices to drop more. The stock market crashed completely on October 29, 1929. Many investors lost all of their money. ✓

✓ Checkpoint

List the industries that were declining before the stock market crashed.

____

____

____

____

The Great Depression Begins

The stock market crash contributed to the Great Depression, which lasted 12 years. One cause of the Depression was **overproduction**, which occurs when there are too many goods produced and not enough buyers. A banking crisis was another cause. Rural banks lost money because farmers could not repay their loans. Many city banks lost huge sums in the crash. Thousands of banks closed, and depositors lost their money. A downward spiral developed. People had less money to buy goods, so factories cut jobs. The unemployed had even less money to spend. Many businesses declared **bankruptcy**, or financial failure caused by a company's inability to pay its debts. Because of international loans and trade, the Depression spread worldwide. ☑

The Human Cost

Between 1929 and 1933, unemployment rose from 3 percent to 25 percent, with some 13 million people out of work. Even people with jobs had salaries cut. Poverty and misery gripped the country. Many people lost their homes and lived in makeshift dwellings. The magnitude of the crisis was so great that many schools closed from lack of funds. ☑

Hoover Responds

Hoover's advisers thought the economy would bounce back on its own. When it did not, Hoover encouraged businesses and local governments and charities to help those in need. Finally, in 1932 Hoover created the Reconstruction Finance Corporation to provide money to local governments and key industries. The Depression continued to worsen, however. Hoover's popularity fell after the Bonus Army incident in June 1932. World War I veterans marched on Washington to demand a $1,000 **bonus**, or extra payment, promised for their military service. Some veterans refused to leave, and the military fired on them. The country was outraged. ☑

Check Your Progress

1. What were two causes of the Great Depression?

____

____

2. How did the loss of jobs make the Depression worse?

____

____

✓ Checkpoint

Explain why the Depression spread worldwide.

____

____

Vocabulary Builder

Magnitude means "great size, significance, or importance." List two examples of how human suffering showed the magnitude of the Depression.

____

____

✓ Checkpoint

Identify the unemployment figures of the Great Depression.

____

____

✓ Checkpoint

Name two measures President Hoover took in response to the Depression.

____

____

Section 1 Notetaking Study Guide

Question to Think About As you read Section 1 in your textbook and take notes, keep this section focus question in mind: **Why did the economy collapse after the stock market crash?**

► Use this chart to record key information from the section. Some information has been filled in to get you started.

Hoover and the Crash

The Collapsing Economy

- Problems with the U.S. economy started in the late 1920s.
- Major industries were declining, but stock prices were still ______. This encouraged risky investments by ______.
- When stock prices started falling, margin buyers ______.
- The stock market crashed on ______, known as Black Tuesday.

The Great Depression Begins

- The Great Depression was a major economic and ______ disaster that affected the entire country.
- The Great Depression lasted ______ years and was triggered by the ______.
- One problem that caused the Great Depression was ______. Factories produced more goods than people could afford to buy.
- The ______ crisis also contributed to the Depression. Banks closed because farmers could not repay loans and from losses in the stock market crash.
- People had less money because ______.

The Human Cost

- From 1929 to 1933, the unemployment rate went from ______ to ______ percent.
- The number of people without jobs was about ______.
- With little or no money, many people lacked adequate food, shelter, and clothing.
- The Great Depression was a time of widespread ______.

Hoover Responds

- At first, President Hoover's advisers recommended doing ______. They believed the Depression was temporary.
- Hoover's first measures encouraged businesses and local governments—but not the ______ government—to take the lead to help people. He also urged private ______ to set up ______.
- As the Depression worsened, he created the ______ in 1932 to provide ______ to key industries and local governments.
- The treatment of the ______ further damaged Hoover's popularity.

Refer to this page to answer the Chapter 23 Focus Question on page 363.

Section 2

Roosevelt and the New Deal

Section 2 Focus Question

How did President Roosevelt respond to the Great Depression? To begin answering this question,

- Learn how FDR won the 1932 presidential election.
- Read how the New Deal tried to help economic recovery.
- Note what new laws regulated the economic system.
- Identify problems and criticisms faced by the New Deal.

Section 2 Summary

Franklin D. Roosevelt, known as FDR, took office in 1933 and provided hope and action. His program, the New Deal, included many reforms. The New Deal had critics and mixed results, yet FDR became a popular President.

Franklin D. Roosevelt

Roosevelt, a Democrat and governor of New York, was elected President in 1932. FDR was a wealthy cousin of Theodore Roosevelt. He was disabled from polio, yet he was never shown in his wheelchair. In his 1933 inaugural speech, he offered hope by stating: "the only thing we have to fear is fear itself. . . ." His first action was to declare a bank holiday, a four-day closing of all banks. Then he introduced the Emergency Banking Relief Act, which restored confidence in the nation's banks. FDR also began his **fireside chats,** which were national radio broadcasts to explain his measures and reassure the public. ✓

Relief for the Jobless

FDR's New Deal measures had three key goals: relief for the jobless, economic recovery, and reforms to prevent future depressions. The Federal Emergency Relief Administration (FERA) provided financial help for the unemployed. The Civilian Conservation Corps (CCC) hired jobless men to work on environmental projects in national parks, forests, and wilderness areas. The Works Progress Administration (WPA) hired people to build or repair schools, post offices, roads, bridges, and airports. Even artists and writers were employed for government arts and writing projects. ✓

Key Events

1929	Stock market crash marks the beginning of the Great Depression.
1933	President Roosevelt launches the New Deal.
1935	Congress passes the Social Security Act.
1941	Great Depression ends as the United States prepares for war.

✓ Checkpoint

Name the method FDR used to reassure the public.

____

✓ Checkpoint

Name two federal programs that gave work to the jobless.

____

____

✓ Checkpoint

Identify FDR's two priorities for economic recovery.

✓ Checkpoint

Explain why the FDIC was established.

Reading Strategy

Reread the bracketed paragraph. Underline the cause of a roadblock FDR faced. Draw an arrow to FDR's reaction (the effect).

Mark the Text

✓ Checkpoint

List three critics of FDR's New Deal.

Promoting Economic Recovery

FDR established federal agencies to help industry and agriculture. The National Recovery Administration (NRA) aimed to keep prices stable while increasing employment. The Public Works Administration (PWA) hired people for major public works projects, such as building the Lincoln Tunnel in New York City. The Tennessee Valley Authority (TVA) built dams along the Tennessee River to provide jobs and electricity in a poverty-stricken region. These programs generally accomplished their goals. They failed to significantly improve the economy, however. ✓

Reforming the Economic System

FDR's reform measures aimed to prevent another depression. Companies were now required to report honestly about their stock. The Federal Deposit Insurance Corporation (FDIC) was created to protect bank deposits. Federal agencies were established or strengthened to set fairness and safety standards for various industries. ✓

Obstacles to the New Deal

Many Americans supported FDR's New Deal. He easily won reelection in 1936. Yet, he faced roadblocks. One challenge came from the judicial branch. The Supreme Court declared some of his programs unconstitutional. In response, FDR tried to "pack" the court by proposing to add six additional judges who would support him. Congress defeated the plan. However, in 1937, FDR was able to appoint a liberal justice when a conservative resigned.

FDR's critics included conservatives who complained about regulations on business, as well as liberals who wanted more done for the poor. Among his loudest critics was Louisiana Senator **Huey Long,** who called for taxing the rich and giving their wealth to the poor. Still, FDR remained popular and kept most of the country's trust. ✓

Check Your Progress

1. What was Roosevelt's first action after taking office?

2. What were the three goals of FDR's New Deal program?

Section 2 Notetaking Study Guide

Question to Think About As you read Section 2 in your textbook and take notes, keep this section focus question in mind: **How did President Roosevelt respond to the Great Depression?**

► Use the chart to record key information from the section. Some information has been filled in to get you started.

Roosevelt and the New Deal		
Franklin D. Roosevelt took office in ________. Three goals of FDR's New Deal measures: • ________ • ________ • ________		
New Deal Measures		
Act	**Abbreviation**	**Purpose**
Emergency Banking Relief Act	(none)	Provided more careful government regulation of banks
Federal Emergency Relief Administration		
	CCC	
	WPA	
National Recovery Administration		
	PWA	
	TVA	
Truth-in-Securities Act	(none)	
Federal Deposit Insurance Corporation		
Federal Power Commission		Helped control the oil and gas industries
Obstacles to the New Deal		
Roosevelt was reelected in 1936, showing that many Americans ________ the New Deal. However, the Supreme Court declared the ________ and other measures ________. When FDR tried to add justices who would support his programs, his plan to ________ the court was defeated. Three famous critics of the New Deal were ________, ________, and Charles Coughlin.		

Refer to this page to answer the Chapter 23 Focus Question on page 363.

Section 3

Life in the Great Depression

Key Events

1929	Stock market crash marks the beginning of the Great Depression.
1933	President Roosevelt launches the New Deal.
1935	Congress passes the Social Security Act.
1941	Great Depression ends as the United States prepares for war.

Section 3 Focus Question

How did the Great Depression affect daily life? To begin answering this question,

- Read how the Depression affected minorities.
- Learn about the causes and effects of the Dust Bowl.
- Understand how art and media informed and entertained people during the Depression.

Section 3 Summary

The Great Depression made life more difficult for nearly everyone. However, some people experienced special hardships. Their challenges were related to gender, racial or ethnic background, or where they lived.

Women in the Depression

Women took on extra responsibilities during the Depression. Many had to get jobs to support their families. Some were secretaries and salesclerks, more secure jobs than men's factory work. However, women in factory jobs were usually cut before men. Those who were maids also lost positions when families could no longer afford paid help. At home, women made their family's clothing to save money. One very busy woman was First Lady **Eleanor Roosevelt.** She traveled the country to report conditions to the President and to help evaluate needs. She also supported women's rights and racial equality. ✓

✓ Checkpoint

Explain what First Lady Eleanor Roosevelt did to help during the Depression.

____

____

____

African Americans in the Depression

African Americans experienced more hardships than most whites during the Depression. Whites competed for jobs that African Americans traditionally held. African American workers were often the first to be cut in layoffs. As a result, African American unemployment was 50 percent or higher in the South and in northern cities like New York. Through the influence of the First Lady, FDR appointed some 100 African American leaders to government posts. Some served as his informal "Black Cabinet." ✓

✓ Checkpoint

Give two reasons that caused high unemployment for African Americans.

____

____

Other Americans in the Depression

Mexican Americans and Native Americans also faced special challenges. Mexicans who were **migrant workers,** or those who moved about picking crops, were threatened by whites who wanted their jobs. Many Mexicans, including some who were U.S. citizens, were deported. Native Americans were among the poorest people in the United States before the Depression. A program called the Indian New Deal provided jobs for them. It also aimed to give them greater control of their reservations, encouraged Indian schools, and stopped the sale of tribal lands. Still, they remained very poor. ✓

The Dust Bowl

Farmers in the southwestern Plains faced a new problem when a severe drought hit in 1930. Crops failed. With no plants to hold the topsoil in place, it blew away in giant dust storms called "black blizzards." This disaster lasted five years. It turned the region into what was called the Dust Bowl. Oklahoma was especially hard hit. Thousands of "Okies" abandoned their ruined farms and moved to California to find work. There they suffered more hardships as they competed for low-paying jobs. ✓

Arts and Media of the Depression

Some artists and writers used the Depression as a theme in their work. Photographers and painters captured visually the suffering of people. **John Steinbeck's** *The Grapes of Wrath* described the experiences of Dust Bowl Okies in California. Some movies also depicted people's struggles. But most helped ordinary Americans escape their miseries. Mickey Mouse and child star Shirley Temple were very popular. People listened to radio for entertainment, for news, and for FDR's fireside chats. Continuing dramas sponsored by soap companies created the birth of soap operas. ✓

Check Your Progress

1. List the people who were hardest hit by the Depression.

____

____

2. Name three groups of people who captured the experience of the Great Depression.

____

____

Reading Strategy

Circle the main idea of the bracketed paragraph. Underline two sentences that provide supporting details.

✓ Checkpoint

Explain why many Mexican Americans were deported.

____

____

✓ Checkpoint

Name the region that became the Dust Bowl.

____

✓ Checkpoint

List three reasons why people listened to the radio.

____

____

____

Section 3 Notetaking Study Guide

Question to Think About As you read Section 3 in your textbook and take notes, keep this section focus question in mind: **How did the Great Depression affect daily life?**

► Use this chart to record key information from the section. Some information has been filled in to get you started.

Life in the Great Depression		
Women in the Depression Women who were secretaries and ______ often kept their jobs, but those who were ______ or ______ workers lost theirs.		
African Americans in the Depression African Americans suffered more unemployment, ______, ______, and ______ than did whites.		
Other Americans in the Depression Mexicans and Mexican Americans were forced out of ______ and sometimes deported. Native Americans were among the ______ when the Depression began.		
The Dust Bowl was located in the ______. The dust storms began in 1930 and lasted ______, turning ______ into wasteland. Many farm families were forced to go to ______ to find work.		
Arts and Media of the Depression The movies helped people ______, while radio was a vital part of ______.		
Important People of the Depression		
Key Person	**Position or Role**	**Why Important**
1.	First Lady	Championed women's and minorities' rights
2. Mary McLeod Bethune	Educator and member of FDR's "Black Cabinet"	
3.		Promoted the "Indian New Deal"
4. John Steinbeck		
5.	Photographer for Farm Security Administration	
6.		WPA murals captured lives of ordinary people
7.	Popular child actress	

Refer to this page to answer the Chapter 23 Focus Question on page 365.

Section 4

Legacy of the New Deal

Section 4 Focus Question

What were the long-term effects of the New Deal? To begin answering this question,

- Find out how Social Security began.
- Learn how the New Deal reformed labor relations.
- Identify the main arguments for and against the New Deal.

Section 4 Summary

Social and labor reforms increased the size and influence of the federal government. These changes gave the New Deal its lasting legacy.

Social Security

One of the most important legacies of the New Deal is Social Security. The Social Security Act was passed in 1935 to help old people, children, the disabled, and the unemployed. Old-Age Insurance was a key part of the Social Security Act. It guaranteed a pension to retired people. The pension was funded by a **payroll tax,** or a tax that removes money directly from workers' paychecks. Businesses were required to match the amount withheld from their employees.

The Social Security Act also included Aid to Dependent Children (ADC), which provided money for children without fathers at home. It let mothers stay home to raise their children. Social Security also gave financial help to disabled people and offered the states federal money to give short-term payments to unemployed workers. ✓

Lasting Labor Reforms

FDR had the first woman Cabinet member, **Frances Perkins.** As secretary of labor, she supported reforms that gave workers more rights. The 1935 National Labor Relations Act gave employees the right to organize unions. It also allowed **collective bargaining,** or the right of unions to speak for all workers in labor negotiations. The 1938 Fair Labor Standards Act set a minimum wage and maximum hours for the work week. It established the idea of extra pay for overtime work. It also ended some kinds of child labor.

Key Events

- **1929** Stock market crash marks the beginning of the Great Depression.
- **1933** President Roosevelt launches the New Deal.
- **1935** Congress passes the Social Security Act.
- **1941** Great Depression ends as the United States prepares for war.

✓ Checkpoint

List four types of payments that Social Security provided.

____

____

____

____

Reading Strategy

Ask and answer a question about labor unions.

Question:

____

____

Answer:

____

____

✓ Checkpoint

List three key benefits that the Fair Labor Standards Act established for all workers.

____

____

____

Vocabulary Builder

Synonyms for the word *impact* include "influence" and "effect." List two influences or effects of the New Deal on government.

____

____

✓ Checkpoint

State when the Great Depression finally ended, and why.

____

____

____

Union membership increased as unions became more powerful. More women and African Americans became union members through the new Congress of Industrial Organizations (CIO). Formed by **John L. Lewis,** the CIO included all workers, skilled and unskilled, in each industry. A new labor tactic was the **sit-down strike,** in which employees would stay on the job but stop working. The sit-down strike was successful for auto workers, although it was later ruled illegal by the Supreme Court. ✓

Scorecard on the New Deal

The New Deal had a strong and lasting impact on the federal government. The size of government was increased along with its role in solving social problems. There was much debate over whether this was good or bad. Arguments against the New Deal included concerns that a powerful federal government threatened individual freedom and free enterprise. The cost of the New Deal programs led to **deficit spending.** This occurs when the government spends more money than it receives in taxes. Some critics also questioned the effectiveness of New Deal programs. They argued that preparing for war in 1941—not New Deal programs—pulled the country out of the Depression.

Supporters of the New Deal pointed to the millions of new jobs it created and how it ended the banking crisis. It also reformed the stock market and improved working conditions. Buildings, roads, and bridges were improved or created. About 12 million acres of national parks were improved through New Deal programs. Rural America had electricity for the first time, and great works of art emerged. Many Americans also felt greater confidence in their government. Supporters of the New Deal believed that the programs helped save democracy in the United States when other countries in Europe and Asia turned to dictatorships. ✓

Check Your Progress

1. Explain why the New Deal had a lasting legacy.

____

____

2. Identify at least two arguments for and two arguments against the New Deal.

____

____

____

Section 4 Notetaking Study Guide

Question to Think About As you read Section 4 in your textbook and take notes, keep this section focus question in mind: **What were the long-term effects of the New Deal?**

► Use these charts to record key information from the section. Some information has been filled in to get you started.

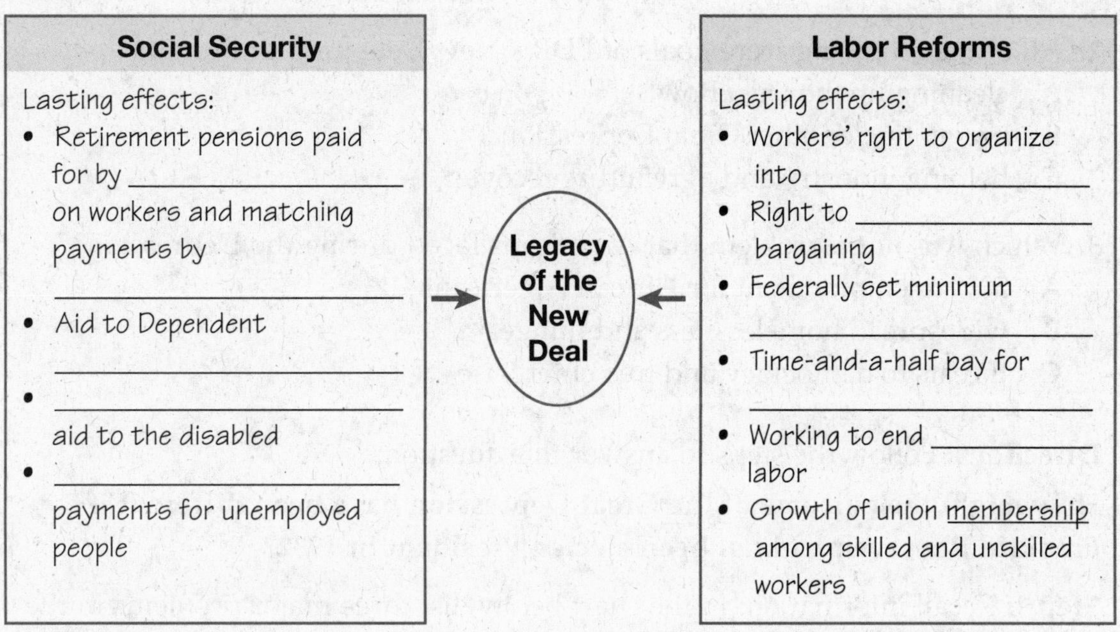

Scorecard on the New Deal	
Arguments against the New Deal	**Arguments in favor of the New Deal**
Powerful federal government threatened individual freedom	Employed millions and improved _____ conditions on the job
Powerful federal government threatened free _____	Ended the _____ crisis and reformed the _____ market
Increase in national debt through _____ spending	• Built dams and bridges • Preserved _____ million acres of parkland • Provided _____ to rural areas
New Deal programs did not fulfill their goal of full _____	Restored Americans' _____ in government

Refer to this page to answer the Chapter 23 Focus Question on page 363.

Chapter 23 Assessment

Directions: Circle the letter of the correct answer.

1. Which of the following did *not* cause the Great Depression?
   - **A** The stock market crashed on October 29, 1929.
   - **B** Bonus Army veterans demanded their payments.
   - **C** Overproduction forced jobs to be cut and factories to close.

2. All of the following were goals of FDR's New Deal program *except*
   - **A** cleaning up the Dust Bowl.
   - **B** preventing another Great Depression.
   - **C** helping industry and agriculture recover.

3. Which was *not* a problem that Americans faced during the Depression?
   - **A** 50% unemployment for African Americans
   - **B** widespread homelessness and hunger
   - **C** threats to democracy and free enterprise

Directions: Follow the steps to answer this question:

How might the outcome of the Great Depression have been different if Franklin Roosevelt had not been elected President in 1932?

Step 1: Recall information: In the chart below, list three major problems in the country that developed from 1929 to 1932. Include statistics that you remember.

Downward Spiral from 1929 to 1932
• • •

Step 2: List examples of how FDR gave hope and took action to solve problems.

FDR Takes Office in 1933
• Hope: • Action:

Step 3: Complete the topic sentence that follows. Then write two or three more sentences that support your topic sentence.

The outcome of the Great Depression might have been different without FDR as President because ____

____

____

____

Chapter 23 Notetaking Study Guide

Now you are ready to answer the Chapter 23 Focus Question: **How did the Great Depression affect the American people and change the role of government?**

▶ Complete the charts to help you answer this question. Use the notes that you took for each section.

Great Depression: Effects on American People		
Aspect of Life	**Problems Caused by the Great Depression**	**Improvements as a Result of New Deal**
Jobs	• Widespread job loss • High unemployment with no relief for the unemployed • Poverty and ______________	• Job programs provided employment • Labor reforms provided a __________ wage and workers' right to join ______________ • Federal money to states provided ______________ funds to the unemployed
Communities	• People lived in makeshift areas called ______________ • Dust Bowl farms were ruined and abandoned • Schools ______________ ______________	• WPA projects built ______________ • PWA financed large public-works projects • TVA provided ______________ ______________
Savings and investments	• Margin buying in stocks wiped out investors' money • Banks ______________ ______________	• FDIC ______________ ______________ • Truth-in-Securities Act ______________

Changing Role of Government		
Aspect of Federal Government	**Before the Great Depression**	**After the Great Depression**
Size	Smaller	
Role in solving economic and social problems	Local governments, charities, and businesses solved problems	
Control of business practices and industry standards	• Risky stock speculating allowed • Overproduction in manufacturing unchecked	Larger role in setting regulations and passing laws to protect workers
Relationship of people to federal government	Less connection and involvement in people's lives	

Refer to this page to answer the Unit 8 Focus Question on page 392.

Chapter 24

The World War II Era (1935–1945)

What You Will Learn

World War II was the bloodiest conflict in history, with fighting in Europe and the Pacific. Both U.S. soldiers and civilians made major contributions to winning the war.

Chapter 24 Focus Question

As you read this chapter, keep this question in mind: **What were the causes and effects of World War II?**

Key Events

1939	Germany invades Poland; World War II begins.
1941	United States enters war after Japan attacks Pearl Harbor.
1945	U.S. plane drops atomic bomb on Hiroshima. World War II ends.

Section 1

Aggression Leads to War

Section 1 Focus Question

What events led to the outbreak of World War II? To begin answering this question,

- Learn why dictators gained power after World War I.
- Find out how Germany, Italy, and Japan went on a path of military conquest.
- Read how the United States tried to remain neutral.
- Understand how World War II began in Europe.

Section 1 Summary

The Great Depression led to dictatorships in Germany, Italy, and Japan. Those dictators took military actions against other countries. American policy aimed to remain neutral.

The Rise of Dictators

After World War I, many nations thought democracy was too weak to solve their hardships. In the Soviet Union, Italy, Germany, and Japan, the citizens turned to dictators to rule their countries. In the Soviet Union, **Josef Stalin** held total control of the country. In Italy, **Benito Mussolini** used **fascism**—a form of rule based on militarism, radical nationalism, and blind loyalty—to take power. In Germany, **Adolf Hitler** and his Nazi Party rose to power. Nazism was a form of fascism. Hitler argued that Germans were a "master race." He preached anti-Semitism, or hatred of Jews. In Japan, military leaders also used racism to justify the invasion of nearby countries. ✓

✓ Checkpoint

Name the dictator in each country.

Soviet Union: ________________

Germany: ________________

Italy: ________________

Military Aggression

The League of Nations was founded after World War I to stop **aggression**, or warlike actions against another country without cause. But the League failed to act when Japan, Italy, and Germany showed aggression. In 1931, Japan took over Manchuria in China. In late 1937, Japanese troops invaded China, killing about 250,000 people in the city of Nanjing alone. In 1935, Italy invaded Ethiopia in Africa. Hitler invaded the Rhineland in 1936 and Austria in 1938. When he threatened Czechoslovakia, Britain and France finally stepped in. To avoid war, they tried to appease Hitler by signing the Munich Pact. This gave him a German-speaking area of Czechoslovakia. Soon, however, Hitler took all of the country. ✓

American Neutrality

The United States declared itself neutral in order to stay out of the growing conflicts. The Neutrality Act of 1935 forbade the United States from providing loans, arms, or other assistance to any nation at war. The United States also took steps to improve relations with Latin America. FDR started the Good Neighbor Policy, which withdrew U.S. troops from Nicaragua and Haiti. ✓

War Begins in Europe

As Hitler eyed Poland, France and Britain realized that their policy of **appeasement**, or agreeing to tolerate aggression to avoid war, had failed. Germany and the Soviet Union, former enemies, pledged not to attack each other. On September 1, 1939, German troops attacked Poland. Britain and France declared war on Germany. Hitler's army soon crushed Poland and much of western Europe. France fell in June 1940. Only Britain remained unconquered. Led by Prime Minister **Winston Churchill**, the British withstood German bombing. Hitler gave up his invasion plans. In June 1941, he attacked the Soviet Union, which soon allied with Britain. ✓

Check Your Progress

1. How did the rise of dictators lead to World War II?

____

____

2. Why was appeasement a failure in preventing war?

____

____

✓ Checkpoint

Name the country that invaded each nation.

Austria: _______________

Manchuria: _______________

Czechoslovakia: _______________

China: _______________

Ethiopia: _______________

✓ Checkpoint

Explain what the Neutrality Act of 1935 did not allow.

____

____

Vocabulary Builder

Tolerate means "to allow something to exist." What did France and Britain tolerate, and why?

____

____

✓ Checkpoint

Name the British leader who withstood Germany.

____

Section 1 Notetaking Study Guide

Question to Think About As you read Section 1 in your textbook and take notes, keep this section focus question in mind: **What events led to the outbreak of World War II?**

▶ Use this chart to record key information from the section. Some information has been filled in to get you started.

Aggression Leads to War	
Event	**How It Contributed to World War II**
1. Economic problems and social unrest after World War I	Encouraged the rise of dictators who took control of their countries.
2. Fascism takes hold in Italy and Germany.	_______ was appointed Italy's prime minister. He turned Italy into a Fascist state, which is a political system based on militarism, extreme nationalism, and _______.
3. Adolf Hitler becomes the leader of Germany.	He created a _______ state and passed anti-Semitic laws against the Jews.
4. Japan invades China.	Japan became an aggressive force in the _______ region.
5. Italy invades Ethiopia.	The emperor, _______, appealed to the League of Nations for aid, but Ethiopia fell to Italy.
6. Hitler violates the Treaty of Versailles without punishment and rebuilds Germany's armed forces.	It gave Germany _______ might and it showed Hitler that the _______ were weak.
7. Britain and France sign the Munich Pact with Germany.	They were following a policy of _______ that failed to stop Hitler's aggression. Hitler occupied the _______ in Czechoslovakia.
8. U.S. Congress passes the Neutrality Act.	Forbade the United States from _______ involved in war.
9. Germany and the Soviet Union sign the Nazi-Soviet Pact.	They pledged not to _______ and secretly agreed to _______.
10. Britain and France pledge support to Poland.	When Germany attacked Poland on _______, they _______.

War Begins in Europe

- By June 1940, Britain _______.
- In June 1941, Hitler invaded _______.

Refer to this page to answer the Chapter 24 Focus Question on page 377.

Section 2

The United States at War

Section 2 Focus Question

How did the United States move from neutrality to full involvement in the war? To begin answering this question,

- Understand how the United States prepared for war.
- Discover why the United States finally entered World War II.
- Learn how the Allies turned the tide of battle.

Section 2 Summary

The United States stayed out of World War II until it was attacked by Japan in 1941. Soon the United States was fighting with the Allies against Germany in Europe and against Japan in the Pacific. The Allies were losing until key victories came in 1942 and 1943.

Moving Toward War

In 1940, Franklin Roosevelt became the first American President to run for and win a third term in office. He promised that the United States would remain neutral. However, when Britain stood alone against Germany, the United States allowed the British to buy war goods. Then the Lend-Lease Act of 1941 allowed Britain to "borrow" them. America also stepped up its own war readiness by creating the first peacetime draft in 1940. At the same time, the Tuskegee Airmen were organized as the first African American combat unit under the command of black officers.

In August 1941, Roosevelt and Britain's Prime Minister Winston Churchill issued the Atlantic Charter, which set postwar goals. Both countries agreed that they would not seek territory after the war. They called for an international organization to replace the League of Nations. ✓

The United States Enters the War

Japanese aggression forced the United States to enter World War II. The Japanese invaded Indochina in July 1941. In turn, President Roosevelt limited U.S. oil sold to Japan and banned the sale of scrap metals. The loss of these materials propelled Japan to set a course for war with the United States. On December 7, 1941, Japanese planes attacked the American naval fleet at Pearl Harbor, Hawaii.

Key Events

1939	Germany invades Poland; World War II begins.
1941	United States enters war after Japan attacks Pearl Harbor.
1945	U.S. plane drops atomic bomb on Hiroshima. World War II ends.

✓ Checkpoint

List two "firsts" that occurred in 1940 that showed the United States was moving toward war.

____

____

Vocabulary Builder

Which of the following words is the best synonym for the word *propelled* as used in the underlined sentence?

a. forced
b. steered
c. targeted

✓ Checkpoint

Name the location where the United States was first attacked in World War II.

____

Soon the United States was in a global fight. Germany, Italy, Japan, and six other nations made up the Axis powers. America joined some 50 countries that made up the Allies. Together, all were involved in **total war,** as not only armies, but as civilians, too, were caught up in the conflict. ✓

Europe and North Africa

In Europe, Germany's early victories and large gains of territory made the war a hard and bloody struggle. However, the Allies made some advances. In late 1941, Soviet fighters and the fierce Russian winter halted the Germans outside of Moscow. After a second major defeat at Stalingrad in 1942, Hitler's army began to be pushed back.

In October 1942, the British defeated the German forces at the Battle of El Alamein in Egypt. The German tank commander Erwin Rommel was pushed westward. General **Dwight D. Eisenhower** arrived with fresh American troops in November. Trapped by both the Americans and the British, Rommel's army surrendered in May 1943. ✓

✓ Checkpoint

Name two battles that helped turn the tide of war against Germany.

____

____

Japan Sweeps Through the Pacific

After Pearl Harbor, Japan attacked other Pacific islands. The Japanese invaded the U.S.-governed Philippine Islands. A Filipino-American force under General **Douglas MacArthur** resisted bravely. MacArthur was ordered to leave the Philippines but vowed to return. Some 70,000 soldiers and civilians surrendered. Their forced 65-mile march to a Japanese prison camp became the "Bataan Death March."

Reading Strategy

Underline the main idea of the bracketed paragraph.

[In 1942, naval battles helped turn the tide. In May, the Battle of the Coral Sea became the first battle fought by planes launched from aircraft carriers. At the Battle of Midway Island in June, U.S. forces sank four Japanese carriers and shot down 322 planes. Japan's navy suffered a severe blow. ✓]

✓ Checkpoint

Name the general who vowed to return to the Philippines.

____

Check Your Progress

1. How did the Lend-Lease Act show U.S. support of one side of the war in Europe?

____

____

2. Why did the United States end its neutrality and enter the war?

____

____

Section 2 Notetaking Study Guide

Question to Think About As you read Section 2 in your textbook and take notes, keep this section focus question in mind: **How did the United States move from neutrality to full involvement in the war?**

▶ Use this chart to record key information from the section. Some information has been filled in to get you started.

The United States at War

Moving Toward War

- President Roosevelt was reelected for a third term in 1940. He sympathized with the ______ in Europe.
- The ______ supported the British by allowing them to obtain American war goods without paying for them directly.
- Meanwhile, the United States passed the first ______ to build up its armed forces.
- Roosevelt and British Prime Minister ______ showed their alliance by meeting and issuing the ______.
- On ______, the ______ waged a surprise attack on U.S. naval forces at ______. As a result, the United States declared war.
- In turn, ______ and ______ declared war on the United States.
- The main Axis powers were Germany, Italy, and ______.
- The main Allied powers were Britain, France, ______, ______, and ______.

Europe and North Africa

- In the Soviet Union, key victories that stopped the German push took place near Moscow in 1941 and at ______ in 1942.
- In North Africa, the British began pushing back the German tank corps after the victory at ______ in Egypt.
- The United States entered its first ground combat troops and occupied ______ and ______ under the command of ______.

Japan Sweeps Through the Pacific

- Japanese troops invaded country after country in the Pacific region, including ______, which were governed by the United States and had U.S. bases.
- General ______ became commander of the U.S. troops in the region.
- The Bataan Death March followed the defeat in ______ and took the lives of U.S. and ______ prisoners.
- Two historic naval battles that turned the tide of the war in the Pacific were the Battles of the Coral Sea and ______. Both were important because the United States ______.

Refer to this page to answer the Chapter 24 Focus Question on page 377.

Section 3

The War at Home

Section 3 Focus Question

How did the home front respond to American participation in the war? To begin answering this question,

- Find out how the United States built its military and changed its economy to meet wartime needs.
- Learn how American women contributed to the war effort.
- Discover how World War II affected Japanese Americans and other groups of people at home.

Key Events

1939	Germany invades Poland; World War II begins.
1941	United States enters war after Japan attacks Pearl Harbor.
1945	U.S. plane drops atomic bomb on Hiroshima. World War II ends.

Section 3 Summary

Daily life in the United States changed dramatically after war was declared in 1941. Millions of men joined the service, while women filled jobs producing war goods. For some, the war brought serious restrictions and new tensions at home.

Organizing for War

Americans quickly realized that all of the country's resources had to be committed to supporting the armed forces. Volunteers and draftees of all ethnic and religious backgrounds swelled the ranks of the military. Some 15 million men fought. Hundreds of thousands of women filled noncombat roles. They served as nurses and also as pilots who ferried bombers, towed targets, and taught men to fly.

The War Production Board directed the change as factories began producing war goods. Millions of new jobs ended the unemployment of the Depression. Americans accepted **rationing,** or limits on the purchase of specific items, such as certain foods, rubber, and gasoline that were needed for the war effort. Planting victory gardens and buying war bonds were other ways people helped. ✓

✓ Checkpoint

Name three ways that Americans on the home front contributed to the fight.

____

____

____

Women in Industry

Minorities and women took over traditionally male jobs in factories and shipyards, such as welders and riveters. Women also became bus drivers, police officers, and other key workers in their communities. As a result, women gained better working conditions and generally received the same pay as men for the same work. ✓

✓ Checkpoint

Identify two benefits women gained as a result of their wartime work.

____

____

Ordeal for Japanese Americans

For Japanese Americans, World War II created a painful situation. Erroneous fears that they would spy for Japan led to prejudice. Anti-Japanese feelings were widespread. In February 1942, President Roosevelt issued an order to **intern,** or temporarily imprison, Japanese Americans in the United States. About 110,000 were forced to sell most of their possessions and live in internment camps until the end of the war. Barbed wire and guards made the camps seem very much like prison camps. No evidence of Japanese American disloyalty was ever found. On the contrary, the 17,000 Japanese Americans who fought in Europe were among the most honored for bravery. Both at the time and later, there was criticism of the internment. In 1990, the government formally apologized to Japanese Americans. Surviving internees were each given a $20,000 payment. ✓

Tensions at Home

German Americans and Italian Americans also faced some restrictions. Several thousand who were not U.S. citizens were held in camps as "enemy aliens." Despite job gains, African Americans still experienced discrimination in employment. Some African American leaders demanded change. They pointed to the irony of the United States fighting for democracy while allowing injustice at home. President Roosevelt set up the Fair Employment Practices Committee to enforce racial equality in hiring.

Young Mexican Americans also served in the armed forces. In the United States, Mexican Americans, as well as **braceros,** or Mexican laborers, supported the war effort. Yet their language, culture, and flashy "zoot suits" set them apart. Riots occurred after some Mexican Americans were attacked by sailors on leave in Los Angeles. Eleanor Roosevelt blamed these "Zoot Suit Riots" on longstanding discrimination against Mexican Americans. ✓

Check Your Progress

1. Give examples of American unity on the home front.

____

____

2. Give examples of prejudice on the American home front.

____

____

Vocabulary Builder

Erroneous describes something that is based on an incorrect idea. Circle two sentences in the bracketed paragraph that explain why fears of Japanese Americans acting as spies were erroneous.

✓ Checkpoint

Explain why Japanese Americans were interned.

____

____

Reading Strategy

Reread the bracketed paragraph. Underline the cause of African American leaders demanding change. Circle the result of their demand.

✓ Checkpoint

Name the committee that President Roosevelt set up to combat racial discrimination in hiring.

____

____

Section 3 Notetaking Study Guide

Question to Think About As you read Section 3 in your textbook and take notes, keep this section focus question in mind: **How did the home front respond to American participation in the war?**

▶ Use this chart to record key information from the section. Some information has been filled in to get you started.

The War at Home		
Building the Military	**The Wartime Economy**	**Supporting the War Effort**
• More than ________ men served in the U.S. military. • Hundreds of thousands of women served as nurses and in ________ roles. For example, they ________________.	• U.S. factories shifted from producing ________ goods to creating ________ goods. • The ________________ was a government agency that supervised that change and set ________. • U.S. military output nearly ________.	• Americans followed ________ of scarce goods like sugar, shoes, and gasoline. They used ________ to buy these goods. • They also bought ________ to show support. • Maintaining strong ________ at home was also key to fighting the war.

Americans on the Home Front		
Group	**Experience**	**Positive or Negative Outcomes**
Women	Millions went to work in industry to fill needed ________ in factories and ________.	They gained: • • •
Japanese Americans	Some 110,000 were interned in prison-type camps for the duration of the war.	They lost their freedom and ________, even though there was never evidence of ________ against the United States.
African Americans	They still faced ________________.	The Fair Employment Practices Committee was set up to ________________.
Mexican Americans	They experienced ________ in America. In Los Angeles, they were attacked by ________________.	After the ________, Eleanor Roosevelt called attention to the problem of ________ against them.

Refer to this page to answer the Chapter 24 Focus Question on page 377.

Section 4
Toward Victory

Section 4 Focus Question

How did the Allies win World War II and what were the results? To begin answering this question,

- Learn how the Allies were finally able to defeat Germany.
- Discover how a powerful new weapon brought the war in the Pacific to a close.
- Explore the horrors of the Holocaust.
- Understand the immediate effects of World War II.

Section 4 Summary

The battles that stopped the Axis powers in 1942 turned the tide of the war. With determination and sacrifice, the Allies achieved victory in 1945. The war's unspeakable acts of brutality led to the first trials for war crimes.

Victory in Europe

In 1942, German movements into the Soviet Union and North Africa had been stopped. Russia was still facing heavy fighting from Germany, however. Stalin urged the Americans and the British to invade France to bring German troops west. Instead, the United States and Britain invaded Italy in July 1943. They knocked Mussolini from power. German troops in Italy continued to fight there, however.

On June 6, 1944—D-Day—the long-awaited campaign to retake France began. Under Allied commander Dwight Eisenhower, American, British, and Canadian troops landed at Normandy, in western France. Some 2,500 American soldiers were killed that day on Omaha Beach. By August, the Allies were able to free Paris from the Germans.

The German army regrouped for a last offensive at the Battle of the Bulge in December. By then, however, the Germans were short of supplies and soldiers. In January 1945, Allied troops invaded Germany from the west. The Soviets closed in from the east. By April 1945, both Berlin and victory were in sight. Tragically, President Roosevelt died of a stroke on April 12. On April 30, Hitler committed suicide, freeing his generals to make an unconditional surrender. V-E Day, May 8, 1945, celebrated the end of war in Europe. ✓

Key Events

1939	Germany invades Poland; World War II begins.
1941	United States enters war after Japan attacks Pearl Harbor.
1945	U.S. plane drops an atomic bomb on Hiroshima. World War II ends.

Reading Strategy

Ask and answer a question about the bracketed paragraph.

Question:

____

____

Answer:

____

____

✓ Checkpoint

List three major events that led to Allied victory in Europe.

____

____

____

Victory in the Pacific

The Japanese offensive was halted at the Battle of Midway in 1942. Japan had conquered many islands in the Pacific. The Allies used a strategy of **island hopping**, targeting islands to capture that would create a path for an invasion of Japan. MacArthur returned to the Philippines in January 1945. Famous battles in the Pacific included Iow Jima and Okinawa, islands closest to Japan. Still, the Japanese were fierce fighters. Japanese **kamikaze** pilots committed suicide by crashing into Allied ships. There was great fear that invading Japan would bring high American casualties. This worry convinced the new President, **Harry Truman**, to drop the atomic bomb on the Japanese cities of Hiroshima and Nagasaki. The two blasts instantly killed an estimated 165,000 people. Five days after the second bomb was dropped, the Japanese surrendered. August 14, 1945, is known as V-J Day. World War II finally ended with Japan's official surrender to General MacArthur on September 2, 1945. ✓

Vocabulary Builder

The word *kamikaze* means "divine wind" in Japanese.

✓ Checkpoint

Explain the term "island hopping."

____

____

The Holocaust

World War II took the lives of up to 60 million people, including 400,000 Americans. After the Germans were defeated, the Allied armies came upon "death camps" in Poland. Hitler had planned to kill all of Europe's Jews. His "final solution" was **genocide**, or the deliberate attempt to wipe out an entire nation or group of people. Railway cars carried men, women, and children to the death camps. Most were killed in gas chambers. Others were tortured. Some six million Jews were murdered in the Holocaust.

The Allies charged the German and Japanese leaders with **war crimes**. These are wartime acts of cruelty and brutality that are judged to be beyond the accepted rules of war and human behavior. Nuremberg, Germany, saw the first trials for war crimes. Trials were also held in Tokyo and Manila. Several Axis leaders were sentenced to death. ✓

✓ Checkpoint

Identify the goal of Hitler's "final solution."

____

____

Check Your Progress

1. How did the Allies win the war in Europe?

____

____

____

2. How did the Allies win the war in the Pacific?

____

____

Section 4 Notetaking Study Guide

Question to Think About As you read Section 4 in your textbook and take notes, keep this section focus question in mind: **How did the Allies win World War II and what were the results?**

▶ Use this chart to record key information from the section. Some information has been filled in to get you started.

<table>
<tr><th colspan="2">Toward Victory</th></tr>
<tr><th>Victory in Europe</th><th>Victory in the Pacific</th></tr>
<tr><td>Italy Surrenders
• Invasion of Sicily in July 1943
• Surrendered on ______
D-Day
• Date: ______
• Commanded by General Eisenhower
• Goal: ______
• Americans landed on ______.
• Number killed: ______
• Success: Allies entered Paris on ______.
Battle of the Bulge
• Date: ______
• Outcome: Germany's defeat showed that the Allies had more ______ and ______ to keep fighting.
Germany Invaded
• Date: January ______
• Allies invaded from the ______.
• ______ invaded from the east.
• Allies used ground troops and bombs.
Victory
V-E Day: ______
Aftermath
• Nazi death camps discovered
• Nazis who committed war crimes were tried at ______.</td><td>Island Hopping
• Strategy: Capture some islands and go around others to create a stepping stone to Japan.
Battles:
• Guadalcanal
• Luzon and ______ in the Philippines
• Iwo Jima
• ______
The Atomic Bombs
• President ______ ordered bombings.
• Goal: To avoid ______ if United States invades Japan
• First bomb: Hiroshima on ______ killed ______
• Second bomb: ______ on ______ killed 30,000 instantly
Victory
• V-J Day: ______
• Who announced surrender: Emperor of Japan
• Official end of World War II: General ______ accepted surrender on the battleship ______.
Aftermath
• War crimes trials in ______ and Manila forced responsibility on the leaders who created the ______ machine.</td></tr>
<tr><td colspan="2">• Which Allied leader did not live to see the end of World War II, and when did he die?
______</td></tr>
</table>

Refer to this page to answer the Chapter 24 Focus Question on page 377.

Chapter 24 Assessment

Directions: Circle the letter of the correct answer.

1. Which world event contributed most directly to the start of World War II?

- **A** Italy invaded Ethiopia.
- **B** Germany invaded Poland.
- **C** Military leaders came to power in Japan.

2. Which is ***not*** an accurate description of World War II?

- **A** It demonstrated the failure of appeasement.
- **B** It was total war.
- **C** The main allies were the United States and Britain.

3. Which is ***not*** true of the U.S. home front during World War II?

- **A** There was proof of spying by Japanese Americans.
- **B** Some foods and other items were rationed.
- **C** Millions of women filled jobs in industry.

Directions: Follow the steps to answer this question:

How might the outcome of the war in Europe have changed if Germany had kept the nonaggression pact and not invaded the Soviet Union?

Step 1: Recall information: In the chart, identify details that describe the countries and their relationship before the war.

Germany and Russia Before the War
• Their Leaders: ______________________
• Terms of Nazi-Soviet Pact: ______________________

Step 2: List three examples of how the Soviet Union helped defeat Germany.

Soviet Union in the War
•
•
•

Step 3: Complete the topic sentence that follows. Then write two or three more sentences that support your topic sentence.

The outcome of the war in Europe might have been different if Germany had not attacked the Soviet Union because ______________________

____

____

Chapter 24 Notetaking Study Guide

Now you are ready to answer the Chapter 24 Focus Question: **What were the causes and effects of World War II?**

▶ Complete the charts to help you answer this question. Use the notes that you took for each section.

Causes			
Economic Factors	**Totalitarian Governments**	**Racist Theories**	**Failed Organizations and Policies**
______ ______ caused people in many countires to lose faith in ______ governments.	Dictators took control in Germany, Italy, and ______. Militarism and ______, which promotes extreme nationalism and ______, took hold.	The idea of superior peoples who have the right to conquer ______ ones spread in Italy, Japan, and Germany. Hitler preached extreme ______ against Jews.	The ______ ______ failed to act to stop invasions of China and Ethiopia. Britain and France tried ______ with Hitler by signing the ______ ______.

World War II

Effects	
In the United States	**In the World**
• War production solved the unemployment problems of the ______. • Women gained jobs with better working conditions and pay because they were needed in industry. • ______ of scarce goods required sacrifice of all Americans. • Prejudice created shameful experiences for ______, ______, and ______. • The United States gained power as "the great arsenal of ______."	• Global conflict spread throughout ______ and ______. • Total war affected millions of ______ and ______. • Hitler's "final solution" murdered ______ Jews in the ______. • The first ______ were used in warfare, on ______ and ______. • The first trials to prosecute ______ followed victory by the Allies.

Refer to this page to answer the Unit 8 Focus Question on page 392.

Chapter 25

The United States in the Cold War

(1945–1963)

What You Will Learn

After World War II, the United States faced new challenges in the world as well as economic and social changes at home. Conflict with the Soviet Union developed into a Cold War.

Chapter 25 Focus Question

As you read this chapter, keep this question in mind: **What key foreign and domestic issues affected the United States after World War II?**

Key Events

- **1947** The Truman Doctrine and Marshall Plan change U.S. foreign policy.
- **1950** The Korean War begins.
- **1962** The United States faces the Soviet Union in the Cuban missile crisis.

Section 1

Roots of the Cold War

Section 1 Focus Question

How did the United States respond to the early stages of the Cold War? To begin answering this question,

- Learn about the growing distrust of Russia after the war.
- Discover how the United States tried to limit communism.
- Find out about three new international organizations.
- Read how the events of 1949 shook America's confidence.

Section 1 Summary

A new conflict developed immediately after World War II. A Cold War of tension grew as the United States and its allies faced off with the Soviet Union and other Communist nations.

Growing Distrust

Soviet troops occupied most of Eastern Europe at the end of World War II. Stalin agreed to allow free elections in those countries. Then he broke his promise. He wanted Communist governments in Eastern Europe to help his goal of making the Soviet Union the chief world power. Churchill described the result as an "**iron curtain,**" or barrier to understanding and information, across Europe. By 1948, Eastern Europe was filled with Communist **satellites,** or countries ruled by another nation. The dispute between the Communist and non-Communist nations became known as the Cold War. ✓

✓ Checkpoint

State the term Churchill used to describe Soviet expansion.

____

Containing Soviet Expansion

President Truman outlined the "Truman Doctrine," which opposed the spread of communism. He began the policy of **containment,** or limiting Soviet expansion. In 1947, the Marshall Plan gave $12 billion to European nations to rebuild from the war and weaken Communist influence.

The next standoff was in Germany. It was divided into four zones after the war. The Soviets controlled the eastern zone. It included the German capital, Berlin. Berlin was also divided, with the Soviets controlling East Berlin. When the Western powers wanted to reunify Germany in 1948, Stalin chose to confront the Allies. He set up a blockade to control West Berlin. The Allies responded with a huge **airlift,** sending cargo planes to deliver tons of supplies to West Berliners. In 1949, the Allies combined their zones to form West Germany. The Soviet zone became East Germany, with Berlin still divided. In 1961, the Communists began building a wall to keep East Berliners from escaping to the West. The Berlin Wall became a symbol of the Cold War. ✓

International Organizations

The United States turned from isolationism by leading the creation of the United Nations (UN). This was an international organization to maintain peace and to settle disputes. The United States also joined a military alliance. The Western powers formed the North Atlantic Treaty Organization (NATO). The Soviets and Eastern Europeans created the Warsaw Pact. ✓

The Shocks of 1949

In 1949, U.S. security was shaken by two events. First, the Soviet Union exploded its own atomic bomb. Second, Communists in China came to power under Mao Zedong. Mao established the People's Republic of China. The Chinese Nationalists, America's allies in World War II, retreated to Taiwan. The United States viewed them as the legal Chinese government. ✓

Check Your Progress

1. What was the purpose of the Truman Doctrine?

____

2. What two organizations turned the United States from isolationism?

____

____

Vocabulary Builder

To *confront* is "to challenge face to face." Identify what Stalin did in 1948 to confront the Allies.

____

____

✓ Checkpoint

List two purposes of the Marshall Plan.

____

____

✓ Checkpoint

List two goals of the UN when it was founded.

____

____

✓ Checkpoint

Identify the two events in 1949 that shocked Americans.

____

____

Section 1 Notetaking Study Guide

Question to Think About As you read Section 1 in your textbook and take notes, keep this section focus question in mind: **How did the United States respond to the early stages of the Cold War?**

► Use these charts to record key information from the section. Some information has been filled in to get you started.

Roots of the Cold War
• Conflict developed immediately following World War II when the Soviet Union refused to allow free elections in ______________ and created Communist satellites there. • Winston Churchill called the Soviet threat an ______________ across Europe.

U.S. Responses to the Cold War	
U.S. Policies 1947 to 1949	**U.S. Actions 1947 to 1949**
• The Truman Doctrine stated that the United States would ______________ ______________. • The U.S. policy of limiting Communist expansion was called ______________. • The United States demonstrated a turn away from isolationism by supporting two organizations. • The United States took a leading role in creating the ______________. Like all members, it had a vote in the General Assembly. The United States became one of five countries that are permanent members of the more powerful ______________. • The United States also helped establish a military alliance with other Western nations known as NATO, the ______________ ______________. Its purpose was to ______________ ______________.	• In 1947, President Truman requested military aid to stop Communist threats to Greece and ______________. • In 1947, Secretary of State George Marshall proposed the ______________ to provide ______________ to postwar Europe. Growing Communist parties in ______________ and Italy was one reason the United States stepped in to help with $______________ in aid. • In 1948, the Soviet Union ______________ ______________ around West Berlin. The United States played a major role in the Berlin airlift by ______________ ______________. • In 1949, the United States joined with Britain and France to combine the areas of Germany that they controlled into ______________. In turn, the Soviets created East Germany. • In 1949, Communists under ______________ came to power in China. The United States refused to recognize the People's Republic of China, insisting that the government of ______________ was the ______________ Chinese government.

Refer to this page to answer the Chapter 25 Focus Question on page 391.

Section 2
A Time of Prosperity

Section 2 Focus Question

How did the American economy and society change after World War II? To begin answering this question,

- Identify the problems of the postwar economy.
- Explain the effects of a changing society during the 1950s.
- Contrast life in the suburbs with life in the cities.

Section 2 Summary

The postwar years saw changes as the country adjusted to peacetime. By the 1950s, the economy was booming. Television had an impact on family life. Growing suburbs sent cities into decline.

Adjusting to Peacetime

With peace came significant changes on the home front. Millions of soldiers returned. Congress passed the GI Bill of Rights, which gave soldiers money to start businesses, buy homes, and pay for college. U.S. industry switched from producing military goods to consumer goods. After the sacrifices of the war years, people wanted consumer goods. Demand for these goods soon exceeded the supply. Inflation resulted, which caused prices to rise. This caused workers to demand higher pay, and labor unrest followed. President Truman at first backed employers, fearing that higher wages would lead to more inflation. That made the unions angry. When he supported higher wages, prices rose. Then consumers became angry.

Truman's Democrats lost the 1946 mid-term election, and Republicans gained control of Congress. The Republicans wanted to undo many New Deal labor reforms. Congress passed the Taft-Hartley Act, which cracked down on strikes. The act also banned the **closed shop,** a workplace in which only union members can be hired.

By the presidential election of 1948, Truman seemed unlikely to win. The Republicans nominated New York's governor, Thomas Dewey. Truman's party, the Democrats, was divided. Truman campaigned hard, however. He focused Americans on the problem of the "do-nothing"

Key Events

1947	The Truman Doctrine and Marshall Plan change U.S. foreign policy.
1950	The Korean War begins.
1962	The United States faces the Soviet Union in the Cuban missile crisis.

Reading Strategy

Reread the bracketed paragraph. Underline the sentence that gives the main idea. Circle phrases that support the main idea.

Republican Congress. In a surprise victory, Truman was reelected. The Democrats regained control of Congress. Truman passed some of his "Fair Deal" proposals, such as a higher minimum wage and low-income housing.

In 1952, Truman chose not to run again. The presidency went to World War II General Dwight Eisenhower. He was more conservative. Eisenhower won again in 1956 on a campaign promise of "peace, progress, and prosperity." His achievements included the Interstate Highway Act of 1956, which provided funds for a vast system of highways. ✓

✓ Checkpoint

Name the act that helped returning soldiers.

____

____

A Changing Society

The 1950s were good times for much of America. Inflation fell as more goods became available. New technologies helped increase **productivity.** This meant that workers were able to work more efficiently and produce more goods. Many Americans <u>prospered</u> and purchased homes. They bought freezers, clothes dryers, and air conditioners. The **standard of living** rose, which is the measure of how comfortable life is for a person, group, or country. The postwar birthrate soared, a phenomenon called the **baby boom.** People lived longer thanks to new vaccines.

More families had cars. With the new highway system, more people had the freedom to live outside of cities. Suburbs grew rapidly, especially in western states.

Television replaced the radio as the focus of family entertainment. By the early 1960s, most homes had at least one television. Young people also enjoyed **rock-and-roll.** This music was a blend of blues and country music. The most popular rock-and-roll singer was **Elvis Presley.**

Vocabulary Builder

One meaning of *prosper* is "to be successful in a financial way." Use clues in the bracketed paragraphs to identify four types of purchases that reveal how Americans were prospering in the 1950s.

____

____

In many cities, life became worse. The tax base eroded as people moved to the suburbs. Without the money to make repairs and ensure city services, urban areas deteriorated. Crime rose. Those left in the **inner cities,** or centers of older cities, tended to be poor and less educated. ✓

✓ Checkpoint

Identify two urban problems that resulted from the growth of suburbs.

____

____

Check Your Progress

1. What were three effects of inflation after the war?

____

____

2. What changes did families experience in the 1950s?

____

____

Section 2 Notetaking Study Guide

Question to Think About As you read Section 2 in your textbook and take notes, keep this section focus question in mind: **How did the American economy and society change after World War II?**

▶ Use these charts to record key information from the section. Some information has been filled in to get you started.

Adjusting to Peacetime

- Two economic challenges that the United States faced after World War II were absorbing millions of ______________ into a peacetime economy and changing the economy from producing war goods to ______________.
- The ______________ helped to solve the first problem by providing money for starting businesses, buying homes, and paying for college.
- Americans were eager to buy consumer goods, and demand soon exceeded ________, causing ______________. As prices rose, workers demanded higher wages, and a wave of ______________ swept the nation.
- When a Republican Congress took control, it passed the Taft-Hartley Act, which gave the government power to delay a strike. Truman managed to win the presidential election in ________, and the ______________ gained control of Congress. It passed Truman's "Fair Deal" proposals that helped workers, such as a higher ______________.

A Changing Society

Dwight Eisenhower was elected president in __________ and reelected in __________. He believed in smaller government with less control of the ______________.

Economic Changes in the 1950s	Social Changes in the 1950s
• Once the peacetime economy got underway, the 1950s were ______________ for many Americans. • Soaring employment and increased ______________ helped workers produce more goods for consumers to buy. • The U.S. standard of living ______________. More people owned their own ________ and ______________. • However, cities experienced an economic downturn as ______________ and ______________ moved to the suburbs, leaving ______________ people behind. Cities lost money to pay for ______________ and services, and ______________ increased.	• A postwar increase in population was caused by a ______________ and by new antibiotic medicines and ______________ that helped people live longer. • More cars and a new system of ______________ linking America fueled the growth of suburbs located ______________ cities. • Entertainment changed as ______________ became the most important family activity, and new styles of music such as ______________ became popular. • Social critics worried that Americans were feeling more pressure to ______________. They also criticized consumers' collecting of ______________ possessions.

Refer to this page to answer the Chapter 25 Focus Question on page 391.

Section 3

The Korean War Period

Key Events

1947	The Truman Doctrine and Marshall Plan change U.S. foreign policy.
1950	The Korean War begins.
1962	The United States faces the Soviet Union in the Cuban missile crisis.

Vocabulary Builder

Which of the following words is a synonym for the underlined word *retreating*: advancing, withdrawing, or repeating?

____

Section 3 Focus Question

How did the United States respond to the invasion of Korea and its aftermath? To begin answering this question,

- Read how the Korean War became the first Cold War conflict.
- Describe how the Korean War ended.
- Explain how the Cold War led to a Red Scare in the United States.

Section 3 Summary

In 1950, the United States led United Nations troops in the Korean War. Spy cases and a U.S. senator fueled fear of Communists inside America.

Conflict in Korea

After World War II, Korea was divided into two countries along the 38th line of latitude. Communists took control in North Korea. On June 25, 1950, North Korean troops invaded South Korea. They reached Seoul (sole), South Korea's capital, within three days. President Truman urged the UN to rush military aid to South Korea. The UN force included soldiers from 16 different countries. It was mostly made up of American troops, however. General MacArthur, the former World War II commander, led the force.

At first the war went badly for the UN troops. Then more soldiers and supplies arrived. They pushed the North Koreans back over the 38th parallel. MacArthur sent his forces after the retreating North Koreans. The UN troops almost reached the Yalu River, the border between North Korea and Communist China. The Chinese were threatened and attacked with a large force. They pushed the UN troops back to the South Korean border and into a military **stalemate**, a situation in which neither side wins.

MacArthur was frustrated at this outcome. He said he could win the war by bombing bases in China that were supplying the North Koreans. Truman wanted to avoid war with China. He warned MacArthur to stop making these statements. When MacArthur complained that politicians were preventing him from winning, Truman fired him.

The Korean conflict remained a stalemate for two years. The killing continued while peace talks were held. Finally, in July 1953, a cease-fire was reached. Each side agreed to a **demilitarized zone,** an area that neither side controls. This zone still separates North and South Korea today. About two million Koreans died in the war. More than 30,000 Americans died, and another 100,000 were wounded. ✓

✓ Checkpoint

Name the country that MacArthur wanted to bomb in order to win the Korean War.

____

Fears at Home

With Cold War tensions high, fear of communism increased in the United States. Americans worried that the country could not defeat communism. Worse, they thought that Communists inside the United States might overthrow the government. Those fears were fueled by two famous spy cases. In 1948, a former Communist named Whittaker Chambers accused a former State Department employee named Alger Hiss of being a spy. Chambers said that Hiss passed secrets to the Soviets in the 1930s. To prove it, Chambers produced copies of papers that Hiss had given him. The second case made headlines in 1950. Julius and Ethel Rosenberg were found guilty of passing secret information to the Soviets. They were executed in 1953. At the time, many people were outraged by the executions. Years later, however, the U.S. government released messages that proved the guilt of the Rosenbergs and Hiss.

Reading Strategy

Mark the Text

Circle three words or phrases in the underlined text that describe American society during the Cold War.

In this fear of the 1950s, a U.S. senator from Wisconsin, **Joseph McCarthy,** gained fame for hunting down Communists. He made sensational charges against people in government and other fields, often with no evidence. Many lives were ruined. After four years, he lost popularity. In televised Senate hearings, he made false charges against U.S. Army leaders. Congress voted to **censure,** or condemn, him for his behavior. Since that time, *McCarthyism* has come to mean accusing someone of disloyalty without evidence. ✓

✓ Checkpoint

Name the person who led the hunt for Communists in America in the 1950s.

____

Check Your Progress

1. How did the Korean War end?

____

____

2. What did many Americans fear most about the idea of having Communists in the United States?

____

____

Section 3 Notetaking Study Guide

Question to Think About As you read Section 3 in your textbook and take notes, keep this section focus question in mind: **How did the United States respond to the invasion of Korea and its aftermath?**

► Use these charts to record key information from the section. Some information has been filled in to get you started.

The Korean War		
Causes/Expansion	**Decisive Actions**	**Outcomes**
• After World War II, Korea was divided into ______ and ______ at the 38th parallel. • The Soviet Union backed a Communist government in ______. The United States backed ______. • On ______, North Korea invaded South Korea. • President Truman called on the United Nations to send military aid. The United States led a force of soldiers from ______ countries, although ______ were American. The commander was General ______.	• Within three days after the invasion, the North Koreans reached ______, the capital of South Korea. • The UN forces did badly at first. Then more soldiers and ______ arrived, and the UN ______ line held. • MacArthur ordered an advance that sent the North Koreans back over the ______. • MacArthur pushed his troops to the ______ border. • A counterattack by ______ and North Korean forces sent the UN troops back to ______.	• War ended in a ______. A cease-fire in 1953 created a ______, an area that neither side controlled. • More than ______ Koreans died in the war, mainly ______. U.S. casualties were ______ killed and ______ wounded. • A disagreement between MacArthur and President Truman developed. Truman ______ MacArthur after he called for the bombing of ______. • Korea remained ______.

Fears at Home		
Three events that caused Americans to become worried about Communists at home: • • •	Two famous spy cases that seized public attention: • Alger Hiss, a former State Department official, was accused of spying for the Soviets in the 1930s. •	• ______ gained a following of Americans by hunting Communists in ______ and in the U.S. Army. • The term ______ came to mean accusing someone without evidence.

Refer to this page to answer the Chapter 25 Focus Question on page 391.

Section 4

Global Concerns in the Cold War

Section 4 Focus Question

How did the Cold War increase tensions around the world? To begin answering this question,

- Learn how the Cold War turned into an arms race.
- Understand why emerging countries became targets.
- Read how communism gained influence in Latin America.
- Explain why Cuba became a crisis during the Cold War.

Section 4 Summary

In the 1950s and 1960s, the United States and Soviet Union competed to have the most nuclear arms and influence. The Cold War nearly exploded into a nuclear war over Cuba.

The Arms Race

The death of Stalin in 1953 brought Nikita Khrushchev (KROO shawf) to power. New leadership did not improve relations with the United States. By then, both countries had exploded the hydrogen bomb. Both were on their way to becoming **superpowers,** or countries whose military, economic, and political strength are so great that they can influence events worldwide. The two countries began an **arms race**—a contest in which nations compete to build more and more powerful weapons. China, France, and Britain joined the arms race when they developed nuclear weapons. No country wanted to use the weapons, so they **stockpiled,** or collected, them. The United States and Soviet Union had enough missiles stockpiled to destroy each other many times.

Space also became an area of competition between the two countries. In October 1957, the Soviets launched *Sputnik*, a satellite, into Earth's orbit. Congress then created NASA, the National Aeronautics and Space Administration, to begin a U.S. space program. It also passed the National Defense Education Act to train scientists and teachers. ✓

Emerging Nations

After World War II, many colonies gained independence. The Soviet Union aimed to spread communism to these new countries, and the United States continued its efforts at containment. In 1961, President **John F. Kennedy** proposed

Key Events

1947	The Truman Doctrine and Marshall Plan change U.S. foreign policy.
1950	The Korean War begins.
1962	The United States faces the Soviet Union in the Cuban missile crisis.

✓ Checkpoint

Name the first satellite launched into space.

____

Reading Strategy

Recall the U.S. policy for limiting the spread of communism. Circle the name of the policy where it appears in the underlined sentence. Then, on the next page, circle an example of how the United States was following that policy.

the Peace Corps to build friendships with developing countries. The Peace Corps sent skilled American volunteers to help in villages throughout Asia, Latin America, and Africa.

In Africa, the Congo was one area of conflict. Soon after Congo gained independence from Belgium, a civil war erupted. The United States backed one side, and the Soviet Union supported the other. The war became more violent with the weapons supplied by the two superpowers.

The United States gave the Philippines their independence in 1946. Communist rebels began fighting there but were defeated. In the French colony of Indochina, the United States supported France in its battle with Ho Chi Minh. He was a Soviet-backed Communist who sought independence for Vietnam. In 1954, Ho's forces gained control of what would become North Vietnam. ✓

✓ Checkpoint

List three countries in which forces supported by the United States fought Communist-backed forces.

___

___

___

Latin America and the Cold War

Poverty and corrupt leaders created unrest in many Latin American countries. In 1959, Fidel Castro staged a successful revolution in Cuba and set up a Communist government. The Soviet Union promised aid. Two years later, Cubans who had left the country tried to retake control by invading with the support of the United States. Known as the "Bay of Pigs," the invasion failed and made tensions higher.

The Soviet Union backed Castro with aid and arms. This led to the Cuban missile crisis of 1962. The United States gained evidence of nuclear missiles in Cuba. President Kennedy demanded that the missiles be removed. He also ordered a naval blockade of Cuba to stop Soviet ships from delivering more missiles. The potential for nuclear war grew as Soviet ships steamed toward Cuba. The world watched in fear. Finally, the ships turned back, and a compromise was reached. The Soviet Union agreed to withdraw the missiles, and the United States pledged not to invade Cuba. ✓

Vocabulary Builder

Potential refers to the possibility or capability of something happening. In the bracketed paragraph, identify one action by the United States and one by the Soviet Union that caused the potential for nuclear war to increase.

___

___

✓ Checkpoint

Name the failed invasion of Cuba.

___

Check Your Progress

1. What are two reasons the arms race increased tensions?

___

___

2. What agreement ended the Cuban missile crisis?

___

___

Section 4 Notetaking Study Guide

Question to Think About As you read Section 4 in your textbook and take notes, keep this section focus question in mind: **How did the Cold War increase tensions around the world?**

▶ Use this chart to record key information from the section. Some information has been filled in to get you started.

Global Concerns in the Cold War

The Arms Race

- Josef Stalin died in 1953 and was replaced by ______________.
- Both the United States and Soviet Union exploded ______________ in the early 1950s, which they ______________ in dangerous collections.
- The arms race got more crowded as ______________, ______________, and ______________ developed nuclear weapons.
- The Soviet Union launched ______________, expanding the arms race. Now the goal was also to control ______________.
- Two responses by the United States were the establishment of NASA and the ______________.

Emerging Nations

- The ______________ was established for the purpose of building ______________ with developing countries and encouraging their economic growth.
- New countries emerged following ______________. Most were former colonies in ______________ and ______________ that gained independence.
- The United States backed one side and the Soviets the other in the Congo. Each side supplied ______________, ______________, and technical advisers. As a result, the war became more ______________.
- The U.S. colony of ______________ also gained independence. Communist rebels were ______________ there.
- The United States backed ______________ forces against a Communist fight for independence in Vietnam. Communists under ______________ won control of northern Vietnam.

Latin America and the Cold War

- Revolts in Latin America brought ______________ groups to power.
- When ______________ took power in Cuba, he created a ______________ state and began encouraging revolution in other parts of Latin America.
- The ______________ invasion failed and made ______________ more popular.
- Soviet aid to Cuba included building ______________ and providing nuclear missiles.
- During the Cuban missile crisis, the two key opposing leaders were ______________ and ______________. There were fears of nuclear war if Soviet ships ran the American blockade. The crisis ended when the Soviets agreed to ______________, and the United States agreed not to ______________.

Refer to this page to answer the Chapter 25 Focus Question on page 391.

Chapter 25 Assessment

Directions: Circle the letter of the correct answer.

1. Which of the following was *not* a U.S. foreign policy issue after World War II?
   - **A** fighting inflation
   - **B** helping Europe recover economically
   - **C** building up nuclear arms

2. Which event did *not* happen in the United States during the 1950s?
   - **A** Joseph McCarthy led the hunt for U.S. Communists.
   - **B** Watching television took over family life.
   - **C** A baby boom forced a drop in the standard of living.

3. What caused the greatest threat to the United States during the Cold War?
   - **A** Communists in China
   - **B** Communists in Cuba
   - **C** Communists in Vietnam

Directions: Follow the steps to answer this question:

Why was President Truman a good leader at the start of the Cold War?

Step 1: Recall information: In the chart, identify places in the world where communism spread while President Truman was in office.

Communism Spreads	
• • •	• •

Step 2: In the chart, explain how Truman responded to Cold War threats.

President Truman's Statements and Actions
• Statements:
• Actions:

Step 3: Complete the topic sentence that follows. Then write two or three more sentences that support your topic sentence.

President Truman was a good leader for the United States at the start of the Cold War because ____

____

____

____

Chapter 25 Notetaking Study Guide

Now you are ready to answer the Chapter 25 Focus Question: **What key foreign and domestic issues affected the United States after World War II?**

► Complete the charts to help you answer this question. Use the notes that you took for each section.

Foreign Issues Affecting U.S.	How the United States Responded
Spread of communism	• Sets policy of ________________ • Funds $12 billion ________________ to prevent growth of communism in ________________ Europe • Fights war in ________________, with ________________ Americans killed and ________________ wounded
Arms race	• Explodes a more powerful ________________ bomb • Competes with ________________ in stockpiling ________________ • Establishes ________________ to compete in space • Comes to brink of nuclear war during the ________________
International organizations	• Abandons policy of ________________ • Leads in establishing ________________ • Joins ________________ to prevent Soviet attacks
Developing nations	• Spreads influence with military support against ________________ forces • Establishes the ________________, sending skilled ________________ to promote friendships and provide ________________ help

Domestic Issues Affecting U.S.	Positive or Negative Outcomes
Inflation	• Negative because:
Peacetime economy	Positive when: the economy gets rolling and productivity increases, leading to a rise in the standard of living for many Americans
Growth of suburbs	• Positive for: • Negative for:
Fear of communism	• Negative because:

Refer to this page to answer the Unit 8 Focus Question on page 392.

Unit 8 Pulling It Together Activity

What You Have Learned

Chapter 23 The Great Depression was the worst economic crisis in American history. Millions of people lost their jobs, homes, and savings. President Franklin Roosevelt responded with a wide range of measures called the New Deal.

Chapter 24 World War II was the bloodiest conflict in history. Both U.S. soldiers and civilians at home made major contributions to winning the war.

Chapter 25 After World War II, the United States faced new challenges in the world and economic and social changes at home. Conflict with the Soviet Union developed into a Cold War.

Think Like a Historian

Read the Unit 8 Focus Question: **How did the United States deal with crises in domestic and foreign affairs?**

► Use the organizers on this page and the next to collect information to answer this question.

How did the United States deal with domestic crises in the Great Depression and war? Read the problems and issues identified on the organizer below. Then review your section and chapter notes to help you list the solutions to, or effects of, each.

U.S. Domestic Crises: Problems and Issues

The Great Depression	World War II Home Front	Postwar/Cold War Era
• 25% unemployment	• Meeting war production	• Millions of returning soldiers
• Bankrupt businesses and industries	• Supporting the war effort	• Fear of Communists in the United States
• Stock market crash and bank failures	• Anti-Japanese feelings and fears	• Competing in the space race

What types of crises in foreign affairs did the United States deal with, and how did it respond? Major ones are identified here. Review your section and chapter notes to help you complete the organizer.

U.S. Foreign Crises: American Responses	
World War II	**The Cold War**
• German Aggression in Europe	• Spreading Soviet Threat
	• Korean War
• Japanese Aggression in the Pacific	
	• Cuban Missile Crisis

Unit 9

Moving Toward the Future

What You Will Learn

Chapter 26 In the 1950s and 1960s, the civil rights movement made great strides. President Johnson's "Great Society" program sought to end poverty. African Americans and other groups organized for civil rights.

Chapter 27 Vietnam became a major battlefield in America's fight against communism. America's involvement in the Vietnam War grew during the 1960s, and opinion was divided on the war and how it ended.

Chapter 28 Ronald Reagan ushered in a conservative era. The Cold War ended, leaving the United States as the sole superpower. Middle East tensions posed challenges.

Chapter 29 The September 11, 2001, attacks led to a war on terrorism. Today, the United States faces foreign policy, economic, and environmental challenges.

Focus Your Learning As you study this unit and take notes, you will find the information to answer the questions below. Answering the Chapter Focus Questions will help you build your answer to the Unit Focus Question.

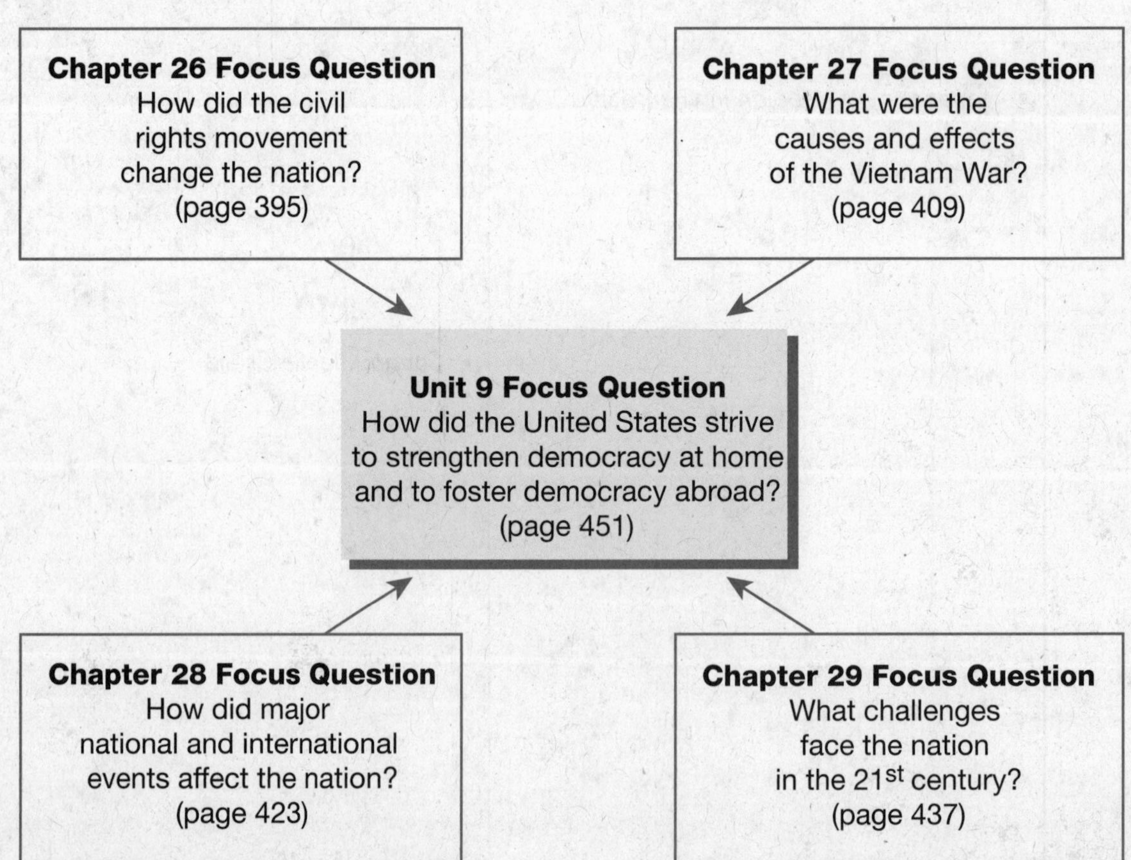

Chapter 26 Focus Question
How did the civil rights movement change the nation? (page 395)
Chapter 27 Focus Question
What were the causes and effects of the Vietnam War? (page 409)
Unit 9 Focus Question
How did the United States strive to strengthen democracy at home and to foster democracy abroad? (page 451)
Chapter 28 Focus Question
How did major national and international events affect the nation? (page 423)
Chapter 29 Focus Question
What challenges face the nation in the 21st century? (page 437)

Chapter 26

The Civil Rights Era (1945–1975)

What You Will Learn

African Americans made important civil rights gains after World War II. Their movement inspired women, Latinos, and Native Americans to protest for better treatment.

Chapter 26 Focus Question

As you read this chapter, keep this question in mind: **How did the civil rights movement change the nation?**

Section 1

Beginnings of the Civil Rights Movement

Section 1 Focus Question

What key events marked the beginning of the civil rights movement in the 1950s? To begin answering this question,

- Learn about racial barriers in the North and South.
- Read about the integration of baseball and the military.
- Find out about *Brown* v. *Board of Education of Topeka.*
- Note the importance of the Montgomery bus boycott.

Section 1 Summary

There were many racial obstacles for African Americans. Changes occurred after World War II. In the 1950s, the Supreme Court made historic desegregation rulings.

Separate but Unequal

African Americans faced racial barriers throughout the country. In the North, prejudice limited jobs and housing. In the South, laws kept African Americans separate from whites in many public places, including schools.

The National Association for the Advancement of Colored People (NAACP) worked to end segregation and discrimination. In 1938, the talented lawyer **Thurgood Marshall** took charge of the NAACP's legal efforts. He fought for **integration**, or an end to racial segregation. ✓

Barriers Begin to Crumble

African American soldiers fought bravely in World War II, as did other minorities. After the war, they wanted discrimination

Key Events

1954	Supreme Court strikes down school segregation in *Brown* v. *Board of Education*.
1955	African Americans stage a bus boycott in Montgomery, Alabama.
1965	United Farm Workers union is founded.
1966	National Organization for Women is founded.

✓ Checkpoint

Explain what the NAACP fought against.

____

____

to end. The color barrier fell in Major League Baseball in 1947. The Brooklyn Dodgers hired **Jackie Robinson** to play for their team. Robinson faced terrible treatment by other players and baseball fans. Eventually, however, his talent and courage earned him many admirers. In 1948, President Truman ordered an end to military segregation. As commander in chief, he could do so without needing congressional approval. ✓

✓ Checkpoint

Name two institutions that desegregated during the 1940s.

______

______

Desegregating the Schools

In 1951, Oliver Brown sued the Topeka, Kansas, board of education. He wanted his daughter to attend a nearby public school. At the time, the school allowed only white students. Thurgood Marshall took the case, *Brown* v. *Board of Education of Topeka,* before the Supreme Court. He argued that segregated schools were not equal to all-white schools. In addition, they made African Americans feel inferior. The Court ruled that schools needed to be integrated.

[Whites resisted school integration. In 1957, nine African Americans tried to attend an all-white high school in Little Rock, Arkansas. They faced hostile mobs. President Eisenhower sent federal troops to protect them.] ✓

Vocabulary Builder

Reread the bracketed paragraph. Use context clues to write a definition of *hostile*.

______

______

✓ Checkpoint

State why Oliver Brown sued the Topeka board of education.

______

______

The Montgomery Bus Boycott

In 1955, **Rosa Parks** refused to give up her seat to white passengers on a bus in Montgomery, Alabama. She was arrested. As a result, African Americans **boycotted**, or refused to use, the city's buses. At the time, nearly 75 percent of Montgomery's bus riders were African Americans. Leaders like **Martin Luther King, Jr.**, urged the boycott to continue until bus segregation stopped. Angry whites bombed King's house. Other leaders were falsely arrested. Still, the boycott continued 381 days. In November 1956, the Supreme Court ruled against segregation on buses. ✓

✓ Checkpoint

Name two people closely associated with the Montgomery bus boycott.

______

______

Check Your Progress

1. How did the Supreme Court help to end segregation?

______

______

2. What led to the Montgomery bus boycott, and why was it effective?

______

______

Section 1 Notetaking Study Guide

Question to Think About As you read Section 1 in your textbook and take notes, keep this section focus question in mind: **What key events marked the beginning of the civil rights movement in the 1950s?**

▶ Use this chart to record key information from the section. Some information has been filled in to get you started.

Beginnings of the Civil Rights Movement

- The 1896, the Supreme Court ruling *Plessy v. Ferguson* strengthened segregation.
- The National Association for the Advancement of Colored People (NAACP) was organized to fight discrimination.

The 1940s

- After serving in the armed services in ______________, minorities wanted justice between the races at home.
- When Branch Rickey hired ______________, he helped to integrate ______________.
- President Harry Truman ordered desegregation of the ______________.

The 1950s

Segregation in the Schools

- Thurgood Marshall argued for school ______________ in the Supreme Court case ______________.
- In this case, the Court ruled to end school segregation.
- In 1957, nine African American students tried to enter Central High School in ______________.
- Governor ______________ called in the state's National Guard to keep them out.
- President ______________ called in federal troops to protect the students.

Montgomery Bus Boycott

- ______________ was arrested when she refused ______________ on a bus to a white passenger.
- The Women's Political Council organized a ______________ of buses on Parks' trial day.
- ______________ urged African Americans to continue the boycott.
- Some white leaders were outraged by the boycott. Some even ______________ King's home.
- After the boycott went on for more than a year, the Supreme Court ruled that ______________.

Refer to this page to answer the Chapter 26 Focus Question on page 408.

Section 2

An Expanding Role for Government

Section 2 Focus Question

What was the "Great Society"? To begin answering this question,

- Learn about Chief Justice Earl Warren's Supreme Court.
- Find out about the domestic goals of John F. Kennedy.
- Read about Lyndon Johnson's plans for social reform.

Section 2 Summary

The role of the federal government expanded during the 1960s. This was partly due to the actions of the Supreme Court. It was also caused by President Kennedy's and President Johnson's programs for social reform.

The Warren Court

President Eisenhower appointed **Earl Warren** as Chief Justice of the Supreme Court in 1953. Warren broke with past decisions if he believed they were unfair. He did not depend on the precise words of the Constitution to make his decisions. This approach to law has become known as "judicial activism." It led to the landmark decision ending school segregation in *Brown* v. *Board of Education of Topeka.*

The Warren Court generally supported the rights of individuals. In the 1966 decision *Miranda* v. *Arizona,* the Supreme Court ruled that police must inform arrested persons of their right to remain silent and to have a lawyer. In the 1969 decision *Tinker* v. *Des Moines School District,* the Court expanded freedom of speech. It ruled that school administrators could not punish students for wearing black arm bands in protest of the Vietnam War. ✓

Kennedy's Brief Presidency

John F. Kennedy ran for President against Richard Nixon in 1960. Kennedy, a Roman Catholic, beat Nixon in a very close election. He became the youngest President in U.S. history.

Kennedy believed that social reforms were necessary. He had a strong domestic agenda. Kennedy wanted people to have equal treatment under the law. He also wanted to eradicate poverty and improve health conditions. Congress did not pass most of his legislation. They did approve some antipoverty programs. Kennedy's most successful accomplishment was the

Key Events

- **1954** Supreme Court strikes down school segregation in *Brown* v. *Board of Education*.
- **1955** African Americans stage a bus boycott in Montgomery, Alabama.
- **1965** United Farm Workers union is founded.
- **1966** National Organization for Women is founded.

✓ Checkpoint

Name three cases decided by the Warren Court.

____

____

____

Reading Strategy

Reread the bracketed text. Define *domestic;* then circle 3 examples of *domestic* issues.

____

____

____

nation's space program. His goal was to place a man on the moon by the end of the 1960s.

Kennedy's administration was brought to a tragic end when he was assassinated in Dallas, Texas, on November 22, 1963. Lee Harvey Oswald was arrested for the murder. He, too, was shot and killed two days later. ✓

Johnson's Great Society

After Kennedy was assassinated, Vice President **Lyndon Johnson** took over as President. In 1964, Johnson was elected President by a landslide. Johnson had grown up in a poor family in Texas, and he wanted to eliminate poverty in the United States.

Johnson began his presidency by pushing for laws that Kennedy had promoted. Soon he came up with his own ambitious plan for social and economic reform that he named the Great Society. As part of the Great Society, Johnson promoted an antipoverty agenda that he called the War on Poverty. The table below shows his major programs.

Great Society and the War on Poverty

Program	Purpose
Economic Opportunity Act	To address causes of poverty
Head Start	To provide preschools for needy children
Food stamps	To provide food vouchers for the poor
Welfare	To give cash payments to the poor
Department of Housing and Urban Development	To build housing for the poor and middle-income
Medicare	To help the elderly pay medical bills
Medicaid	To help poor people (not covered by Medicare) pay medical bills

✓

Check Your Progress

1. Define "judicial activism." Name one of the cases decided by the Warren Court, and describe its impact.

____

____

2. What were some of the goals of Johnson's Great Society?

____

____

✓ Checkpoint

Name two issues that Kennedy was successful at promoting.

____

____

✓ Checkpoint

Name two programs that were part of Johnson's War on Poverty.

____

____

Section 2 Notetaking Study Guide

Question to Think About As you read Section 2 in your textbook and take notes, keep this section focus question in mind: **What was the "Great Society"?**

▶ Use this organizer to record key information from the section. Some information has been filled in to get you started.

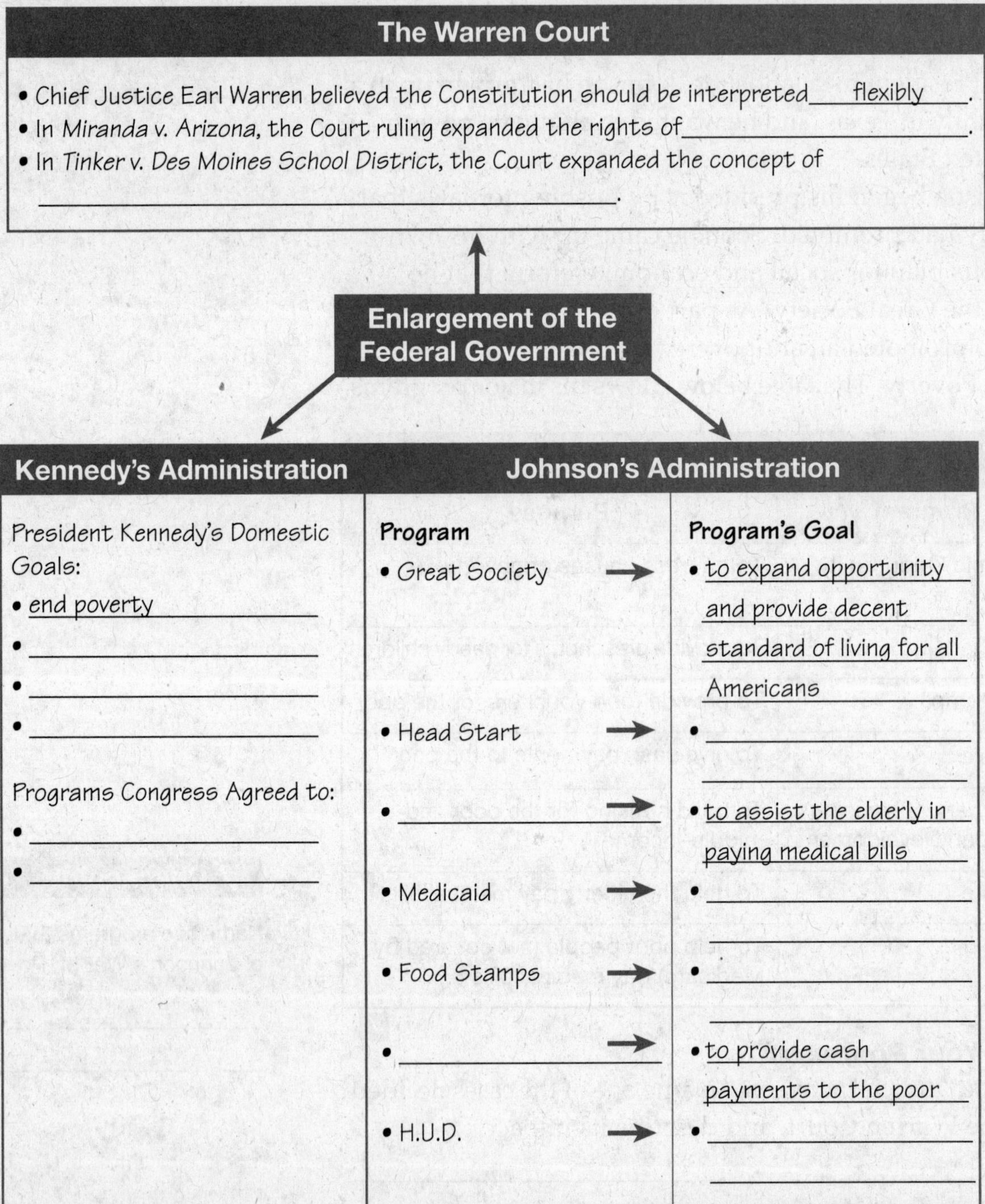

The Warren Court
• Chief Justice Earl Warren believed the Constitution should be interpreted flexibly.
• In *Miranda* v. *Arizona*, the Court ruling expanded the rights of ________.
• In *Tinker* v. *Des Moines School District*, the Court expanded the concept of ________.
Enlargement of the Federal Government
Kennedy's Administration
President Kennedy's Domestic Goals:
• end poverty
•
•
•
Programs Congress Agreed to:
•
•
Johnson's Administration
Program
• Great Society
• Head Start
•
• Medicaid
• Food Stamps
•
• H.U.D.
Program's Goal
• to expand opportunity and provide decent standard of living for all Americans
•
• to assist the elderly in paying medical bills
•
•
• to provide cash payments to the poor
•

Refer to this page to answer the Chapter 26 Focus Question on page 408.

Section 3

The Civil Rights Movement Continues

Section 3 Focus Question

How did the civil rights movement gain momentum? To begin answering this question,

- Read about Martin Luther King, Jr., and civil disobedience.
- Discover which legislation helped further civil rights.
- Learn about the new leaders and effects of the movement.

Section 3 Summary

Protests using civil disobedience led to important changes. Later, the civil rights movement splintered. President Johnson pushed major civil rights laws through Congress.

King's Strategy of Nonviolence

Martin Luther King, Jr., believed in **civil disobedience**, or peaceful refusal to obey unjust laws. King's ideas came from Jesus and Christian teachings. He was also influenced by Mohandas Gandhi and A. Philip Randolph, an African American labor leader. In 1957, King and other African American church leaders formed the Southern Christian Leadership Conference (SCLC). They led many protests. ✓

Nonviolent Protest Spreads

African Americans protested segregation in several ways. One method began in 1960. It was the **sit-in**, in which African Americans sat and refused to leave "whites only" areas. Freedom Rides were another type of protest. African Americans rode buses with whites to check that interstate travel was desegregated. Freedom Riders faced violence.

In 1963, the SCLC organized massive marches in Birmingham, Alabama, to protest the city's segregation policies. The city's police violently attacked the marchers. The brutality was seen on television, horrifying viewers.

President Kennedy tried to get Congress to pass a sweeping civil rights act in 1963. To publicize the bill, the civil rights community organized the March on Washington. Almost 250,000 people came to the demonstration, where King moved the crowd with his famous speech, "I Have a Dream." ✓

Key Events

1954	Supreme Court strikes down school segregation in *Brown* v. *Board of Education*.
1955	African Americans stage a bus boycott in Montgomery, Alabama.
1965	United Farm Workers union is founded.
1966	National Organization for Women is founded.

✓ Checkpoint

Name three people who influenced Martin Luther King, Jr.

____

____

____

✓ Checkpoint

Name two types of protests used during the early 1960s.

____

____

✓ **Checkpoint**

List two pieces of civil rights legislation passed under Johnson.

____

____

Reading Strategy

Circle three words that note sequence in the bracketed text.

Mark the Text

✓ **Checkpoint**

Name two leaders who disagreed with King's approach.

____

____

✓ **Checkpoint**

Define affirmative action.

____

____

Civil Rights Legislation

President Johnson pushed the Civil Rights Act of 1964 through Congress. This act integrated public facilities, outlawed job discrimination, sped up school desegregation, and helped to protect rights of voters. Even so, African Americans had trouble registering to vote in the South. In 1965, King organized a march from Selma to Montgomery, Alabama, to publicize the problem. State troopers viciously attacked the peaceful marchers. In response, Johnson pushed the Voting Rights Act of 1965 through Congress. This law banned discriminatory voting practices and allowed federal officials to register African Americans in the South. ✓

The Movement Splinters

[Some African Americans began to disagree with King's slow, nonviolent approach. **Malcolm X** at first believed in total black separatism rather than integration. He later supported a white-black brotherhood. He was murdered before his new ideas were fully formed.] **Stokely Carmichael** believed in "black power." He urged African Americans to support black businesses and to feel pride in being black.

Many African Americans lived in **ghettos**, or poor, run-down neighborhoods. In Watts, a Los Angeles neighborhood, African Americans reacted to police brutality with massive rioting in 1965. Other cities also erupted in riots. In 1968, Martin Luther King, Jr., was shot to death. Riots took place all over the country. ✓

Summing Up the Civil Rights Era

The civil rights movement ended legal segregation, removed barriers to voting, and led to more African Americans holding political office. **Affirmative action**, a policy by which businesses and schools give preference to groups discriminated against in the past, increased the number of African Americans in colleges and in professions. ✓

Check Your Progress

1. What did the Civil Rights Act of 1964 do?

____

____

2. What were three successes of the civil rights movement?

____

____

Section 3 Notetaking Study Guide

Question to Think About As you read Section 3 in your textbook and take notes, keep this section focus question in mind: **How did the civil rights movement gain momentum?**

▶ Use this chart to record key information from the section. Some information has been filled in to get you started.

Timeline of the Civil Rights Movement

Date	Events
1957	Martin Luther King, Jr. joins with other African American church leaders to form the ________________.
1960	Four African American college students refuse to leave a lunch counter, starting a type of protest known as a ________________.
1961	________________ take place to desegregate public transportation across state lines.
1962	________________ tries to attend the University of Mississippi, and riots break out.
1963	• Massive demonstrations take place in Birmingham, Alabama, and police respond with violence. • Nearly 250,000 people come together to support civil rights legislation in the famous ________________.
1964	President ________________ pushed the ________________ through Congress. This act ________________ ________________.
1965	• In King's march for voting rights, people walk from ________________ to ________________. State troopers set upon marchers with ________________. • Congress passes the ________________, which removes barriers to voting and allows federal officials to register African Americans. • ________________, once a believer in black separatism, is killed. • Riots occur in the ________________ neighborhood of Los Angeles in response to ________________.
1967	________________ becomes the first African American Supreme Court justice.
1968	________________ is killed. ________ occur throughout the country.
1970s	________________, a program through which groups who were previously discriminated against get preferential treatment, is established. Critics argue that ________________.

Refer to this page to answer the Chapter 26 Focus Question on page 408.

Section 4

Other Americans Seek Rights

Key Events

1954	Supreme Court strikes down school segregation in *Brown* v. *Board of Education*.
1955	African Americans stage a bus boycott in Montgomery, Alabama.
1965	United Farm Workers union is founded.
1966	National Organization for Women is founded.

Section 4 Focus Question

What other groups were swept up in the spirit of reform? To begin answering this question,

- Learn about the gains of the women's rights movement.
- Find out about Mexican Americans' struggles for change.
- Read how older Americans, the disabled, and Native Americans formed groups to seek fairer treatment.

Section 4 Summary

As African Americans struggled for civil rights, other groups also began to organize. Women, Mexican Americans, Native Americans, the disabled, and older Americans tried to improve their own economic and social conditions.

Women's Rights Movement

In the 1960s, women were inspired by **Betty Friedan's** book *The Feminine Mystique.* Friedan argued that women were unhappy because of their limited roles in society. She and other leaders in the women's rights movement founded the National Organization for Women (NOW) in 1966. NOW fought for fairer treatment under the law, better professional opportunities, and day-care for working mothers. NOW also led the fight for the Equal Rights Amendment (ERA), which would outlaw sex discrimination. Congress passed the ERA in 1972, but 38 states had to ratify it for it to become law. Eventually, the ERA failed to be ratified by enough states, and it died.

The women's movement did have important successes. These included the 1963 Equal Pay Act, which made sure that men and women doing the same job received equal pay. The Civil Rights Act of 1965 banned discrimination based on sex. More and more women went to college and got jobs outside of their homes. In politics, many women were elected to important offices. ✓

Civil Rights for Mexican Americans

Mexican Americans were segregated in the Southwest, especially in schools. Mexican American children had to attend deficient "Mexican schools." Mexican Americans also

✓ Checkpoint

List three goals of the National Organization for Women.

____

____

____

Vocabulary Builder

The word *deficient* comes from the Latin *deficiens*, which means "to be wanting." In what ways do you think the "Mexican schools" were found wanting?

____

____

faced discrimination in housing and in the workplace. In 1948, Mexican American World War II veterans formed the American GI Forum to legally challenge discrimination. An important victory came in the Supreme Court case *Hernández* v. *Texas.* In *Hernández,* the Court determined that excluding Mexican Americans from juries was illegal.

In 1965, **César Chávez** helped to form the United Farm Workers (UFW). This was a labor union for migrant workers, many of whom were Mexican Americans. Growers refused to recognize the union, however. In response, Chávez organized a successful national boycott of California grapes. The boycott led to increased wages and improved working conditions for migrant workers.

The Voting Rights Act of 1975 ensured that foreign-language speakers could vote by requiring bilingual elections. **Bilingual** means "in two languages." Laws promoting bilingual education were also passed. ✓

Organizing for Change

Other groups organized to work for equal rights. Native Americans formed the National Congress of American Indians to regain land, mineral, and water rights. The American Indian Movement (AIM) was more militant. AIM sought to make people realize how badly the U.S. government had historically treated Native Americans.

Older Americans formed the American Association of Retired Persons (AARP) in 1958. They promoted health insurance for the elderly. AARP has continued to work on many causes for older Americans.

Americans with disabilities pushed for easier access to public buildings. Congress passed laws for equal education for disabled children. In 1990, Congress passed the Americans With Disabilities Act. It outlawed job discrimination against persons with disabilities. ✓

Check Your Progress

1. What were some successes of the women's rights movement?

____

____

2. What groups fought for change during the 1960s and 1970s?

____

____

Reading Strategy

Ask and answer a question about César Chávez.

Question:

____

____

Answer:

____

____

✓ Checkpoint

Explain why the UFW organized a grape boycott.

____

____

✓ Checkpoint

Name one difference between the National Congress of American Indians and AIM.

____

____

Section 4 Notetaking Study Guide

Question to Think About As you read Section 4 in your textbook and take notes, keep this section focus question in mind: **What other groups were swept up in the spirit of reform?**

▶ Use this chart to record key information from the section. Some information has been filled in to get you started.

Reform Movements

The Women's Rights Movement

- Betty Friedan's _The Feminine Mystique_ criticized _women's limited role in society_.
- NOW's goals were ____.
- Arguments for the ERA: ______________________________
- Arguments against the ERA: _would undermine traditional values, could force women into combat, could lessen women's right to alimony, laws already gave women equality_
- The 1963 Equal Pay Act ensured ______________________________.
- ______________________________ of 1965 banned discrimination based on sex.
- In the 1960s and 1970s, the number of women working outside the home __________.

Mexican Americans

- In the Southwest, many Mexican American children went to ______________.
- Mexican American World War II veterans formed the ______________ to challenge discrimination.
- In *Hernández* v. *Texas*, the Supreme Court ruled that ______________.
- ______________ was one of the founders of the United Farm Workers. He organized a nationwide boycott of California ______________. The boycott led to ______________________________.
- The Voting Rights Act of 1975 was important because ______________.
- Legislation for ______________ education was passed.

Native Americans

- _The National Congress of American Indians_ had some success in regaining land, ______________, and ______________ rights for Native Americans.
- The ______________ was more militant. Armed members went to ______________ ______________________________. Its goal was ______________________________.

Older Americans

- Mandatory retirement means ______________________________.
- The ______________ championed health insurance for retired Americans.
- Maggie Kuhn formed the ______________ to fight age discrimination.

Americans With Disabilities

- Organizations for the disabled championed laws that ______________.
- The Education for the Handicapped Act of 1975 guaranteed ______________.
- The Americans With Disabilities Act made it illegal to ______________.

Refer to this page to answer the Chapter 26 Focus Question on page 408.

Chapter 26 Assessment

Directions: Circle the letter of the correct answer.

1. Which of the following Supreme Court cases ended segregation in schools?
   - **A** *Hernández* v. *Texas*
   - **B** *Plessy* v. *Ferguson*
   - **C** *Brown* v. *Board of Education of Topeka*
2. Martin Luther King, Jr.'s, strategy for protest and change was known as
   - **A** separatism. **B** civil disobedience. **C** Black Power.
3. Betty Friedan and other leaders of the women's movement organized the
   - **A** Women's Lib Movement.
   - **B** Great Society.
   - **C** National Organization for Women.

Directions: Follow the steps to answer this question:

In what ways did the U.S. government help the civil rights movement to achieve its goals?

Step 1: Recall information: List some of the goals of the civil rights movement.

Goals of Civil Rights Movement
•
•
•
•

Step 2: List court cases and legislation, and their effects, that were related to the civil rights movement.

Court Cases & Legislation	Effects

Step 3: Draw conclusions: Complete the topic sentence that follows. Then write two or three more sentences that support your topic sentence.

The American government helped the civil rights movement to achieve its goals in that ______________________________

____

____

Chapter 26 Notetaking Study Guide

Now you are ready to answer the Chapter 26 Focus Question: **How did the civil rights movement change the nation?**

▶ Fill in the following chart to help you answer this question. Use the notes that you took for each section.

Civil Rights Movements Change the Nation

Education

- In *Brown v. Board of Education of Topeka*, the Supreme Court ruled that ______________________________.
- Head Start, one of President Johnson's Great Society programs, provided ______________________________.
- When students get bilingual education, they are taught ______________________________.
- The Education for the Handicapped Act of 1975 ensured that all children, regardless of disabilities, get a free education.

Transportation

- The Montgomery bus boycott started after ______________ was arrested for refusing to ______________________________.
- The Supreme Court decided that segregation on public buses was ______________.
- Freedom Rides took place to ______________________________.

Workplace

- The Civil Rights Act of 1964 banned ______________________________.
- The 1964 Equal Pay Act stated that ______________________________.
- César Chávez led the struggle for ______________________________.
- The Americans With Disabilities Act made it illegal to ______________ in hiring based on ______________________________.

Public facilities

- At sit-ins, protesters ______________________________.
- The Civil Rights Act of 1964 banned segregation of public facilities.
- Organizations for the disabled have successfully fought to have ______________ to public facilities.

Voting

Purpose of the Voting Rights Act of 1965

- ______________________________
- ______________________________

Purpose of the Voting Rights Act of 1975

- ______________________________

Public Health

- Medicare is a program that ______________________________.
- Medicaid is a program that ______________________________.
- The American Association of Retired Persons fought for ______________________________.

Refer to this page to answer the Unit 9 Focus Question on page 451.

Chapter 27

The Vietnam Era (1954–1976)

What You Will Learn

When the United States became involved in a war in Vietnam, the nation was divided in its opinion of the war. After the U.S. withdrew, Vietnam was taken over by a Communist government. Richard Nixon's presidency, which occurred during the last years of the war, ended in scandal.

Chapter 27 Focus Question

As you read this chapter, keep this question in mind: **What were the causes and effects of the Vietnam War?**

Key Events

1961	Kennedy sends military advisers to South Vietnam.
1964	Congress passes the Gulf of Tonkin Resolution.
1968	Antiwar demonstrations disrupt the Democratic National Convention.
1974	Nixon resigns from office as a result of the Watergate scandal.

Section 1

The War Begins

Section 1 Focus Question

How did Vietnam become a major battlefield in the war against communism? To begin answering this question,

- Learn how Vietnam became a focus of conflict.
- Find out how U.S. involvement in Vietnam increased.

Section 1 Summary

The U.S. helped France to oppose Vietnamese independence. When the French were defeated, the U.S. feared the spread of communism and backed South Vietnam.

Origins of the Conflict

France had ruled Vietnam, a small country in Southeast Asia, since the 1800s. During World War II, Japan took over, but after the war, the French regained control. **Ho Chi Minh**, a Communist leader, opposed the French. He and his followers, known as the Vietminh, occupied Hanoi and proclaimed Vietnam's independence. France refused to give up Vietnam. Ho Chi Minh asked the United States for help. America, distrusting Communists, gave money and supplies to France. The fighting between the Vietminh and France lasted nearly eight years. During this war, Ho Chi Minh acquired more and more followers. In 1954, the Vietminh finally forced the French to surrender after a battle at Dien Bien Phu. ✓

Vocabulary Builder

Use context clues to determine which of the following is a synonym for *acquired*.

a. collected
b. destroyed
c. supported

✓ Checkpoint

Explain the U.S. role in the French-Vietnamese conflict.

____

____

The War Spreads

After World War II, the United States worried about the spread of communism. China was taken over by a Communist government in 1949. Then in 1950, the Korean War began after Communist North Korea attacked South Korea. Leaders in the United States watched the Communists' power grow. They thought that if Ho Chi Minh gained control of Vietnam, much of Southeast Asia would fall under Communist rule. This argument, called the **domino theory,** reasoned that if one country fell to Communists, neighboring countries would follow.

When the French gave up power in Vietnam, an international conference took place in Geneva, Switzerland. There it was decided under the Geneva Accords that Vietnam would be divided. Ho Chi Minh's Communist government would rule North Vietnam from its capital of Hanoi. **Ngo Dinh Diem's** non-Communist government would hold power in South Vietnam from its capital of Saigon. Under the Geneva Accords, elections would be held to unite the country within a few years. Diem, however, prevented these elections from taking place. In 1959, the South Vietnamese organized to oppose him. **Guerrillas,** or fighters who carry out hit-and-run attacks, began strikes against Diem's government. These guerrillas, called the Vietcong, were supplied with weapons by North Vietnam.

During Eisenhower's and Kennedy's administrations, the United States supported South Vietnam with aid and military advisers. As time went on, it became clear that Diem's government was corrupt. Diem's actions were causing the Vietcong to gain followers. Finally, in 1963, Kennedy pulled his support from Diem. The South Vietnamese military then took over the government and shot Diem. Soon after, Kennedy was assassinated in the United States, and Vice President **Lyndon Johnson** became president. ☑

Reading Strategy

Reread the bracketed text. It describes a cause and an effect. Underline the cause and circle the effect.

✓ Checkpoint

State the argument of the domino theory.

____

____

Check Your Progress

1. Why did Ho Chi Minh fight the French?

____

____

2. What happened to Vietnam as a result of the Geneva Accords?

____

____

Section 1 Notetaking Study Guide

Question to Think About As you read Section 1 in your textbook and take notes, keep this section focus question in mind: **How did Vietnam become a major battlefield in the war against Communism?**

► Use this chart to record key information from the section. Some information has been filled in to get you started.

The War Begins

Vietnam's History

- Vietnam is located in Southeast Asia.
- Since the 1800s, Vietnam had been ruled by the French as part of the colony of ____________.
- In World War II, Japan gained control of Vietnam.
- After World War II, ____________, a Communist leader, led the fight for Vietnamese independence. His followers were called ____________.
- The United States supported ____________ during the war in order to stop ____________.
- The fighting lasted nearly ____________ years.
- France's major defeat came at the battle of ____________.

A Battleground Against Communism

- The domino theory argued that ____________.
- Under the Geneva Accords, Vietnam ____________.
- Ho Chi Minh's Communist government was to rule North Vietnam from its capital of ____________.
- ____________ was to rule South Vietnam from its capital of ____________.
- Guerrillas are ____________.
- Guerrillas in South Vietnam were called ____________.
- Ngo Dinh Diem's government in South Vietnam was ____________.
- The United States responded to Diem's governing by ____________.
- In November 1963, ____________ of South Vietnam took over the government and shot Diem.
- Three weeks later, American President ____________ was shot.
- Vice President ____________ was sworn in as President.

Refer to this page to answer the Chapter 27 Focus Question on page 422.

Section 2

American Involvement Grows

Key Events

1961	Kennedy sends military advisers to South Vietnam.
1964	Congress passes the Gulf of Tonkin Resolution.
1968	Antiwar demonstrations disrupt the Democratic National Convention.
1974	Nixon resigns from office as a result of the Watergate scandal.

✓ Checkpoint

Name the act that gave President Johnson the authority to step up American involvement in Vietnam.

____

____

Section 2 Focus Question

How did the demands of greater involvement in Vietnam divide the nation? To begin answering this question,

- Learn how Johnson increased U.S. involvement in the war.
- Read how the United States tried to win this unconventional war.
- Discover how hawks and doves reacted to the war.

Section 2 Summary

Determined not to lose Vietnam to communism, Johnson sent hundreds of thousands of American troops to the war. Some Americans protested to end U.S. involvement. Others wanted an even greater military response.

A Wider War

During Johnson's early days as President, South Vietnam was in turmoil. The Vietcong, supported by the Soviet Union and China, were gaining strength. Johnson believed that saving South Vietnam from communism was vital. As a result, he sent more money and military advisers there.

In August 1964, it was reported that North Vietnam had torpedoed American destroyers twice in the Gulf of Tonkin. It was later revealed that the second attack may not have occurred. Still, Johnson asked Congress to pass a resolution that would permit the United States to respond to aggression. The act, called the Gulf of Tonkin Resolution, let Johnson **escalate**, or step up, involvement in Vietnam. ✓

An Unconventional War

President Johnson successfully ran for reelection in 1964. He said he would not send American troops to Vietnam. When the Vietcong attacked an American base in South Vietnam and killed eight soldiers, Johnson responded with more air strikes against North Vietnam. It soon became clear that air strikes alone would not be enough to stop North Vietnam. Johnson decided to send American soldiers. By 1968, half a million American troops were in Vietnam.

Nguyen Cao Ky, a military leader, took over South Vietnam in 1965 and dealt harshly with his opponents. With him firmly in control, South Vietnam could focus more on the war. Americans used new weapons, such as bombs with **napalm,** a jellylike substance that burst into flames and stuck to people's bodies. Another weapon was Agent Orange. It was an herbicide that killed plant life and was used to destroy enemy hiding places. Some claim that Agent Orange caused health troubles for Vietnamese and U.S. troops.

None of this stopped the Vietcong. They knew the countryside and could recognize the enemy. In contrast, U.S. troops were not sure who was or wasn't a member of the Vietcong. Americans tried new strategies, including search and destroy missions. Instead of trying to gain territory, they tried to kill as many Vietcong as they could.

January 31, 1968, was Tet, the Vietnamese New Year holiday. During the celebrations, the North Vietnamese and Vietcong launched massive attacks on every major city in South Vietnam. By the end of February, U.S. and South Vietnamese forces had retaken the cities. However, the magnitude of the Tet offensive made people no longer sure that the U.S. could win. Support for the war declined. ✓

A Nation Divided

As more troops were sent to Vietnam, the U.S. reaction was divided. **Hawks** supported the war, and some even wanted to increase U.S. military involvement. **Doves** believed the Vietnam War could not be won and was morally wrong. They wanted the United States to withdraw its troops. Doves held huge protests against the war. Sometimes they came into conflict with police.

Some men resisted being drafted into the military by burning their draft cards. Others were **conscientious objectors,** or people who oppose war because of religious or philosophical beliefs. About 100,000 people went to live in Canada to avoid military service in Vietnam. Throughout the war, television brought horrible images of war into people's homes. ✓

Check Your Progress

1. Why did Johnson escalate U.S. involvement in Vietnam?

____

____

2. How did young Americans avoid going to war?

____

____

Vocabulary Builder

The word *magnitude* has different meanings depending on its context. Which definition below is closest to its usage in the underlined sentence?

a. volume of sound
b. greatness of size or extent

✓ Checkpoint

List two effects of the Tet offensive.

____

____

____

✓ Checkpoint

Name the two "sides" at home that conflicted over the war.

____

____

Section 2 Notetaking Study Guide

Question to Think About As you read Section 2 in your textbook and take notes, keep this section focus question in mind: **How did the demands of greater involvement in Vietnam divide the nation?**

► Use this chart to record key information from the section. Some information has been filled in to get you started.

United States in Vietnam	
Event	**U.S. Response**
North Vietnam attacks American destroyers in the Gulf of Tonkin.	Johnson responds by calling for: • Gulf of Tonkin Resolution • air strikes against North Vietnam
Johnson runs for reelection, vowing not to send Americans to Vietnam.	• Johnson ______ the 1964 election in a ______.
North Vietnam attacks American base at Pleiku.	• Johnson responds by launching more ______ ______.
The Vietcong continue their attacks.	• Americans develop new weapons, including ______ and ______. • Americans try to kill massive numbers of enemy troops in missions called ______.
The North Vietnamese launch the ______ on the New Year holiday.	• Americans and South Vietnamese troops retake cities and win the battle. • Americans at home react with ______ ______.
The war continues for several years.	• Hawks ______ ______. • Doves ______ ______.
Opposition to the war increases.	• Some resisters ______ their draft cards. • Some claim to be ______ ______, who disagree with war for religious or philosophical reasons. • Many flee to ______.
Antiwar movement evolves.	• First, protests are mainly ______. • Later, violence between protesters and ______ becomes more common.

Refer to this page to answer the Chapter 27 Focus Question on page 422.

Section 3
The War Ends

Section 3 Focus Question

What were the causes and effects of American withdrawal from Vietnam? To begin answering this question,

- Learn about the 1968 presidential election.
- Read how U.S. involvement changed under Nixon.
- Find out how South Vietnam fell to Communist control.
- Discover the effects of the war on the United States and Vietnam.

Section 3 Summary

Nixon won the 1968 presidential race, promising to bring peace. Antiwar protests continued. U.S. troops withdrew. Two years later, Communists ruled South Vietnam.

Election of 1968

With American support for the Vietnam War weakening, Johnson decided not to run for reelection in 1968. Instead, Vice President Hubert Humphrey, who supported Johnson's policies, ran for the Democrats. At the Democratic convention in Chicago, antiwar protesters held a huge demonstration. When police attacked the protesters, the nation watched the turmoil on television. The Republican candidate was **Richard Nixon.** He promised to bring "peace with honor" in Vietnam. In a close election, Nixon won. ✓

The War Winds Down

In a policy called Vietnamization, Nixon cut America's role by having South Vietnamese troops do more fighting. Yet Nixon took the war into Cambodia, bombing Communist bases there that supplied the Vietcong. This had little impact on the enemy, but it did result in protests at home. During antiwar protests at Kent State University, the Ohio National Guard killed four students. Other protests also ended tragically.

Peace talks in Paris between the United States and North Vietnam dragged on for three years. **Henry Kissinger,** the national security adviser, met secretly with a North Vietnamese leader in 1970. The United States withdrew thousands of troops. As the 1972 presidential election drew near, Kissinger said the two sides were close to an agreement. South Vietnam did not agree to Kissinger's plan, but

Key Events

1961	Kennedy sends military advisers to South Vietnam.
1964	Congress passes the Gulf of Tonkin Resolution.
1968	Antiwar demonstrations disrupt the Democratic National Convention.
1974	Nixon resigns from office as a result of the Watergate scandal.

✓ Checkpoint

State Nixon's campaign promise.

____

____

Vocabulary Builder

Impact means "having a strong effect." Why did Nixon think bombing Cambodian bases would impact the war?

____

____

____

✓ Checkpoint

Name Nixon's policy of giving South Vietnam responsibility of fighting the war.

____

✓ Checkpoint

Explain what the Convoy of Tears was.

____

____

____

Reading Strategy

Congress passed legislation in 1973 to limit the president's power in going to war. Circle the name of this legislation. Underline the text describing its provisions.

Mark the Text

✓ Checkpoint

List U.S. losses in the Vietnam War.

____

____

an agreement was finally signed on January 27, 1973. By March, the last American troops in Vietnam had come home. ✓

The Final Years of Conflict

After United States forces left Vietnam, conflict continued. According to the Paris Peace Accords, the North Vietnamese could keep 150,000 troops in South Vietnam. Communists used these troops to take control, forcing the South Vietnamese army to retreat. This retreat, during which many South Vietnamese soldiers and civilians died, became known as the Convoy of Tears. When North Vietnamese troops got close to Saigon in April 1975, the United States sent helicopters to help U.S. workers and South Vietnamese supporters leave. U.S. ships rescued thousands who fled on boats. ✓

Vietnam Balance Sheet

For America, the Vietnam War had lasting effects. The United States was defeated in a foreign war for the first time. More than 58,000 Americans died in battle. Another 300,000 were injured. The war hurt the U.S. economy for years. Veterans lacked support when they got home. America's faith in its government weakened. Secret documents, known as the Pentagon Papers, were published in 1971. They revealed that U.S. leaders had misled Americans about the war. Congress passed the War Powers Act in 1973. This said that presidents needed the approval of Congress before sending U.S. troops into combat for longer than 60 days.

In Vietnam, the war had awful costs. More than 350,000 South Vietnamese died in combat. Between 500,000 and a million North Vietnamese died. When Communists took power in 1975, over a million people tried to leave Vietnam. Those who attempted to escape in small boats were called **boat people,** and some 200,000 died. Many Vietnamese came to the United States and other countries. ✓

Check Your Progress

1. How did bombing Cambodian bases affect the United States?

____

____

2. What happened after U.S. troops left Vietnam?

____

____

Section 3 Notetaking Study Guide

Question to Think About As you read Section 3 in your textbook and take notes, keep this section focus question in mind: **What were the causes and effects of American withdrawal from Vietnam?**

▶ Use this chart to record key information from the section. Some information has been filled in to get you started.

Events During the Vietnam War	
Cause	**Effect**
Johnson does not run for reelection.	• Hubert Humphrey runs for the Democrats.
Nixon promises to bring "peace with honor."	• ________ wins the 1968 presidential election.
Nixon pursues a policy of ________.	• American troops withdraw, giving the South Vietnamese more responsibility for the war.
Nixon calls for bombing Cambodian bases.	• For the outcome of the war, the effect is small. • For Cambodia, the bombings cause ________. • The attacks trigger ________ in the United States.
Henry Kissinger meets with a North Vietnamese leader to work out a peace agreement.	• Before the 1972 presidential election, Kissinger promises that ________. • In fact, the South Vietnamese rejected the proposed agreement.
________ are signed in January 1973.	• The last U.S. combat troops leave Vietnam by ________.
North Vietnamese are allowed to keep 150,000 troops in South Vietnam.	• North Vietnamese troops proceed to ________.
South Vietnamese troops retreat.	• Thousands of soldiers die and civilians flee in what became known as the ________.
South Vietnamese government surrenders.	• Vietnam is united under a ________ government. • Saigon is renamed ________.
Number of killed and wounded	• ________ Americans die in battle. • About ________ South Vietnamese die in battle. • North Vietnamese dead are between ________. • ________ people in South Vietnam are left homeless.
Some South Vietnamese want to flee.	• Some try to escape by sea and are called ________. • About ________ die at sea or in refugee camps.

Refer to this page to answer the Chapter 27 Focus Question on page 422.

Section 4
A Time of Uncertainty

Key Events

1961 — Kennedy sends military advisers to South Vietnam.

1964 — Congress passes the Gulf of Tonkin Resolution.

1968 — Antiwar demonstrations disrupt the Democratic National Convention.

1974 — Nixon resigns from office as a result of the Watergate scandal.

Vocabulary Builder

The word *priority* comes from the Latin word *prior*, meaning "first." Why do you think easing Cold War tensions might have been one of Nixon's first concerns?

____

____

✓ Checkpoint

State two of Nixon's successes.

____

____

Section 4 Focus Question

What successes and failures marked Nixon's presidency? To begin answering this question,

- Learn about Nixon's foreign and domestic policies.
- Find out about the Watergate scandal.
- Read about President Gerald Ford.

Section 4 Summary

Richard Nixon had successes in foreign policy, including easing tensions with China and the Soviet Union. After the Watergate scandal broke, however, Nixon was forced to resign. Vice President Gerald Ford became President.

Richard Nixon in Office

When Richard Nixon won the presidency in 1968, the country was in turmoil. A bright spot occurred on July 20, 1969, when American astronaut Neil Armstrong became the first person to walk on the moon. Still, most Americans were concerned with the war and with **inflation**, or a steady rise in prices. High unemployment and a recession also hurt the economy. To help ease inflation, Nixon took an unusual step, especially for a Republican. He froze prices, wages, and rents. Unfortunately, the freeze did not curb inflation.

Nixon had greater success with foreign policy. He opened relations between the United States and Communist China, which had long been strained. In 1972, Nixon visited mainland China and met with Chairman Mao Zedong. Easing tensions with the Soviet Union was also a priority. Nixon signed the Strategic Arms Limitation Treaty (SALT). It limited how many and what kind of nuclear weapons the United States and the Soviet Union could build. ✓

Watergate Scandal

Nixon was reelected in the 1972 presidential election. Within months, however, a political scandal erupted that would end Nixon's presidency. During the presidential campaign, Nixon's team tried to gather information about their opposition, the Democrats. Police arrested five men who broke into the Democratic Party offices located in the Watergate apartment complex in Washington, D.C. White House officials tried to pay the burglars so that they would not talk about the break-in. Still, the story became public.

Televised Senate hearings on the Watergate scandal took place in May 1973. A former White House counsel, John Dean, testified that Nixon was involved in the attempt to cover up the burglary. Another witness revealed that Nixon had tapes of all of his conversations. The Supreme Court ordered Nixon to give up the tapes. They showed that Nixon was involved in the coverup operation. In July 1974, Nixon faced impeachment by the House of Representatives. He knew that there were enough votes to remove him from office. Within a month, Nixon resigned. ✓

The Ford Presidency

Vice President **Gerald Ford** became President. His first act was unpopular—he pardoned Richard Nixon. Another action concerned the continuing high inflation. Ford tried to lower it through Whip Inflation Now. This was an unsuccessful program of voluntary wage and price controls. The country slipped into a recession. Ford pushed Congress to cut taxes to help spur the economy. It took the economy a long time to recover from the recession.

Ford continued Nixon's policies in China and the Soviet Union, working to ease Cold War tensions. Although American troops were out of Vietnam, when Communist troops got near Saigon, Ford arranged an airlift that helped more than 50,000 South Vietnamese to leave the country. Ford had other crises as well. Cambodian Communists seized an American merchant ship. Ford sent U.S. marines to Cambodia to save the crew. In the 1976 presidential election, Ford ran as the Republican candidate. Democratic candidate **Jimmy Carter** won the race, however. ✓

Check Your Progress

1. What led to Nixon's resignation?

____

____

____

2. What prompted Ford to continue U.S. involvement in Southeast Asia?

____

____

Reading Strategy

Reread the two paragraphs under the "Watergate Scandal" heading. Underline the words or phrases that reveal the sequence of time.

✓ Checkpoint

Name the activity that Nixon tried to cover up.

____

____

✓ Checkpoint

Name Ford's program to beat inflation through voluntary price controls.

____

____

Section 4 Notetaking Study Guide

Question to Think About As you read Section 4 in your textbook and take notes, keep this section focus question in mind: **What successes and failures marked Nixon's presidency?**

▶ Use this chart to record key information from the section. Some information has been filled in to get you started.

President Richard Nixon

Important Events

- In 1969, Neil Armstrong became the first person to walk on the moon.

Domestic Policy

- Throughout his presidency, Nixon had to deal with the following economic problems: ________, ________, and ________.
- Nixon ________ wages, rents, and prices to curb inflation. The policy ________ work.

Foreign Policy

- In 1972, Nixon visited ________, which surprised many people.
- While there, Nixon met with Chairman ________.
- Nixon and Soviet leaders signed the ________.
- The agreement that Nixon reached with Soviet leaders limited ________.

Watergate

- In order to obtain information during the 1972 presidential elections, burglars broke into the ________ offices in the ________ apartment complex.
- ________ paid the burglars so that they would not tell the story of the burglary.
- ________ held hearings to investigate the scandal.
- ________, a former White House counsel, testified that Nixon had approved the coverup.
- The Supreme Court ordered Nixon to turn over tapes of his conversations.
- The House of Representatives took steps to ________ President Nixon.
- On August 9, 1974, Nixon ________.

President Gerald Ford

- The public felt less trust in Ford because he ________.
- Ford's voluntary program of wage and price controls was called ________.
- To spur the economy, Congress approved a ________.
- When Communist troops drew near to Saigon, Ford ________.
- In 1976, Ford lost the presidential election to ________.

Refer to this page to answer the Chapter 27 Focus Question on page 422.

Chapter 27 Assessment

Directions: Circle the letter of the correct answer.

1. The idea that once one country falls to communism, neighboring countries will follow, is called
   - **A** search and destroy.
   - **B** the domino theory.
   - **C** Vietnamization.
2. In 1968, this candidate won the U.S. presidential election, saying he would bring "peace with honor."
   A Richard Nixon **B** Lyndon Johnson **C** Gerald Ford
3. When North Vietnamese and Vietcong troops coordinated attacks on major cities in South Vietnam, it was called the
   - **A** Tet offensive.
   - **B** Gulf of Tonkin attack.
   - **C** *Mayaguez* incident.

Directions: Follow the steps to answer this question:

Why did the United States keep changing its goals throughout the Vietnam War?

Step 1: Recall information: Briefly list some of the goals of the United States during the Vietnam War.

U.S. Goals at Beginning of Vietnam War	U.S. Goals During the War Under Nixon
• Stop the spread of communism	•
•	•

Step 2: List factors that might have had an impact on these goals.

U.S. Difficulties in Vietnam	U.S. Reaction to War
•	•
•	•

Step 3: Complete the topic sentence that follows. Then write two or three more sentences that support your topic sentence.

The U.S. goals in Vietnam changed as time went on, from ____________

____

____

____

Chapter 27 Notetaking Study Guide

Now you are ready to answer the Chapter 27 Focus Question: **What were the causes and effects of the Vietnam War?**

► Complete the charts to help you answer this question. Use the notes that you took for each section.

The Vietnam War
Causes
• Beginning in the 1800s, France ruled Vietnam as part of the colony of Indochina. • When France took control of Vietnam again after World War II, ________ led the Vietnamese fight for independence. His followers were called ________. • The ________ were defeated at the battle of Dien Bien Phu. • U.S. leaders believed that if one country fell to communism, its neighbors would follow, an idea known as ________. • Vice President Lyndon Johnson became President after ________. • After North Vietnam attacked American destroyers, Congress passed the ________, allowing the President to use the military to respond to acts of aggression. • New types of weapons were used by the U.S. military, including ________ and ________.
Effects
• U.S. opinion of the war was divided. ________ believed that the war was justified. ________ believed that the war was morally wrong. • The antiwar movement grew, and ________ between protesters and police became more common. • ________ realized how unpopular the war was, and he decided not to run for reelection. • ________ won the presidential election of 1968 and pursued a policy of ________, whereby the South Vietnamese took on more responsibility for fighting. • U.S. troops left Vietnam after the ________ Accords were signed in 1973. • After U.S. troops left, North Vietnamese troops attacked South Vietnam. • In 1975, South Vietnam was united with North Vietnam under a ________ government. • During the war, ________ American soldiers died in combat. • The South Vietnamese lost ________ in battle. • The North Vietnamese lost between ________ and ________ soldiers in battle. • ________ tried to escape the new regime by sea. • As a result of the war, some Americans lost faith in the government, and this feeling intensified as a result of Nixon's presidential scandal, known as ________.

Refer to this page to answer the Unit 9 Focus Question on page 451.

Chapter 28

New Directions for a Nation (1977–2000)

What You Will Learn

Ronald Reagan began a conservative movement. The Soviet Union collapsed, ending the Cold War and changing America's foreign policy goals. The Middle East posed challenges to the nation's leaders.

Chapter 28 Focus Question

As you read this chapter, keep this question in mind: **How did major national and international events affect the nation?**

Section 1

A Conservative Surge

Section 1 Focus Question

How did the growing conservative movement help reshape American politics? To begin answering this question,

- Learn about Jimmy Carter's difficult presidency.
- Read about Reagan's and George H. W. Bush's terms.
- Note the prosperity and scandal of Clinton's presidency.
- Find out about the conservative goals of George W. Bush.

Section 1 Summary

Carter faced inflation at home and a hostage crisis abroad. Reagan began a conservative movement in 1980. Clinton brought prosperity, but scandal weakened his presidency. George W. Bush made tax cuts and educational reforms.

Carter's Troubled Presidency

President Jimmy Carter was elected in 1976. He had to confront inflation at home and difficult issues abroad. Revolutionaries seized the American embassy in Iran and held 53 American hostages. For over a year, Carter failed to gain their freedom, which weakened his presidency. ✓

The Conservative Movement

Liberals believed the federal government could solve problems in the tradition of the New Deal. Political conservatives wanted to reduce government power and lower taxes. Social

Key Events

1979	Militants take 53 Americans hostage in Iran.
1987	United States and Soviet Union agree on an arms control treaty.
1991	United States leads the coalition against Iraq in the Persian Gulf War.

Vocabulary Builder

Read the underlined sentence. Based on context clues, what do you think the word *confront* means?

____

✓ Checkpoint

Name two challenges President Carter faced.

____

____

✓ Checkpoint

Name three points of the 1980 Republican Party platform.

____

____

____

✓ Checkpoint

Name two ways that Reagan cut the federal budget.

____

____

✓ Checkpoint

Name two ways in which Clinton reduced the deficit.

____

____

conservatives felt that traditional family values must be priorities. Conservatives gained control of the Republican Party by 1980. They promised tax cuts, deregulation of business, and a **balanced budget,** meaning that government spends only as much money as it collects. They nominated Ronald Reagan, who beat Carter. ✓

Reagan's Presidency

President **Ronald Reagan** pushed large tax cuts through Congress. By slashing federal jobs and social programs, he cut $40 billion from the federal budget. He also **deregulated** industries, or scaled back federal rules for businesses. However, his tax cuts and military spending caused a huge federal **deficit.** This occurs when government spends more money than it collects. Critics charged that he helped the wealthy but hurt the poor and the environment. Still, he limited the growth of federal government and cut inflation.

Reagan's Vice President, **George H. W. Bush,** was elected in 1988. He vowed not to raise taxes. Later he needed to do so to cut the deficit. Conservatives were outraged. A **recession,** or temporary economic slump, took place. ✓

The Clinton Years and George W. Bush

In 1992, **Bill Clinton** defeated George H. W. Bush and became President. He pushed through tax increases for the wealthy and reduced federal spending, thus cutting the deficit. Clinton's policies brought prosperity and a **surplus,** in which government collects more than it spends. A scandal during his second term weakened his presidency. Because he seemed to lie under oath, the House of Representatives impeached him. The Senate did not convict Clinton.

In 2000, Vice President Al Gore ran against **George W. Bush.** Although Gore won more popular votes, Bush won the electoral vote in the controversial election. He pushed through tax cuts and education reforms. ✓

Check Your Progress

1. What were the strengths of Reagan's presidency?

____

____

2. What were the strengths of Clinton's presidency?

____

____

Section 1 Notetaking Study Guide

Question to Think About As you read Section 1 in your textbook and take notes, keep this section focus question in mind: **How did the growing conservative movement help reshape American politics?**

▶ Use this chart to record key information from the section. Some information has been filled in to get you started.

President Jimmy Carter
President Carter had to deal with the economic problem of inflation.
Carter's major foreign policy crisis was ______.
The Conservative Movement and President Ronald Reagan
A political conservative believes in cutting federal government, deregulating business, and lowering taxes.
A social conservative believes ______.
Reagan's arguments for cutting government spending and taxes: ______
Reagan's successes include being successful at communicating his optimism, and helping to cut inflation and slow the growth of the federal government.
Reagan's critics charged ______.
President George H. W. Bush
Bush broke his promise not to raise taxes because ______.
A recession is ______.
President Bill Clinton
Bill Clinton was a "New Democrat." This meant that ______.
Clinton's economic policies included ______.
Clinton's welfare reform included ______.
A surplus is ______.
Clinton's presidency was weakened during his second term when ______.
President George W. Bush
The presidential election of 2000 was controversial because Democrats believed the election in Florida was unfair and they wanted a recount. The Supreme Court stopped the recount and Bush won.
Bush's major domestic priorities included ______.

Refer to this page to answer the Chapter 28 Focus Question on page 436.

Section 2

End of the Cold War

Key Events

1979 Militants take 53 Americans hostage in Iran.

1987 United States and Soviet Union agree on an arms control treaty.

1991 United States leads the coalition against Iraq in the Persian Gulf War.

Section 2 Focus Question

How did the Cold War end? To begin answering this question,

- Learn why détente with the Soviet Union ended.
- Read how the Soviet Union weakened both economically and militarily, and how Gorbachev introduced reforms.
- Discover how the Cold War ended.

Section 2 Summary

Carter ended his policy of détente when the Soviets invaded Afghanistan. President Reagan increased military spending and fought communism. The Soviet Union broke apart in 1991, which ended the Cold War.

The End of Détente

Presidents Nixon and Carter believed in the policy of détente with the Soviet Union. But in 1979, the Soviet Union invaded Afghanistan. Carter showed his disapproval by pulling an arms agreement from the Senate, boycotting the 1980 Moscow Olympics, and imposing trade restrictions.

President Reagan supported the Islamic fighters in Afghanistan who fought the Soviet Union. He increased military spending and oversaw major weapons programs. Reagan believed in funding the Strategic Defense Initiative. This defense system would use lasers to shoot enemy missiles before they hit the United States. Critics believed the program was too expensive.

Reagan fought communism in Central America by secretly supporting the Contras, guerrillas who fought the Sandinistas in Nicaragua. The Sandinistas were tied to Cuba and the Soviet Union. The Contras were believed to be brutal, however. Congress outlawed further support to them. When seven Americans were taken hostage in Lebanon, Reagan officials sold arms to Iran and used the money to help the Contras. When this agreement, known as the "Iran-Contra deal," became public, many were scandalized. Reagan claimed that he knew nothing of the agreement, but the controversy marred his second term. ✓

Vocabulary Builder

List three synonyms for the underlined word *marred.*

____

____

____

✓ Checkpoint

List three actions Reagan took to fight communism.

____

____

____

The Soviet Union in Decline

The Soviet Union tried to match U.S. military spending. Because so much had been spent on the failed war in Afghanistan, this new buildup caused an economic decline. Meanwhile, resistance to Communist rule was growing in Eastern Europe. **Mikhail Gorbachev** took over the Soviet government in 1985 and began economic reforms. He introduced a policy known as **glasnost,** or speaking openly about Soviet problems. Gorbachev and Reagan agreed to a treaty calling for the destruction of short-range and intermediate-range nuclear missiles.

At the same time, the Soviet-controlled governments of Eastern Europe faced rising opposition. Communist governments fell in Poland, Hungary, Romania, and Czechoslovakia. In 1989, students and workers destroyed the Berlin Wall. Soon there was one united Germany. Other national borders changed as well. Czechoslovakia became the two countries of the Czech Republic and Slovakia. Yugoslavia divided into several loosely joined republics. ✓

✓ Checkpoint

Name two important actions Gorbachev made as the leader of the Soviet Union.

____

____

The Cold War Ends

The fall of Communist governments sparked independence movements. The Soviet Union dissolved in 1991, and each republic became an independent state. Boris Yeltsin became president of Russia. He worked to strengthen the economy and achieve democratic reforms. Yet Russia still faced crime and corruption. Independence for the Yugoslav republics led to a four-year civil war. Hundreds of thousands of Croatians, Bosnians, and Albanians were killed.

The Cold War, which had lasted for 45 years, ended with the breakup of the Soviet Union. Americans were relieved. The Cold War had cost the United States trillions of dollars in military spending. Worse, thousands had died in the conflicts of Korea and Vietnam. ✓

Reading Strategy

Mark the Text

Reread the bracketed text. Circle two actions Yeltsin took to improve Russia. Underline two problems that continued to exist.

✓ Checkpoint

Describe the American reaction to the end of the Cold War.

____

____

Check Your Progress

1. What happened to cause an end to détente?

____

____

2. How did Reagan's military policies affect the Soviet Union?

____

____

Section 2 Notetaking Study Guide

Question to Think About As you read Section 2 in your textbook and take notes, keep this section focus question in mind: **How did the Cold War end?**

► Use this chart to record key information from the section. Some information has been filled in to get you started.

The Cold War Ends	
Cause	**Effect**
Nixon and Carter pursue détente with Soviet Union.	Cold War tensions ease.
Soviet Union invades Afghanistan.	President Carter responds by: • stopping arms control agreement • ______ • ______
Conservative Reagan is elected President of the United States.	Tries to fight communism by: • ______ • ______ • ______
Sandinistas overthrow Somoza in Nicaragua.	• Reagan responds by supporting ______.
Seven Americans taken hostage in Lebanon by Iranian-backed militants.	• Reagan officials sell arms to ______ so that hostages will be freed. Officials use the money to buy arms for ______.
Reagan builds up military.	• Soviet Union responds by building up its own military.
Soviet Union increases military spending.	• Soviet economy ______.
Gorbachev allows glasnost.	• Soviets want ______.
Gorbachev wants better relations with the West.	He meets with Reagan in 1987, and they agree on ______ treaty.
Soviet Union stops supporting unpopular Eastern European Communist leaders.	• Communism loses power in ______, ______, ______, ______, and Yugoslavia. In East Germany, people tear down the ______.
Soviet republics want independence.	• Soviet Union ______.
The Cold War ends.	• Americans feel ______.

Refer to this page to answer the Chapter 28 Focus Question on page 436.

Section 3

A New Role in the World

Section 3 Focus Question

How did the United States use its influence after the Cold War ended? To begin answering this question,

- Learn about U.S. goals for peace and democracy.
- Read how the United States attempted to promote change in South Africa, Northern Ireland, China, and Cuba.
- Note how the U.S. dealt with nuclear arms.

Section 3 Summary

Presidents George H. W. Bush and Clinton worked for peace and the spread of democracy. The United States promoted change in South Africa, Northern Ireland, China, and Cuba. America also tried to halt the spread of nuclear weapons.

Promoting Democracy and Peace

After the Cold War ended, the United States became the world's only superpower. Presidents Bush and Clinton felt it was key to use that power in the causes of peace and democracy.

For years, U.S. lawmakers wanted to end South Africa's policy of **apartheid,** or racial separation and inequality. Over Reagan's veto, Congress voted for **sanctions,** penalties applied against a country in order to pressure it to change its policies. The sanctions forbade U.S. businesses to invest in South Africa or to import its products. In 1991, because of the sanctions and internal protests, South Africa ended apartheid. Free elections in 1994 put black leaders in office.

British-ruled Northern Ireland experienced years of violence between the Protestant majority and the Catholic minority. The United States helped negotiate a 1998 power-sharing agreement between these groups.

In 1989, Chinese students and workers protested in Tiananmen Square for democratic reforms. The Communist government assaulted the protesters. President George H. W. Bush tried to persuade China to introduce reforms. Clinton pressed China to change human rights policies.

Cuba posed a different problem. After the Soviet Union broke apart, Cuba lost a major source of economic aid. When Cuba's economy crashed, the United States considered trading with its neighbor. George W. Bush has vowed to continue

Key Events

1979	Militants take 53 Americans hostage in Iran.
1987	United States and Soviet Union agree on an arms control treaty.
1991	United States leads the coalition against Iraq in the Persian Gulf War.

Vocabulary Builder

When a computer "crashes," it fails completely. When an economy crashes, what do you think happens to the value of the currency, or money?

____

____

____

✓ Checkpoint

Name the strategy the U.S. Congress used to pressure South Africa to change its policy of apartheid.

____

____

sanctions against Cuba, however. He wants to weaken its Communist dictator Fidel Castro. ✓

Easing the Arms Race

The first arms control agreement between the Soviet Union and the United States was signed in 1972. Since then, both countries have worked to reduce their nuclear weapons.

Arms Control Agreements Between United States and Soviet Union		
Treaty	**Year Signed**	**Agreement**
Strategic Arms Limitation Treaty (SALT)	1972	Reduced number of nuclear warheads and long-range missiles to be built
SALT II	1977	None—Carter withdrew the treaty after the Soviet invasion of Afghanistan
Strategic Arms Reduction Treaty (START)	1991	Thirty percent reduction in existing nuclear weapons
START II	1993, revised 1997	Two-thirds reduction in existing long-range nuclear weapons

After the Cold War ended, new problems arose. The former Soviet Union had nuclear weapons in four now-independent republics. Each of these, including Russia, agreed to uphold the Soviet Union's treaties. The United States sent support so that the weapons could be stored or destroyed.

Britain, France, and China had held nuclear weapons for a long time. Israel had a nuclear weapon by the late 1960s. Nuclear weapons spread to other countries, increasing the danger of nuclear war. U.S. intelligence reports indicated that Iran, Iraq, and North Korea were trying to build nuclear weapons. Especially troubling was the fact that India and Pakistan, feuding neighbors, both built nuclear bombs. ✓

Reading Strategy

Underline the sentence that tells you about two feuding countries that acquired nuclear weapons. Draw an arrow to the phrase that tells you why the spread of nuclear arms is dangerous.

Mark the Text

✓ Checkpoint

Name one difference between the START treaties and the SALT treaty.

____

____

Check Your Progress

1. Name a country that the United States has tried to influence, and describe the progress that has been made.

____

____

2. Why are nuclear weapons a continuing threat?

____

Section 3 Notetaking Study Guide

Question to Think About As you read Section 3 in your textbook and take notes, keep this section focus question in mind: **How did the United States use its influence after the Cold War ended?**

► Use this chart to record key information from the section. Some information has been filled in to get you started.

Promoting Democracy and Peace	
Countries	**United States Uses Its Influence**
South Africa	• Applied sanctions in order to end ______
Philippines	• Sent ______ to freely elected government after the dictator Ferdinand Marcos lost power
Northern Ireland	• Helped negotiate an agreement between ______
China	• Tried to ______ the government to reform after the brutal crackdown at ______
Cuba	• Banned trade to weaken leader ______

Arms Control	
Strategic Arms Limitation Treaty (SALT) Countries Involved: U.S., Soviet Union Year: ______ What Was Agreed to: ______	**SALT II** Countries Involved: ______ Year: ______ What Was Agreed to: no agreement, Carter withdrew treaty in protest
Strategic Arms Reduction Treaty (START) Countries Involved: ______ Leaders: ______ Year: ______ What Was Agreed to: ______	**START II** Countries Involved: ______ Year: ______ Year Revised: ______ What Was Agreed to: ______

The Nuclear Threat Continues

- Four former Soviet states agreed to ______.
- The United States sent aid to ______ or ______ weapons.
- ______ and ______ tested nuclear weapons for the first time in 1998.
- The United States is concerned about more countries obtaining nuclear weapons because ______.

Refer to this page to answer the Chapter 28 Focus Question on page 436.

Section 4

Conflict in the Middle East

Key Events

1979	Militants take 53 Americans hostage in Iran.
1987	United States and Soviet Union agree on an arms control treaty.
1991	United States leads the coalition against Iraq in the Persian Gulf War.

Section 4 Focus Question

How have tensions in the Middle East posed concerns for the United States? To begin answering this question,

- Learn about the importance of the Middle East to the United States.
- Find out about the conflict between Arabs and Israelis.
- Read about U.S. activity in the region.

Section 4 Summary

The Middle East is important as a site of major world religions and for its oil reserves. Conflicts between Arabs and Israelis remain unresolved. The United States has been involved in negotiation and war in the region.

A Vital Region

The Middle East is an important crossroads for Europe, Asia, and Africa. Judaism, Christianity, and Islam all began in the Middle East. Conflict between members of these faiths has gone on for centuries. Today the region is important due to its oil. Oil production and price levels are set by the Arab nations that form the Organization of Petroleum Exporting Countries (OPEC). The United States has a strong relationship with Israel. Yet it has also tried to maintain relations with Arab nations that do not support Israel. ✓

✓ Checkpoint

Give two reasons why OPEC is important.

____

____

Arab-Israeli Conflict

Many Jews began settling in Palestine in the late 1800s. They wanted to establish a Jewish state. This put them at odds with the Arabs who lived there. Nazism and the Holocaust led thousands more Jews to settle in Palestine. Arab nations opposed the formation of the state of Israel in 1948, and war began. With Israel's victory, hundreds of thousands of Palestinian Arabs lost their homes. They lived in refugee camps in neighboring Arab nations. Other wars followed. Israel invaded Egypt in 1956, but left due to international pressure. In 1967 and 1973, Arab countries attacked Israel. Israel gained land in Egypt, Jordan, and Syria as a result of these wars. Israelis settled in the newly acquired regions. Arabs called these lands "occupied territories."

Reading Strategy

Reread the bracketed paragraph. Underline two causes of Jewish settlement in Palestine. Then circle two effects of the establishment of the state of Israel.

Mark the Text

In 1978, President Carter brought Egyptian leader Anwar el-Sadat and Israeli leader Menachim Begin to Camp David in Maryland. They signed the Camp David Accords. Egypt recognized Israel, and Israel returned the Sinai Peninsula to Egypt. However, the Palestinian Liberation Organization (PLO), led by **Yasir Arafat,** declared that there should be a Palestinian state run by Palestinians.

President Clinton hosted leaders from Israel and the PLO in 1993. They signed an agreement that gave Palestinians limited self-rule in the Gaza Strip and part of the West Bank. In return, Arafat agreed to renounce violence and recognize Israel. Yet extremists on both sides did not want to comply with this agreement. Arab extremists committed suicide bombings in Israel, and the Israeli military was called in. Israeli troops surrounded Arafat's compound, believing he supported the bombers. Some Israelis and Palestinians have kept working for peace. A year after Arafat died in 2004, a cease-fire was declared. ✓

Increasing Tensions

There have been other sources of tension with Muslim nations. The revolutionaries who gained power in Iran were part of a new kind of Islam. These Islamists, including Iran's leader, Ayatollah **Ruholla Khomeini,** limited women's rights and rejected Western ideas and culture. Islamists did not want American forces in Saudi Arabia. Sometimes they attacked Americans and other Westerners.

Iraq, ruled by dictator **Saddam Hussein,** invaded Kuwait in 1990. President George H. W. Bush worked with 28 other countries to make Iraq pull out of Kuwait. After Hussein refused, these countries attacked Iraq, beginning the Persian Gulf War. Within weeks, Hussein withdrew his forces from Kuwait. The UN enforced sanctions against Iraq, but Hussein stayed in power. ✓

Check Your Progress

1. Why is the Middle East important to the United States?

____

____

2. How did President George H. W. Bush respond to Iraq's invasion of Kuwait?

____

____

Vocabulary Builder

The underlined word *comply* means "to follow or obey." Why do you think extremists did not want to follow the terms of the agreement?

____

____

✓ Checkpoint

State the position taken by Palestinian Arabs in opposing the creation of the state of Israel.

____

____

✓ Checkpoint

List reasons that Islamists pose a problem for the United States.

____

____

Section 4 Notetaking Study Guide

Question to Think About As you read Section 4 in your textbook and take notes, keep this section focus question in mind: **How have tensions in the Middle East posed concerns for the United States?**

▸ Use this chart to record key information from the section. Some information has been filled in to get you started.

The Middle East

- The Middle East is a European term for Southwest Asia, and it also often includes Egypt and ________.
- Three major religions that began in the Middle East are ________, ________, and ________.
- The Middle East is of vital interest today because of its ________.

Arab-Israeli Conflict

- Jews moved to Palestine to establish a Jewish state.
- In 1948, Jews formed ________.
- After war with Israel, Palestinian Arabs became ________.
- Wars in 1967 and 1973 resulted in Israel gaining more land from other nations.
- The Camp David Accords were an agreement between ________ and Israel.
- The PLO under Yasir Arafat wanted ________. They led a mass protest known as the ________.
- After meeting with Clinton and Israel's leader in 1993, Arafat agreed to ________. Israel agreed to let Palestinians ________.
- After the agreement, some Arab extremists launched ________ in Israel. Israel responded by using military force.
- A year after Arafat died in 2004, a ________ was announced.

Islamist Extremism

- In Iran, many people opposed the Shah of Iran, who was an ally of the United States.
- Revolutionaries in Iran banned ________.
- Followers of an extreme form of Islam are called ________.
- These extremists resent the United States for the following reasons: ________

The Persian Gulf War

- When Iraq invaded Kuwait in 1990, President George H. W. Bush responded quickly.
- The American forces in the Persian Gulf War were led by ________ and ________.
- After six weeks of war, Saddam Hussein ________.
- The United Nations imposed ________ on Iraq.

Refer to this page to answer the Chapter 28 Focus Question on page 436.

Chapter 28 Assessment

Directions: Circle the letter of the correct answer.

1. Who of the following ushered in the conservative movement in U.S. politics?
   A Jimmy Carter
   B George H. W. Bush
   C Ronald Reagan

2. The period of détente between the United States and the Soviet Union ended when
   A the Soviet Union invaded Afghanistan.
   B the United States boycotted the Moscow Olympics.
   C the Soviet Union allowed glasnost.

3. To what country did the United States apply sanctions to protest its policy of apartheid?
   A Iraq **B** South Africa **C** Cuba

Directions: Follow the steps to answer this question:

How did U.S. foreign policy goals change under President George H. W. Bush and President Bill Clinton with the end of the Cold War?

Step 1: Recall information: Briefly list the major goals of U.S. foreign policy during the Cold War.

Cold War Goals
•
•
•

Step 2: List the major goals of U.S. foreign policy after the Cold War ended.

Bush's Foreign Policy Goals	Clinton's Foreign Policy Goals
•	•
•	•
•	•

Step 3: Draw conclusions: Complete the topic sentence that follows. Then write two or three more sentences that support your topic sentence.

After the Cold War ended, U.S. foreign policy goals ______________________

____

____

____

____

Chapter 28 Notetaking Study Guide

Now you are ready to answer the chapter 28 Focus Question: **How did major national and international events affect the nation?**

▶ Complete the charts to help you answer this question. Use the notes that you took for each section.

National Events Change the Nation

President Jimmy Carter struggled with the economic problem of ______________.
President Reagan made the following economic changes:

- ______________
- ______________

President George H. W. Bush faced an economic ______________.
President Bill Clinton made the following economic changes:

- ______________
- ______________
- ended federal welfare payments

International Events Affect the Nation

President Reagan fought communism by ______________, ______________, and ______________.
The Soviet Union's economy was weakened when ______________.
Some changes under Gorbachev included: ______________, ______________, ______________, and lack of support for Communist regimes in Eastern Europe.
The Cold War ended when ______________.

Other Major World Events

In South Africa, the United States applied ______________ to end ______________.
In China, the United States responded to the crackdown at Tiananmen Square by ______________.
After the Cold War ended, the United States worried about the spread of ______________.
Two neighboring countries that tested nuclear weapons for the first time in 1998 were ______________ and ______________.

Tensions in the Middle East

Palestinian Arabs were unhappy in 1948 when Jews formed ______________.
The PLO was led by ______________. The PLO wanted a ______________ state run by ______________.
In 1993, leaders from Israel and the PLO met with Clinton and made the following agreement:
Palestinians would get ______________. In return, the PLO would ______________.
Islamists are ______________.
The Persian Gulf War occurred after ______________ invaded ______________.

Refer to this page to answer the Unit 9 Focus Question on 451.

Chapter 29

Challenges for a New Century

(1980–Present)

What You Will Learn

After terrorist attacks in 2001, the United States began a global war against terrorism. The nation faced many other challenges, including an increasingly global economy, environmental problems, and a changing population.

Chapter 29 Focus Question

As you read this chapter, keep this question in mind: **What challenges face the nation in the 21st century?**

Section 1

The Threat of Terrorism

Section 1 Focus Question

How did the war on terrorism affect American actions at home and abroad? To begin answering this question,

- Read about terrorist strikes against Americans.
- Find out about the terrorist attack on September 11, 2001.
- Understand the war on terrorism.
- Learn about the presidential election of 2004.

Section 1 Summary

When terrorism spread to the United States, the nation joined a global effort to combat this violence.

Terrorism on the World Stage

Terrorism is the use of violence, often against civilians, to force political or social change. Middle Eastern extremists use terrorism to reduce Western influence. The first terrorist attacks against Americans occurred abroad. In 1993, however, a truck bomb exploded under the World Trade Center in New York City, killing six people. In 1995, a truck bomb exploded near a federal office building in Oklahoma City, killing 168 people. The terrorists in this second attack were two young American men who resented the federal government. ✓

Key Events

1970	President Nixon forms the Environmental Protection Agency (EPA).
2001	Terrorists attack New York's World Trade Center and the Pentagon, killing thousands of people.
2003	Latinos, or Hispanics, become the largest ethnic minority in the United States.

✓ Checkpoint

Name one way the bombing in 1993 was different from previous terrorist attacks against Americans.

____

____

The Nation Is Attacked

On September 11, 2001, Arab terrorists hijacked four passenger jets from Boston. The terrorists crashed two of the planes into the World Trade Center in New York City. They crashed a third plane into the Pentagon in Washington, D.C. The fourth jet crashed into a field in Pennsylvania. Both towers of the World Trade Center collapsed. Nearly 3,000 people were killed in New York, at the Pentagon, or on the airplanes. President George W. Bush took steps to protect America. He made it a priority to promote **counterterrorism**, action taken against terrorists. In 2002, Bush signed the Patriot Act. It gave authorities the power to investigate and jail people suspected of having terrorist ties. Suspects could be held indefinitely without being charged or being allowed to consult a lawyer. ✓

✓ Checkpoint

List two ways President Bush responded to the attacks of September 11, 2001.

______

______

The War on Terror

Osama Bin Laden was a wealthy Saudi Arabian who ran a worldwide terrorist network called al Qaeda (al KI duh). He was suspected of perpetrating the September 11th attacks. He took refuge in Afghanistan, ruled by the Taliban, a group of extremists. The Taliban refused to give him up, so the U.S. attacked. The Taliban lost power, but Bin Laden escaped.

President Bush next targeted Iraqi dictator Saddam Hussein as a threat. Bush accused Hussein of having ties with Bin Laden and developing weapons of mass destruction (WMDs), such as nuclear weapons. In March 2003, the U.S. led an attack on Iraq. On May 1, Bush announced the end of major combat. Yet war continued even after Hussein was captured late in 2003. ✓

Vocabulary Builder

To *perpetrate* is to "commit" or "carry out." Reread the bracketed paragraph. How might Bin Laden have helped perpetrate the 9/11 attacks?

______

______

✓ Checkpoint

Name the two countries the United States attacked in order to combat terrorism.

______

______

Election of 2004

The Iraq war was a major issue in the 2004 presidential election. The Democrats nominated Senator **John Kerry** of Massachusetts. Kerry accused Bush of mishandling the war in Iraq. Bush said that Kerry lacked the determination to fight terrorism. Bush won the election. Republicans also won greater majorities in both houses of Congress. ✓

✓ Checkpoint

Name one issue on which Bush and Kerry disagreed.

______

______

Check Your Progress

1. What is the difference between terrorism and counter-terrorism?

______

______

2. Who was Osama Bin Laden?

______

Section 1 Notetaking Study Guide

Question to Think About As you read Section 1 in your textbook and take notes, keep this section focus question in mind: **How did the war on terrorism affect American actions at home and abroad?**

▶ Use these charts to record key information from the section. Some information has been filled in to get you started.

Terrorism on the World Stage		
When	**Where**	**Event**
1988	Scotland	explosion on airplane kills 270 people (189 Americans)
1993		
1995		

The Nation Is Attacked		
When	**Where**	**Event**
2001	New York City, Washington, D.C.	Four passenger jets are hijacked by ________. Two of the jets ________. One crashes into ________. As a result, President Bush promotes counterterrorism, which is ________. He also signs the Patriot Act, which ________.

The War on Terror	
Afghanistan	**Iraq**
Osama Bin Laden: leader of al Qaeda terrorist network The Taliban: ________	Saddam Hussein: ________ WMDs: weapons of mass destruction such as nuclear and chemical weapons

Election of 2004	
George W. Bush's position on Kerry: ________	John Kerry's position on Bush: ________
Outcome: ________	

Refer to this page to answer the Chapter 29 Focus Question on page 450.

Key Events

1970 President Nixon forms the Environmental Protection Agency (EPA).

2001 Terrorists attack New York's World Trade Center and the Pentagon, killing thousands of people.

2003 Latinos, or Hispanics, become the largest ethnic minority in the United States.

Vocabulary Builder

The word *advocate* includes the Latin root *voc*, which means "voice." Use this fact and clues from the underlined sentence to write a definition of *advocate*.

____

____

✓ Checkpoint

List two different strategies for dealing with economic competition between countries.

____

____

Section 2
Economy and the Environment

Section 2 Focus Question

How do economic and environmental issues link the United States and the world? To begin answering this question,

- Understand how globalization affects the U.S. economy.
- Read about the growth of the environmental movement.
- Examine the energy supply.
- Learn about the issue of global warming.

Section 2 Summary

As economic ties between nations grew stronger, the United States faced growing economic and environmental challenges.

A World Linked by Trade

Globalization is the process of creating an international network. Foreign trade accounts for about 25 percent of the American economy. Foreign goods are cheaper because workers in Latin America, Eastern Europe, and Asia are generally paid less than American workers. A **trade deficit** occurs when a country buys more from other nations than it sells to them. The U.S. trade deficit reached almost $500 billion in 2003. As a result, American companies have begun **outsourcing,** or having work done in other countries. This allows companies to use cheap labor outside the United States. Critics of outsourcing say it hurts American workers.

Tariffs and free trade are two different strategies for dealing with foreign competition. Some people believe that raising tariffs on foreign goods will protect American profits and jobs. Others who support **free trade** advocate the removal of trade barriers. In 1994, President Clinton signed the North American Free Trade Agreement (NAFTA). It removed trade barriers between the United States, Mexico, and Canada. NAFTA has increased trade and generated jobs. However, opponents of free trade argue that it weakens workers' rights and harms the environment. ✓

The Environment

The environmental movement began when biologist **Rachel Carson** published *Silent Spring* in 1962. The book led to laws restricting the use of DDT, a chemical pesticide that was killing birds and fish. Then in 1969, an oil spill polluted water off the coast of California. Smog blanketed many cities. In response, the Environmental Protection Agency (EPA) was set up. New laws targeted auto emissions, lakes, and rivers for cleanup. Local groups started recycling programs. Critics argue that these laws are costly.

Natural disasters also can harm the environment and the economy. On August 29, 2005, Hurricane Katrina tore into Louisiana, Mississippi, and Alabama. An estimated $100 billion worth of damage resulted. As many as a million people were driven from their homes. ✓

The Energy Supply

In 1973, OPEC cut off Middle Eastern oil supplies to the United States for a year. The price of oil quadrupled. Laws ordered car makers to improve fuel efficiency. The government created a reserve to protect against future shortages. People also began to look for other sources of energy. Coal supplies are plentiful. However, it is expensive to reduce the acid and smoke that coal produces. **Renewable resources** are energy resources that are more easily restored by nature, such as water, solar, and wind. But water power is available only in areas with rivers. The equipment for solar energy takes up too much space to be used on a large scale. Wind power is not a steady source. Nuclear power plants can provide near-limitless energy, but they are costly and produce radioactive waste. Accidents in nuclear plants in Pennsylvania and the Soviet Union showed the world the danger of radiation. ✓

The Question of Global Warming

Global warming is a worldwide rise in temperatures. Many scientists blame the current trend of global warming on gases emitted by cars, factories, and homes. The United States signed the Kyoto Protocol in 1997 to reduce carbon dioxide emissions. President Bush rejected this protocol in 2001. He argued that little evidence of global warming did not justify the cost to U.S. businesses. ✓

Check Your Progress

1. Why did some American companies turn to outsourcing?

____

____

2. What were some responses to OPEC's actions of 1973?

____

____

✓ Checkpoint

List three areas of focus for the environmental movement.

____

____

____

Reading Strategy

Reread the bracketed text. Underline the disadvantage of water power. Circle the disadvantage of solar power. Draw an arrow next to the disadvantage of wind power.

✓ Checkpoint

Name three renewable energy resources.

____

____

____

✓ Checkpoint

Name the source that many scientists believe is responsible for the increase in global temperatures.

____

____

Section 2 Notetaking Study Guide

Question to Think About As you read Section 2 in your textbook and take notes, keep this section focus question in mind: **How do economic and environmental issues link the United States and the world?**

▶ Use these charts to record key information from the section. Some information has been filled in to get you started.

A World Linked by Trade		
Term	**Definition**	**Why It Is Important**
globalization	creating an international network	
trade deficit		
outsourcing		
free trade		

The Environment		
Early Awareness	**Environmental Actions**	**Critics of the Movement**
In 1962, Rachel Carson's book *Silent Spring* criticized ________. In 1969, ______ spilled off the coast of ________ and smog blanketed many cities.	The Nixon administration formed the ________. Legislation targeted ________ ________. Local governments ________ ________.	Some critics argue that ________ ________.

The Energy Supply	
Cause	**Effects**
In 1973, OPEC ________ ________ ________.	The price of oil ________. Car makers started to improve ________, and people conserved energy by ________ ________. Alternative energy sources were explored, including ________ ________, ________, ________, and ________.

The Question of Global Warming
Global warming is ________. Environmentalists argue that ________. Critics of this theory argue that ________.

Refer to this page to answer the Chapter 29 Focus Question on page 450.

Section 3

Science and Technology

Section 3 Focus Question

How have science and technology transformed modern society? To begin answering this question,

- Learn how computers led to an information revolution.
- Read about important advances in medical science.

Section 3 Summary

Computer technology and advances in medical science have contributed to many important changes in American life.

The Computer Age

The computer has revolutionized daily life in America. Computers make it possible to store, analyze, and share vast amounts of information in a flash. Before the 1970s, most computing was done by machines called mainframes. They were very large and expensive. Only governments, universities, and big business used them. The invention of transistors, or circuits on tiny silicon chips, made smaller computers possible. In 1977, Apple introduced the first computer for home use. International Business Machines (IBM) marketed its own personal computer four years later. During the 1970s, Bill Gates developed software to help ordinary people run computers. He cofounded Microsoft, today one of the world's most successful businesses. By 1990, Americans were buying 7 million computers every year.

In 1969, the U.S. Department of Defense began to link its computers with those in several American universities. This electronic network formed the basis for the Internet. The Internet helped to create an information revolution. By 2003, more than half of all Americans used the Internet to search for information, to communicate, and to purchase goods. **E-commerce,** or buying and selling online, grew rapidly. Companies used the Internet to advertise and do business. Satellite technology also added to the information revolution. Telecommunications satellites orbit the Earth, carrying millions of radio and television signals.

Not all of the changes caused by technology have been positive. Privacy can be threatened by "hackers" who tap into computers. This contributed to a new crime known as

Key Events

1970	President Nixon forms the Environmental Protection Agency (EPA).
2001	Terrorists attack New York's World Trade Center and the Pentagon, killing thousands of people.
2003	Latinos, or Hispanics, become the largest ethnic minority in the United States.

Vocabulary Builder

Suffixes change word forms. The noun *computer* and the verb *compute* share the same base word. The suffix *–ing* is added to the verb form to show a gerund, which names an action. Use your knowledge of words to define *computing.*

identity theft. The use of cellular phones, introduced in 1973, also threatened privacy. Many Americans favor restrictions on cell phone use in public places and when driving, because cell phone use has been blamed for many auto accidents. ✓

✓ Checkpoint

List three examples of technology that has been available in American homes for less than 40 years.

____

____

____

Medical Advances

Technology has helped doctors to detect and treat many medical problems. A **laser** is a powerful beam of focused light. Lasers have become critical tools for surgeons. They are more flexible than scalpels and can be focused on very small areas. Doctors use lasers to perform delicate eye and skin surgery. Magnetic Resonance Imaging (MRI) provides an accurate view of internal organs. MRIs help doctors identify injuries or illnesses and reduce the need for surgery.

Acquired Immune Deficiency Syndrome (AIDS) first appeared in the 1980s. The AIDS epidemic has killed millions of people in the United States and worldwide. In some African countries, 20 percent of the population is infected with the virus that causes AIDS. New drugs have extended the lives of many AIDS sufferers. However, they are too expensive for most people in developing countries. In 2003, President Bush promised a $15 billion program to distribute these medicines worldwide.

Reading Strategy

Reread the bracketed paragraph. What is the problem it discusses? What is the proposed solution to solve the problem?

Problem:

____

____

Solution:

____

____

Cloning is the process of making a genetic double of a plant or an animal. This controversial scientific process made headlines in 1997 when a Scottish researcher cloned a sheep named Dolly. In 2004, South Korean scientists cloned a human embryo. Cloning research may help find cures for people with serious medical conditions. Yet many people worry about the biological and ethical dangers that could result if this led to the cloning of human beings. In 1997, President Clinton prohibited federal funding of the cloning of human cells. ✓

✓ Checkpoint

Name two recently developed tools that help doctors diagnose and treat illnesses.

____

____

Check Your Progress

1. Explain what is meant by the "information revolution."

____

____

2. How has AIDS affected the global population?

____

____

Section 3 Notetaking Study Guide

Question to Think About As you read Section 3 in your textbook and take notes, keep this section focus question in mind: **How have science and technology transformed modern society?**

▶ Use these charts to record key information from the section. Some information has been filled in to get you started.

The Computer Age	
Computer Technology	• Before the 1970s, computers were very ______ and ______. • When the ______ was developed, computers became smaller. • The first home computer was introduced by ______ in ______.
The Internet	• This technology was developed to link computers in the Department of ______ and computers in ______. • ______ proposed the World Wide Web in 1989. • By 2003, more than half of all Americans used the Internet. • E-commerce is ______.
Privacy Issues	• Hackers can ______. • Identity theft is ______. • Most Americans favor restricting the use of cell phones in ______.

Medical Advances		
New Tools	**AIDS**	**Cloning**
• Lasers are ______ ______ ______. • Doctors use them to ______ ______. • MRI stands for ______ ______. • MRIs are used to ______ ______ ______.	• The first AIDS cases appeared in ______. • AIDS has killed millions of people worldwide. • AIDS sufferers in Africa often go without medication because ______ ______ ______.	• Cloning is ______ ______ ______. • Dolly was ______ ______ ______. • In 1997, Clinton ______ ______ because ______ ______.

Refer to this page to answer the Chapter 29 Focus Question on page 450.

Key Events

1970 President Nixon forms the Environmental Protection Agency (EPA).

2001 Terrorists attack New York's World Trade Center and the Pentagon, killing thousands of people.

2003 Latinos, or Hispanics, become the largest ethnic minority in the United States.

Vocabulary Builder

Which two of the following words are synonyms for the underlined word *incentive*?

motivation	regulation
admiration	disadvantage
hardship	encouragement

____

____

✓ Checkpoint

List seven countries from which refugees fled after 1965.

____

____

____

____

____

____

____

Section 4

A Changing Society

Section 4 Focus Question

How have new immigration and population patterns increased diversity? To begin answering this question,

- Understand immigration patterns after 1965.
- Learn about key shifts in the U.S. population.
- Find out how opportunities have expanded for African Americans, women, and Native Americans.
- Identify challenges faced by young Americans.

Section 4 Summary

The American population has changed as immigration trends shifted and diversity has grown.

Changing Immigration Patterns

Immigration to the United States is at its highest rate since the early 1900s. Some immigrants are attracted to the United States by the <u>incentive</u> of economic opportunities. Others are **refugees,** people who flee war or persecution in their own countries.

After 1965, refugees from Vietnam and China came to escape war or oppression. Education and employment attracted people from India, Korea, and the Philippines.

The largest source of immigration is Latin America. Refugees fled dictators in Cuba and Chile and civil wars in El Salvador, Guatemala, and Nicaragua. Poverty drove people from Mexico, Central America, and the Caribbean. Many immigrants have also come from Eastern Europe and the former Soviet Union.

Undocumented workers are laborers who enter the country without legal permission. The Immigration Reform and Control Act of 1986 penalized employers who hired undocumented workers. The attacks of September 11, 2001, raised new concerns about immigration. In 2004, President Bush proposed allowing more **guest workers,** or temporary immigrant workers, to enter the country. ✓

A Changing Population

In 2003, Latinos, or Hispanics, became the largest ethnic minority in the United States. They make up 12.5 percent of the population. In 2003, the House of Representatives included 23 Latino members. The number of Latino-owned businesses increased dramatically over the past 20 years. However, almost 40 percent of Latino children were living in poverty.

Birthrates have declined, and people live longer due to improved medical care. As a result, the average age of the American population has increased. Health care and Social Security are major concerns. The number of people collecting Social Security is rising faster than the number of people paying Social Security taxes. The centers of population have shifted from the Northeast and Midwest to the warmer climates of the Sunbelt—the South and Southwest. ✓

Expanding Opportunities

The civil rights movement produced economic and political gains for African Americans. By 2000, more were earning college degrees, and fewer were living in poverty. Over 10,000 African Americans held public office. However, African American unemployment was twice as high as that for whites. Three times as many African American, as opposed to white, children lived in poverty.

Women also expanded their roles in the workplace and government. Many became professionals or elected officials.

The 2000 census counted more than 4 million Native Americans. One-third lived on reservations. Indian communities today still have high rates of unemployment, poverty, and juvenile delinquency. Indians have made progress, however. Businesses such as factories and casinos are strengthening reservation economies. ✓

Challenges for the Young

Young Americans face difficult challenges. These include violence in schools and the use of illegal drugs, including steroids. People often disagree about how to solve these problems. Still, Americans share key values that define the nation: faith in democracy, respect for individual rights, tolerance, and the opportunity to build a better future. ✓

Check Your Progress

1. How do undocumented and guest workers differ?

____

____

2. Why has the average age of the U.S. population changed?

____

____

Reading Strategy

Underline one positive gain made by Hispanic Americans. Circle a challenge the Latino population still faces.

✓ Checkpoint

Name three ways in which the U.S. population has changed.

____

____

____

✓ Checkpoint

List two gains made by African Americans since the civil rights movement.

____

____

✓ Checkpoint

Name two issues that affect young people directly.

____

____

Section 4 Notetaking Study Guide

Question to Think About As you read Section 4 in your textbook and take notes, keep this section focus question in mind: **How have new immigration and population patterns increased diversity?**

► Use these charts to record key information from the section. Some information has been filled in to get you started.

Changing Immigration Patterns	
Sources of Immigration	**Immigration Policies**
• After 1965, the fastest growing immigrant group was Asians. • The largest source of immigration was ______. • ______ flee war or persecution. • Other immigrants seek ______ ______ in America.	• In 1965, President Johnson signed a law that ______ ______. • In 1986, an act imposed penalties on ______. • In 2004, President Bush proposed allowing more guest workers.

A Changing Population			
Latinos	**Asian Americans**	**Older Population**	**Population Center**
In 2003, Latinos became ______ ______. Miami became the first U.S. city ______ ______. Challenges: poverty, unemployment	By 2000, more than ______ Americans were of Asian descent. Challenges: employment	The percentage of older Americans has increased because ______ ______ ______. Challenges: Social Security, health care	People have moved from ______ ______ to ______ ______. This region is called ______.

Expanding Opportunities		
African Americans	**Women**	**Native Americans**
Gains: ______ ______ Challenges: ______ ______	Gains: ______ ______ Challenges: ______ ______	Gains: ______ ______ Challenges: ______ ______

Challenges for the Young	
Violence	**Illegal Drugs**
• Increase in violent attacks in schools Possible solutions: ______ ______	• Illegal drug use, including steroids Possible solutions: ______ ______

Refer to this page to answer the Chapter 29 Focus Question on page 450.

Chapter 29 Assessment

Directions: Circle the letter of the correct answer.

1. What was the goal of the Patriot Act?
- **A** to encourage immigration
- **B** to place tariffs on foreign goods
- **C** to help authorities investigate terrorists

2. What is the result when a country buys more from foreign countries than it sells to them?
- **A** tariffs **B** globalization **C** trade deficit

3. What is the largest minority in the United States today?
- **A** Latinos
- **B** Asian Americans
- **C** African Americans

Directions: Follow the steps to answer this question:

How might the United States be different in 25 years if current patterns of change continue?

Step 1: Recall information: Describe three patterns of change that you have read about. You might consider the threat of terrorism, the economy, technology, or the population.

Three Important Changes
• • •

Step 2: Now choose two changes from your list and predict how they might continue in the next 25 years.

How Two Changes Could Continue
• •

Step 3: Complete the topic sentence that follows. Then write two or three more sentences that support your topic sentence.

If current patterns continue, in 25 years the United States will ____________

____

____

____

____

Chapter 29 Notetaking Study Guide

Now you are ready to answer the Chapter 29 Focus Question: **What challenges face the nation in the twenty-first century?**

▶ Complete the following chart to help you answer this question. Use the notes that you took for each section.

The Threat of Terrorism	
On September 11, 2001, ______________________________.	→ In response to these attacks, the United States ______________________________.

Economy and the Environment	
Trade Deficits	Trade deficits occur when ____________. Outsourcing is ____________.
Free Trade	Free trade is ____________.
Environmental Movement	This movement has called attention to problems such as air and water pollution and the misuse of limited resources.

Science and Technology	
Computer Technology	**Medical Science**
The information revolution began when ____________. The Internet helps Americans ____________.	Medical science has developed new tools, such as ________ and ________, but also faces new challenges such as the ________ epidemic.

A Changing Society	
Immigration	Immigration increased from regions such as ____________ and ____________.
Ethnic Changes	____________ have become America's largest minority.
Aging Population	Declining birthrates and longer life spans have led to ____________.
Population Shift	The population has moved from ____________ to ____________.

Refer to this page to answer the Unit 9 Focus Question on page 451.

Unit 9 Pulling It Together Activity

What You Have Learned

Chapter 26 The civil rights movement gained momentum after World War II, with organized protests, court decisions, and elected leaders all creating changes.

Chapter 27 The United States became involved in Vietnam, and Americans were sharply divided about the war. Under Nixon, the Watergate affair brought more turmoil.

Chapter 28 Reagan's presidency advanced the conservative movement. The Cold War ended. Conflicts in the Middle East and Islamic extremists posed challenges.

Chapter 29 After September 11, 2001, the United States led a war against terrorism. Other challenges facing the United States include the global economy and environmental issues.

Think Like a Historian

Read the Unit 9 Focus Question: **How did the United States strive to strengthen democracy at home and to foster democracy abroad?**

► Use the organizers on this page and the next to collect information to answer this question.

What are some examples of strengthening democracy at home? Some of them are listed in this organizer. Review your section and chapter notes. Then complete the organizer.

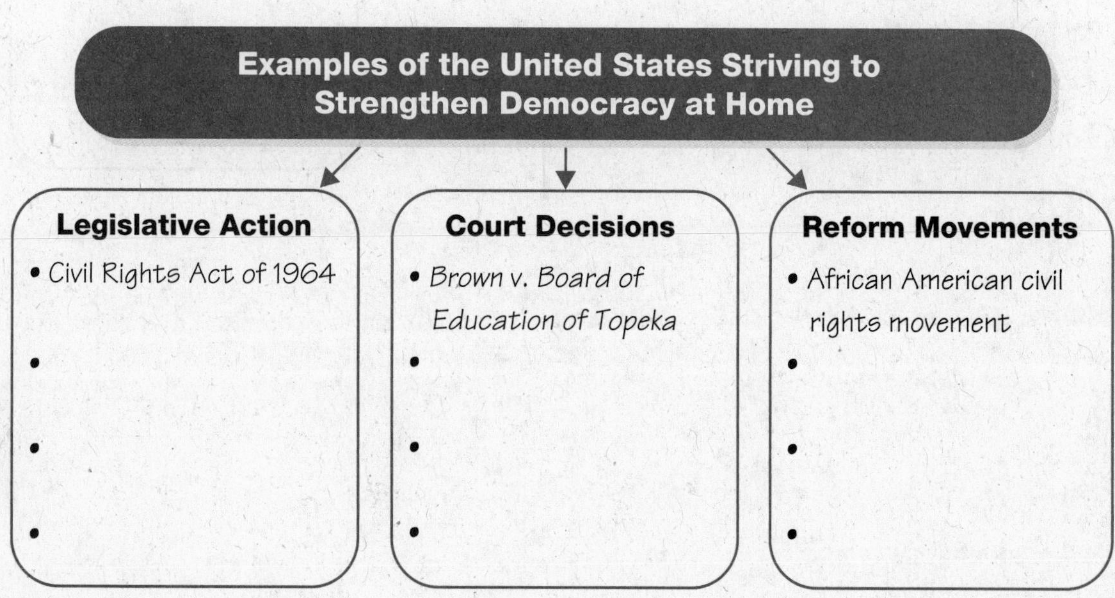

Look at the second part of the Unit Focus Question. It asks how the United States strove to foster democracy abroad. The organizer below gives you a part of the answer. Review your section and chapter notes. Then fill in the rest of the organizer.

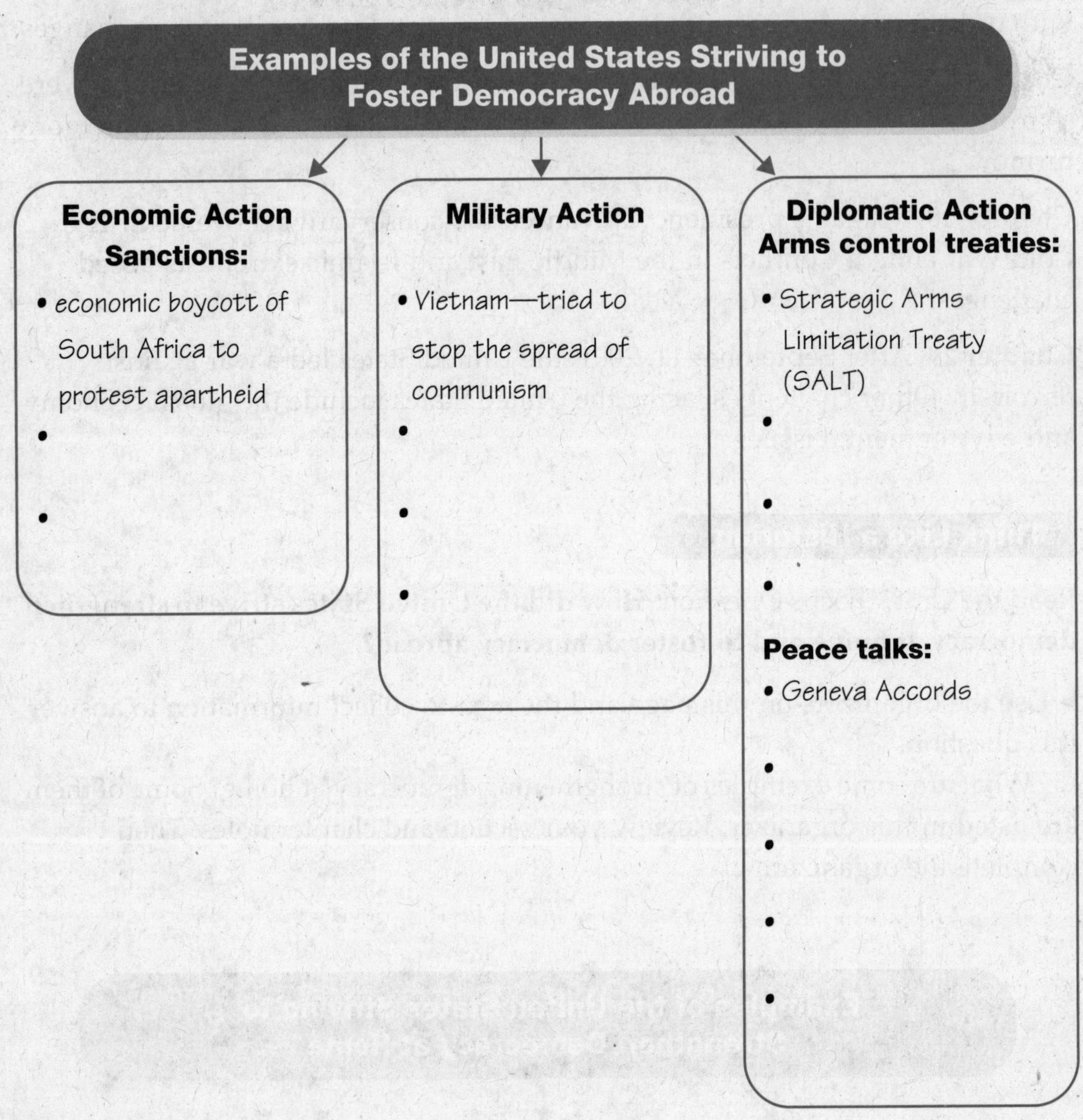